Theology and the Practice of Responsibility

THEOLOGY AND THE PRACTICE OF RESPONSIBILITY

Essays on Dietrich Bonhoeffer

Edited by
Wayne Whitson Floyd Jr. and Charles Marsh

Trinity Press International
Valley Forge, Pennsylvania

Trinity Press Edition 1994

Trinity Press International
P.O. Box 851
Valley Forge, PA 19482-0851

Cover design by Gene Harris

Library of Congress Cataloging-in-Publication Data

Theology and the practice of responsibility : essays on Dietrich
    Bonhoeffer / edited by Wayne Whitson Floyd Jr. and Charles Marsh. — 1st
    ed.
        p.   cm.
    Includes bibliographical references and index.
    ISBN 1-56338-077-3
    1. Bonhoeffer, Dietrich, 1906–1945. 2. Theology–History–20th
century. I. Floyd, Wayne W. Jr. II. Marsh, Charles, 1958–   .
BX4827.B57T47 1994
230′.044′092–dc20   94-15801
                                                                 CIP

Printed in the United States of America
94   95   96   97   98   6   5   4   3   2   1

CONTENTS

EDITORS' INTRODUCTION

This volume commemorates the fact that a half-century ago, on April 30, 1944, Dietrich Bonhoeffer penned the first of his distinctly *theological* letters from Tegel Prison, asking from the context of the horror of the Holocaust a Christian's questions about the tradition of Western religiosity and the meaning of the modern age. Indeed, it was these writings by Bonhoeffer which first caught the imagination of twentieth-century theology.

In the present moment, at the end of a most pained and troubling twentieth century, we should not be surprised to find that contemporary theology has become preoccupied with the "end of metaphysics," the "end of modernity," and even the "end of history." Especially at such a time as this, we might do well to listen with a renewed sense of significance to Bonhoeffer's theological musings about the modern world: his reflections about the "end of religion," the need to "speak of God – without religion," beyond what he called the "presuppositions of metaphysics, inwardness, and so on" – in a word, the themes of his *Letters and Papers from Prison*.

Yet provocative as these writings often were – and still can be – they have always begged for more sustained reflection. "I must break off for today . . ." Bonhoeffer concluded that first theological letter. Most of the letters contained only such incomplete formulations, fragments of a vision which have spurred a wide variety of interpretations and speculations. A popular readership encountered Bonhoeffer first through *The Cost of Discipleship* and *Life Together,* the writings of his underground seminary experiences at Zingst and Finkenwalde. These were found to be intimately tied to his theological explorations in *Creation and Fall, Christ the Center,* and his unfinished *Ethics*. But Bonhoeffer the pastor, teacher, and ecumenist was discovered also to have been Bonhoeffer the scholar, the author of such academic theological studies as *Sanctorum Communio* and *Act and Being*. The result was the realization of the need for a critical edition of all of Bonhoeffer's writings, the sixteen-volume, still-emerging *Dietrich Bonhoeffer Werke*, already in the process of translation into English through the labors of the *Dietrich Bonhoeffer Works* translation project. Now a new generation of scholarly voices, not only in Europe and North America, but also in Central and South America, Africa, and Japan, is demonstrating its discovery in Bonhoeffer of a resource for a surprisingly diverse array of modern and postmodern theologies. Refusing the temptation to try to systematize this quintessential unsystematic thinker, such new approaches to Bonhoeffer—by both established scholars and younger thinkers—are engaging his legacy with a variety of alternative critical tools and perspectives, such as critical social theories, political philosophy, and philosophical hermeneutics.

The essays in this volume represent, therefore, a new direction in the interpretation of Dietrich Bonhoeffer's theology. While the main concern of most scholarly literature has been to understand Bonhoeffer in historical context, this volume demonstrates the power of his life and thought to reach beyond his own milieu into new historical and intellectual territory. Of course, it is not the editors' intention to ignore the important work of previous scholars. If anything, the condition of the very possibility of the present volume is the foundation laid by more than four decades of difficult historical research. Nonetheless, the promise of Bonhoeffer's theology, not only for the academy, for the churches, and for interfaith conversations, but also for diverse forums of civic debate, remains unclaimed as long as his wide-ranging intellectual interests are not given their full consideration. A richer, more developed understanding of Bonhoeffer's theology depends on locating new ways of reading and appropriating his texts. If it is pursued well, the image of Bonhoeffer that comes into focus is one of a theologian more sophisticated and conceptually nuanced than hitherto imagined.

Part 1, "Making Sense of Modernity," positions Bonhoeffer as an essential voice in the conversation about the shaping of the modern world. Bonhoeffer's important contribution is his insistence on a theological account of modernity that neither identifies faith and the secular nor absorbs modernity into theology's own categories. Rather, he wishes to understand theologically the modern world in its *autonomy*. Wolfgang Huber's important distinction between a modern theology and a theology of modernity is apropos of this task. In conversation with figures ranging from Vaclav Havel to Charles Taylor and Klaus-Michael Kodalle, Huber models a theology of modernity that is at the same time a critique of modernity, combining both analytical precision and responsible engagement. Steven Schroeder focuses specifically on a debate between Bonhoeffer's critique of modernity and Francis Fukuyama's *The End of History*. Barry Harvey—an avid reader of Nicholas Lash, Rowan Williams, Stanley Hauerwas, and John Howard Yoder—asks whether a postmodern Bonhoeffer is not finally the advocate of the church's responsible participation in God's own messianic suffering. And Douglas John Hall deepens such questioning about the *ecclesia crucis*, daring to ask whether the church in North America has a future at all if it cannot learn to distinguish discipleship from religion, to affirm Christianity's world-orientation versus otherworldliness, and to choose suffering with God in the world versus spiritual security.

Part 2, "Social Analysis and Liberation," extends Bonhoeffer's theological account of modernity into the specific task of confronting economic and social inequities. While it is agreed that Bonhoeffer's witness in resistance against Hitler offers inspiration in the concrete pursuit of human liberation, his own thinking appears limited with respect to the task of analyzing ideology, economic power, and global bureaucracy. The central question in this unfinished task is how to connect Bonhoeffer's theological protest against the idols of nationalism with other social analyses that use more sophisticated tools and concepts. In other words, is the difference between Bonhoeffer and liberation theologians primarily one of historical context or social location? Despite his numerous polemics against religious liberalism, must Bonhoeffer still be described as a bourgeois theologian whose solidarity with revolutionary movements will always be cut short by his unyielding class allegiances? Or does this assessment betray an unfair revisionism that asks too much of any theological figure now a half-century after his death? Otto Maduro raises some difficult, yet unavoidable, questions about what he calls "the fracture separating modern, liberal theologies from liberation theologies," thus questioning the precise manner in which any European theologian can still contribute to postcolonialist theological or social movements. Geffrey Kelly compares and contrasts Bonhoeffer with the life and thought of Archbishop Oscar Romero, seeing in each a critique of idolatry and a prophetic call for concrete action that links this bourgeois German and his peasant-activist Salvadoran counterpart. Stephen Plant places Bonhoeffer in dialogue with the South African theologian Itumeleng J. Mosala, showing the ways in which Mosala's materialist hermeneutics extend the range of Bonhoeffer's theological analysis. And Clifford Green examines the interpretation of Bonhoeffer in the work of Gustavo Gutierrez, particularly the latter's understanding of Bonhoeffer as a "modern" theologian as well as a critic of "modernity."

Part 3, "Refiguring Community," offers an indirect answer to the question of how to connect Bonhoeffer's theological protest against nationalism with other analyses of power by renewed consideration of his ecclesiology. Bonhoeffer's christological axiom, *"Christus als Gemeinde existierend"* ("Christ existing as community"), is intended not only to emphasize the sociality of revelation, but equally to describe the new patterns of human relationality "in Christ." No longer does the person exist in isolation from others in solitariness (what Luther called the *cor curvum in se*), but the person exists for and with the other in life together. The model of human selfhood implicit in this transformation is unexpectedly complex and offers a rich alternative to the models of selfhood bequeathed by the Kantian tradition of the self-reflective subject. Luca D'Isanto, drawing upon the work of Carl Heinz Ratschow, Gianni Vattimo, and others, proposes that the community of faith, the church, be understood as "the historical *Gestalt* of God's hidden presence in the world" and thus as the center of any theological hermeneutics. L. Gregory Jones, reexamining Bonhoeffer's *The Cost of Discipleship,* lays out the shape of a trinitarian theology of forgiveness rooted in communal discipline and worldly discipleship. Vigen Guroian takes a theological analysis of community beyond the bounds of the church to the question of nationhood, employing the story of the national church in Armenia as a case study. And Luca Bagetto explores the influence of Bonhoeffer's contemporary, Gerhard Leibholz, on Bonhoeffer's notion of responsible decision, tracing the philosophical roots of this strand of Bonhoeffer's thought in Kant and Heidegger.

Part 4, "Postmodern Perspectives," might at first glance seem like a break in the continuity of the volume's structure, a tear in the seam of the narrative. However, in several critical though too often unexplored ways, many themes in Bonhoeffer's theology, both early and mature, push us beyond the aporias of the metaphysical theisms and transcendental theologies of the modern period to a decisively *postmodern* or *postmetaphysical* theological discourse. Walter Lowe undertakes a conversation between Bonhoeffer's theology and Jacques Derrida's deconstructionism. Thinking along with Derrida, Mark Taylor, Jean-Luc Nancy—as well as Karl Barth—Lowe examines Bonhoeffer's contributions to a theology of the incarnate word which at the same time aims to be a theology of the crucified *logos.* In debate with Alasdair MacIntyre, Richard Rorty, and Gianni

Vattimo, Hans van Hoogstraten inquires into the model of selfhood implicit in Bonhoeffer's theology—one that by force of its own demands seeks a description that overcomes the excesses and quandaries of the modern identity. Wayne Floyd sees Bonhoeffer's critique of metaphysics in the very style of his theological writing. The fragmentariness of the essay, to use an insight drawn from the aesthetics of Theodor Adorno, sustains—or even may help make possible—the antisystematic critique of all totalitarianisms that is so central not only to Bonhoeffer's early works, such as *Act and Being*, but also to his entire theological project. Robert Scharlemann draws fertile connections between Bonhoeffer's work and its Heideggerian roots, suggesting in the process that Bonhoeffer's project was moving toward "a theological ontology different from the better known ones of Bultmann and Tillich and also . . . still capable of being developed." The central question in this entire section is how Bonhoeffer's new theological and anthropological horizons come to expression, and in turn take form in a certain discourse. Must the discourse be ever broken and fragmented amid the dissonance of the age, or can it graduate into a general ontological description of being in Christ?

Part 5, "Repentance and the Practice of Responsibility," brings the consideration of Bonhoeffer's theology to the urgent needs of responsible action in a world come of age. Although it seems edifying to say that the church is the church when it exists for others, it is quite another matter to explain exactly what this means, in North America, in South Africa, and in the time—our time—after Auschwitz. Jean Bethke Elshtain brings to Bonhoeffer the skill and questions of a political philosopher, refusing to allow easy theological responses to the demands our age places upon any proposals concerning human freedom and responsibility. John de Gruchy argues that Bonhoeffer should be commemorated primarily through responsible acts of critical solidarity, by confessing guilt and practicing responsibility in the midst of the concrete struggles for human dignity. Finally, Christian Gremmels draws our attention back to the context from which Bonhoeffer's own practice of responsibility arose—the struggle of all those who resisted and especially those who fell victim to the genocide of National Socialism.

Our choice of the title *Theology and the Practice of Responsibility* emphasizes Bonhoeffer's lifelong attempt to bring two elements into unity, namely, theology, that certain kind of reflection that thinks after the truth of the reconciling God, and practice, that mode of being in the world that seeks concrete expression of humanity's reconciliation to God by being for and with others. Bonhoeffer did not wish to conflate reflection and action, nor did he privilege the one at the expense of the other. Rather, reflection and action dialectically enrich each other; theological thinking informs responsible actions, while actions in turn make concrete demands of reflection.

The papers in this volume were presented in an earlier form in August 1992 in the course of the Sixth International Bonhoeffer Conference at Union Theological Seminary in New York City. The general theme of that conference—and an enduring concern of this volume—was Bonhoeffer's theological interpretation of modernity, an issue sharpened by liberation and by other theologians who have declared the end of the modern period in theology, as well as by lively debate in the humanities concerning the idea of the postmodern. It was the hope of the conference organizers not only to bring together an international cast of Bonhoeffer specialists but also to expand the scope of our conversation by including many other influential scholars whose work has been substantively shaped by Bonhoeffer's life and thought. We hope that this volume extends to a broader readership the stimulating and challenging array of thinkers that gathered then to commemorate Dietrich Bonhoeffer.

We were assisted by many individuals and institutions in the preparation of this manuscript. Hal Rast and Laura Barrett of Trinity Press International have spirited the volume toward publication at a pace not even the editors could match. Will Love, Patrick Minges, and Pamela Eisenbaum—the editors at *Union Seminary Quarterly Review,* in which these essays originally appeared—assisted immeasurably in preparing these essays for publication, as did Larry Rasmussen and Clifford Green. We are also grateful to the following for financial support of the Sixth International Bonhoeffer Conference and thus, indirectly, of this volume as well: Lutheran Brotherhood; Second Ponce de Leon Baptist Church in Atlanta; the Vesper Society; Theological Horizons; the Trull Foundation; Prince of Peace Lutheran Church in Brooklyn Park, Minnesota; Story-Langdon Foundation, Inc.; and the Consulate General of the Federal Republic of Germany. Finally, a special thanks goes to all of the people who participated in the New York conference, both those whose work appears here and those unnamed, all of whose contributions illuminated new directions of inquiry in the rich promise of Bonhoeffer's theological legacy.

Wayne Whitson Floyd Jr.   Charles Marsh
Lutheran Theological Seminary   Loyola College
Philadelphia   Baltimore

THEOLOGY AND THE PRACTICE OF RESPONSIBILITY
Essays on Dietrich Bonhoeffer

Part I:

Making Sense of Modernity

BONHOEFFER AND MODERNITY

WOLFGANG HUBER

The theme "Bonhoeffer and Modernity" leads us into the center of Bonhoeffer's theology and at the same time confronts us with the task of a comprehensive diagnosis of our present time. The *theology of Dietrich Bonhoeffer* is at its core a critical theology of modernity that begins with his dissertation on *Sanctorum Communio* and its telling sub-title: A dogmatic investigation on the sociology of the Church,[1] and it ends with the *Letters and Papers from Prison*[2] and their reflections on the world come of age. The whole of his literary work is directed towards issues related to the specific structures of modernity. His life was shaped by the experience of modernity: growing up in an enlightened, liberal, bourgeois family, confronted early on with the coining vigor of modern science, and finally fighting with a modern political phenomenon, namely a totalitarian regime. However one defines modernity itself, there is no doubt that Bonhoeffer is a theologian of modernity in an extraordinary sense. His turn to a theology of revelation coincides with the turn to the problems of modernity. Whereas others understand the concept of revelation as premodern and think that a modern theology has to rely on experience instead of revelation, Bonhoeffer develops a critical theology of modernity in the way of a theology of revelation. Our theme "Bonhoeffer and Modernity," taken seriously, requires an interpretation of Bonhoeffer's theology as a whole.

On the other hand, the *concept of modernity* is highly debated. For some it designates a limited epoch in history, now behind us, after which we entered the "postmodern" period. For others it points to a historical project, namely the project of freedom and autonomy—a project which will never be finished as long as persons experience oppression and the lack of freedom. Under a different perspective, finally, modernity is understood as modernization—a process which is determined by the progress of science and technology and mostly structured by the capitalistic organization of economic power. This process is highly ambivalent: the increase of technological possibilities and the growth of the standard of life in some parts of the world are paid for by the fact that the majority of the world population grows poor and that non-human life is devastated to an unimaginable degree.[3] Modernity as limited epoch, as unfinished project or as ambivalent process: the keyword of modernity, taken seriously, requires a diagnosis of our present time in an embracing sense.

None of these tasks—neither an interpretation of Bonhoeffer's theology as a whole nor a diagnosis of our present time—can be fulfilled in an essay. So I choose a different way: I will start with a contextual analysis of some problems of modernity. I will ask what we—as Germans and Europeans— had to experience and to learn about the problems of modernity in the developments around the year 1989. From this contextual background I will ask how Bonhoeffer's theology can help us to understand and to better interpret our own experience of modernity.

Of course this reflection will happen within a hermeneutical circle. It is obvious that already my personal perception of our immediate past is shaped by categories and perspectives which I learned from Dietrich Bonhoeffer. But it could also be that the experiences of our days open our eyes to some aspects in Bonhoeffer's thinking which thus far have not been heard at the center of our interpretative awareness.

I

During the past few years all of us witnessed tremendous historical changes with unforeseeable consequences. In a specific sense this is true for those living in Europe. The political structures of the continent which were formed by the war period of 1914 to 1945 were dissolved; the cold-war-confrontation between East and West came to an end; one of the world's hegemonic powers with its center in the Kremlin disappeared; its satellites entered a period of disintegration and partly—in the former Yugoslavia—of cruel and bloody war. Western Europe, including a larger Germany and with some new satellites in the East, strengthens its global economic role with obvious consequences for its influence in world politics. What do these changes mean for our perception of modernity? Let me distinguish four main challenges, for which I will use four Bonhoefferian keywords: reality, responsibility, freedom, and the Church.

1. The change of 1989 has often been interpreted as the decision between two alternative concepts of modernization. Both of them have in common the idea that modernity is determined by the progress of science and technology. For both of them modernity and progress are twins. Both of them follow the idea that you have to build a scientific model of reality and then form reality according to your model. The opposite concepts were the concept of the market economy, on the one hand, and that of a centrally planned economy, on the other hand. There is no doubt about the result of this conflict: the market economies are the winner. But such a description misses the deeper dimensions of the processes we are witnessing in our days. We approach these deeper dimensions when we begin to realize that Western democracies did not find any convincing answer to the breakdown of so-called existing socialism and its centrally planned economy. The reason is that the change of 1989 is only interpreted as the victory of one model of modernization. It is not yet interpreted in the framework of the crisis of modernization itself.

Many in the West are so fixed on the concepts of progress, feasibility, and economic effectiveness that they are not aware of the depth of the incision which we experience in our days. However the signals are evident. The most important signals have to be seen in the lack of answers to the questions of the economic injustice between North and South, in the incompatibility between the economic model of Western societies and the elementary demands of global ecological sustainibility, and in the general depolitization of the public in Western societies.

The crisis of our days relates not only to our behavior towards nature or technology or to our acting in the political arena or in social structures, but moreover to our perception of these realities as such. The end of communism signals much more than the end of a specific perversion of modern scientific thinking. We experience the crisis of this way of thinking itself. It is no longer sufficient to take our models and our scientific constructions as the reality itself. For we have to learn to distinguish our models of the world from its reality. What we are asked is to open our experience and our thinking anew to the reality itself.

The extent to which our models not only uncover but also cover reality can easily be seen. The hunger in the poverty belt of the globe, the growing misery in the urban centers of highly industrialized countries, or the devastation of the global environment: all these traits of our present reality mostly play only a marginal role in the influential scientific models of our world.

From the models to reality itself: this is the first direction of the new orientation which is required today. What Vaclav Havel said about the politician is true about us all: "A politician must again become a person, that means someone who trusts not only in a scientific model and an analysis of the world, but in the world as such."[4]

2. In the collapse of East European regimes we experienced in a specifically drastic form the system of organized irresponsibility as a sign of scientific modernity. It is remarkable to observe that those who were responsible for decades of economic mismanagement cannot be identified, that those who systematically distorted civil liberties cannot be prosecuted, that those who really played decisive roles in the state security system move into business and enjoy a new kind of security without being called to account. In Germany, Erich Honecker was indicted in a symbolic trial for the shooting order at the Berlin Wall. But this trial dealt only with a small segment of all brutalities executed in the name of the former GDR. Today the German public concentrates more on the involvement of some church leaders with the state security system than on the crimes against humanity executed by fulltime functionaries of the former regime.

The crisis of responsibility which can be shown by this example is by no means restricted to the former East. It is under different conditions true also for the West. That is demonstrated by the dramatic decline of political authority in the Western democracies since 1989. The credibility of persons in political office seems to be nearly exhausted — mainly because they have arranged a system of thinking and behaviour in which they personally are not accountable for what happens in the public arena. Politics has assumed a symbolic character and tends to be more and more separated from the real events. That constitutes what I call, using an expression borrowed from the sociologist Ulrich Beck, organized irresponsibility.[5]

This system of organized irresponsibility can easily undermine democratic structures; it can delegitimate the system of parliamentary representation. It will then end up in a new wave of authoritarian regimes dominated by economic interests. If you intend to prevent such a development, then the task is to establish realistic responsibility instead of a system of organized irresponsibility.

3. Some people interpret the turn of 1989 as the definite victory of an individualistic concept of freedom. The concept which originated in the times of the Renaissance and found its first full expressions in the theory of possessive individualism and in the utilitarian concept of ethics seems to reach its final victory in the triumph of market economies over the collectivism of centrally planned economies. Francis Fukuyama even identifies this victory with "the end of history."[6] The end of history means in this case that history no longer has to be made; rather it has simply to be executed.

This victorious attitude hides only temporarily the ambiguity of the underlying concept of freedom. The ambivalent consequences of the individualistic concept of freedom are clearly shown by Robert Bellah and his colleagues in their two volumes *Habits of the Heart* and *The Good Society.*[7] The results of their research are in my view important not only for the United States but for all Western societies. I interpret these results in two ways. On the one hand, an individualistic concept of freedom dissolves the integrity of the human person, because it fails to acknowledge that this integrity develops in processes of obliging interaction and exchange between persons. On the other hand, an individualistic concept of freedom hollows out the institutions of the common life; they are used as long as they exist, but nothing is done for their renewal and their revitalization. But the self is not formed in an unstructured social environment; it depends on the nourishment of institutions which encourage the exercise of freedom but demand also the exercise of responsibility. The "sources of the self," to quote the extraordinary book by Charles Taylor,[8] are not found in the isolated individual itself, but develop in the way that the individual takes part in the stories of interpretative communities which contribute to the person's integrity.

What we are witnessing today is a sharpening conflict between two concepts of freedom. The individualistic interpretation of freedom is favored by those processes of individualization which are introduced and facilitated by technological innovations and economic differentiations. The obvious ambiguity of this individualism evokes new efforts to clarify the interrelatedness of freedom and solidarity, the individual and its communities, the personal and the social, as the two sides of the same coin of human life. For this alternative concept of freedom I will use the term "communicative freedom."[9]

4. In a last analytical reflection let me turn to the churches. If I am not mistaken they find themselves today in different parts of the world in a posture of defensiveness. Some of our churches sound the retreat to inwardness, some diminish their ecumenical involvement: some proclaim again a seeming political neutrality, many of them try to find in one way or the other their peace with highly effective but at the same time highly unjust economic structures. The decision of Leonardo Boff to lay down his priesthood and to leave the order of Saint Francis is, independent of all personal aspects, a tremendous signal not only for the Catholic Church and not only for Brazil, but for ecumenical Christianity as a whole. When he explains his decision in his "Open Letter" of July 1992, he formulates the criteria for a church which can be in solidarity with the liberation of the oppressed. That is only possible, says Boff, if the church "overcomes

in her own life all those structures and modes of behaviour, which lead to the discrimination of women, the marginalization of lay people, the distrust against modern freedoms and the spirit of democracy and the forced concentration of sacral power in the hands of priests."[10] Boff painfully missed this liberation of the church itself in the Catholic Church. But that does not mean that this liberation is realized in other churches. Do not even the churches of the reformation, who claim Christian freedom as their specific heritage, wait for a liberation which is still expected? Also for us non-Catholics the hope is not yet fulfilled which Boff terms the hope for a society "in which cooperation and solidarity find less obstacles because the praxis of Jesus and the inspiration by the Spirit invite us to do so," and the hope for a church which lives "in conformity with the gospel, growing in compassion and humanity, obliged to the freedom and the liberation of the sons and daughters of God."[11]

II

My contextual reflection on some aspects of modernity which arise from our specific experience in Europe during the past few years leads to the following result: in the crisis of modernity we need a turn from the models of reality to reality itself, from the system of organized irresponsibility to realistic responsibility, from an individualistic concept of the human person to a new understanding of communicative freedom, and finally from the church on the defensive to the liberation of the church. With this fourfold turn in mind, we might ask, what is the specific contribution of Bonhoeffer's critical theology of modernity to a better understanding of our own situation?

In passing I wish to underline again the intention of my deliberations. My question is not whether Bonhoeffer is representative for *modern theology*, but whether he contributes to a *theology of modernity*.

For my purpose I distinguish modern theology and a theology of modernity. *Modern theology* applies the premises of modernity to theology. It takes, for instance, the criteria of progress or autonomy as decisive criteria for theological truth. This modern theology is what Bonhoeffer calls *liberal theology*. Its specific weakness is, according to him, "that it conceded to the world the right to determine Christ's place in the world; in the conflict between the Church and the world it accepted the comparatively easy terms of peace that the world dictated."[12]

A *theology of modernity*, in comparison, trys to clarify the problems of modernity by theological means. It establishes a critical relationship between biblical concepts and the premises of modernity. With the help of this critical relationship it uncovers the ambiguities of modernity as well as the traditional religious captivity of biblical concepts. So it initiates a liberating process in both directions.

The times of modern theology as described above are not at all over. To the contrary, the efforts of resuscitation are numerous. However, this modern theology is a phenomenon of the past. With its one-dimensional positive reception of the premises of modernity, it underestimates the ambiguity of modernity. The analysis of this ambiguity is one of the central theological tasks of our day. For that we need a theology of modernity which equips us with categories for a critical evaluation, an independent judgement and a practical orientation in the midst of the processes of modernization. Seen from this perspective the theologies of liberation and the theology of Dietrich Bonhoeffer are both critical theologies of modernity.

Their task is not at all fulfilled. The agenda of postmodernity, which was fashionable for a few years and still has some adherents in theology, should not mislead us. Postmodern theology is nothing else than a new variant of modern theology; it accepts the criterion of plurality as a central criterion for Christ's presence in the world. Besides that, the thesis that we have left the epoch of modernity and entered the epoch of post-modernity is simply harmless. For the majority of people life is still determined by the processes of modernization, rationalization and econo-mization. For the majority of people the project of modernity—freedom from need and oppression—is not at all fulfilled simply because a class analysis rightly applies to a theoretical construct that is true for many variants of "postmodernism." Postmodernism is a meaningful ideology for those who profit from the affluence of affluent societies. For all the others a critical theology of modernity is still needed.[13]

In my effort to go some steps further in this endeavor, I will use in a selective way the insights of Dietrich Bonhoeffer, partly from his *Ethics* and partly from the *Letters and Papers from Prison*. I organize these insights following once again our four keywords: reality, responsibility, freedom, and the Church. Following these keywords I am more interested in what Bonhoeffer's thinking can contribute to a theory of modernity than in what is lacking in Bonhoeffer.

1. Reality and responsibility are the two focal points of Bonhoeffer's 'Ethics.' The research done for the new edition of the *Ethics*[14] shows with high probability that Bonhoeffer began his writing with the chapter 'Christ, Reality, and the Good.' This chapter contains the hermeneutical key for his whole endeavor. He writes: "The reality of God discloses itself only

by setting me entirely in the reality of the world, and when I encounter the reality of the world, it is always sustained, accepted and reconciled in the reality of God. This is the inner meaning of the revelation of God in the human being Jesus Christ. Christian ethics enquires about the realization of this divine and wordly reality which is given in Christ, in our world."[15]

From the beginning, it is characteristic of Bonhoeffer's theology that he starts not with possibilities which have to be realized but with a reality which has to be actualized.[16] This reality is found neither in an outerworldly reality of the transcendent God nor in an innerworldly godless reality. Moreover, this reality is defined as the unity of the reality of God and the reality of the world.

This concept of reality has critical implications for more than one traditional way of theological thinking. These critical implications are most obvious for the neo-Lutheran two-kingdoms doctrine. Using a Kantian model of thinking, the two-kingdoms doctrine separates the two realities of the world and of God, or the two orders of creation and of salvation. In separating two realities it evades the conflict within reality itself. Therefore, the two-kingdoms doctrine is an anxious way of doing theology. In opposition to this evasive way of thinking, Bonhoeffer starts with an incarnational christology which provides access to an integral understanding of reality. Its most important consequence is that we have to locate the central conflicts of human existence not between different realities but within reality itself.

There are certain theological consequences of this decision.[17] To understand God as the one who entered wordly reality in faithfulness to the divine creation and for the sake of its fulfillment means to see the conflicts in reality—the conflicts between death and life, isolation and community, hatred and love, violence and peace, guilt and grace—from the perspective of the vivid and life-giving divine spirit, whose presence in the world is instantiated by the incarnation, the cross and the resurrection of Christ. Human participation in the conflicts of reality is therefore oriented toward enacting parables of life and community, of love and peace, and, so, parables of grace, in a reality still overshadowed by death and isolation, by hatred and violence and so by guilt.

Bonhoeffer's incarnational christology forms the foundation for his central concept of "correspondence to reality."[18] I propose to interpret this concept in the sense of a critical participation in the conflicts of reality, a participation in the ongoing struggle to bring the criteria of humanity to bear under the given and ambiguous conditions emerging in the historical character of society. So an incarnational christology leads to a perception of the conflicting character of history with the "view from below," as described in Bonhoeffer's famous text "After Ten Years."[19]

When we turn from *Ethics* to the *Letters and Papers from Prison* we encounter a new tone in Bonhoeffer's speaking about the world. This new tone is concentrated in the formula of the world come of age. The new reflection is determined not only by Wilhelm Dilthey's analysis of the genesis of the modern mind,[20] but also by Carl Friedrich von Weizsäcker's analysis of the worldview of modern physics.[21] It is therefore a reaction to a better understanding of modernity in a twofold sense.[22] Not only does Bonhoeffer accept the historization of our normative orientations, called human autonomy; he also accepts that we have to understand the reality of the external world, *etsi deus non daretur*.[23] Instead of the God-hypothesis we have to accept as a hypothesis for the understanding of reality "that God is not given." In my reading the relationship between the concept of reality in *Ethics* and the understanding of the world come of age in the *Letters and Papers from Prison* is one of the most moving challenges for every interpreter of Bonhoeffer.[24] I have to restrict myself to two indications.

a) It must again and again be emphasized that Bonhoeffer's interpretation of the world without God as a working hypothesis is not a withdrawal from the theological argument, but its intensification. In christological terms this intensification takes the form of Bonhoeffer's unfolding his theology of incarnation as a radical theology of the cross. The key for that theological decision can be found in the letter of July 16, 1944.[25]

The basis for the *theologia crucis* of this letter is the conviction that it is really God himself who is suffering on the cross. It is not only the human person Jesus with whom, as the crucified, God identifies himself in the resurrection – a way of speaking often used in theology. No, it is God, in the human person Jesus, who is suffering and dying on the cross. So it is God himself who is crying on the cross: "My God, my God, why hast thou forsaken me?" (Mark 15.34, one of the two biblical quotations in the letter of July 16). It is extremely strange to imagine that God himself complains that he abandoned himself. But it symbolizes that God himself experiences being abandoned by God. God himself participates in a world without God. So the cross is the place with respect to which it is not a self-contradiction to say: "Before God and with God we live without God."

b) Looking back from this letter from Tegel to the manuscripts for the *Ethics* we detect already there a characteristic combination of a theology of the cross and the affirmation of worldliness. At different instances of the *Ethics* Bonhoeffer develops his christology in the three steps of incarnation, crucifixion and resurrection. The most embracing form of this concept can be found in the latest of these manuscripts, written early in 1943, immediately before his imprisonment. It is the passage on "the concrete commandment and the divine mandates." Here he modifies the three christological steps in the following way: Jesus Christ, the eternal Son with the Father for all eternity; Jesus Christ the crucified Reconciler; and Jesus Christ, the risen and ascended Lord. At the center of this reflection we find Jesus Christ as the crucified Reconciler. The way which is opened up by him is the way of genuine worldliness. "A life in genuine worldliness is possible only through the proclamation of Christ crucified; true worldly living is not possible or real in contradiction or side by side with it, that is to say, in any kind of autonomy of the secular sphere ['Eigengesetz-lichkeit' is Bonhoeffer's term here]; it is possible and real only 'in, with and under' the proclamation of Christ."[26]

The comparison of this text with the letter of July 16, 1944 shows that in the theological letters from Tegel, Bonhoeffer becomes more consistent in his reception of a genuinely modern concept of the world—namely the explanation of the world without God as working hypothesis. But he continues to interpret the divine presence in this world in christological terms—namely in a *theologia crucis*. It is exactly the proclamation of the cross which allows us to overcome the religious captivity of Christian faith and to live this faith in genuine worldliness. This approach allows us to address the conflicts in reality itself and to overcome the restrictions of our perception of reality determined by our models of scientific explanation. A critical theology of modernity uses scientific explanations as working hypotheses. But it demythologizes scientism as the religion of modernity. Only beyond this scientism can a genuine worldliness begin. For the turn from the models of reality to reality itself, Bonhoeffer's theological concept of genuine worldliness is eminently important.

2. Bonhoeffer's "Ethics" forms an ellipse with two focal points. The first is the concept of reality, the second the concept of responsibility. How they are interrelated is evident already from the key formulation for the concept of responsibility:

> The notion of responsibility means the comprehensive unity of the response to the reality which is given to us in Jesus Christ in distinction to the partial responses that the human person could give for instance out of calculation of utility or out of some specific principles. In view of the life which encounters us in Jesus Christ, those partial answers do not suffice, for what is at stake is the unique and comprehensive response of our life.[27]

Responsibility is grounded in the responsiveness of human life. Responsibility is not a specific act as such but the answer given by our life as a whole. But to what do we answer? We answer to reality. More narrowly this reality is defined as "the reality which is given to us in Jesus

Christ." The interpretation of reality already reflected above helps us to explain this even more precisely: Responsibility is the answer of our life as a whole to the unity of divine and worldly reality given to us in Jesus Christ.

Responsibility has a twofold structure. It is responsibility *to* and responsibility *for*. In comparison to other uses of this distinction, it is characteristic that Bonhoeffer does not simply speak of a responsibility to God and for humans. His concept is more complex. He speaks of a responsibility to God and for God as well as to humans and for humans.[28] This is a starting point for a complex theory of responsibility, of which I emphasize only two elements.

a) "Responsibility for" is often interpreted as care. Bonhoeffer himself seems to favor such an interpretation with his concept of "existence for others" or proexistence. But "responsibility for" involves more. It is not simply care ("Fürsorge"), but prospective care ("Vorsorge"), namely the prospective care for a shared realm of living together. This is precisely the sense in which Bonhoeffer summarizes his ethics of responsibility in the text "After Ten Years": "The ultimate question for a responsible person to ask is not how he or she is to extricate him- or herself heroically from the affair, but how the coming generation is to live. It is only from this question, with its responsibility, that fruitful solutions can come, even if for the time being they are very humiliating."[29]

Responsibility as prospective care for the future of a shared realm of living seems to me to be a clear alternative to the system of organized irresponsibility which is predominant in our days. The self-limitation of the living generation in the interest of the life-conditions of future generations, and with respect to the dignity of nature, is the most urgent concrete form of this responsibility.[30]

b) The idea of responsibility has its original place in the sphere of law. "Responsibility to" originally means responsibility to a judge. The transfer of this idea from the sphere of law to the sphere of ethics was historically possible only under the influence of the Christian idea that all humans have to give a last account to a divine judge at the end of history, in the fullness of time. Universal history as such became the ultimate horizon of human responsibility.

The Christian tradition links this universalization of responsibility back to the life of the individual. Here the parable of the last judgement (Mt. 25:31–46) has a fundamental as well as an exemplary function.[31] On the one hand, this parable portrays the last judgement as the fulfillment of time, when the actions of all individuals can receive their definitive meaning in light of the actions of all other individuals. But, on the other hand, it portrays a present situation on the basis of which one's actions are judged—namely the needs of the weak and the oppressed, the fears and hopes of our poor and marginalized brothers and sisters. The legitimacy or illegitimacy of our actions is decided in our interactions with those who are weaker than we are. That seems to me to be the adequate explication of Bonhoeffer's notion of "existence-for-others" in the framework of an ethics of responsibility.

3. In Germany we just started the discussion of a newly published and partly stimulating criticism of Bonhoeffer's theology, written by Klaus-Michael Kodalle.[32] At its core this book criticizes Bonhoeffer in the name of modernity. The criticism is directed against the authoritarian elements in his theology, the dominance of collectivistic over individualistic categories, the legitimation of structures of "above" and "below" as divine mandates.

Kodalle's critique has a double basis. One part is a specific reading of Kierkegaard. According to Kodalle, Kierkegaard understands faith as the movement of pure, absolute communication with God, as the most intense form of the genesis of the individual self. Theology in this understanding seems to be the most radical theory of individuality. The other part of Kodalle's thesis is a certain interpretation of the American experiment. Individual freedom, tolerance, rule of law and democracy are the main elements of the liberal spirit of America in Kodalle's interpretation.

One of Kodalle's main points of criticism is that Bonhoeffer had an insurmountable prejudice against the revolutionary tradition and the liberal spirit of America. His return from Union Theological Seminary to Germany in 1939 shows that the participation with his own destiny in the destiny of his people was for him more important than the new horizons of individual freedom and open possibilities in the new world.[33]

My criticism of Kodalle has two main points. First, Kodalle misunderstands Bonhoeffer's decision of 1939, because he has no access to a concept of responsibility which binds a person's responsibility to a certain historical situation, to a certain point in space and time. Second, Kodalle works with a simplistic and ideological alternative between individualism and collectivism. All reflections on the sociality of human life are seen by him as expressions of an anti-individualistic collectivism. Whereas I agree with his criticism of Bonhoeffer's legitimation of structures of above and below, I do not agree with his interpretation of Bonhoeffer as a collectivist. Kodalle's simplistic alternative of individualism and collectivism is in itself an expression of modern theology, but it is not a contribution to a critical theology of modernity.

I mention this debate because it leads us to the interpretative task before us. The key for the debate lies in Bonhoeffer's concept of freedom. When you look at his understanding of freedom as the central element of responsibility[34] or when you meditate on the "Stations on the Road to Freedom"[35] you will observe an understanding of freedom which is close to the concept of communicative freedom mentioned earlier. Bonhoeffer urges us to overcome the ideological opposition between individualism and collectivism. He helps us to understand human existence as a unity of individuality and solidarity, of lonely life and life together, of purposeless joy and prospective care. This complex unity of human freedom is a much richer concept than the atrophic apologies of individualism favored by some of the modern theologians of our days.

4. Finally, let me conclude with a comment on the Church. At the end of his life, Bonhoeffer returned to the theme of his beginnings, to the theme of the Church. For the book which he started to write in the cell of Tegel, he announced three chapters: "A Stocktaking of Christianity"; "The Real Meaning of Christian Faith"; and "Conclusions." The theme of the "Conclusions" was, as the "Outline for the Book" indicates, the Church. The starting sentences are famous and sound like an answer to Leonardo Boff's letter cited earlier:

> The Church is the Church only when it exists for others. To make a start, it should give away all its property to those in need. The clergy must live solely on the free-will offerings of their congregations, or possibly engage in some secular calling. The Church must share in the secular problems of ordinary human life, not dominating, but helping and serving. It must tell persons of every calling what it means to live in Christ, to exist for others. . . . It is not abstract argument, but example, that gives its word emphasis and power.[36]

Personally, I know local communities living according to this vision. But I do not know an institutional ecclesial body which really has changed its structures according to Bonhoeffer's proposal. What are the reasons for that? Are they simply to be found in the laziness of the human heart or in the power-interests of the church leadership? Or is there a tension in Bonhoeffer's concept itself which has to be taken more seriously than we did in most of our interpretations so far? The tension which I have in mind is the tension between the Church as a community of followers and the public vocation of the Church.[37] To fulfill its public vocation the Church participates in the social conditions which structure the public arena. But a community of followers is independent from those social conditions. In a so-called Christian culture the Church could seemingly accept on easier terms the social structures of which it was a part itself. But the process of modernization led to the result that all variants of "Christian culture" lie behind us. The self-contradictory global civilization of our days allows no room for enclaves of Christian culture anywhere. Nowhere is Christian faith simply identical with the cultural assumptions of a given lifeworld. The Gospel has to be proclaimed anew, articulated and lived out as a strange truth. And so the Church has to accept being a strange reality in a post-Christian world. For that we have to find new models, models in which the faithfulness of a following community and the Church's public vocation are bound together in a new way. Bonhoeffer did not offer a blueprint for that, but he formulated the question. That, again, was a lasting contribution to a critical theology of modernity.

Notes

1. Dietrich Bonhoeffer, *Sanctorum Communio: Eine dogmatische Untersuchung zur Soziologie der Kirche*, herausgegeben von Joachim von Soosten (*Dietrich Bonhoeffer Werke*, 1; Munich: Chr. Kaiser, 1986). See Dietrich Bonhoeffer, *The Communion of Saints*, trans. Ronald G. Smith et al. (New York: Harper & Row, 1963).
2. Dietrich Bonhoeffer, *Widerstand und Ergebung: Briefe und Aufzeichnungen aus der Haft*, herausgegeben von Eberhard Bethge (Munich: Chr. Kaiser, 1990). See Dietrich Bonhoeffer, *Letters and Papers from Prison: The Enlarged Edition*, trans. R. H. Fuller, John Bowden, et al. (New York: Macmillan, 1972).
3. For my own understanding of modernity see Wolfgang Huber, "Der Protestantismus und die Ambivalenz der Moderne," in *Religion der Freiheit: Protestantismus in der Moderne*, herausgegeben von Jürgen Moltmann (Munich: Chr. Kaiser, 1990), 29–65.
4. Vaclav Havel, "The End of the Modern Era," *New York Times*, March 1, 1992, sec. 4, p. 15, col. 2.
5. Ulrich Beck, *Gegengifte: Die organisierte Unverantwortlichkeit* (Frankfurt a.M.: Suhrkamp, 1988).
6. Francis Fukuyama, *The End of History* (New York: The Free Press, 1992).
7. Robert N. Bellah, Richard Madsen, William M. Sullivan, Ann Swidler, Steven M. Tipton, *Habits of the Heart* (Berkeley: University of California Press, 1985); *The Good Society* (New York: Alfred Knopf, 1991).
8. Charles Taylor, *Sources of the Self: The Making of the Modern Identity* (Cambridge, MA: Harvard University Press, 1989).
9. My use of the term depends on Michael Theunissen, *Sein und Schein: Die kritische Funktion der Hegelschen Logik* (Frankfurt a.M.: Suhrkamp, 1978), 37–50, 433–71.
10. *Publik-Forum* 13, July 17, 1992, 14, translation mine.
11. *Publik-Forum* 13, July 17, 1992, 14, translation mine.
12. *Widerstand und Ergebung*, 172; *Letters and Papers*, 327.
13. The most reflected "postmodern" theories are *de facto* critical theories of modernity themselves, cf. Jean-François Lyotard, *The Differend: Phrases in Dispute*, trans. Georges Van Den Abeele (Minneapolis: University of Minnesota Press, 1988).
14. Dietrich Bonhoeffer, *Ethik*, herausgegeben von Ilse Tödt, Heinz Eduard Tödt, Ernst Feil und Clifford Green (*Dietrich Bonhoeffer Werke*, 6; Munich: Chr. Kaiser, 1992).

15. *Ethik*, 40, trans. Ilse Tödt in Clifford Green et al., "Textual Research for the New Edition," in *Bonhoeffer's Ethics: Old Europe and New Frontiers*, ed. Guy Carter et al. (Kampen, Netherlands: Kok Pharos, 1991), 36.
16. *Sanctorum Communio*, 87–139.
17. I use here formulations from my earlier article, "Toward an Ethics of Responsibility" (forthcoming).
18. *Ethik*, 221–3, 256–75f.
19. *Widerstand und Ergebung*, 26; *Letters and Papers*, 17.
20. Wilhelm Dilthey, *Weltanschauung und Analyse des Menschen seit Renaissance und Reformation*, in *Gesammelte Schriften*, 2 (Stuttgart: Teubner and Vandenhoeck & Ruprecht, 1960).
21. Carl Friedrich von Weizsäcker, *Zum Weltbild der Physik* (Stuttgart: Hirzel, 1970).
22. Cf. Ernst Feil, *Die Theologie Dietrich Bonhoeffers* (Munich: Chr. Kaiser, 1991), 355.
23. *Widerstand und Ergebung*, 191; *Letters and Papers*, 360.
24. I am grateful for an important discussion with Alberto Gallas (Milano) on this topic. A work-in-progress by Gallas will provide a detailed interpretation of the relationship mentioned above.
25. *Widerstand und Ergebung*, 191–2; *Letters and Papers*, 360–1.
26. *Ethik*, 404f.; *Ethics*, trans. Neville Horton Smith. (New York: Macmillan, 1965), 297.
27. *Ethik*, 254, my translation; see *Ethics*, 222. I discussed Bonhoeffer's concept of responsibility more in detail in Wolfgang Huber, "Sozialethik als Verantwortungsethik," in *Konflikt und Konsens: Studien zur Ethik der Verantwortung* (Munich: Chr. Kaiser, 1990), 135–57; "Toward an Ethics of Responsibility," (forthcoming).
28. *Ethik*, 255; *Ethics*, 223.
29. *Widerstand und Ergebung*, 14; see *Letters and Papers*, 7.
30. See for this argument Wolfgang Huber, "Rights of Nature or Dignity of Nature?," *The Annual of the Society of Christian Ethics* (1991): 43–60; "Selbstbegrenzung aus Freiheit: Über das ethische Grundproblem des technischen Zeitalters," *Evangelische Theologie* 52 (1992): 128–46.
31. For the relevance of the parable in Bonhoeffer's 'Ethics' see *Ethik*, 155, 321–2.
32. Klaus-Michael Kodalle, *Dietrich Bonhoeffer: Zur Kritik seiner Theologie* (Gütersloh: Gütersloher Verlagshaus Gerd Mohn, 1991).
33. Kodalle, 74–5.
34. *Ethik*, 283–9.
35. *Widerstand und Ergebung*, 197–8; *Letters and Papers*, 370–1.
36. *Widerstand und Ergebung*, 206–7; *Letters and Papers*, 382–3.
37. Cf. Larry Rasmussen with Renate Bethge, *Dietrich Bonhoeffer: His Significance for North Americans* (Minneapolis: Fortress, 1990), 72–88.

THE END OF HISTORY
AND THE NEW WORLD ORDER

Steven Schroeder

Two concepts, the "end of history" and the "new world order," have become prominent as we approach the end of what Christians immodestly refer to as the second millennium and the beginning of the 500th anniversary of what Europeans and Americans have equally immodestly designated the discovery of the New World. It is interesting to speculate on whether this is due to serendipity or an apocalyptic madness peculiar to times that dominant cultures call millennial. Given the entanglement of mission and conquest in Columbus and in the culture that took up his mantle with the founding and expansion of the United States, I suspect the latter. And I suspect that responsibility in a new world will require us to attend to the confusion between that order which is reflected in the division and measurement of time by dominant cultures and an Order supposed to be inherent in Nature. Bonhoeffer's later work, particularly *Ethics* and *Letters and Papers from Prison,* is a resource uniquely suited to this task. Since the end of history and the new world order have coalesced in a contemporary interpreter of Hegel such as Francis Fukuyama, Bonhoeffer's discussion of orders in conversation with interpreters of Hegel and Luther among *his* contemporaries is timely.

In the first section of this paper, I will explore Bonhoeffer's reading of the history of the west as developed in his *Ethics* and in the prison correspondence, with special attention to his caution against confusing the penultimate with the ultimate and to his understanding of order, formation, and conformation. In the second section, I will explore Francis Fukuyama's influential reading of the history of the west, with special attention to his appropriation of Hegel by way of Alexandre Kojève. In the

21

third and final section, I will explore the differences between Bonhoeffer
and Fukuyama and seek to show the difference they make as a corrective
to the triumphalism that has accompanied European-American attitudes
toward new worlds at least since the time of Columbus.

I

The section of Bonhoeffer's *Ethics* entitled "Ethics as Formation" is his
most extended reading of the history of the west.[1] Less extended, but also
important, is a series of letters to Eberhard Bethge written from Tegel during
1944.[2] Taken together, these selections constitute the primary sources with
which to begin an analysis of Bonhoeffer's reading of the history of the
west in the last five years of his life.

"Ethics as Formation" begins with a timely reflection on the absence
of concern for theoretical ethics precipitated, Bonhoeffer suggests, by the
fact that most people at the time he was writing (around 1940) were too
deeply embroiled in the pressing problems posed by practical ethics to
concern themselves with the theoretical. Preoccupation with the practical,
to the extent that it means giving precedence to the concrete rather than
the abstract, is critically important to Bonhoeffer's own approach to ethics.
But he is concerned with the extent to which the popular preoccupation
was entangled with a "failure of *reasonable* people to perceive either the
depths of evil or the depths of the holy."[3] Writing from the depths of Hitler's
Germany, Bonhoeffer himself is preoccupied with the failure of ethics, as
understood by "reasonable" people, to sustain resistance. There are obvious
reasons for that preoccupation—which became the basis for a realistic ethic
grounded in a careful reading of history—in the last years of his life.

Bonhoeffer points to the failure of reason, will, conscience, duty,
freedom, and private virtue as bases for ethics, then proposes a christological alternative that is consistent with his earlier writing.[4] The only
adequate basis for Christian ethics, he insists, is Christ; and this means
that it is grounded not in a general or abstract principle but in a particular
and concrete encounter with God in humankind. God, Bonhoeffer insists
more than once, did not become an abstract principle; God became a
human being. The christological alternative is thus also incarnational, and
it is this incarnational character of ethics that makes it so important to *read*
history rather than simply to be swept along by it. If human history is where
we meet God, then human history is of central importance from a theological as well as an anthropological perspective.

Bonhoeffer understands the failure of all those noble bases for human ethics in the context of the struggle that ensues when "an old world ventures to take up arms against a new one and when a world of the past hazards an attack against the superior forces of the commonplace and mean."[5] The patron saint of this struggle is Don Quixote, and there is good reason to take a second look at that patron of impossible causes. The second look, as has been recently suggested by Kirkpatrick Sale,[6] might lead us to read *Don Quixote* rather than the *Aeneid* as the foundation myth of western culture.

The problem posed by Don Quixote's struggle on behalf of the old world against the new is how to see the world as it is. Bonhoeffer asserts that the wise person is precisely the one "who sees reality as it is, and who sees into the depths of things."[7] To see reality as it is, to see into the depths of things, is to see reality in God. There are hints here both of the Hegelian shape of Bonhoeffer's historical and epistemological outlook and of the limitation of that shape. Though Bonhoeffer may be reluctant to follow Hegel in explicitly affirming that without the world, God would not be God, he is more than willing to insist that without God, the world would not be the world. His reluctance to follow the seemingly more radical version of Hegel's assertion stems from a clear-sighted understanding of the dangerous tendency to deify the world; it does not prevent him from later recognizing that the hypothesis of God may have no place in a world come of age. If one is to see God, one must look at the world; and if one is to see Jesus, one must look at humankind. "Jesus," Bonhoeffer writes, "is not *a* man. He is *man*."[8] That this is an ethical as much as an epistemological problem becomes progressively clearer over the four or five year span from the composition of this text to the last of the prison letters to Bethge. The problem is not how to be redeemed from the world (or to be given a place outside the world from which to move it, as Bonhoeffer repeats many times) but how to be redeemed *into* it. And that means both how to be empowered to live in it and how to be enabled to recognize it. For Bonhoeffer, "to be conformed with the Incarnate is to have the right to be the man [or woman] one really is."[9]

Bonhoeffer does not proceed in a linear fashion from beginning to end, because he is inclined (as in his early lectures on *Creation and Fall*[10]) to insist that the end is in the beginning. We live *from* the end of time because the eschatological event of incarnation, God's taking on of human flesh, has already happened. This means that "the point of departure for Christian ethics is the body of Christ."[11] And it means, because "the Church is nothing but a section of humanity in which Christ has really taken form," that the point of departure is "the form of Christ in the form of the Church." The latter form, of course, became increasingly problematic for Bonhoeffer in the course of the *Kirchenkampf*, and this problematization of the form of the church is one of his great strengths. To the extent that the church is the body of Christ, it is a living being, that, like all living beings, is not only formed but also in formation. The important thing, as Bonhoeffer wrote in one of his letters from prison, "is that we should be able to discover from the fragment of our life how the whole was arranged and planned, and what material it consists of."[12] We confront the church in the world; it is not an Archimedean point. We confront it both as a crucified, broken body that challenges us to discern the whole in the parts and as a resurrected body that "takes form among us here and now."[13]

Bonhoeffer (like Hegel, like Luther, and like the Hebrew prophets) reads history because that is where we meet God. He also reads it with the consciousness that our history sets us "objectively in a definite nexus of experiences, responsibilities and decisions from which we cannot free ourselves again except by an abstraction. We live, in fact, within this nexus, whether or not we are in every respect aware of it."[14] Bonhoeffer reads history because that is where we–both as individuals and as communities–become who we are.

Those are not, by the way, two different reasons for reading history, but two aspects of one reason. In our encounter with history, we encounter God (whether we know it or not, Bonhoeffer suggests), and it is that encounter that empowers us to be who we are. We should keep in mind that when he speaks a bit later about the penultimate and the ultimate, Bonhoeffer explains that the penultimate must always precede the ultimate temporally; that the ultimate is not, however, to be understood as resulting from the penultimate; and that the penultimate (even though it comes first in a temporal sense) is entirely dependent on the ultimate. Without God the world would not be the world–nor would "we" be "we." But before we encounter God, we encounter the world in history, and it is in the encounter that we *become*–the encounter *is* the becoming. Bonhoeffer is closer to Luther and the Hebrew prophets at this point than was Hegel, insofar as Hegel saw the abstraction by which we free ourselves as the point of our historical/philosophical inquiry. To the extent that Hegel saw history as a process within which consciousness becomes conscious of itself and thereby transcends itself, he departed from the profound this worldliness that Luther appropriated from Hebrew Scripture. Bonhoeffer would be more inclined to describe the process as one of conformation in which human being comes into being in encounter with the fully human reality embodied in Christ. This, I think, is what he must have had in mind in the prison letters when he told Eberhard Bethge that Christianity is not a religion of redemption. "Redemption myths," he wrote, "arise from human boundary experiences, but Christ takes hold of a man [or woman] at the center of his [or her] life."[15] Hegel, unlike Bonhoeffer, may have lost sight of the characteristically Lutheran focus on the cross which, as Bonhoeffer was aware, was not a morbid preoccupation with death but a potentially empowering preoccupation with the presence of God in the fullness of humanity (and the creation of the fullness of humanity in the presence of God).

That our reading of history is an *encounter* may identify it as an action or as a passion. It is probably most accurate to read Bonhoeffer as intending both identifications. As an action, it is formation: we make history, and we are most likely to make it in our image. Bonhoeffer, like Kierkegaard before him, was rightly critical of Hegel's tendency to see his own time and place as the end point toward which all previous history had developed and in which all previous history took shape. But, like Kierkegaard, he was also conscious of the fact that to the extent that we become *subjects* of history we can only see it—and make it—from the places and times in which we stand. We cannot step outside the world, and to claim that we have done so is to deify our place and time while despising humanity in a way that Bonhoeffer, following Luther, identifies as decidedly unchristian. As a passion, it is conformation: we are made by history, and to the extent that God is the subject of history we are made in God's image. Bonhoeffer was acutely conscious of the extent to which the deification of the human as subject of history could result in profound deformation and dehumanization of the human as its object. For evidence, he had only to look at the total state of National Socialism.

Bonhoeffer's consciousness of the profound deformation and dehumanization so prevalent as a product of the historical nexus within which he lived is the backdrop against which he speaks of the Christian west. For Bonhoeffer, that backdrop is one in which God's action in history is obscured and which therefore poses two practical questions: What is it about the history of the Christian west that has obscured God as the subject of history? And what can be done to facilitate encounter with God in the context of this history? Both questions contribute to a definition of the church and its work, though the first does this only by defining the larger context within which the church and its work exists. Bonhoeffer's answer to the first question goes some way toward describing what he sees as the order of the old world that struggles against the new world constituted by the form of Christ in the church. Bonhoeffer's reading of the old world is shaped in part by that world (as indicated, perhaps, in his choice of the word "inheritance" [*Erbe*] which had both biological and historical dimensions in the ideology of National Socialism); it is predicated on the assumption that the old world renders responsibility difficult to the extent that it places obstacles in the way of encountering (and therefore responding to) God. The form of the church, for Bonhoeffer, is that space in the world that enables encounter with and therefore response to God. It is the *response* to God in the world (and therefore in humankind) that constitutes responsible action.[16]

Bonhoeffer distinguishes the west from the rest of the world by suggesting that we look back to our forbears not as "ancestors who are made the object of worship and veneration" but as "witnesses of the entry of God into history."[17] Jesus, according to Bonhoeffer, is "the continuity of our history." This obviously involves a certain degree of exclusivity that bears further examination, but it does not lead him to an exclusive or facile focus on Christian Scripture to the exclusion of Hebrew Scripture (a focus that was undeniably tempting to Christian theologians in the Nazi context). Instead, it leads him first to a christocentric, then to a more broadly incarnational, interpretation of Hebrew Scripture and to a reminder that "an expulsion of the Jews from the west must necessarily bring with it an expulsion of Christ. For Jesus Christ was a Jew."[18] This is important not only as a repudiation of Hitler's attack on the Jewish community of Europe, but also because it establishes one source of the inheritance of the west in Bonhoeffer's reading of history. He looked to Hebrew Scripture and to Judaism as one of the sources out of which this entity called the west was born. It is, significantly, the Jewish community to whom we look first as witnesses.

Greco-Roman antiquity is a second source in Bonhoeffer's reading that is subsequently transformed into several sources with several distinct implications. As he tells the story, the *Roman* Hellenistic world is important because it is the "time when the time of God was fulfilled," and because it is "the world which God took to Himself in the incarnation."[19] This suggests that God became incarnate not just in a particular person (Jesus) but also in the world within which that person lived. That may seem obvious, but it has important implications for Bonhoeffer's incarnational approach: when God became human, God took on the whole world. This parallels the theme repeated several times in *Ethics* of Jesus as all humanity rather than *a* human being. It also amounts to a reaffirmation of the characteristically Hegelian (and characteristically Lutheran) connection between God and the world.

Though Bonhoeffer gives special significance to the Greco-Roman heritage of the west, he splits it by identifying the Roman heritage as coming to represent "the combination and assimilation of antiquity with the Christian element" and the Greek heritage as coming to represent

"opposition and hostility to Christ."[20] Given the role of the Roman government in the crucifixion, this may seem a bit odd, but Bonhoeffer appears
to have in mind the identification of the church with Rome that gradually
occurred over the first several centuries of Christianity that coincided with
the emergence of the papacy. And he appears to have in mind the tendency
of western thinkers who wanted an alternative to Christianity to look to
the Greeks and their mythology as a pre-Christian and often anti-Christian
option. This had particular importance in his context because of Nietzsche's
appropriation of Greek philosophy and its employment by some architects
of Nazi ideology.

Bonhoeffer traces this approach to the Greek tradition back to the
German Reformation. The Roman tradition had been passed on to Europe
in general and Germany in particular in a more or less unbroken line. In
fact, Bonhoeffer points out with some justification that the histories of
Europe *began* in the encounter with Rome and that, as Rome became inextricably identified with Christianity in the west, those histories began
in the encounter with Christ transmitted through the medium of Rome.
Western Europe saw itself as the inheritor of Roman antiquity and therefore
appropriated Roman Christianity and Roman foundation myths (including
the *Aeneid*, reinterpreted through Christian eyes, with Christ substituted
for Augustus). Luther's turn *away* from Rome meant a turn *toward* Greece
because there were only two western alternatives.

In Bonhoeffer's reading, there is one inheritance with four sources,
three of which are joined together in the historical figure of Jesus and one
of which is viewed as pre-Christian: first is the Jewish tradition, particularly
the tradition of the Hebrew prophets; second is the Greek tradition, particularly the tradition of Greek philosophy and tragic drama interpreted
as humanistic; third is the Hellenistic tradition, which is a melding of Greek
and Roman tradition and which is the world into which Jesus was born;
fourth is the Roman tradition, which is the tradition of Roman Christianity. Of course, Bonhoeffer could argue that the person of Jesus ties all these
sources together to the extent that the Greek tradition is appropriated
through the Hellenistic world. But he is interested in the consciously anti-
Christian (not just anti-Roman) conjuring of the Greek heritage that he
sees as characteristic of Germany's attitude toward antiquity.

The Reformation shattered "the *corpus christianum*, the historical order
of the Christian west, which was ruled and held together by Emperor and
Pope in the name of Jesus Christ."[21] Bonhoeffer attributes this to Luther's
conviction that the unity of the faith could not reside in any political power,
which gave rise to the Lutheran understanding of two kingdoms. Bonhoeffer insists that, while Luther did not lose sight of the fact that God

is the sovereign of both kingdoms, many Lutherans and others misunderstood the two kingdoms as implying "the emancipation and sanctification of the world and of the natural."[22] He perhaps underplays the tension that existed between Emperor and Pope long before Luther, but Bonhoeffer sees the Lutheran Reformation as providing the background against which a proper distinction of two spheres of God's activity in the world (a distinction that Luther and Bonhoeffer would insist existed but was denied with increasing regularity before the Reformation) could be transformed into a vision of the world as consisting of one sphere in which God is sovereign and one sphere in which God is not. This split becomes an important theme for his ethical analysis and has been an important tool with which to explain the Lutheran and more broadly Protestant tradition of withdrawal into quietism and personal piety that played so disastrously into Hitler's hands in Germany.

The misunderstanding of two kingdoms as an "emancipation and sanctification of the world and of the natural" is seen as the basis for the emergence of western technology as *mastery* rather than service. To the extent that the natural becomes independent of God, there is a renewed western emphasis on dominating it, as though the issue of sovereignty is in doubt and must be established primarily through technological means. Bonhoeffer does not reject western technology and is in fact critical of those who do. He asserts that "the age of technology is a genuine heritage of our western history. We must come to grips with it. We cannot return to the pretechnical era."[23] This poses the obvious problem of how, precisely, to come to grips with it, a problem that still plagues us.

For Bonhoeffer, then, the Lutheran Reformation is the starting point of an independent secular sphere from which God is excluded and a religious sphere to which the church is increasingly confined. It is also the moment of birth of a western technological tradition of dominance over nature in the name of humankind, as opposed to service to humankind through nature in the name of God. This is not, of course, to say that Bonhoeffer believed Luther intended these consequences; he expressly denied this in a Reformation Day letter to his parents written in 1943.[24] But he became increasingly conscious of the power of unintended consequences and secondary motivations during his time in prison.

Bonhoeffer cites the French Revolution as the moment of birth of modern nationalism.[25] He distinguishes the nation (which is organic) from the state (which is institutional) and identifies France with the former, Prussia with the latter. "Prussia," Bonhoeffer asserts, "wished to be neither nationalistic nor international. In this respect its thought was more western than was that of the Revolution."[26] In the defeat of Prussia by France,

Bonhoeffer sees the triumph of technology, mass movements, and nationalism which became the inheritance bequeathed by the revolution to the western world. His reading suggests that the Reformation opened the way to a misunderstanding that was then transformed by the French Revolution into this deadly inheritance. That it is deadly in Bonhoeffer's eyes results in part from the bitter conflict it contains: "The masses and nationalism," he writes, "are hostile to reason. Technology and the masses are hostile to nationalism. Nationalism and technology are hostile to the masses."[27]

It is not surprising that Bonhoeffer reads the French Revolution through the lens of the German Reformation. "Luther's great discovery of the freedom of the Christian man," he writes, "and the Catholic heresy of the essential good in man combined to produce the deification of man. But, rightly understood, the deification of man is the proclamation of nihilism."[28] That nihilism, it would seem, is embodied for Bonhoeffer in Nazi Germany.

In his *Ethics*, it is clear that Bonhoeffer sees the Christian church as the guardian of the western inheritance against the nihilism embodied in Nazism. The western inheritance he has in mind is the form of Christ, the dwelling of God with humankind that is communicated by both Hebrew and Christian Scripture and which the West first encountered in the Roman Church. The decay of the West derives from its refusal "to accept its historical inheritance for what it is."[29] That this vision continues in the prison correspondence is evidenced by the fact that the worldly Christianity Bonhoeffer was struggling to articulate there was directed toward enabling humankind to encounter God in the very center of the world—even when the hypothesis of God had been discarded.

Bonhoeffer's reading of history is Hegelian, but it is also radically christocentric, incarnational, and concrete. These characteristics, I believe, gave it a critical edge that the later Hegel and many of his followers lost in their absolutization of the system and their virtual sanctification of the existing state of affairs.[30] I will return to this later, but for now it is sufficient to note once again that Bonhoeffer's critical edge, the ground under his feet that sustained and supported his resistance, consisted in his willingness to embrace the world rather than attempting to overcome or transcend it.

II

Francis Fukuyama's understanding of the end of history, and the reading of the history of the west that accompanies it, is derived from Hegel by way of Alexandre Kojève, a Russian emigré contemporary with Bonhoeffer who went to France and became an influential teacher of postwar political thinkers covering the political gamut from left (Jean Paul Sartre) to right (Raymond Aron).[31] That Allan Bloom shared Fukuyama's assessment of Kojève and based his praise particularly on Kojève's single-minded devotion to a single book—the *Phenomenology*—is further testimony to his influence as an interpreter of Hegel. Fukuyama sees the recovery of Kojève as a way to offer a corrective to the Marxist lens through which most of us have been exposed to Hegel and by which (he would have us believe) Hegel's impact on our understanding of history has been distorted.

When Fukuyama applies his Hegelian framework to contemporary events, he sees not "the end of ideology" but the "end of history": "What we may be witnessing is not just the end of the Cold War, or the passing of a particular period of postwar history, but the end of history as such: that is, the end point of [hu]mankind's ideological evolution and the univer-salization of western liberal democracy as the final form of human government."[32]

Fukuyama credits Hegel as the originator of the concept of the end of history. More exactly, he contends that it was Hegel who gave us "the concept of history as a dialectical process with a beginning, a middle, and an end. . . . Hegel believed that history culminated in an absolute moment—a moment in which a final, rational form of society and state become victorious."[33] In those terms, Fukuyama and Kojève contend that Hegel declared history to have come to an end in 1806 with Napoleon's victory over the Prussian monarchy at the Battle of Jena. He could make this proclamation because he saw in Napoleon's victory "the victory of the ideals of the French Revolution, and the imminent universalization of the state incorporating the principles of liberty and equality."[34] Neither Kojève nor Fukuyama rejects Hegel's declaration in the light of what has happened in the almost two centuries since. Instead, both contend that it was essentially correct, that the struggles that have followed the Battle of Jena have been struggles to consolidate the victory in that battle of the ideas represented by the French Revolution. Both see Europe and North America as a vanguard existing at the end of history while the rest of the world struggles to catch up.

Fukuyama, like Hegel and Kojève, intertwines teleology with eschatology. Both have to do with the end, but the first is more concerned with direction and purpose while the second is more concerned with space and time. Although sometimes it appears that the teleological aspect (concerned with the direction of history) is more important to Fukuyama than the eschatological aspect (concerned with our place in it), it generally appears to be the case that his language about the present and about international relations in the future is shaped by his perception of our place on the vanguard. It even appears at times that his perception of our place in space and time as the vanguard plays a major role in shaping his understanding of history's direction.

Fukuyama's interpretation of Hegel's idealism depends on the conviction that the contradictions that drive history exist on the level of *ideas*. Consciousness shapes the material world, not the other way around. Marx criticized this argument from a materialist perspective, insisting that it is the material world which shapes consciousness, and asserted that, rather than turning Hegel upside down, he had found Hegel standing on his head and put him on his feet. Bonhoeffer was increasingly in agreement with this criticism and increasingly inclined to see Hegelianism as standing on its head as he moved toward a worldly interpretation of Christianity. But Fukuyama categorizes this as an influential distortion which ultimately diminishes the importance of ideas and downplays the significance of consciousness and culture.[35]

Fukuyama enlists Max Weber as an ally, arguing that he inverted Marx's analysis by describing the material mode of production as superstructure built up on the base of consciousness and culture, including religion. Like Weber, Fukuyama associates the rise of capitalism with Protestantism. Oddly enough, however, he also associates socialism with Catholicism. He cites a proverb which says that Protestants eat well while Catholics sleep well and uses it to emphasize the association of a Protestant devotion to profit (not work!) with economic success and a Catholic devotion to asceticism and discipline with economic failure. Ultimately, this has the effect of associating individualism and competition with economic success, collectivism and disciplined cooperation with economic failure.

Fukuyama's understanding of Hegel leads him to assert that history is directional and purposive, that history's *direction* is toward a rational, economic, political and social system that is the embodiment of the ideals of the French Revolution and capitalism, and that its *purpose* is to realize such a system. Because he is convinced, like Hegel and Kojève, that history ended at the Battle of Jena, he is led to assert that a universal homogenous state has been achieved by history, and that this state represents history's end. He summarizes the content of this universal homogenous state as "liberal democracy in the political sphere combined with easy access to VCRs and stereos in the economic."[36]

Much of Fukuyama's argument is devoted to the assertion that there have been two challenges to liberalism in the past century, fascism and communism, and that both have been thoroughly discredited, not so much because of moral revulsion against them, but because they do not work.

Fukuyama dismisses fascism too cavalierly, I am afraid, because he fails to view it consistently as a particularly virulent and destructive strain of nationalism. He simply equates communism with the Soviet Union and dismisses it as irrelevant. But this identification fails to take socialism into account as a possible alternative that has yet to be put into actual practice. He reads developments since Hegel's declaration of the end of history as a march toward a universal homogenous state which he identifies with liberalism and capitalism. This is not because the evidence supports that kind of developmental reading so much as because that kind of developmental ideology provides a convenient framework within which to organize the evidence. The relationship between the framework and the evidence is a problem to which I will return in the last section of the paper.

Fukuyama lists two additional alternatives to liberalism: religion and nationalism. Added to the ones discussed before, these alternatives result in an odd collection that is neither consistent nor systematic in its principles of categorization. It is not really clear what Fukuyama means by liberalism, though it appears likely that he intends a universal homogeneous state consisting of liberal democracy and easy access to consumer goods. But liberal democracy drops out of the picture altogether in his substitution of "a truly universal consumer culture"[37] (from which he is reluctant to exclude even the People's Republic of China after Tiananmen Square) for the universal homogeneous state. Access to consumer goods, not access to democracy, is the single most salient feature.

Fukuyama pictures the dialectic of history since Hegel's declaration of its end as a series of struggles: first between liberalism and fascism, then, when liberalism triumphs, between liberalism and communism. Two additional struggles may ensue, one with nationalism, the other with religion. Unfortunately, it is not clear how these struggles fit together or why their resolution is to be seen as development toward an end.

This lack of clarity is related to the fact that Fukuyama's liberalism, as suggested above, is not so much liberal democracy as consumerism. Greater clarity could be introduced into the Hegelian reading of events since the end of history in 1806 by arguing that the development in question is toward political democracy, not consumerism. The struggles Fukuyama describes may be more properly characterized as struggles between the *universal* and the *tendency to universalize various particulars*. The latter tendency is seen in consumerism (Fukuyama's universal), in all forms of nationalism (including fascism), in religious fundamentalism, and in state socialism (including the Marxist-Leninist variety).

Development toward political democracy is only a moment in the process of development toward human liberation, and we are hardly at the end of that process—though we *may* be able to view what we are doing now in the light of that process as an end.

III

In this third and final section I will explore the differences between the two readings with which we've been concerned so far and take a look at why they matter. Let me remind the reader that I offer this exploration as a tentative step toward a corrective to the triumphalism that has accompanied European-American attitudes toward new worlds at least since the time of Columbus.

An obvious and important difference is in the relative weight accorded the French Revolution and the Lutheran Reformation. Fukuyama and Kojève emphasize the former, while Bonhoeffer emphasizes the latter. It is tempting, and at least partly correct, to attribute this difference to the times and places of the two readings. Bonhoeffer, of course, wrote in Germany *during* the Second World War while Kojève wrote in France *after* the war. Fukuyama simply follows Kojève, though his post-Cold War vantage point is undoubtedly a significant contributing factor in his easy appropriation of Kojève's emphasis, particularly to the extent that he conflates the French and American Revolutions.[38] It is also tempting—and, again, partly correct—to refer the mediation of this difference to scholarship on Hegel, to the extent that our concern is whether *Hegel* emphasized the reformation or the revolution. But Hegel scholars are divided on the issue, because Hegel emphasized both—and so did Bonhoeffer. Bonhoeffer seems to have read the Reformation as a part of the inheritance of the West that crystallized in the revolution—particularly since he sees Napoleon's victory over Prussia as a victory of the nation (and Nationalism) over the state—into a process of decay, while Kojève and Fukuyama seem to have seen the former as preparatory for the latter and the latter as the beginning of the end—not as decay, but as *telos.*

A second difference involves our place vis-à-vis history. Fukuyama's appropriation of Hegel by way of Kojève puts the West on the vanguard, at the end of history, and leaves the rest of the world struggling to catch up. Many readers of Hegel have noted his tendency to place Europe at the pinnacle of historical development, with Germany at the pinnacle of Europe. In Fukuyama as in much post-Cold War discourse, the United States supplants Germany. As a thoroughly aristocratic and generally conservative German, Bonhoeffer was partly inclined to adopt Hegel's Germanocentrism[39] more or less unconsciously. As a German Lutheran theologian, he could also be expected to attribute great importance to the Lutheran Reformation. But as a reflective opponent of National Socialism, he seems to have taken note of the danger of placing one's own time and place on the vanguard. He returned again and again to the idea of being in the middle, and this took increasingly concrete form as he began to develop the idea of a worldly Christianity. For Bonhoeffer, our place is *in* history, and we can claim to live from the end only to the extent that we recognize that this end is also in history. We live from (not at or toward) the end, but only because the end has entered into the middle. For Fukuyama, our place is at the end of history, transcending it through our consciousness of and participation in the universal homogeneous state. To the extent that we live within our consciousness, we live beyond the end.

This has a direct impact on a third difference, which has to do with Hegel's orientation. Bonhoeffer seems to have increasingly come to agree with Marx that Hegel ended up standing on his head. This does not mean that Bonhoeffer arrived at Marx's materialist reading, though his worldly Christianity has strong affinities with it. What it means is that he insisted on beginning with the concrete rather than the abstract (and in this he is probably closer to Kierkegaard than to Marx). Fukuyama is convinced that when Marx (or Kierkegaard or Bonhoeffer) turned Hegel over, they left him upside down. This is particularly significant, I think, because it largely determines where and how we stand. For Fukuyama, we stand beyond (or transcend) history in our consciousness, in our ideas; that, then, is where we really live. For Bonhoeffer (as for Marx), we stand in history in our concrete encounter with other human beings.

A fourth difference, which grows to some extent out of the third, consists in the emphasis of individualism and competition (as in Fukuyama) over collectivism and disciplined cooperation (as in Marx—but also, I think, in Bonhoeffer). Fukuyama's argument results in an embrace of a universal consumer culture that places its faith in the market.[40] In a curious sense, the market becomes the embodiment of Reason in history (taking the place of Christ in the Hegelian scheme) and therefore transcends the need for application of human reason to history. I think Jeffrey Friedman's libertarian argument[41] extends Fukuyama's liberal argument to its logical conclusion: rational economic planning fails because it distorts the reason of the market which proceeds on the basis of unbridled competition among individuals pursuing their own interests, hence the emphasis on individual freedom and competition. Bonhoeffer's argument results in a struggle to discern the form of Christ in the form of the church—and to do it inside rather than outside history. Christ is embodied in history, but not as an abstract principle. This means that the encounter with Christ in history is the encounter with concrete human beings, and that it always has the fragmentary character of a form that is in formation. Bonhoeffer's vision of the church is a confessional vision in which individuals speak *with* rather than *against* one another.

A fifth difference, reflected in the relationship between framework and evidence, also grows out of the third. To the extent that we live beyond the end of history, we have access to a framework (or a system) that can simply be applied as an abstract principle to the concrete evidence and events of our lives. We form history in the image of the system by incorporating it into the system. Whatever is outside the system simply ceases to exist. Bonhoeffer, like Kierkegaard and Marx, was extremely critical of this type of idealism. For Bonhoeffer, there is no abstract system or framework to be applied to the concrete. We live in the concrete, and we struggle to discern the form of Christ that takes form only there. The difference, again, is not so much between idealism and materialism as between the abstract and the concrete.

The last difference is perhaps the most significant because it is a difference in identification of the end. Fukuyama, Kojève, Marx, and Bonhoeffer are all Hegelians; but that fact should not be allowed to mask profound differences in their understanding of the end. For Fukuyama, the end is a universal homogeneous state by which he means a universal culture of consumerism. As a good Hegelian, he views reason as the end of history, but he equates reason with the market. The final triumph of the market with the dissolution of the Soviet Union becomes the embodiment of reason in history, and responsible action, action in accordance with reason, means participation in the market. For Bonhoeffer, the end is Christ, God's incarnation in history. This makes Bonhoeffer, too, a good Hegelian—and a christocentric one. But, because he refuses to see Christ as the embodiment of an abstract principle, he sees responsible action as an encounter with God in humankind, in a living form that—because it is living—is always in formation.

Bonhoeffer's emphasis on the Lutheran Reformation is an emphasis on Luther's great insight that we are *bound* to freedom and to one another.[42] To emphasize this insight over the triumph of the French Revolution is intended to give prominence to passion over action and faith over reason. I do not mean by this that Bonhoeffer devalued reason in favor of emotion or that he discounted action in favor of passivity. As Bonhoeffer was aware, both possibilities crept into Lutheran (and more broadly Protestant) interpretation rather quickly. But his point, I believe, was to emphasize that

God enters history in the concrete form of freedom, and that we encounter that freedom as both gift and task, as something that we receive as well as something that we do. This is a potentially important corrective to the deification of humankind that does not move to the opposite extreme of contempt for humanity, because it recognizes the other as the concrete *subject* of God's action rather than the *object* of our action.

The emphasis on the reformation over the revolution is also intended as a corrective to the separation of the world into two spheres, one of which is separate from God. Bonhoeffer saw this separation as the direct result of a misunderstanding of Luther's doctrine of the one God's two rules, but he also saw the French Revolution as the logical culmination of that misunderstanding, as driving a wedge between the extraordinary and otherworldly realm in which God acts and the ordinary and worldly realm in which human beings act.

Bonhoeffer's insistence that we are *in the middle of history* is a corrective to the additional separation of the heroic realm of those who have reached the end from the ordinary realm of those who have not yet arrived. The temptation to see our own place and time as the end toward which all history tends, and to which other places and times are expected to conform, is countered by a reminder that we are only at the end in our encounter with Christ, and that we encounter Christ only in the midst of the world, where Christ takes form. This is carried further in Bonhoeffer to the insistence that we know reality only in encounter with the world, and that true Christianity is therefore the most profound and thoroughgoing worldliness. The point is not to be saved *from* the world but to be saved *into* it, to encounter it and embrace it as fully as possible.

For Bonhoeffer, this means not only that the end is Christ, but also that the end is human liberation. The incarnation means that we encounter God as a fully human being, and that to conform to Christ is to become fully human. Anything that stands in the way of becoming fully human, anything that dehumanizes or devalues human being, is therefore a denial of the work of the church—and it is that against which we are compelled to struggle.

Notes

1. Dietrich Bonhoeffer, *Ethics* (New York: Macmillan, 1965), 64–119.
2. Dietrich Bonhoeffer, *Letters and Papers from Prison*, ed. Eberhard Bethge (New York: Macmillan, 1972), 324–29, 335–37, 339–42, 343–47, 357–63, and 369–70.

3. *Ethics*, 65.
4. Cf. Dietrich Bonhoeffer, *Christ the Center*, rev. trans. Edwin H. Robertson (New York: Harper & Row, 1978). It is also consistent with his reading of Hegel. See *Dietrich Bonhoeffers Hegel-Seminar 1933*, nach den Aufzeichnungen von Ferenc Lehel, herausgegeben von Ilse Tödt (Munich: Chr. Kaiser, 1988). For an important analysis of Hegel's Christology that sheds additional light on Bonhoeffer's reading, see James Yerkes, *The Christology of Hegel* (Missoula, MT: Scholars Press, 1978).
5. *Ethics*, 68.
6. Kirkpatrick Sale, *The Conquest of Paradise* (New York: Knopf, 1990).
7. *Ethics*, 68.
8. *Ethics*, 72.
9. *Ethics*, 81.
10. Dietrich Bonhoeffer, *Creation and Fall. Temptation,* trans. John C. Fletcher and Kathleen Downham (New York: Macmillan, 1966).
11. *Ethics*, 83.
12. *Letters and Papers*, 219.
13. *Ethics*, 84, 85.
14. *Ethics*, 87.
15. *Letters and Papers*, 336-7.
16. Cf. *Ethics*, 222-54.
17. *Ethics*, 89.
18. *Ethics*, 90. For an important discussion of Bonhoeffer's appropriation of Hebrew scripture, see Martin Kuske, *The Old Testament as the Book of Christ: An Appraisal of Bonhoeffer's Interpretation,* trans. S. T. Kimbrough, Jr. (Philadelphia: Westminster, 1976).
19. *Ethics*, 90.
20. *Ethics*, 90.
21. *Ethics*, 94.
22. *Ethics*, 96. This makes it tempting to remind ourselves that Luther was no more a Lutheran than Hegel was a Hegelian!
23. *Ethics*, 99.
24. *Letters and Papers*, 123.
25. *Ethics*, 100.
26. *Ethics*, 100, 101.
27. *Ethics*, 102.
28. *Ethics*, 103.
29. *Ethics*, 108.
30. This is, of course, to build on Herbert Marcuse's discussion of "positive" philosophy in *Reason and Revolution* (Boston: Beacon, 1960).
31. An earlier version of this section appeared in "It's the End of the World as We Know It (And I Feel Fine): 'The End of History,' Marxist Eschatology and the New World Order," *Journal of Social Philosophy* 33 (Fall 1992): 127-41.
32. Francis Fukuyama, in *A Look at "The End of History?,"* ed. Kenneth M. Jensen (Washington, DC: United States Institute of Peace, 1990), 2.
33. Fukuyama, 3. Bonhoeffer made a similar point in correspondence with Bethge from Tegel Prison in 1944 (see *Letters and Papers*, 230).
34. Fukuyama, 4.
35. Fukuyama, 8.

36. Fukuyama, 10.
37. Fukuyama, 13.
38. Something that Bonhoeffer, interestingly enough, does not do. (Cf. *Ethics*, 104ff.)
39. Or, more properly, I suppose, "Prussocentrism."
40. Cf. Hugo Assmann, "JPIC and the 'Warm God' of the Global Market," *Ecumenical Review* 42 (January 1990): 48–60.
41. Jeffrey Friedman, "The New Consensus: I. The Fukuyama Thesis," *Critical Review* (Summer 1989): 373–410.
42. "A Christian is a perfectly free lord of all, subject to none. A Christian is a perfectly dutiful servant of all, subject to all." *A Treatise on Christian Liberty*, trans. W. A. Lambert, and rev. Harold J. Grimm (Philadelphia: Fortress Press, 1957), 7.

A POST-CRITICAL APPROACH TO 'RELIGIONLESS CHRISTIANITY'

Barry A. Harvey

> True discipleship, to which many Christians may once again be called, does not lead men back to religion.
>
> Max Horkheimer

Dietrich Bonhoeffer's criticism of the concept of religion as the proper genus under which to categorize Christian faith provides an important point of departure for developing a post-critical theological critique of a rationalized society. More specifically, I propose a rereading of key motifs and criticisms from Bonhoeffer's last works within our (post)modern context. When we improvise upon Bonhoeffer's provocative motifs and criticisms, we discover that religion and secularization, far from designating conflicting impulses within society, are actually complementary artifacts of the modern world which together serve to weave the whole of creation into the rationalized fabric of Western culture. Religion, on this account, is an intrinsic feature of the process of cultural rationalization—the differentiation of culture into autonomous value spheres (science, religion, morality, art)—where it functions as the primary mode of confinement and utilization for the Christian practice of everyday life. In addition, Bonhoeffer's discussion of religionless Christianity, articulated around the question of "who Christ really is . . . for us today,"[1] strives to fashion an alternative picture of the way Christians see themselves in relation to the whole of human life, to the rest of creation, and thus to God.

I. Bonhoeffer's Critique of 'Religion' in a (Post)modern Context

In an outline to a book he never had the chance to write, Bonhoeffer elaborates on what I take to be an ironic use of the phrase "a world come of age." He describes humanity's maturation as consisting in the safe-guarding of life against accidents and blows of fate. The aim of these efforts, writes Bonhoeffer, is to make human life independent of the menace of nature. This menace had formerly been dealt with through spiritual means, but in the modern era it has been "conquered . . . by technical organization of all kinds." Consequently, our immediate environment is no longer nature, but organization. "But with this protection from nature's menace," Bonhoeffer warns, "there arises a new one—through organization itself." Sadly, we no longer possess the spiritual force to cope with this peculiarly modern menace. The question that plagues us, then, is: "What protects us against the menace of organization? Man is again thrown back on himself. He has managed to deal with everything, only not with himself. He can insure against everything, only not against man."[2]

Thus for good and for ill, humanity's coming of age begins with Enlightenment, with Renaissance, and with Reform. As William Poteat observes, we are the products of criticism, revolution, self-inflicted amnesia: "Not only have we turned our backs upon the past, tradition, inherited ways, the harmonious balance between man and nature. We have been tempted, as we have de-divinized nature . . . to divinize ourselves; and there has thus ensued a ripening flirtation with godhood, with infinity, restlessness, tumult, and madness."[3] Only in retrospect are we discovering that human beings have come to dominate a world in which there is no sign that we still exist, save for our concern to maintain the powers of our sovereignty.[4] All our activities and achievements, all our doings and our knowings, are focused by a will to power, which Joseph Rouse accurately defines as "a continual striving for increased control and more precise determination of ourselves and the world, that is *never* subordinated to any other concern." To complicate matters further, every attempt on the part of modernity to get a fix on who we are and what is at issue in our practices has only perpetuated the endless expansion of calculative rationality and the mechanisms which are the bearers of such instrumental reasoning, resulting in the continuing subjection of ourselves, our neighbors, and our world to more precise manipulations and control. In short, the will to power inevitably results in the constant annihilation of any stable field of meaning that might provide coherence to our lives.[5] Poteat eloquently concludes:

[Even] our "humanism" is very often the despairing offspring of this impiety . . . [embodying] a strain of self-hatred in our . . . protests against dehumanization, a bad faith that shows itself more the more mordant and shrill the protest, as if we have to still with the sound of our own voices the deeper doubt that there is anything genuinely and intrinsically human to be defended. . . . Our humanism keeps a mistress whose name is Nihilism.[6]

If the rise of modern culture has traditionally been associated with the "disenchantment of the world" (a name assigned to modernity by Max Weber), then the current "disenchantment with disenchantment"[7] is an ambiguous phenomenon that is aptly named (post)modernism. Philosopher Stanley Rosen puts it well when he states that (post)modernism is only "the rhetorical frenzy of the latest attempt of the self-contradictory nature of Enlightenment to enforce itself as a solution to its own incoherence."[8] On the other hand, (post)modern criticism reveals much about the world which Bonhoeffer describes as having come of age. Above all, (post)modern writers and artists have demonstrated that the evolution of the modern world was not the realization of latent universal tendencies gestating in the womb of Western civilization, but "the result of the contingent emergence of imposed interpretations."[9] In other words, the modern world is a fiction in the strict sense of the word, i.e., something that has not merely been arranged by human imagination, but which is a historically determinate series of practices, social roles, disciplinary techniques, material forces, institutions, and political configurations that, in its efficient anonymity, is both the instrument *and* effect of human intelligence and craftsmanship. (Post)modern critics have shown that the modern world, and especially its celebrated secularity, are but a contingent array of practices, institutions, technologies, and social relations, orchestrated by a *mythos* disguised as the necessary laws of the natural and human sciences.

(Post)modernism, to put the matter in Bonhoeffer's terms, has exposed a world come of age to an unexpected light, showing that it is indeed godless, and thereby bringing it closer both to God's judgment and God's grace. By depriving the institutions, discourses, techniques, and social dynamics of modernity of all foundations, by shattering every assumption of rational certainty, stability, and security, by calling into question any attempt to assign the status of the given to its contingent impositions, (post)modern writers have helped us understand the modern world better than it has heretofore understood itself. In particular, (post)modernism has helped us to see that the particulars of a world come of age are not so much *facts* (in the modern sense of that word) but *artifacts*. (It is interesting to note at this point that the English words fact and artifact are both derived from the Latin *factum*, signifying a deed, act, event, or accomplishment).

(Post)modern thought also makes explicit something that is implied in Bonhoeffer's statements about humanity's coming of age, which is that who we are as persons is the outcome of our productive activity. As Nicholas Lash puts it, "the whole complex, conflictual, unstable process of human history is a matter of the production and destruction of the 'personal.'"[10] There is no safe haven of meaning, no substantial self immune from the particularities of history and its contingent networks of power, no Hegelian *a priorism*, which supplies an incorrigible identity and purpose to our contingent existence or to what we do and achieve. Who we are as human beings, therefore, is not what we are inwardly and privately, always under attack by the external world. The self is at any given moment a made self (not to be confused with the mistaken notion of modernity that each of us is, in the end, self-made), "whose present range of responses are part of a developing story."[11] To the extent that each of us is somebody, therefore, we are, both individually and corporately, the products of our common history, scripted by stories and crafted by practices, social roles, institutions, and goals which in a sense possess us. Paradoxically, it is this productive activity which also enables us to be intentional, purposeful beings. If the initial trajectories of religionless Christianity contained in Bonhoeffer's prison letters are to converge into a coherent and credible response to a (post)modern world, they must, first, effectively disclose that the contingencies of history constitute the process of human selfhood. Secondly, they must function as a school or laboratory for the production of the person, a school whose pedagogical goals and a laboratory whose methods of inquiry have been forged upon the anvil of suffering. Finally, they must bear witness that the goal of this process is the achievement of a "counter-history of peace regained through atoning suffering."[12]

That human beings, along with everything else in the world, are the products of history leads us to another important disclosure of a (post)modern scholarship which sharpens the focus on Bonhoeffer's criticism of "religious methodism" and the reliance on psychotherapy and existentialist philosophers as "God's pioneers," namely, the extension and consolidation of power which is entrenched in the *factum*, the artifacts, of the modern world. As I noted above, the *factum* of the modern world is constituted by strategic networks of institutions, disciplinary mechanisms, and material forces. Embedded in and animating these networks are relations of power which constrain us, govern our conduct, and invest our lives in a political field, wherein we are compelled to produce signs of our own presence and behavior. Power relations thus permeate the smallest and most ordinary of our doings, thoroughly reconfiguring the interconnectedness and the style of who we are and what we do. These relations of power do not determine particular actions, but they do govern the range of alternative possibilities open to us. The control which is exercised over us is therefore anonymous and indirect, but for this reason all the more pervasive and total. A world come of age is thus accurately represented as a contingent style of being which has us, that is, a particular and concrete mode of existence which determines the range of alternative responses among which we are free to choose. But as we exercise this freedom we unwittingly extend and consolidate its hold over us. The relations of power that sustain this way of life lead to an ambiguous sense of ourselves both as quasi-divine subjects of power and as tragic objects of power. On the one hand, we moderns have come to see ourselves as constructing society according to our own designs. Yet, on the other hand, we recognize only in retrospect that it is the form and coherence of our own existence which has been constructed, entangled within a web of power we helped to create yet over which we have no control. In the end, it is we who have been compelled to produce signs of our presence and behavior.[13]

The primary object and target of these relations of power is the human body, which has been manipulated, supervised, transformed, and used; in a word, the body has been masterfully subjected. By means of a variety of techniques that govern its range of possibilities, the body's integrity, motility, sentience, and intentionality have been carefully crafted and reinvested in the political field of modernity. Moreover, it is through this field that the body is involved in a complex web of economic relations, for as Foucault notes, "it is largely as a force of production that the body is invested with relations of power and domination . . . [and] its constitution as labour power is possible only if it is caught up in a system of subjection . . . the body becomes a useful force only if it is both a productive body and a subjected body."[14]

Control is thus obtained over the presence and conduct of individuals in a world come of age, not by the explicit and often unreliable use of force exercised directly on the body, but primarily through the creation of the modern soul by the various knowledges of modernity. This soul is the creation, instrument, and effect of what Foucault refers to as a political anatomy: "a set of material elements and techniques that serve as weapons, relays, communication routes and supports for the power and knowledge relations that invest human bodies and subjugate them by turning them into objects of knowledge."[15] These knowledges, for which relations of power are the precondition and not merely the effect, determine who we are and what is at stake in our lives, insofar as they circumscribe the range of possible responses to the world. Hence, what is at stake for us in our activities and achievements is not a value which we posit for ourselves, something over which we as autonomous self-possessing subjects exercise authority. These values are posited for us by the political anatomy of a secularized world, which comprises the logic and rationality, the style and coherence, of what we as individuals and as a society do.

This modern soul is somewhat similar to that which Thomas Aquinas carefully sets forth in the *Summa Theologica,* in that both are regarded as the form of the body. Thus both transcribe a kind of metaphysical order which integrates the body's individual faculties, "interconnecting them and subordinating them to a uniform method of accountability, supplying the combined operation of all these components with rules of the game, that is, with certain regulations, limitations, and legalities . . . guarantee[ing] the inner coherence of the [hegemonic] power structure."[16] By means of this soul, perhaps the single most important invention of a rationalized society, the differentiation of modern culture into autonomous value spheres is reproduced within the body, allowing it to be worked retail rather than wholesale, thereby increasing its utility and optimizing its productive potential through the efficient ordering of its multiplicities. In short, a strange inversion of an early Christian heresy characterizes a world come of age, for it is now the soul that constitutes the prison of the body.[17]

The "contingent emergence of imposed interpretations" which characterizes the modern world is made possible by a gradual paradigm shift in styles of social hegemony from a straightforward juridical mode to an epistemological mode grounded in the metaphysical soul of the subject. Apart from this shift it is impossible to grasp the significance of Hugo Grotius's assertion that the world could be known *etsi deus non daretur,* which, as Bonhoeffer recognizes, distinguishes a world come of age from its predecessors. The shift to an epistemological mode of social hegemony permeates the various technological, bureaucratic, political, and economic mechanisms in ways which for the most part eliminate the need for more explicit and coercive modes of supervision and utilization. In short, the imagining of this subject was a crucial moment in the rationalization of modern culture into autonomous domains of fact and value (science, religion, morality, art), and thus was essential to the perpetuation of the entrenched political apparatus over a world come of age.

With the unmasking of the convergence of knowledge and social domination in a world come of age we have returned full circle to Bonhoeffer's contention that, whereas humankind has been thrown back upon itself in the attempt to protect itself from the menace of nature, now it lacks the spiritual force necessary to protect itself from the menace of organization.[18] Foucault refers to the convergence of knowledge and power as the technological threshold of modernity. According to Foucault, this threshold was reached when human practices attained a level at which the celebrated advance of knowledge and the much sought-after increase of power reinforced each other in a reciprocating fashion: "It is a double process, then: an epistemological 'thaw' through a refinement of power relations; a multiplication of the effects of power through the formation and accumulation of new forms of knowledge."[19] In short, the production of knowledge in a world come of age is inseparable from the techniques and disciplines entrenched within the cultural practices and social institutions of modernity. The will to knowledge that is the engine of enlightenment has exacted a terrible price from us—it has required of us our very soul.

The practices and institutions of Christianity were among the first to be targeted by the political anatomy of modernity, for as Marx observes, "the criticism of religion is the premise of all criticism."[20] The reconfiguration of the church's practice of everyday life, against which much of Bonhoeffer's criticism of religion is directed, takes place at several levels, each level affording a microcosmic cross-section in terms of which the expansion and consolidation of power that takes place as the world comes of age may be accurately displayed. The traditional discourse about God, for example, is abstracted from its teleological context within the social anatomy of the church. It is, then, *reinscribed* within the political field of modernity as a series of causal hypotheses about a most sublime entity ("the highest, most powerful, and best Being imaginable"[21]), whose attributes may be rigorously specified as these hypotheses are entertained by solitary, non-historical subjects. As a result of this process of reinsciption, modern epistemology and metaphysics deprive humankind of a mode of discourse capable of articulating the unity and form, sense and significance of everyday life.

In similar fashion, confining the concept of "faith," as Bonhoeffer laments, to "the sphere of the 'personal,' the 'inner,' and the 'private,'"[22] was accomplished by modifying the infrastructure of the human subject, resulting in the invention of the autonomous realm of the religious. The reconfiguring of traditional Christian piety as a discrete facet of subjective human experience essentially unrelated to knowing and doing (i.e., as a "spiritual substance" that can be placed under surveillance, and its movements tracked and recorded) not only privatized what had been located during the Middle Ages and Renaissance in the public realm of civic virtue and ecclesiastical discipline, but it also assigned it to a series of specialized discourses. Thus "religion" as a formal, self-same, universal phenomenon rooted in the human subject was imagined.

The significance of the transformation of the practice of piety into religion within the structures and institutions of a rationalized world cannot be underestimated. As John Milbank has recently noted, prior to the Enlightenment there was no secular in the sense of an autonomous sphere or domain in which the purely natural and human could be ascertained *etsi deus non daretur.* "Instead there was the single community of Christendom, with its dual aspects of *sacerdotium* and *regnum.* The *saeculum,* in the medieval era, was not a space, a domain, but a time – the interval between fall and *eschaton* where coercive justice, private property and impaired natural reason must make a shift to cope with the unredeemed effects of sinful humanity." Moreover, within medieval society the idea of religion, as found for example in the title of John Calvin's *magnum opus, The Institutes of the Christian Religion,* did not specify an autonomous domain of value devoid of substantive criteria. But with its incorporation into the purview of the modern subject, the fiction of the *homo religiosus* was simultaneously created and delimited as private and discrete, and thereby subjected to rational management. Milbank rightly states that "The more 'matters of the soul' concern a private realm which is always the same, then the more public discourse concerning such things can detach itself from tradition, and declare itself to be both universal and scientific." As Bonhoeffer had anticipated in his criticism of theology's reliance on existentialist philosophy and psychotherapy to act as "God's pioneers," the widely celebrated "religious pluralism" of the (post)modern world is carefully bracketed at the level of the individual subject and at the level of society as a whole by these knowledges of religion.[23]

The modern distinction between public and private spheres which reproduces at the social level the neo-Kantian dichotomy between the realms of facts and values emerged in tandem with the transformation of the discipline of politics from a substantive discussion about the goods which society's members should pursue in common into a formal process through which an optimum amount of coexistence among people who shared little in common is secured by means of a range of bureaucratic controls, disciplinary techniques, and economic adjustments. While this distinction between public and private realms of life was deemed necessary to protect and promote the latter from unwarranted interventions on the part of public authorities, it also required that individuals subordinate their allegiance to whatever private concerns they might have to the public requirements of a rationalized social order, and hence effectively confining these private concerns to the margins of a secular world. In a striking inversion of the biblical mandate, in a (post)modern society one must fear the emperor and honor God (cf. 1 Peter 2:17).

What is particularly noteworthy about the confinement of faith by the epistemic strategies of the modern world is that it was initially achieved, not by sociologists, philosophers, political economists, and other secularists, but by theologians such as Schleiermacher, Ritschl, and Harnack. What was originally intended as a movement of emancipation from institutional corruption and dogmatic rigidity became the primary mechanism for confining the habits and relations of Christianity within the contours and dynamics of modernity. The invention of religion as a private facet of human experience, an invention for which theologians entrusted with the teaching office of the church were largely responsible, became "an inadvertent service on behalf of the coercive tendencies of modern society—a way of supervising and containing the ['religious'] by keeping it enclosed in its own space, a mode of self-policing, as it were."[24]

I am not suggesting that the church attempt the *salto mortale* (the deathleap), as Bonhoeffer puts it, back to the clericalism of the Middle Ages. Not only would this be impossible to achieve, it would indeed signal "a counsel of despair . . . at the cost of intellectual honesty." The changes which took place in the life of the church through the so-called "Constantinian shift" formed the basic tendencies of the religious a *priori* which Bonhoeffer rightly takes to task in *Letters and Papers from Prison.*[25] Nevertheless, the unravelling of the medieval synthesis of *regnum* and *sacerdotium*, exemplified by the institutional separation of church and state in liberal democratic societies, was not, as it has often been presented, the realization of desacralizing tendencies that were always gestating in the womb of Judeo-Christianity (whatever that is). At best, the church meekly acquiesced to the fragmentation of reality into autonomous domains of value, which are then reintegrated into a social whole by an instrumental rationality that restricts any expression of humanity to the margins of society. As Bonhoeffer himself intimates in his comments regarding the displacement of God from the public aspects of life, it was due to the rationalization of modern culture that our relation to the divine came to be regarded as one particular object among many. Our relationship to the infinite was henceforth conceived as a religious quest to be pursued alongside the economic quest for full employment, the scientific quest for a cure for cancer or the secrets of the atom, the moral quest for racial equality, etc. The failure of this quest in the public realm, in the guise of "a working hypothesis in morals, politics, or science," increasingly led to methodism, "the attempt to keep [Gods'] place secure, at least in the sphere of the 'personal,' the 'inner,' and the 'private.'"[26] At its worst, however, the church was, and continues to be, a full-fledged participant in the process of secularization, supervising and containing its own practice of everyday life by keeping it enclosed in the space of the religious.

The unwitting involvement of the church in the parturition of a world come of age ironically perpetuates one of the fundamental errors of medieval Christendom, which was to identify the rule of God with one particular social configuration, in this case, with the techniques and tendencies of liberal democratic capitalism. A (post)modern reading of Bonhoeffer's critique of religion must therefore avoid what is a tempting yet false dichotomy, namely, that the church must either swallow whole the modern world's self-characterization as an autonomous sphere in which nature and humanity can truthfully be encountered *etsi deus non daretur*, or take the deathleap back to the religious a *priori* of Christendom. While the church must come to terms with the artifact of social differentiation, religionless Christianity must resist the temptation to ascribe ontological status to cultural rationalization. It must, in other words, refuse to accept the present ordering of the world as a *given*, ordained by heavenly powers. The role of theology, on this account, is not to tinker with the self-designation of a world come of age, which finally is nothing more than a *de facto* legitimation of its basic techniques and tendencies, but to help the church understand its own distinctive grasp of how to deal with the world. It accomplishes this role, not by embracing the autonomy of the secular world, but providing a way for the church to name, confront, and (ultimately) subvert this particular artifact of enlightenment with the claims of God's messianic rule manifested in the weakness and suffering of Jesus.

II. A Post-critical Religionless Christianity

Bonhoeffer, with his initial reconnaissance into the contours and dynamics of religionless Christianity, is attempting to sketch an alternative picture of how a Christian is to see herself in relation to herself, to her neighbors, to creation as a whole, and to God. It is an understanding of the world that is rooted in concrete discipleship to the suffering messiah, which is located in the integrity and intentionality of the body, rather than in the religiosity of a discarnate subject. The basic shape and direction of Christian discipleship is intimated in Bonhoeffer's famous meditation for his godson's baptism. In an important allusion to what he elsewhere refers to as the church's "arcane discipline," Bonhoeffer tells his godson that "Today you will be baptized a Christian. All those great ancient words of the Christian proclamation will be spoken over you, and the command of Jesus Christ to baptize will be carried out on you, without your knowing anything about it." His reflections on the significance of this rite drives him back, as he says, "to the beginnings of our understanding. Reconciliation and redemption, regeneration and the Holy Spirit, love of our enemies, cross and resurrection, life in Christ and Christian discipleship – all these things are so difficult and so remote that we hardly venture any more to speak of them." Nevertheless, he adds, "In the traditional words and acts we suspect that there may be something quite new and revolutionary, though we cannot as yet grasp or express it." It is this something new and revolutionary in the church's ancient practices which constitutes the core of religionless Christianity, something that will enable the church "so to utter the word of God that the world will be changed and renewed by it."[27]

The goal of religionless Christianity, therefore, is not to provide an account of the modern world in order that the community of faith might with a good conscience embrace its basic techniques and strategies as autonomous and grace-imbued domains, but to put the church in a position to confront this contingent world. It means, as Bonhoeffer was quoted above, "so to utter the word of God that the world will be changed and renewed by it." Bonhoeffer does not regard the process of secularization, as some have argued, as simply "the result of a transformation of the self-understanding of man . . . a process which not only coincides perfectly with a Christian vision of man, of history and of the cosmos; it also favors a more complete fulfillment of the Christian life insofar as it offers man the possibility of being more fully human."[28] The type of worldliness that Bonhoeffer advocates begins with the recognition that the church needs to understand the world better than that world understands itself, "on the basis of the gospel and in the light of Christ." By "living unreservedly in life's duties, problems, successes and failures, experiences and perplexities," the church is to expose the polity and policies of the *pax moderna* to an unexpected light, demonstrating how the exclusive claim to our allegiance on the part of a world come of age directly conflicts with the crucified messiah who "claims for himself and the Kingdom of God the whole of human life in all its manifestations."[29]

Consequently, writes Bonhoeffer, "I should like to speak of God not on the boundaries but at the centre, not in weakness but in strength; and therefore not in death and guilt but in man's life and goodness . . . God is beyond in the midst of our life. The church stands, not at the boundaries where human powers give out, but in the middle of the village."[30] Religionless Christianity thus pertains to the practices and skills of a group of people whose relationship to God's mystery and presence in the world is not constructed (or deconstructed) through sophisticated philosophic engineering related to a disembodied, non-historical subject striving to comprehend life's boundaries (which, as I have argued, has historically been the site of faith's subjection to the relations and habits of modernity). Such a relationship is exhibited in the style and interconnectedness that characterizes, in Bonhoeffer's words, "the polyphony of life."[31] This polyphonic style of everyday life, which Larry Rasmussen rightly labels "the shape of grace and the means to maturity,"[32] embodies a performative grasp of how to deal with the concerns and celebrations that occur in the middle of the human village. As we have seen, the world has tried systematically to exclude the church from dealing directly with these concerns by restricting its sphere of operations to religious matters. However, it is only when we attend to the actions and passions that characterize daily existence, in all their particularity and contingency, a world, as John Howard Yoder puts it, "in which people eat bread and pursue debtors, hope for power and execute subversives,"[33] that humans have to do with God's "beyond."

If the church is to stand in the middle of the (post)modern global village and not at its religious boundaries, it must first look to its primary vocation: to be the church, i.e., to be the corporate structure of God's eschatological rule embodied in and bodied forth by Jesus as messiah. This vocation only sounds self-serving when we neglect the fact that the church exists for the sake of God's kingdom and that its calling is the same as its servant-king: to open the world to its destiny in this kingdom.[34] To neglect this calling would be to abandon the world (and ourselves along with it) to the hopelessness that pervades the present age. Religionless Christianity in a (post)modern world means, first of all, that the messianic community must refuse its confinement as a religious association, and rediscover, as Bonhoeffer states in *The Cost of Discipleship*, that it possesses a distinctively "political character."[35] The community of the crucified messiah, to put the matter in its proper eschatological perspective, is the social and political manifestation, in the midst of the present age, of the age to come. Apart from the distinctive habits and relations nurtured within the church's societal framework, what Bonhoeffer's close friend and colleague Paul Lehmann calls the "laboratory of the living word," the world has no way of developing and refining the imaginative skills that will provide it with the critical traction it needs to make sense of the "blooming, buzzing confusion" (William James) which is the whole complex, conflictual, unstable, and irreducible story of creation. The church, in other words, allows the world to know the truth about itself and its history. In short, the only way the particularity and contingency of Jesus' life, death, and resurrection can address the contours and dynamics of a world come of age is through his community of followers, "the corporate structure of God's activity in the world."[36]

Apart from the motifs that distinguish "the polyphony of life" in the body of Christ, the church has very little if anything to offer to the world that the world does not already possess, or at least to which it does not already have access. It is only *as* the church that the people of Christ can be for the world a sacrament, a herald, a mystical communion, a servant, in short, as those who exist for others.[37] It is in the non-religious identity and activity of the church as the social laboratory of human maturity that gives the world the means to grasp its destiny in the kingdom of God. When the community is faithful to its vocation, the presence and activity of God's spirit transfigures the facts (*factum*) and possibilities of a world come of age into the presence of the *pax christi*, the peace of God proleptically realized in the midst of a world come of age.[38] Shorn of its eschatological contours and ecclesial discipline, however, the church is reduced to the anemic position of promising that it can run the policies and programs of the world better, and make better sense of its distinctive habits and relations, than the "pagans" who initially developed them.

Two matters of concern in our (post)modern world are truthfully grasped only within the political anatomy of the church. First, we learn within this community that human selfhood is not merely the outcome of productive activity (though it cannot be disassociated with such activity), but that in the course of our production by the contingencies and particularities of history we are *addressed* by the mystery of our existence. The mystery of God, "God's 'beyond,'" as Bonhoeffer puts it, "is not the beyond of our cognitive faculties. The transcendence of epistemological theory has nothing to do with the transcendence of God."[39] Put differently, God's incomprehensibility and ineffability are not functions of the metaphysics and epistemological strategies of Cartesian subjectivity. The divine mystery, rather, confronts us in the messianic suffering of Christ, addressing us with both a word of judgment and of redemption.

Secondly, the church's distinctive grasp of how to relate to the world also provides the basis on which Christians respond to the "other," the one whom the Bible refers to as the foreigner or alien: those of other races, cultures and traditions, of other Christian confessions, with whom we must live and work, struggle and celebrate, and together with whom we must forge our lives before the God who is beyond our grasp, yet who in Jesus Christ has addressed us. There are those who would insist that no one should be regarded as a foreigner, yet the refusal to let the other *be* other, to be strange and alien to us, marks one of the most tragic features of a

world come of age. The God of Jesus Christ does not call us to confine
the other within the disciplinary structures of a (post)modern world, but
as both Old and New Testament bear witness, to recognize in her or him
the measure of our concern for the justice of God's reign.⁴⁰

Allowing the other to be unknown to us, while at the same time seeing
in the stranger, the enemy, and the unwelcomed the rule of our involvement in God's struggle for a just and peaceable existence for all creation,
also clarifies the nature of Bonhoeffer's admonition to "costly worldly
solidarity," as Larry Rasmussen puts it, on the part of Christians in a world
come of age.⁴¹ Such solidarity avoids the false alternative between sectarian
withdrawal, on the one hand, and on the other, the imperialist assumption that any form of discourse is capable of transcending its own particularity and therefore provide a general account of human experience.
Sectarian withdrawal is not a possibility, for as Stanley Hauerwas has
recently noted, how can the church withdraw when it necessarily finds
itself surrounded, having no place of its own to which it can retreat.⁴² By
the same token, a general account of human experience presupposes a
universal community of humankind, a truly ecumenical body which does
not yet exist even for Christians.

Because the church has no place of its own from which it can advance
a comprehensive strategy of containment, its laboratory of the social (configured by the church's *disciplina arcani*) has always been crafted from
materials already at hand, not from scratch or with materials revealed from
on high. The early church, for example, adopted many of the social roles,
institutions, and practices of late antiquity, all of which predate the Christian movement, but it also adapted and redirected these practices toward
very different ends.⁴³ The early church, in other words, constituted itself
through the reconfiguration of these structures as a society-in-microcosm
in which a set of relations, habits, and sensibilities might be fostered that
could not otherwise be realized within the established ordering of the world
of late antiquity. Its practices were not esoteric rituals but publicly accessible activities in which virtually all human beings participate in some form.⁴⁴
In other words, the basic "stuff" of their everyday existence was also the
context of Christian discipleship; but it is also this "stuff," the particulars
of our mundane existence as God's people, which is the icon of God's
mystery in the world. Thus, when configured as a community in which
every aspect of its members' lives is integrated into a distinctive pattern
of relations and habits, the church becomes the social manifestation of what
Bonhoeffer refers to as the *Gestalt Christi*, the form or image of Christ.⁴⁵

The messianic reconfiguration of societal practices, goals, habits and
relations constitutes the group of believers into a social body, creating

within the microcosm of the church an alternative social reality. Not surprisingly, the sacraments of baptism and eucharist play important roles within the core practices and equipment of this laboratory, but the non-religious (i.e., political) context and significance of these sacramental signs must be recovered in our own social settings. The sacraments, as I have already intimated, originated among a group of practices which constituted a distinctive pattern of social process within the early church. This process pertained to both the internal relations of the gathered congregation and the ways the church interacted with the world.[46] The emphasis, therefore, was upon the *societal* rather than the *sacerdotal* relation of God and God's people.[47] The eucharist, for example, was originally an economic activity, the sharing of bread by those who have it with those who do not, thereby extending the boundaries of economic solidarity which are normally are restricted to the family to include the widow, the orphan, the alien, and the poor. The distribution of material goods within the household as charity or hospitality (rather than accumulating it as surplus to use as capital, as modern society does) signifies the presence of a counter-historical ordering of the world.[48] The peace that is then shared at the beginning of the eucharist takes on material substance as the crucified and risen messiah distributes bread around the table in the role of the family head, thereby "project[ing] into the post-Passion world the common purse of the wandering disciple band whose members had left their prior economic bases to join his movement."[49]

The eucharist, however, is never simply a fellowship meal with Jesus or with our neighbors, but concretely embodies the divine summons, as Bonhoeffer puts it, "to share in God's sufferings at the hands of a godless world." The words of institution recorded in Scripture consistently set the origins of this fellowship meal in the context of Jesus' betrayal by his followers on the night before his death. The political anatomy of the eucharist, therefore, does not ignore the tragic suffering associated with the practice of everyday life, nor does it cover over our complicity in this tragedy, but incorporates these within its costly solidarity with the world. In Rowan Williams' words, the imagery of the eucharist "always and necessarily operates between the two poles of Maundy Thursday and Easter Sunday, between Gethsemane and Emmaus, between the Upper Room before the crucifixion and the Upper Room to which the risen Jesus comes." The anatomy of our "participation in the sufferings of God in the secular life" takes concrete form in the eucharistic celebration, signifying the restoration of a fellowship broken time and again by human infidelity, hence "the wounded body and the shed blood are inescapably present."[50]

There is another important dimension to the eucharist which concretizes the sense of Bonhoeffer's dictum, growing out of his own social location, that "Only he who cries out for the Jews may sing Gregorian chants." Eucharistic solidarity nurtures what Johann Baptist Metz calls the memory of suffering, in the light of which "it is clear that social power and political domination are not simply to be taken for granted but that they continually have to justify themselves in view of actual suffering."[51] The Christian practice of everyday life, linked eucharistically by God's own sufferings in Jesus Christ to the victims of suffering and oppression, subversively challenges the hegemony of the (post)modern world to justify itself in light of the human cost which it involves, but it also extends in a concrete manner the divine offer of new life in the servant community, the prefiguring of the peaceable kingdom.

The sacrament of baptism also originally embodied at its core a distinctive social meaning, marking the induction of individuals into a new society, the body of Christ. In this social microcosm all previous definitions of identity based on class and gender were relativized, so that they no longer provided one with her normative social status. In concert with the endowing of every member of the community by the Spirit with her own distinctive role (the divine *charisma*), baptism thus established a new mode of social relations within the community and formed the basis of early Christian egalitarianism, a way of relating which, unlike its modern counterpart, does not regard us as interchangeable cogs in a giant machine. But as with the sacrament of the eucharist, baptism also is set in the context of the death and resurrection of Jesus, and thus in the context of the restoration of a *koinonia* disrupted time and again by human infidelity. To be buried and raised with Christ in baptism is to acknowledge the tragic character of the present moment, and thus of our complicity in this drama, but also to affirm and proclaim God's vindication of suffering in the political anatomy of the crucified.

Other practices of the early church could also be mentioned in this connection—e.g., the interweaving of moral discernment and forgiveness into a process of genuine reconciliation, and the "democratic" patterns of mutual accountability which prevailed in the house churches of Paul.[52] The goal of these distinctive patterns of activity is a community in which a peaceable existence with others, i.e., a just society, becomes a historical possibility owing to God's presence and power in the world. The church is called by God to be the bearer of habits and relations which defies the present darkness by defining this darkness in terms of a promised, but as yet unfulfilled, future, thereby giving shape and direction, sense and coherence, to the present. In the church, the corporate structure of the *pax christi*, God's eschatological reign becomes a historical actuality (to the extent that the church is faithful to its calling). Religionless Christianity is thus squarely located within a politically implicated context: the confrontation of the *pax christi* with the *pax moderna* and its anatomy of power.

One further point needs to be made. Bonhoeffer states that "the starting-point for our 'secular interpretation,'" is that "the God of the Bible . . . wins power and space in the world by his weakness . . . "[53] It is the nonreligious (i.e., social and political) identity and configuration of the messianic community that manifests in concrete form the "political anatomy" of servanthood over against the will to power, the "social grammar" of vulnerability and weakness over against that of domination. The church, by participating in the divine weakness which the Spirit bodies forth among Jesus' followers, exhibits in the middle of the global village the oxymoronic impotence of power, that is, the inability to sustain and therefore to justify itself. Moreover, weakness and servanthood in the moving of God's Spirit are transfigured by the power to sustain and justify not only the community of faith, but the whole of creation as well. Jesus' servant way of life thus opens the way toward a peaceable existence *with* others, a peace which a world come of age has not determined and which it does not comprehend—God's peace, the *pax christi*. This peace is the effect and instrument of the *Gestalt Christi*, the new creation in Christ which invests our bodies in a new political field, inaugurating a new political anatomy governing the possibilities for relating to one another, to creation as a whole, and to God. It is in the occurrence of the Spirit-filled community, i.e., in the redemptive transformation of broken relation into maturity, of power into weakness and weakness into power, that "the reality of God which has become manifest in Christ" is transcribed into the facts and possibilities of a world come of age.[54]

Bonhoeffer's repudiation of religion as a formal strategy by means of which the (post)modern world seeks to supervise the distinctively Christian practice of everyday life, opens the way for us to attend to the concrete ways we might refashion the body politic of the church. Bonhoeffer's deconstruction of religion as a viable theological category is also an invitation to, and an opportunity for, the church to reexamine and reclaim its non-religious (i.e., its political and social) existence and vocation as the body of Christ. In short, religionless Christianity is both a subversive act of noncompliance with the hegemonic ordering of the (post)modern world (i.e., the church's refusal to be confined to the margins, where it had been assigned in a world come of age), and a summons to return to the center of the human village as, to paraphrase John Milbank, "the establishment of a new, universal society, a new *civitas*, in which these intimate relationships are paradigmatic: a community in which we relate primarily to the neighbor, and every neighbor is mother, brother, sister, spouse. What [religionless Christianity] requires, therefore, is a new ecclesiology which would be also a [post-critical] theology.[55] John Howard Yoder might put it this way:

> [Religionless Christianity] tells the world what is the world's own calling and destiny, not by announcing either a utopian or a realistic goal to be imposed on the whole society, but by pioneering a paradigmatic demonstration of both the power and the practices that define the shape of restored humanity. The confessing people of God is the new world on its way.[56]

In short, the church which participates in God's messianic suffering is the vanguard of the new humanity.

Notes

1. Dietrich Bonhoeffer, *Letters and Papers from Prison: The Enlarged Edition*, trans. R. H. Fuller, John Bowden, et al. (New York: Macmillan, 1971), 279.
2. *Letters and Papers*, 380.
3. William Poteat, *Polanyian Meditations: In Search of a Post-Critical Logic* (Durham, NC: Duke University Press, 1985), 4.
4. See Michael Polanyi, *Personal Knowledge: Toward a Post-Critical Philosophy*, corrected ed. (Chicago: The University of Chicago Press, 1962), 380; and Emmanuel Levinas, "Ethics as First Philosophy," *The Levinas Reader*, ed. Seán Hand (Cambridge, MA: Basil Blackwell, 1989), 78.
5. Joseph Rouse, *Knowledge and Power: Toward a Political Philosophy of Science* (Ithaca, NY: Cornell University Press, 1987), 261f.
6. Poteat, *Polanyian Meditations*, 5.
7. Kenneth Surin, "*Contemptus mundi* and the Disenchantment of the World: Bonhoeffer's 'discipline of the secret' and Adorno's 'Strategy of Hibernation',' in *The Turning of Light and Dark: Essays in Philosophical and Systematic Theology* (New York: Cambridge University Press, 1989), 192.
8. Stanley Rosen, *Hermeneutics as Politics* (New York: Oxford University Press, 1987), 11, 49. Hence my parenthetical rendering of the term "postmodern."
9. Hubert L. Dreyfus and Paul Rabinow, *Michel Foucault: Beyond Structuralism and Hermeneutics* (Chicago: The University of Chicago Press, 1983), 108.
10. Nicholas Lash, *Theology on the Way to Emmaus* (London: SCM Press, 1986), 153.
11. Rowan Williams, *Resurrection: Interpreting the Easter Gospel* (New York: Pilgrim Press, 1984), 29.
12. Lash, *Theology on the Way to Emmaus*, 153; see also Lash, *Easter in Ordinary: Reflections on Human Experience and the Knowledge of God* (Charlottesville: University of Virginia Press, 1988), 282–4; John Milbank, "The Second Difference: For a Trinitarianism without Reserve," *Modern Theology* 2 (1986): 227.
13. Rouse, 247.
14. Michel Foucault, *Discipline and Punish: The Birth of the Prison*, trans. Alan Sheridan (New York: Random House, 1979), 25.
15. Foucault, 28.

16. Václav Havel, "The Power of the Powerless," in *Living in Truth*, ed. Jan Vladislav (Boston: Faber and Faber, 1987), 46.

17. Foucault, 28, 30, 136f.

18. *Letters and Papers*, 380.

19. Foucault, 224.

20. Karl Marx, "Contribution to the Critique of Hegel's *Philosophy of Right*," *The Marx-Engels Reader*, ed. Robert C. Tucker (New York: W. W. Norton & Company, 1978), 53.

21. *Letters and Papers*, 381.

22. *Letters and Papers*, 344.

23. John Milbank, *Theology and Social Theory* (Cambridge, MA: Basil Blackwell, Inc., 1990), 9, 109, 128. *Letters and Papers*, 326, 344, 346.

24. Frank Lentricchia, *Criticism and Social Change* (Chicago: University of Chicago, 1983), 54.

25. *Letters and Papers*, 280, 360.

26. *Letters and Papers*, 344.

27. *Letters and Papers*, 299f.

28. Gustavo Gutierrez, *A Theology of Liberation*, trans. Sister Caridad Inda and John Eagleson (Maryknoll, NY: Orbis Books, 1973), 67.

29. *Letters and Papers*, 328f., 342, 370.

30. *Letters and Papers*, 282.

31. *Letters and Papers*, 303.

32. Larry L. Rasmussen, *Dietrich Bonhoeffer: Reality and Resistance* (Nashville, TN: Abingdon Press, 1972), 43, n. 70.

33. John Howard Yoder, *The Priestly Kingdom* (Notre Dame, IN: University of Notre Dame Press, 1984), 62.

34. Rowan Williams, "Postmodern Theology and the Judgment of the World," in *Postmodern Theology*, ed. Frederic B. Burnham (San Francisco: Harper & Row, 1989), 95.

35. Dietrich Bonhoeffer, *The Cost of Discipleship*, trans. R. H. Fuller, rev. Irmgard Booth (New York: Macmillan, 1959), 314.

36. Paul L. Lehmann, *Ethics in a Christian Context* (New York: Harper & Row, 1963), 58, 101, 131.

37. See Avery Dulles, *Models of the Church* (Garden City, NJ: Image Books, 1974), 38–108. The allusion to an existence for others is from *Letters and Papers*, 381.

38. Lash, *Easter in Ordinary*, 282–4.

39. *Letters and Papers*, 282.

40. Genesis 18:1–10; Hebrews 13:2; Matthew 25:31–46.

41. Larry L. Rasmussen, *Dietrich Bonhoeffer: His Significance for North Americans*, with Renate Bethge (Minneapolis: Fortress Press, 1990), 68f.

42. Stanley Hauerwas, *After Christendom?* (Nashville: Abingdon Press, 1991), 18.

43. See Wayne A. Meeks, *The First Urban Christians: The Social World of the Apostle Paul* (New Haven: Yale University Press, 1983), 29–32, 63–80; Milbank, *Theology and Social Theory*, 117.

44. See John H. Yoder, "Sacrament as Social Process: Christ the Transformer of Culture," *Theology Today* 48 (April 1991):31–44.

45. Dietrich Bonhoeffer, *Ethics* (New York: Macmillan 1972), 80–5, and *The Cost of Discipleship*, 337–44.

46. Yoder, "Sacrament as Social Process," 34.

47. Lehmann, *Ethics in a Christian Context*, 103.
48. Wayne A. Meeks, *The First Urban Christians*, 77–84; Milbank, *Theology and Social Theory*, 35, 117.
49. Yoder, "Sacrament as Social Process," 37f.
50. *Letters and Papers*, 361; Rowan Williams, *Resurrection* (New York: The Pilgrim Press, 1984), 40.
51. Johann Baptist Metz, *Faith in History and Society: Toward a Practical Fundamental Theology*, trans. David Smith (New York: The Seabury Press, 1980), 115.
52. Yoder, "Sacrament as Social Process," 37. See also Elisabeth Schüssler Fiorenza, "A Discipleship of Equals: Ekklesial Democracy and Patriarchy in Biblical Perspective," in *A Democratic Catholic Church: The Reconstruction of Roman Catholicism*, ed. Eugene C. Bianchi and Rosemary Radford Ruether (New York: Crossroad, 1992), 17–33.
53. *Letters and Papers*, 346, 361.
54. Lash, *Easter in Ordinary*, 283; *Ethics*, 197.
55. Milbank, *Theology and Social Theory*, 228.
56. Yoder, "Sacrament as Social Process," 44.

ECCLESIA CRUCIS:
THE DISCIPLE COMMUNITY AND
THE FUTURE OF THE CHURCH
IN NORTH AMERICA

Douglas John Hall

Introduction: "Theologische Existenz"

At the end of his seminal study, *The Nature of Doctrine,* George A. Lindbeck concludes his discussion of "postliberal theology" ('inconclusively,' according to his own assessment) by noting that ". . . the intratextual intelligibility that postliberalism emphasizes may not fit the needs of religions such as Christianity when they are in the awkwardly intermediate stage of having once been culturally established but are not yet clearly disestablished."[1]

This is the most succinct summation of the ecclesiastical situation confronting the once-mainline churches of the two northern nations of this continent. So-called 'mainstream' Protestant Christianity has been so thoroughly interwoven with the dominant culture of North America, and especially that of the United States, that it is virtually impossible to distinguish 'Christ and Culture' (to use H. Richard Niebuhr's familiar nomenclature) in this historical experience. With the advent of both cultural and religious pluralism, however, combined with the exodus from 'mainstream' churches and the visible loss of the power of traditions in our society generally, only those Christians who will not see can assume that such an 'established' situation still pertains or could, in the future, be reinstated. Yet the incapacity consciously to absorb and deliberately to act upon the reality of our post-Constantinian condition is not confined to those who are ideologically committed to a Constantinian model of the church and its mission in the world. To one degree or another, all of us are enthralled by a conception of the Christian religion as majority; and our North American fixation upon this imperial model of the church is the more entrenched and adhesive because our sort of establishment has not been one of form but of content—not *de jure* but *de facto*. Moreover, in many if not all situations within our context it is still possible to carry on 'as if' — namely, as if it were still Christendom. We are "not yet clearly dis-established." It is thus a particularly "awkward" period in the history of Christianity in our experience as a (heretofore) mainly European civilization.

It may of course be said that this is an awkward moment for Christianity in Europe as well. It seems to me that those who have remained consciously and seriously within the Christian movement in Europe have been able to appropriate the transition from imperial Christianity to the coming diaspora in ways that are both more realistic and more creative than have we North American Christians. The reasons for this are complex indeed, and this is not the place to elaborate on them extensively. Since my theme is the significance of Bonhoeffer's vision of the disciple community for the future of the church in our North American context, it will be useful to reflect briefly on this comparison.

One reason why European Protestantism may have adapted itself more intelligently than we to the ecclesiastical 'paradigm shift' in question has already been adumbrated. The 'legal' forms of European establishment, while they may foster ironies such as pertain in western Germany, where 95% of the population still belong officially to the church while only 5% have any profound attachment to it, are at least clear-cut. They are a matter of form, and forms can, and usually do, persist well beyond the demise of the visions that begat them. Even unsophisticated people understand this and are ready (as we say) to 'go through the motions' when called upon to do so. By comparison, our 'cultural' establishment on this side of the Atlantic is thoroughly confusing: where does Christianity leave off and the American Dream begin? Candidates for high offices in the United States must still *seem* to be Christian, regardless of their actual state of belief.

To this cause of difference between these two historically familial provinces of the church one may add such considerations as the following. First, in European Christianity, and especially Protestantism, there has always been a strong critical theology at work, ready to distinguish authentic from inauthentic expressions of the faith, whereas in North America activistic and pietistic elements in Christian denominations have ensured the existence of an ongoing suspicion of theology in general and of critical theology in particular. I shall return to this presently.

Since the breakdown of the Middle Ages, European Christianity has witnessed the advent of a whole host of philosophic and political alternatives to the Christian faith, many of them militantly anti-Christian; consequently, generations of serious Christians in that situation have of necessity learned how to dialogue with the rival systems of meaning. In North America, on the other hand, despite the very great reality of a system (individualistic capitalism) inimical to biblical faith at many points, the vast majority of Christians have been able to assume the compatibility if not the identity of Christianity with 'our way of life.'

Or again, as Paul Tillich never tired of pointing out to his North American students, Europe, and especially northern, 'Protestant' Europe, never lost touch with the ancient sense of the tragic and of failure in human existence. In North America, apart from minorities, modernity effectively banished these 'negativities' and insisted upon the triumph of the positive in all phases of life, including religion. Given the official optimism of our culture, a church which could not give evidence of success – and very concrete evidence at that – could hardly be taken seriously.

I draw these contrasts because in every one of them, I think, we can detect intimations of the distinctively European character and Christian self-understanding of Dietrich Bonhoeffer. Therefore we need to recognize, if we are North Americans, that his thought is not immediately transferable to our context – a fact of which he himself, at many points in his meeting with 'America,' was made conscious. This applies, I suspect, to all aspects of his thought; but perhaps it has particular pertinence to his thought about the church. In his provocative essay on North American Christianity, bearing the still-perceptive title, "Protestantism Without Reformation," Bonhoeffer writes:

> American theology and the American church as a whole have never been able to understand the meaning of 'criticism' by the Word of God and all that signifies. Right to the last they do not understand that God's 'criticism' touches even religion, the Christianity of the churches and the sanctification of Christians, and that God has founded his church beyond religion and beyond ethics.[2]

It is precisely this lack of critical theology (and in that sense of 'Reformation') in North American ecclesial life and practice that prevents us from applying Bonhoeffer's insights about the church in a direct way to our context. Perhaps – but only, I think, perhaps – the half-century that has elapsed since the writing of the essay from which I have just quoted has seen the introduction of more critical theology in once-mainline U.S. and Canadian Protestantism. While some professional theology has learned to critique "religion," very few Christians, it seems to me, even amongst those who apply critical theological hermeneutics to ecclesiastical life, have practiced what Bonhoeffer means when he writes that "God has founded his church beyond religion and beyond ethics." In fact, most of our criticism of empirical Christianity as religion emanates from those whose dissatisfactions with the churches stem from their commitment to an ethic more rigorous, more radical, than the bourgeois, individualistic morality dominant in the churches themselves. Reading Bonhoeffer, one cannot escape the impression that his whole approach to the Christian life, corporately as well as personally conceived, proceeds from a theological spirit that is still extremely rare in our context. One feels the presence of this theological mode of thought and being (one could use the term "theologische Existenz"[3]) in the sentence, "American theology and the American church as a whole have never been able to understand the meaning of 'criticism' by the Word of God. . . ." We are apt to hear this as a rather pietistic, perhaps biblicistic sentiment. In reality, it is an expression of the Reformation principle, *semper reformanda*, understood theologically and not only ethically—that is, understood as an ongoing intellectual demand that the church reformulate its profession of faith, its 'gospel,' in obedience to a Spirit that requires us rightly to discern the signs of the times.

In the last analysis, therefore, I propose that what we need most to learn from Dietrich Bonhoeffer as theological servants of churches in the North American context is to appropriate precisely such a form of "theologische Existenz." But this, I realize, is not a lesson which one learns from others. It will emerge, if it does emerge, out of an existential immersion in the *problematique* of our own context and an original exposure to the foundations of the faith—an exposure born of some profound recognition of the need for foundations. This is what happened to Dietrich Bonhoeffer himself, and in that sense he is a model of all authentic theology in the Judeo-Christian mode. However, we need to recognize that he is speaking to us out of the recent past, as one who has already crossed over the invisible but absolutely decisive boundary between professional theology or theology as profession and 'theological existence.' Therefore, his prescription for the church can be appropriated by us only insofar as we, too, find ourselves pushed towards that boundary.

Lindbeck's identification of our "awkwardly intermediate stage" is provocative not only because of its accuracy but because, implicitly, it challenges us to move beyond that stage. No responsible theology can be satisfied to remain in the state of ecclesiastical awkwardness, poised inconclusively between a cultural establishment that is no longer fully real and a post-establishment state that is scarcely imaginable. Theology in North America today, where it has overcome academic gamesmanship and attempted seriously to serve the Christian community, knows that it is obliged to help the church to pass beyond this "awkwardly intermediate stage" into—into what? The term 'disestablishment,' which Lindbeck uses and which I, too, have often employed in this connection, is not satisfactory as a positive conception of a desirable relation of church to society. Disestablishment may describe a process, even a necessary one, but it does not describe the aim of the process. I am somewhat nervous about Stanley Hauerwas's program because I think that disestablishment may be for him an end and not only a means. The "telos" to which the church's disengagement of itself from its host culture and from its own past must serve is a new kind of engagement precisely of that same culture. Disestablishment ought not therefore to suggest abandonment of the dominant society with which, in the present, we are still 'awkwardly' linked; rather, it should lead to a re-engagement of that same society, from a theological-ethical perspective that is sufficiently distinguishable from the culture, its pursuits and its values, in order to address the culture in a prophetic manner.

The question that I want to bring to this discussion, therefore, can now be stated more explicitly: *In what way could the ecclesiastical reflection of Dietrich Bonhoeffer help theology in the North American context to identify specific areas of concentration in the necessary transition from cultural Christianity to new forms of Christian life and witness in the society for which we have a priestly responsibility?* Or, stated in terms of the Lindbeck metaphor: *How might Bonhoeffer, contemplated today by thinking Christians in Canada and the United States, help us to move us from the awkward condition of a no-longer-viable 'establishment' to one of responsible Christian mission?*

I would like to articulate an answer to this question by identifying three prominent contrasts in Bonhoeffer's ecclesiology: discipleship versus religion, world-orientation versus world-ambiguity, and suffering versus spiritual *securitas*. My thesis is that the appropriation of Bonhoeffer's sort of "theologische Existenz" by North American Christians would entail moving from Christianity as religion to Christianity as discipleship, from a posture of ambiguity with respect to the world to one of world-affirmation, and from faith as spiritual security to faith as readiness to suffer with God in the world.

I. Discipleship versus Religion

Forgive me if I begin this first consideration of Bonhoeffer's "theologische Existenz" in a personal way. His book, *The Cost of Discipleship*, was the very first work of serious theology that I ever read. Reginald Fuller's English translation of the abridged edition of *Nachfolge* appeared in 1948, just as I was trying to come to terms with what I later called (in the title of a book) *The Reality of the Gospel and the Unreality of the Churches.*"⁴ I devoured Bonhoeffer's thoughts eagerly! Here was a Christian describing the church as a community of discipleship—discipleship free of the sentimentalism and pietism that I associated with the *methodistisch* 'church-ianity' of my southwestern Ontario village upbringing; discipleship that was critical of the 'religiousness' of which my skeptic father had warned me from my youth up; discipleship that was intellectually alive and at the same time deeply committed to obedience to Jesus Christ.

All the same, the book troubled me. For just prior to its coming into my hands I had read, with growing excitement, three long biographies of Martin Luther; and I had found in Luther a strong deliverer from the awful moralism of my anglo-saxon village Christianity. With Luther's help, I had confirmed for myself at long last what I thought I had been hearing from St. Paul and others (because in those long-forgotten days we actually read and studied the Bible—the text itself!—in Sunday Schools); and it seemed to me not only a victory over my moralistic teachers and elders, but a spiritual breakthrough of the first order, to have discovered in this way "justification by grace through faith—not by works lest anyone should boast!"

Was Dietrich Bonhoeffer, or was he not, upholding this clarion call of unmerited grace? That was my question, and I confess it here because it reinforces in another more concrete way the point that I have made already about the considerable difference between Bonhoeffer's "Sitz im Leben" and our own. His struggle, or the part of it that drove him to write *Nachfolge,* was with a doctrinaire conception of grace that required little by way of praxis; mine—and the struggle of so many of us who have experienced Christian moralism, whether of the Methodist, Calvinist, Catholic or sectarian variety in North America—was to discover whether Christianity was anything more than law and sentiment. Sometimes Bonhoeffer's 'discipleship' came through to me, forty-three summers ago, as an all-too-familiar if differently stated insistence that I should become the very, very nice and good Christian young man that my village pastors and mentors kept harping on!

It was comforting therefore, later on, when I read from Dietrich Bonhoeffer's own hand, the following words: "I thought I could acquire faith by trying to live a holy life, or something like it. It was in this phase that I wrote *The Cost of Discipleship.* Today I can see the dangers of this book, though I am prepared to stand by what I wrote."⁵ The idea of discipleship is not an antidote to Christianity as 'religion' or religious moralism, particularly in the North American context, unless it is formed by a critical biblical theology. Unless the material principle of the Reformation is assumed — existentially and not only intellectually — even Bonhoeffer's skillful exegesis of Christ's "Follow me!" can appear a corroboration of what, for characteristic forms of Christianity in our context, is the very essence of religion: excessive zeal for moral righteousness and exceptional, unquestioning piety!

Clearly, however, Bonhoeffer does assume the absolute priority of grace in his use of 'discipleship,' and when this is understood it becomes, in my view at least, the basis of his critique of 'religion.' I would therefore agree with Professor DeGruchy and others who see Bonhoeffer's work as a remarkable unity despite the obvious 'stages' through which he passed as he encountered new aspects of his fast-changing context. Discipleship for him, it seems to me, refers to the serious Christianity to which, beyond his apparently liberal-bourgeois upbringing, he was led: serious Christianity as distinct from both religious formality and religious 'enthusiasm.'

In this connection, the statement of Eberhard Bethge in his discussion of Bonhoeffer's ecclesiology has seemed to me very helpful. Comparing and contrasting Bonhoeffer's sojourn with that of Paul Tillich, Bethge notes that while Tillich came from the church and discovered the world, Bonhoeffer came from the world and discovered the church; and —

> Having discovered the Church, Bonhoeffer took her more seriously than she was accustomed to being taken, and never ceased to appeal for more appropriate forms of life and witness to replace perverted ones.[6]

From the perspective of serious Christianity — Christianity as discipleship — the later Bonhoeffer, having discovered by now the truly irrelevant if not traitorous character of 'religion,' can write from prison that

> . . . I have found great help in Luther's advice that we should start our morning and evening prayers by making the sign of the cross. There is something objective about it, and that is what I need very badly here. Don't worry, I shan't come out of here a *homo religiosus!* On the contrary, my suspicion and horror of religiosity are greater than ever. I often think of how the Israelites never uttered the name of God. I can understand that much better than I used to do.[7]

Beyond that, it is his sense of discipleship as the fundamental character of Christian existence that enables him almost to rejoice in what he thinks (rather prematurely, as we may now judge) may be the very demise of religion:

> We are proceeding towards a time of no religion at all: [people] as they are now simply cannot be religious any more. . . . Our whole nineteen-hundred-year-old Christian preaching and theology rests upon the 'religious premise'

of [humanity]. What we call Christianity has always been a pattern—perhaps a true pattern—of religion. But if one day it becomes apparent that this *a priori* 'premise' simply does not exist, but was an historical and temporary form of human self-expression, i.e. if we reach the stage of being radically without religion . . . what does that mean for 'Christianity'? . . . How can Christ become the Lord even of those with no religion?[8]

It is for him discipleship—strangely, perhaps paradoxically, the most intensive expression of a Christian life earnestly ('religiously'!) undertaken—which enables him to sit lightly to 'religion' and even welcome its imminent disappearance. "Jesus does not call [people] to a new religion, but to life," he writes on July 18, 1944; and he goes on to define "the nature of that life" as "participation in the powerlessness of God in the world"—the subject which I will address below.[9]

This contrast between discipleship and religion, or however it may be expressed, seems to me the first distinction that would be necessary for Christians in North America to learn from Dietrich Bonhoeffer if they hope to pass beyond the present 'awkwardness' to something more lively by way of relationship with our society. I do not think that this should be interpreted—as the *avant garde* in the churches of the United States and Canada have sometimes interpreted it—as the adoption of 'secular' faith. Bonhoeffer was made the parent of the theology of secularity, of the death-of-God movement, and many other 'theologies of,' but all of these appear to me to bypass the centrality of discipleship in his thought, and quite specifically discipleship of Jesus Christ. Over against the identification of Christianity with religion, or the special interest in religion which has always characterized our cultural establishment, Bonhoeffer insists upon a worldliness that defies the 'religious' impulse to escape the world (more of that later); but also over against mere worldliness he advocates an almost monastic seriousness of devotion to, and obedience towards, the living Christ, testified to by scripture and tradition. One does not avoid the pitfalls of 'religion' by embracing an ideology of secularity. The triumphalism of both conventional Christian religiosity and Western technocratic secularity can only be challenged adequately by a theology of discipleship which entertains an abiding suspicion of all theory and places at the center of faith the living Christ, "who is on his way to the cross."[10]

II. World-Orientation versus Otherworldliness

While (in my opinion) Bonhoeffer's later musings were incorrectly interpreted by those who wanted to claim him for the 'new' post-Christian secularity, because they did not understand his foundations in discipleship and the theology of the cross, the dimension of truth in their interpretation is that Bonhoeffer was driven increasingly towards a theology of world-orientation which constituted, for him, a fundamental break with the otherworldliness and world-ambiguity of conventional Christianity. What I intend by 'world-orientation' is however not at all synonymous with secularity. For the source of Bonhoeffer's affirmation of the world – and precisely at a point in his own life when a strenuous appropriation of the ancient practice of *contemptus mundi* would have been understandable if not even appropriate (!) – lies outside the *saeculum* altogether and is found precisely at the center of the gospel of the incarnation and humiliation of the divine Word.

In fact I would argue – and have done – that what drives Bonhoeffer increasingly towards this world, with all of its duplicity and pain, is his appropriation of the Pauline and Lutheran *theologia crucis*, honed by the worldly events through which he had to pass into a political or, perhaps more accurately, a pre-political theology. Too often in the past, the theology of the cross had been reduced to personalistic and indeed to otherworldly pietism: 'through cross to crown,' 'life in this world is a cross to be borne,' etc. Bonhoeffer realized, in a unique way comparable only to Reinhold Niebuhr in the American scene, the worldly and public implications of a story centered in the suffering of the Messiah.[11]

That he did so is clearly associated with his growing interest in and exposure to the faith of Israel (and this is another link with Niebuhr). For the origin of what Luther named (he did not invent it!) 'the theology of the cross' is to be found, not in Paul – at any rate, not a Paul isolated from his Judaic origins – but in the prophetic tradition. When Abraham Heschel claims as the very essence of that tradition what he calls the sense of "divine pathos," we should know that we are in the vicinity of Golgotha – that the *passio Christi* is a precise, and for Christians of course decisive, enactment of that same "divine pathos."

Bonhoeffer's consciousness of the significance of the Hebraic background of the whole Christian narrative grows visibly in his writings, and with it there is nurtured – quite naturally, as one must surely say – an increasing impatience with Christian hesitancy with respect to this world and an increasing insistence upon the world-orientation of the gospel of the cross. Thus it is no accident that his most poignant statement of this subject comes in the form of reflections on "the Old Testament."

In a letter to Eberhard Bethge from Tegel prison on June 27, 1944, Bonhoeffer writes:

> Now for some further thoughts about the Old Testament. Unlike the other oriental religions, the faith of the Old Testament isn't a religion of redemption.

It's true that Christianity has always been regarded as a religion of redemption. But isn't this a cardinal error, which separates Christ from the Old Testament and interprets him on the lines of the myths about redemption? To the
objection that a crucial importance is given in the Old Testament to redemption (from Egypt, and later from Babylon—cf. Deutero-Isaiah) it may be
answered that the redemptions referred to here are historical, i.e. on this side
of death, whereas everywhere else the myths about redemption are concerned
to overcome the barrier of death. Israel is delivered out of Egypt so that it may
live before God as God's people on earth. The redemption myths try unhis-
torically to find an eternity after death. Sheol and Hades are no metaphysical
constructions, but images which imply that the 'past,' while it still exists, has
only a shadowy existence in the present.[12]

Just at this point, something very dramatic and theologically decisive
happens in this *pensée,* and I doubt very much that its true radicality has
been grasped by many of its North American readers. Realizing that
Christianity—and specifically in its theology of resurrection—has traditionally been considered a "religion of redemption" from finitude, Bonhoeffer boldly reinterprets resurrection as the supremely this-worldly
denouement of the Christian drama:

The decisive factor is said to be that in Christianity the hope of resurrection
is proclaimed, and that that means the emergence of a genuine religion of
redemption, the main emphasis now being on the far side of the boundary
drawn by death. But it seems to me that this is just where the mistake and
the danger lie. Redemption now means redemption from cares, distress, fears,
and longings, from sin and death, in a better world beyond the grave. But
is this really the essential character of the proclamation of Christ in the gospels
and by Paul? I should say it is not. The difference between the Christian hope
of resurrection and the mythological hope is that the former sends a [person]
back to his [or her] life on earth in a wholly new way which is even more
sharply defined than it is in the Old Testament. The Christian, unlike the
devotees of the redemption myths, has no last line of escape available from
earthly tasks and difficulties into the eternal, but, like Christ himself ('My God,
why hast thou forsaken me?') he [she] must drink the earthly cup to the dregs,
and only in his [her] doing so is the crucified and risen Lord with him [her],
and he [she] crucified and risen with Christ. This world must not be prematurely written off.[13]

In this statement, I find the *theologia crucis* carried to its most logical and
most necessary conclusion; for that theological tradition is nothing more
nor less than the recognition of God's abiding commitment to the creation, and as such there is—in our time at least—nothing more needful than
that the redemption theology of Christian faith should be presented as
a statement of God's commitment to and "mending" (Fackenheim) of the
creation!

But as a *theologia crucis* this is implicitly and even explicitly also an *ecclesia crucis;* for what Bonhoeffer counsels here is not merely a message about God's orientation towards the world but the coming to be of a people who, being delivered somewhat from sin—that is, flight from the world!—are learning how to journey towards this world in sacrificial love. This entire emphasis, which seems to me to be the core of Bonhoeffer's later work and the culmination of his christological reflection, is by the same token the heart of what "theologische Existenz" would have to mean in his case. And it seems to me that on this continent we have hardly even begun to grasp this.

On the one hand, 'other-worldliness' continues to haunt all forms of North American Christianity excepting the most liberal; and even amongst the liberals there is a thinly cloaked suspicion that too much worldliness could be a lack of genuine 'spirituality.' On the other hand, we find amongst Christian activists a failure to grasp the rationale of Christian world-orientation, which is not a merely ethical orientation but one which, for Bonhoeffer at least, is decisively theological. The whole source of the wisdom as well as the courage, the courage as well as the wisdom, that Christians require for their journey towards the world is located in their relationship to the crucified one. Their world-keeping is not the consequence of a moral program or a general directive of the divine imperative; it is their baptismal identification with the one who left the security of the father's house and ventured into the far country (Barth).

Nothing is more detrimental to this world-orientation than is the 'resurrectionism' of North American conventional Christianity, whether in its fundamentalist or its bourgeois 'mainstream' attire. And when Bonhoeffer attacks precisely that interpretation of the event of the third day and insists that the resurrection means being sent back into the life of the world with a new exposure to its brokenness and a new concern for its mending, he speaks almost directly to our situation. Almost!

However, between his speaking and our hearing there is a considerable gulf fixed. It is the gulf between his 'theology of the cross' and our 'theology of glory,' which, whether it comes to us via conservative or liberal, conventional (perhaps calvinistic) orthodoxy or radical (perhaps liberationist) theologies, binds us to an ideological triumphalism that, despite external differences, in the end can only corroborate the cultural imperialism of our society. Nothing is more difficult for all forms of North American Christianity to overcome than this predisposition to triumphalism, which, doctrinally and liturgically, locates itself in a resurrectionist interpretation of the gospel that, in superceding the cross, must also turn away from the real world where the cross has not been superceded.

III. Suffering with God in the World versus Spiritual Security

Bonhoeffer's accentuation of the suffering of the church is a consequence of his realism with respect to worldly suffering. It is not—and I
would say decidedly not!—a matter of Christian masochism or what Karl
Barth termed "nordic melancholy." I am sure that Bonhoeffer would have
approved wholeheartedly the opening sentence of Jürgen Moltmann's *The
Crucified God:* "The cross is not and cannot be loved."[14] Bonhoeffer was
certainly conscious of the danger of seeking crosses to bear. His priorities
are clear: the disciple community is not called to suffer but to be obedient—
that is, to follow Christ into the world. Suffering is consequence: the
consequence of discipleship. It will inevitably occur in the pursuit of the
call to follow, because the world still suffers and because God still suffers
for and on account of the world. Moreover, the suffering into which the
church is initiated through its baptismal identification with the Christ is
only a means to a greater end: namely, to the end that suffering may be
overcome:

> Suffering has to be endured in order that it may pass away. Either the world
> must bear the whole burden and collapse beneath it, or it must fall on Christ
> to be overcome in Him. He therefore suffers vicariously for the world. His
> is the only suffering which has redemptive efficacy. But the Church knows
> that the world is still seeking for someone to bear its sufferings, and so, as
> it follows Christ, suffering becomes the Church's lot too. As it follows Him
> beneath the cross, the Church stands before God as the representative of the
> world.[15]

Suffering is for Bonhoeffer, as for Luther, the characteristic mark of
the church, the one indispensable mark. The church may be able to give
evidence of unity, holiness, catholicity and apostolicity; but even if these
traditional marks of the church are present, when "the mark of the holy
cross" is absent, they are worthless. Yet the rationale for this insistence
upon the church's suffering is to be located, not in religious aspirations
(where it has characteristically been found), and not in world-renunciation
(which has been its most frequent earmark), but in the discipleship which
drives the reluctant faithful more and more insistently into God's beloved
world with a view to its healing. For this reason I have come to this aspect
of Bonhoeffer's ecclesiology last, only after laying, in a necessarily minimal
way, the foundations for it in his christology, soteriology and eschatology.
The *theologia crucis,* where it is genuine, necessarily begets an *ecclesia crucis;*
and in this way Bonhoeffer completes, in my view, the work of Luther,
whose followers did not always understand this ecclesiological consequence of 'the theology of the cross.'

The church which follows Jesus Christ into the world will have to experience humiliation; and surely Bonhoeffer understood, what has become more inescapable in the half-century since his death, that this humiliation would have to include, eventually, the very demise of that form of the church which for some sixteen centuries dominated the Western world and still dominates our mental and spiritual processes even when it is quantitatively and qualitatively obsolete. In his "thoughts" on the occasion of the baptism of Dietrich Bethge, Bonhoeffer writes:

> Our church, which has been fighting in these years only for its self-preservation, as though that were an end in itself, is incapable of taking the word of reconciliation and redemption to mankind and the world.[16]

In a similar vein, in his "Outline for a Book," in the first chapter entitled, "A Stocktaking of Christianity," he proposed discussing "The decisive factor: the Church on the defensive. Unwillingness to take risks in the service of humanity."[17] And, in the baptismal reflections, he continues:

> By the time you have grown up, the church's form will have changed greatly. We are not yet out of the melting-pot, and any attempt to help the church prematurely to a new expansion of its organization will merely delay its con-version and purification.[18]

"The humiliation of Christendom," as Albert van den Heuvel later called the de-Constantinianization of the church, is for Bonhoeffer not an end in itself or a program to be undertaken, but a consequence of authentic discipleship, as contrasted with religion and the quest for power and *securitas*. It is necessary for the church to be denied worldly power in order that it may engage the world at the heart of its own life. As John DeGruchy has expressed it (with, it seems to me, insight):

> The church in a world come of age would need to regain its position at the centre of the world, not in a spirit of triumphalism, but in openness to secular people and a willingness to engage with them in the struggles and issues which shape life in society. This meant becoming a 'church for others' in conforming with Jesus Christ, rather than following a path of self-preservation, concrete 'righteous actions' rather than repeating worn-out cliches or enunciating principles.[19]

Today, the once-mainline churches of our own continent are horribly confused by the disestablishment that is happening to them—and it must be stated in that way: 'happening to them.' This is an eventuality so utterly out-of-keeping not only with our ecclesiastical but (even more so) our general cultural expectations that we can only seem to respond to it with revulsion and denial. The most vulgar forms of reaction to our displace-ment go well beyond Bonhoeffer's word about Christian 'defensiveness' and 'self-preservation.' We are now engaged in the creation of so-called "mega-churches," and in the denominations most devastated by the loss of numbers, properties, and social influence, where pathetic attempts at 'church growth' are intermittently undertaken, new depths of depression, debilitation and fatalism about the future are almost palpable.

Quite clearly, all of this falls under Bonhoeffer's assessment, "We are not yet out of the melting-pot, and any attempt to help the church prematurely to a new expansion of its organization will merely delay its conversion and purification."[20] It belongs to our "awkward stage," at least on this continent, that we are able to entertain no viable model of the church beyond the imperial model that, in our democratic society, has had to mean the-church-as-majority.

If we are to move beyond the awkward stage—as I proposed must be the object of every responsible theology—then the specific duty of Christian theologians in our context is to help the churches, or the remnants that remain, to grasp at the spiritual as well as the intellectual level, an alternative model of the Christian community that is both positive and possible. And here Bonhoeffer's vision is perhaps most directly significant for our guidance: the church as a disciple community taken up into its Lord's suffering for the world, explicated in terms of the strange, repressed, hardly allowable suffering of our world, is the only model of the church that can deliver us from eventual oblivion. So I believe.

But ecclesiology is always consequential. One does not begin with a conception of the church and then look for a market for it! If we are to embrace our humiliation and find meaning in it—meaning and new life!— we shall have to begin with another way of understanding the gospel itself. That other way is accurately described by Dietrich Bonhoeffer in the following words:

> Man's religiosity makes him look in his distress to the power of God in the world: God is the *deus ex machina*. The Bible directs man to God's powerlessness and suffering; only the suffering God can help.[21]

Notes

1. George A. Lindbeck, *The Nature of Doctrine* (Philadelphia: Westminster Press, 1984), 134.
2. In John de Gruchy, *Dietrich Bonhoeffer: Witness to Jesus Christ* (London: Collins, 1987), 216.
3. A term coined by Karl Barth and central to the thought of Hans-Joachim Iwand.
4. Douglas John Hall, *The Reality of the Gospel and the Unreality of the Churches* (Philadelphia: Westminster Press, 1975).

5. Dietrich Bonhoeffer, *Letters and Papers from Prison*, ed. Eberhard Bethge, trans. Reginald H. Fuller (London: SCM Press, 1953), 168.

6. Ebehard Bethge, *Bonhoeffer: Exile and Martyr*, ed. John W. De Gruchy (New York: Seabury Press, 1975), 61.

7. *Letters and Papers*, 73.

8. *Letters and Papers*, 122–3.

9. *Letters and Papers*, 167.

10. Dietrich Bonhoeffer, *The Cost of Discipleship*, trans. R. H. Fuller (London: SCM Press, 1959), 51.

11. See my essay on Niebuhr's appropriation of the *theologia crucis* in Richard Harries, ed., *Reinhold Niebuhr and the Issues of Our Time* (London and Oxford: Mowbray, 1986), 183–204.

12. *Letters and Papers from Prison: The Enlarged Edition*, trans. Reginald Fuller, Frank Clarke, et al. (London: SCM Press, 1971), 336.

13. *Letters and Papers: The Enlarged Edition*, 336, my italics.

14. Jürgen Moltmann, *The Crucified God*, trans. R. A. Wilson and John Bowden (London: SCM Press, 1974), 1.

15. *The Cost of Discipleship*, 1948 edition, 76.

16. *Letters and Papers: The Enlarged Edition*, 300.

17. *Letters and Papers*, 1953 edition, 179.

18. *Letters and Papers: The Enlarged Edition*, 300.

19. *Dietrich Bonhoeffer: Witness to Jesus Christ*, 39–40.

20. See above, n. 19.

21. *Letters and Papers: The Enlarged Edition*, 361.

Part II:

Social Analysis and Liberation

THE MODERN NIGHTMARE:
A LATIN AMERICAN
CHRISTIAN INDICTMENT

Otto A. Maduro

Wolf-Dieter Zimmermann, talking about Bonhoeffer's sermons at Finkenwalde, once remarked that there ought to be a shot of heresy in every good sermon, meaning, I take it, that every sermon must drop the doctrinal evenness, become one-sided, take sides, and dare to go beyond the boundaries of what is "permissible." I don't know if what I'm going to say will qualify as a good sermon, but I think it's going to be somewhat of a sermon, with more than a shot of heresy, certainly onesided, blatantly taking sides, and indeed going beyond the boundaries of what seems permissible in many a theological seminary in these times.

Allow me to call this sermon of sorts "The Modern Nightmare: A Latin American Christian Indictment," and to cite a Jewish theologian, Richard Rubenstein – paradoxically a sworn enemy of liberation theologies – to set the tone of what I want to share:

> How utterly mistaken is any view that would isolate Nazism and its supreme expression, bureaucratic mass murder and the bureaucratically administered society of total domination from the mainstream of Western culture.[1]

It is now more than 500 years after 1492, the so-called discovery of America. As Tzvetan Todorov would put it, "Even if every date that permits us to separate any two periods is arbitrary, none is more suitable, in order to mark the beginning of the modern era, than the year 1492."[2] Perhaps no date is more suitable to reflect on what Dietrich Bonhoeffer called "a world-come-of-age," and its ambiguous relation to Christian theology, than this quincentennial – an anniversary that some celebrate as the 500th anniversary of the evangelization and civilization of the Americas, while others, among whom I count myself, insist on commemorating as five hundred years of genocide and resistance.

The year 1492 also marks the year when my paternal Jewish ancestors were expelled from Sepharad—their name for the Iberian peninsula. It was the year, too, when my maternal Native American ancestors started experiencing an ethnocide which reduced their numbers from near 54 million to less than 9 million people in the space of 150 years; and which wiped off the face of the earth 1,700 of the 2,200–odd Native American cultures that were thriving around 1492. It was the year, too, when the European invasion of the Americas prepared the way for changing forever the fate of my maternal African ancestors: shortly thereafter the Western slave trade would wrest nearly 50 million people out of Africa for the Americas, leaving two thirds of them dead in the Atlantic Ocean. The year 1492 was, finally, the year in which my maternal German and Spanish ancestors began to benefit from the wealth wrought from Africa and America by the European invaders—the very same wealth that paid the Spanish foreign debt to Britain and Germany, thus paving the way for the Industrial Revolution and many other modern North Atlantic feats.

To say the least, it is a bit uneasy for a Latin American deeply aware of this history to talk about "a world come of age" when speaking about modernity. Modernity is not a mere fact. It is a process: modernization. Moreover, modernity is not a past process: it is a current, growing, on-going one. It is not, and never was an abstract, neutral process: it is a process that claimed, continues to claim, and apparently will claim while it lasts more victims than victors. In point of fact, the "eighties" —and so far the "nineties" —too were the first decade of this century when every single country south of the Rio Grande endured a sustained impoverishment and growth of its already poor majority. However, never before did those countries export more wealth abroad than during these last twelve years. We have not ceased to repeat it for the last quarter of a century: the so-called "underdevelopment" of the Third World is not an obstacle or an accident alien to modernization; it is but one of the aspects, one of the consequences of modernization. It is, as it were, its hidden, repulsive, shameful facet. The "progress" of both a few countries and of the urban elites throughout the modern world is based upon, requires and generates exploitation and premature death for the many.

"Modernization" is not a natural or inevitable process. Nor is it born out of any conditions whatsoever. "Modernization" is an economic-cultural-political process born within Western Europe and imposed thereafter by open or disguised force upon the rest of humanity. It is a process of subordination and incorporation of the *others* under the sameness of North Atlantic bourgeois domination. And again: this is not a thing of the past. The current International Monetary Fund/World Bank recipe—which fits perfectly the interests of the wealthiest elites of both the First and the Third World—has been the most stringent, inflexible set of demands imposed on us in the last centuries. "Modernization" is not merely, as its naive advocates would want, a "cultural" or at the most technological, scientific, industrial and economic process. It is at its core, too, an expansionist military enterprise an exploitative project which requires brutal force to perpetuate itself. No wonder, first, that the only uncensored item among public expenditures in the IMF-WB recipe happens to be police and military expenditures; no wonder, either, that in the last quarter of a century more than half of the brainpower produced in modern universities throughout the world has been absorbed, directly or indirectly, by the military; no wonder, finally, that the most significant segment of the Third World's foreign debt results from Western loans and sales for military purposes.

In what way does "modern, liberal" theology speak to that? Very little, I am afraid. It is easier to see the horrors of Treblinka as a historical exception due to the racist delirium of a madman, blaming the Gulag on the supposedly anti-modern madness of Soviet communism, justifying My Lai, Den Ying the bloodbath of San Miguelito in Panama, and forgetting the football stadium of Santiago de Chile rather than pondering the complex, contradictory and paradoxical connections between all of the above, while simultaneously acknowledging the measure of singular madness that each one of those instances involve.

My dad told me a story of his youth that has stayed with me for forty years. He was out hunting monkeys with a couple of friends. When they shot their first one they ran to get it. It wasn't quite dead yet. My dad told me that the tormented, supplicating stare he got from that monkey in agony was such that he was never able to kill an animal for the rest of his life. The U.S. army knows better: Salvadoran, Guatemalan, and Honduran minors are recruited by force to serve in their respective armies. Part of the training consists in skinning live monkeys which look exactly like newborn babies afterwards and shooting them then and there: it builds the character of those youths, according to their U.S. trainers, so that they become better soldiers in their struggle against subversion. We don't want to know that. We don't want to know that the delicious tropical fruits sold by Korean merchants in New York city are so cheap because unions are broken in the Central American countryside by green berets. Theology does not want anything to do with that. We do not want to know that there are victims to our freedom, progress, education, consumer goods and tranquility. We do not want to know our victims; we do not want to look them in their eyes—lest we become unable to peacefully sleep and theologize, or whatever, anymore.

Theologizing about the modern world without naming the holocausts and genocides it is based upon, without getting to know the casualties of the freedom and progress of our elites and ourselves, without looking in the eye those who are tormented for our lifestyles is, to say the very least, irresponsible, immature, far away from adulthood and "world come-of-age." Beware: I am not indicting poor Dietrich Bonhoeffer, who did what he could and had to do which was much more than I have done so far for my own. Nor do I want to elicit guilt among my patient audience, either. All I want to suggest is that any responsible, adult, contemporary theology—any theologian who takes seriously Bonhoeffer's conviction that "it is an experience of incomparable value to have learned to see the great events of the history of the world from beneath: from the viewpoint of the useless, the suspect, the abused, the powerless, the oppressed, the despised—in a word, from the viewpoint of those who suffer"³—has to dare the quantum leap of listening carefully to the innocent suffering victims of modernity. True, "There is nothing [we] can do to change history. And [we] should not feel responsible for what others did before [we] were born. However, we . . . do have a responsibility to learn from history. We can choose whether to reverse the legacy of injustice or to continue it."⁴

In my opinion, the fracture separating modern, liberal theologies from liberation theologies is the awareness and central concern of the latter with the continuous, massive human sacrifices required by modernity as opposed to the optimism of the former. True, indeed, this break stems from the fact that the birthplaces of both theological movements are quite different, nay, antithetical: while modern, liberal theology is mainly a product of white, male, North Atlantic intellectuals, sharing in the lifestyles of modern elites unaware of and distant from the victims of modernity, liberation theologies, on the contrary, stem from the experience (included among many white male North Atlantic intellectuals) of the very victims of modernity: the useless, the suspect, the abused, the powerless, the oppressed, the despised, the victims of economic exploitation, sexism, racism, war and torture.

This might be why our questions are not so much, for instance, if God exists or not, but, rather, on whose side is God, and how come God is on the side of the malnourished, the battered women and the tortured; not so much "how to speak of God in a world come of age", but, rather, how to speak of God in a world gone mad; not so much how to worship God in a "non-religious world", but, rather, how to worship God within, despite, and over against churches which ignore, condone, or exercise exploitation and war; not so much why certain people don't believe in God, but, rather, how Efrain Rios Montt, Alexander Haig, Augusto Pinochet, Dan Mitrione, or George Bush are depicted as good Christians; not so much if we have souls, but how are we going to keep our bodies alive; not so much if there is life after death, but, rather, if there is going to be life before death; not so much under what conditions the military, the police, and the guerrillas are morally acceptable, but, rather, how not to loose our marbles under daily, institutionalized violence.

Not that we think that the questions of modern, liberal theologies are irrelevant, superficial or pointless. No! Most of us in Latin America have lived through these questions and have read and appreciated most of the North Atlantic theological attempts to respond to them. It is just that we share other questions which are for us more urgent, burning and grave. It is merely that we are sick and tired of having others telling us what are the questions and the answers that we should ponder. It is simply that we do not share in the experience or the naive conviction that today "we" have more knowledge than ever before in human history. What we see is that today we know less than ever before whether we are going to be able to pay for the rent, the food, the medical care or the schooling of our children than our grandparents did; and we have fewer clues than ever before as to how to guarantee our ability to pay for these things. We do not share in the experience of having more power and control over our lives than before: what we see is that we might lose overnight our jobs, home, health insurance or the savings of a lifetime, despite following all the instructions that the experts gave us at work, school, church, TV and the newspapers. We do not share in the experience of growing security. What we see is that we ourselves and our children are increasingly threatened with homelessness, unemployment, epidemics, arbitrary incarceration, forced displacement and exile. We do not share in the experience of more freedom. All we know is that it is very dangerous to think, talk, write or act differently and that democracies, which are tolerated or taken away at the whim of national and U.S. powers, are nowadays weaker and more restricted than they ever were in the past. While the media chant the final victory of free enterprise over communism most of us, south of the Rio Grande, experience an overwhelming, incomprehensible nightmare. This may be why, of all the modern, liberal Christian theologians, Dietrich Bonhoeffer is the closest to our hearts. Can you understand?

Modernity—for many of us who have already been haunted by its seamy side—is a disease. Inevitable, maybe, not in Hegel's sense, but in a sort of Norman Schwarzkopf's sense. Alien, indeed, at least in its sources.

Full of temptations and, for some, sometimes, of rewards even. But a disease all the same. Part of this sickness is its incapacity to embrace otherness human or divine: its inability to humble itself in face of any real, deep transcendence, historical or otherwise. There is, in fact, a paradoxical intolerance in the modern mindset: a rejection of deep cultural differences; a proclivity to view as intolerance any desire to remain simply and humbly other than modern; an ineptitude to tolerate that some others would want to continue outside of, or only partially within, or simply in mutuality with the "modern world". There is, in the modern Western mindset, an utter inability to realize and accept—for instance, that there are deeply religious, mystic, spiritual, prayerful people in other cultures that have no interest whatsoever in accumulating modern stuff (be it knowledge, gadgets or money), or in competing in modern terms, or in defeating or converting or assimilating anybody to their faith. These are people who do not see their culture as truer, better or stronger than others and, however, feel no qualms, doubts or temptations to shed their ancient beliefs, values and customs.

This intolerance is probably one of the areas where modernity is more of a child of Western Christianity than any other. One of the crucial areas where this is more painfully manifest—at least for us in the Third World—is in the modern grasp of human history as *one*. I am not referring to the idea of the unity of both sacred and human history—a concept at least as dear to liberation theologies as it was to Bonhoeffer, and one which seems to me immensely more faithful to our Jewish heritage, and to Jesus the Jew, than the Manichean dualism separating God's providence and human history. What I refer to is the conception of human history as a single, linear progression conducted by the Christian West: that is, the inability to see the histories of other peoples as anything but previous, underdeveloped, stagnant or primitive stages in the single, one and only history of humankind. Human history could in fact be perceived as a variegated, plural constellation of diverse histories—histories of different, multiple human cultures and societies—which at times intersect, blend, clash, make war, submit, defeat, destroy, dialogue, exchange, separate and/or cross-fertilize each other. This would be, for instance, the way in which many Native American nations see human history. This is not the case for modernity or, more largely, for the Christian West. Actually, it appears to me that the reason for this conception of history, and even more so for its modern version, lies in being the mindset of an expansionist empire: a *Weltanschauung* driven by the resolve to overpower, exploit, swallow and suppress all other societies, cultures and nations. It belies the deep assumption of a "manifest destiny" to force all histories under the history of the

North Atlantic Powers—to make them cry "uncle," kneel in worship and eat the dust before turning them into servants or waste. But, isn't this the very history of modern Western Christianity? Isn't this what began anew, more forcefully than ever before, in 1492?

What do our modern, liberal theologies—or, for that matter, our churches' leadership say to this? Nothing, again, or very little: it might be too hard to look back upon our monotheism, our christologies, ecclesiologies, soteriologies, our dogmatic and moral theologies, and raise the suspicion that some of the deepest roots of our holocausts, from Hernan Cortes' to Hitler's to Stalin's to Teddy Roosevelt's to Rios Montt's, lie at the heart of modern, Western Christianity long before Treblinka, indeed, but perhaps not much before Alexander VI or Luther. Again and possibly not by accident our Jewish sisters and brothers happened to be among the first scapegoats of such a design.

A Latina friend of mine recently attended a mainline Christian service in this city of New York. She was aghast to hear a prayer for deliverance of all guilt: no repentance, no reparation, no humble acknowledgment of our common responsibility for righting the wrongs which are part of our communities. Deliverance of all guilt. To this—I thought to myself—is what the following of Jesus the Jew has been reduced in modern, Western Christianity: "a rich and privileged church that offers cheap grace," if Larry Rasmussen allows me to quote him in this context. Modern, Western Christianity seems to have been turned into cheap counseling requiring no real conversion, no accountability whatsoever, no restitution, no looking at the victims in the eye: just one more therapy in the free market, subject to the interplay of supply and demand; another disposable commodity that neither comforts the afflicted nor afflicts the comfortable.

My own church, the Roman Catholic church, is too busy these days promoting a "new evangelization" on occasion of the quincentennial of 1492. As Bonhoeffer would say, "[o]ur church, which has been fighting in these years only for its self-preservation, as though that were an end in itself, is incapable of taking the word of reconciliation to the world. [. . . A]ny attempt to help the church prematurely to a new expansion of its organization will merely delay its conversion and purification."[5]

There is hope, however, as this current forum proves. There are many people—within and without our churches—pondering these things these days. I have very little to offer other than questions and food for thought—in way of a solution to the tragedies of our time. I don't think that adopting or adapting liberation theologies—as fond as I might be of them—is the solution. In agreement with Rabbi Irving Greenberg, I would converge in suggesting that "[a]fter the Holocaust, there should be no final solutions, not even theological ones."[6]

I feel, however, that liberation theologies are among the little ferments within our churches which might contribute something to the Shalom to which many of us dream and struggle to attain. Again, given the nightmare we go through in Latin America, I might as well close this already too long, not very good sermon, with these words of the modern theologian, victim of modern, bureaucratic mass murder, who gathered us in this place: "We shall have to keep our lives rather than shape them, to hope rather than plan, to hold out rather than march forward."[7]

Notes

1. Richard Rubenstein, *The Cunning of History: The Holocaust and the American Future* (New York: Harper & Row, 1975), 31.
2. Tzvetan Todorov, *The Conquest of America: The Question of the Other* (New York: Harper Perennial, 1992), 5.
3. Dietrich Bonhoeffer, *Gesammelte Schriften*, 2 (Munich: Chr. Kaiser, 1965), 441. See also Gustavo Gutierrez, *The Power of the Poor in History* (Maryknoll, NY: Orbis Books, 1988), 229.
4. "Rethinking Columbus," a special issue of *Rethinking Schools* (1991): 3.
5. See Larry Rasmussen, "Worship in a World Come of Age," in *Dietrich Bonhoeffer. His Significance for North Americans* (New York: Fortress Press, 1990), 59.
6. Irving Greenberg, "Cloud of Smoke, Pillar of Fire: Judaism, Christianity and Modernity after the Holocaust," in *Auschwitz: Beginning of a New Era?*, ed. Eva Fleishner (New York: KTAV, 1974), 11; see also Rasmussen, 116.
7. Dietrich Bonhoeffer, "Thoughts on the Day of the Baptism of Dietrich Wilhelm Rüdiger Bethge," *Letters and Papers from Prison* (New York: Macmillan, 1972), 382; see also Rasmussen, 21.

BONHOEFFER AND ROMERO: PROPHETS OF JUSTICE FOR THE OPPRESSED

Geffrey B. Kelly

I. The Voice of the Voiceless: Solidarity with the Oppressed

To link Archbishop Romero, defender of the poor of El Salvador, with the witness of Dietrich Bonhoeffer, an agitator in the 1930's for a church resistance to Nazism and a conspirator to topple the Nazi government, is to recall the immense compassion of both men for those people whom Nazi and oligarchic ideology had marginalized. In the worst phase of the massacres and the terroristic disruption of Salvadoran village life, Romero became the defender of the poor by his angry protests against those responsible for the oppression. He was their pastor demanding in no-nonsense language an accounting of those taken in the middle of the night and "made to disappear." When the bodies of the "disappeared" were later found mutilated in the dumps and ditches of the country, he was their spokesman who dared to ask why those murdered were always from the ranks of the poor, and why they had been killed without even the formality of a civil trial.

Declarations of solidarity with the victims of injustice from a church leader with some power and influence were precisely what Dietrich Bonhoeffer had demanded from the churches—if their avowed mission to serve Christ among the victims of political ideologies was to have any credibility. In a world seething with hatred, Bonhoeffer goaded the churches finally to act like the true church of Jesus Christ and to defend those brutalized by governmental injustice. His outspokenness on behalf of those whom the Nazis had decreed to be subhuman and, therefore, undeserving of any rights within the Third Reich, would be echoed in the words and deeds of Romero.

There are, in fact, numerous affinities between the German pastor and the Salvadoran bishop. Both had an uncommon sensitivity to the problems besetting an underclass of people. Because of their attempt to change the evil direction of their respective worlds and their having sacrificed their lives in that cause, both are considered an inspiration in the current struggles for liberation and social justice. It is not by accident that Romero was called by his people, "the voice of those who have no voice," ("*la voz de los sin voz*") and that Bonhoeffer justified his daring defense of the Jews by asking in the spirit of Proverbs 31:8: "Who will speak up for those who have no voice?"[1] Romero himself had written that the church would betray its love of God and its mission to preach the gospel were it not to speak up for "those who have no voice."[2]

Romero's bonding with the poor of El Salvador is well known. Bonhoeffer's first encounter with the jagged edges of poverty came during his pastorate in Barcelona. His endeavors there in helping the poor—including begging money for them from his father—carried over into a pastoral concern for those squeezed by forces beyond their control into darkened corners of destitution. How far this compassion should extend can be seen in a portion of his writing on "Jesus Christ and the Essence of Christianity." There he insists that the faces of "Christ existing as community" were those of the grubby poor. He told his parishioners that the way of Christ to God was the divine light shining "down on those who are ever neglected, insignificant, weak, ignoble, unknown, inferior, oppressed, despised; here it radiates over the houses of prostitutes and tax collectors. . . . Here the light of eternity has been cast on the toiling, struggling, and sinning masses. . . ." Bonhoeffer concludes with the observation that Christianity inverts the value systems of society by preaching "the unending worth of the apparently worthless and the unending worthlessness of what is apparently so valuable. The weak shall be made strong through God and the dying shall live. . . ."[3]

Not surprisingly, Bonhoeffer identified with the poverty stricken in the person of the African-Americans of Harlem, whom he met during his year at Union Theological Seminary. That decisive year in America was his first intimation of how poverty could be tied into racism. Through his close friendship with the African-American student, Frank Fisher, Bonhoeffer became attached to the Abyssinian Baptist Church in Harlem. Indeed, he called his association with that community "one of the most decisive and delightful happenings of my stay in America."[4] But, while he admired the deep spirituality of their liturgical hymns, Bonhoeffer also noticed the impatience of young African-Americans at their elders' stoically enduring injustice in a country that bragged of its love of freedom. He believed strongly that, if these young people were ever to become godless because of the rampant racism they encountered and the absence of any real church support on their behalf, "white America would have to acknowledge its guilt."[5]

Bonhoeffer took back to Germany a disgust with the racism to which his friends were subjected and which he himself had witnessed. One of his students in Berlin remembered that "it [the Negro Spirituals and the stories of racial discrimination in America] was for us an entirely unknown, strange and frightening world." Before Bonhoeffer introduced his students to that "strange new world," he prefaced his remarks with the poignant statement that telling them about the racist downside of his American experience was a fulfillment of a promise to his friend, Frank Fisher. "When I took leave of my black friend, he said to me: 'Make our sufferings known in Germany, tell them what is happening to us, and show them what we are like.'"[6] Having absorbed from Fisher a sensitivity to the economic misery of America's blacks, and having tracked their woes not only to racism but also to ecclesiastical apathy, Bonhoeffer was doubly alert to the menace of Hitler's racist ideology. He recognized that in the laws then being concocted to deny the Jewish citizens their fundamental human rights, a contemptuous gauntlet was being thrown down at the churches.

It was in character, then, for Bonhoeffer to hold the churches responsible for their cowardice in failing to respond to Hitler more vigorously on an issue so close to what the gospels depict as Jesus' own identification with the outcasts of his society. The churches of Germany, he said, had jeopardized their integrity by having forsaken their Jewish brothers and sisters. His demands for critical questioning of the Nazi government, for a decision to aid the Jewish victims of the repressive laws, and even for direct acts of opposition aimed at repealing those laws and, that failing, to work for the overthrow of such a criminal government, belong to this period.[7]

In 1939, Bonhoeffer wrote that white people would have to acknowledge their guilt should United States' racism push blacks beyond the brink of their faith in God. In 1940, at the height of Hitler's popularity with the German masses and in the glow of Hitler's greatest military achievements, he crafted a "confession of guilt" charging the churches for their complicity in the sufferings inflicted on the innocent victims of Nazi ideology. His words are a stark reminder of how churches are willing to sell their souls for the porridge of institutional survival.

Finally, in a sobering phrase that could serve as a model for the churches to own up to their responsibility for the hatred of Jews that erupted with unbelievable ferocity in the Holocaust, he asked the churches to confess their guilt in "the deaths of the weakest and most defenseless brothers and sisters of Jesus Christ."[8] This confession amounts to an "indictment" of the churches, by which Bonhoeffer challenges the church leaders to take the more Christlike step of condemning the corrupt political forces that contrive to make life miserable for those branded as subversive or sub-human. His disappointment with the churches was never so keen as when the ecclesiastical leaders were willing to pay with their silence and non-involvement for their privileged existence within the good graces of a criminal state. He wanted more than pietistical platitudes, self-justifying inaction, and fainthearted resolutions from those who were the supposed visible representatives of Jesus Christ on earth. Unlike the six million Jewish victims of Nazism, the churches survived the war with their privileges intact, but only at the price of denying Christ anew.

By the war years, Bonhoeffer had become a near solitary witness against church leaders whose sins of omission had encouraged the Hitlerism from which millions were then suffering. Romero, too, sensed that he was bereft of any solid support either from Rome or from his fellow bishops. His anger at the lack of understanding of the plight of the poor on the part of many church leaders comes through in his Fourth Pastoral Letter on "The Church's Mission Amid the National Crisis." There he lists the three main failures within the church in that time of crisis: the disunity of both leaders and people, the failure to renew and to adapt, and finally, a disregard for the gospel of Jesus Christ. "What is needed," he declared, "is a confession of guilt and a plea for forgiveness, together with the sincere intention to seek out, with each other's help, ways toward unity, and the supernatural courage to follow them."[9] In a phrase reminiscent of the *Ethics*, he added that the hierarchy itself must be included in this "confession of guilt."

Romero's convictions as a church leader on this very point account in part for his willingness to confront those in power who considered themselves above the law precisely because they controlled all the levers of power. His actions were on line with what Bonhoeffer had asked of pastors in his assessment of how the church should react to the anti-Jewish legislation of April 7, 1933. Bonhoeffer wanted these church leaders to critically question the discriminatory laws, to come to the aid of the victims, and to take concrete action against the government if the laws continued in force.[10] Romero engaged in all three steps of resistance. For the desperately poor of El Salvador, Romero was in truth their church, a pastor willing, like Christ, to risk his life in order to protect them from the malevolence of the powerful. In him the church had finally accepted its mission of witnessing to the compassionate presence of Jesus Christ in the modern world.

II. A New Way of Being Church: A Church for Others

There is an irony in Romero's taking up the cause of the peasants and poorly paid laborers in El Salvador. He was appointed Archbishop of San Salvador precisely because the Vatican and the papal nuncio did not expect him to upset the military dictatorship of that country. Indeed, he was directed to placate the military and not to trouble the wealthy few in power, who saw in the ministry to the poor by church people a potential threat to their financial security. Even though the "death squads" of the Salvadoran military embodied a modern-day version of Gestapo terror tactics, the Vatican preferred not to disturb in any radical way the tranquility of the political leaders in that "Catholic" country. Once Romero experienced the "personal conversion" that enabled him to see reality through the eyes of the poor, however, his words and actions forged a new way of being church. Romero offered his people the courageous, Christlike leadership that Bonhoeffer had once envisioned as a powerful church counterforce to a government whose destruction of its "enemies" went in tandem with its ruthless suppression of all dissent.

How Romero reached this degree of prophetic outrage is the story of how he came to identify more and more with the victims of the Salvadoran repression. The massacre by National Guardsmen of protesting peasants at the Plaza Libertad in February 1977, followed a month later by the murder of the Jesuit priest Rutilio Grande along with an old man and a young boy, angered him to the point of a public letter of protest to the President demanding an investigation and declaring that the church would henceforth station itself with the people. Further, Romero refused to appear in any official state function until he received satisfaction on all these counts. When another popular priest, Father Alfonso Navarro, was assassinated less than two months later, Romero knew that the government, run by a corrupt minority, was capable of any brutality in order to protect their moneyed interests. The selective violence against church people and peasants alike moved Romero finally to see things from the viewpoint of the poor.[11]

Archbishop Romero had now experienced what Bonhoeffer once said was at the heart of the German resistance to Hitler. In an essay sent as a Christmas exhortation to his family and fellow conspirators just two months before his imprisonment, he described their newly gained ability to see things from the perspective of the victims of Nazi aggression. "We have for once learned to see the great events of world history from below, from the perspective of the outcast, the suspects, the maltreated, the powerless, the oppressed, the reviled—in short from the perspective of those who suffer."[12] Similarly, in explaining why the repression of the poor by the forces of national security had become a veritable persecution of the churches, Romero pointed to the church's having finally adopted as its own that "view from below," stating that "once again it is the poor who bring us to understand what has really happened. That is why the church has understood the persecution from the perspective of the poor. Persecution has been occasioned by the defense of the poor. It amounts to nothing more than the church's taking upon itself the lot of the poor."[13]

Romero's determination to defend his people impelled him to inform the world of the widespread repression to which the Salvadoran poor had been subjected under the false rubric of maintaining a supposed God-given social and economic order. What such a "world order" really meant to the peasants under his pastoral care was disclosed by Romero in his comments to the National Council of Churches meeting in New York, November 1979. There, citing the Bishops Conference at Puebla, he pointed out that social injustice, more accurately called "structural violence," was the greatest social evil for his people. This structural evil had produced a "'situation of inhuman poverty' finding expression in 'infant mortality, lack of adequate housing, health problems, starvation salaries, unemployment and under-employment, malnutrition, job uncertainty, compulsory mass migrations.'" Even more reprehensible, he added, was the flimsy excuse given by state authorities for continuing such repression: "We have suffered 'repressive violence' from the state, which, justifying itself with the ideology of 'national security,' considers as 'subversive' any attempt at liberation of the people. It pretends to justify murder, disappearances, arbitrary imprisonment, acts of terrorism, kidnapings, and acts of torture, all of which show 'a complete lack of respect for the dignity of the human person.'"[14]

In the face of continued threats against his life, Romero insisted that the mission of the church would remain unchanged. The church was called to follow the way of Jesus Christ, even if that meant embracing the cross and being murdered in his name. He went so far as to proclaim that the church's preferential care of the poor was nothing other than being like Christ "who identified himself with the cause of the poor." If, due to this option, we have lost honors and privileges, he continued, "we feel closer to the heart of our people and in greater harmony with the universal church, which has favored us with many testimonies of solidarity. . . . We feel that unity in Christ is broken only by those who do not seek for Christ in poverty but in their own welfare."[15]

This pastoral reaction by Romero unmasks the "world order," trumpeted in conservative circles of the United States and enforced with armed hostility by U.S. trained security forces in El Salvador. Romero was able to show that greed, not anti-communism, was the inner core of that "order" which had so cruel an impact on the poor. For Bonhoeffer, too, the "world order" proclaimed by Adolf Hitler was a cruel hoax. The heart of a church's witness to Jesus Christ in the frontline of faith, where alone a world order could be grounded, had to include a spirited identification with the "least" of Jesus' brothers and sisters. In his own sermon on a "new order" he reiterated Jesus' rejoinder to the disciples of John the Baptizer that "the deaf hear, the blind see, the lame walk, and the gospel is preached to the poor. . . . So seriously does God take suffering that God must immediately destroy it."[16] In sentiments close to those of Romero in decrying the poverty of his people, Bonhoeffer acknowledged that "there is a depth of human bondage, of human poverty, of human ignorance, which impedes the merciful coming of Christ."[17]

In that same dramatic passage from his *Ethics*, Bonhoeffer made a like connection between the existence of hunger, homelessness, and injustice, stating that such were an affront to God and should arouse to indignation those whose mission was to represent God to the people. The church mandate to prepare the way for the Lord, he said, was

> a charge of immense responsibility for all those who know of the coming of Christ. The hungry need bread and the homeless need a roof; the dispossessed need justice and the lonely need fellowship; the undisciplined need order and the slave needs freedom. To allow the hungry to remain hungry would be blasphemy against God and one's neighbor, for what is nearest to God is precisely the need of one's neighbor. It is for the love of Christ, which belongs as much to the hungry as to myself, that I share my bread with them and that I share my dwelling with the homeless. If the hungry do not attain to faith, then the guilt falls on those who refused them bread. To provide the hungry with bread is to prepare the way for the coming of grace.[18]

For Pastor Bonhoeffer and Archbishop Romero, such a grace would be "costly" enough to exact the ultimate sacrifice of their lives. It bothered Bonhoeffer that the churches of Germany, enjoying their comfort, feared the very cross they preached and avoided taking Christlike risks for the least of Christ's brothers and sisters.

Like Bonhoeffer, Romero's way of being church emerged from a determination to take a stand with the most defenseless of his people against the powerful forces that contrived to keep them in dehumanizing servitude. Romero became for the people a church, as Bonhoeffer put it, coming "out of its stagnation" and willing to "risk saying controversial things."[19] Romero did not offer his people the narcotic of future heavenly rewards when their poverty ridden standard of living contradicted the Salvadoran claim to be a "Christian" nation. Following the massacres of the peasants and the assassinations of priests, religious and lay leaders, he realized that the churches had been part of the problem because they had witlessly sought the places of privilege and had sent the wrong message to the powerful: the poor and the politically and economically weak were less worthy of the church's affections. They did not have the same dignity as those seemingly blessed with abundance. In Hitler's Germany it was almost inconceivable that Christ could be the Jew; in Romero's El Salvador, it was just as preposterous to the reigning minority and the security forces that Christ could be the peasant worker or even the rebel demanding an end to the government-sponsored repression.

Both Bonhoeffer and Romero urged the church to burst the chains of its bondage to political and social ideologies, to become, as Bonhoeffer would insist in his prison letters, a church like Christ existing solely to serve people. That "church must share in the secular problems of ordinary human life, not dominating, but helping and serving. It must tell people of every calling what it means to live in Christ, to exist for others. . . . It must not underestimate the importance of human example (which has its origin in the humanity of Jesus and is so important in Paul's teaching); it is not abstract argument, but example, that gives its word emphasis and power."[20]

These are courageous words that Romero in his own way would put into practice when, not unexpectedly, he abandoned the archbishop's palace and took up residence in rooms adjacent to a cancer hospital run by nuns. He then turned the chancery offices into a meeting place for the laity commission, the national pastoral council, and other pastoral organizations including those the government eyed with suspicion. The photocopying room became a coffee lounge where it could better serve as a center for communication for workers on strike, lay ministers, *campesinos* hounded by the National Guard, a place of refuge for the homeless, and an organizational headquarters for inquiries about those who had been made to disappear, and for all, a "home away from home."[21]

In contrast with the cowardly church leadership in Bonhoeffer's Germany, it was Romero's keen sense of his responsibility to the weakest, most exploited members of his "children," that drew him into ever sharper confrontations with the ruthless power brokers of El Salvador. Soon, their hatred of the peasant began to encircle him too. The slogan, "Be a patriot, kill a priest," that was circulated widely and even painted on the walls of some church buildings, was devised solely to tell the upstart Bishop what he could expect by his agitation on behalf of the poverty stricken, but cheap, labor force of the wealthy few. Through his radio broadcasts Romero took the complaints of his people to an international forum. Everywhere in Latin America he was the prophetic voice denouncing injustice and informing the peoples of the world of the true nature of the repression of his people. Romero forced other nations to take notice of the spiral of violence initiated by the security forces to bedevil a downtrodden peasantry. He called the actions of the security forces a veritable war against the poor. Citing his obligation "to see that faith and justice reign in my country," he even wrote to the President of the United States two months before his assassination asking Mr. Carter to cease arming the military of his nation whose "systematic violation of human rights" had reached such proportions that their "repressive violence" had been reported by the Inter-American Commission on Human Rights.[22]

This letter is of a piece with Romero's prophetic audacity in publicly unmasking the pious charade of the national security forces and their leaders who, behind the facade of fighting communism, had unleashed the death squads on labor leaders, political organizers, innocent peasants and church people alike.[23] The threatened privileged class lost no opportunity to lecture Romero for his "communist subversion." Aware of this and of how Rome's suspicions of liberation theology had compounded his problems, Romero pointed out to those who invoked the Vatican discomfort with his activism that it was equally wrong to preach a transcendent mission if that transcendent mission "loses hold of what is human." It would be sinful for a church, he warned, to be "so concerned with its own identity that this preoccupation gets in the way of its closeness to the world."[24] The "closeness" of which he spoke was to contribute the evangelizing presence of the church to the movement for liberation of his people.

III. The Idolatry of National Security

It is not possible to account for the militarism and savagery that characterized the suppression of dissent and the annihilation of enemies in both Nazi Germany and modern day El Salvador without reference to the national security state. The invocation of the needs of national security has often been the rationale behind the lies and violence engineered by the Central Intelligence Agency and the U.S. State Department to offset conjectured threats to the United States' political and business interests from an unruly peasantry and angry labor force.

Bonhoeffer's denunciation of the churches' unholy alliance with this ideology came early on in his contribution to the ecumenical movement. In a disturbing talk at the ecumenical conference of Gland, Switzerland, he succeeded in goading the assembled delegates to take another look at the consequences of their having uncritically honored the "idol of national security," accepting its violent side as the inescapable price of maintaining a peaceful status quo at home and one's national interests abroad. Bonhoeffer drew their attention to the power this idol exerted over the churches, deterring them from their mission to proclaim unflinchingly the gospel mandate of peace. His remarks on that occasion, fittingly entitled, "The Church Is Dead," are uncanny in their attunement to the problems faced by the people whom Oscar Romero would later defend against the mistreatment they suffered because of their supposed threat to "national security."

Bonhoeffer's words are likewise remarkably prescient of the suffering to befall the German people on Hitler's accession to power through the premise of hate and the promise of making Germany a proud, secure nation once again. Bonhoeffer argued,

> It is as though all the powers of the world had conspired together against peace: money, business, the lust for power, indeed even love for the fatherland have been pressed into the service of hate. Hate of nations, hate of people against their own countrymen. . . . Events are coming to a head more terribly than ever before—millions hungry, people with cruelly deferred and unfulfilled wishes, desperate men who have nothing to lose but their lives and will lose nothing in losing them—humiliated and degraded nations who cannot get over their shame—political extreme against political extreme, fanatic against fanatic, idol against idol, and behind it all a world which bristles with weapons as never before, a world which feverishly arms to guarantee peace through arming, a world whose idol has become the word security—a world without sacrifice, full of mistrust and suspicion, because past fears are still with it.[25]

Few attacks on the idolatry of the national security state have equalled the intensity of these words from Bonhoeffer's ecumenical ministry.

Yet, the bristling denunciation in Romero's Fourth Pastoral Letter, "The Church's Mission Amid the National Crisis," bears several marks of similarity. In this pastoral Romero complained that

> peoples are put into the hands of military elites and are subjected to policies that oppress and repress all who oppose them, in the name of what is alleged to be total war. The armed forces are put in charge of social and economic structures under the pretext of the interests of national security. Everyone not at one with the state is declared a national enemy, and the requirements of national security are used to justify assassinations, disappearances, arbitrary imprisonment, acts of terrorism, kidnappings, acts of torture. . . . The omnipotence of these national security regimes . . . turn national security into an idol,

which, like the god Molech, demands the daily sacrifice of many victims in its name.[26]

Romero dared to trace this idolatry to the greed of the governing elite whose means of maintaining their high standard of living betrayed a crass insensitivity to the ways the security forces kept the peasants and common laborers tightly controlled. Romero held these wealthy, "respectable" churchgoers accountable for the social inequities that had been allowed to fester in the lives of the poor. They had become adept at compartmentalizing their lives into the religious acts that "satisfied" God and the secular decisions that produced the affluence they really coveted. To borrow Bonhoeffer's phrase, they had grown accustomed to "thinking in two spheres," keeping the sacred of church attendance from ever interfering with the profane of worldly success.[27] The idol of national security had so permeated politics and piety that both Romero and Bonhoeffer saw themselves ranged against a majority of church leaders who burned incense on the secular altars of militarism as well as against the governmental sociopaths who were bent on stifling every dissent under the rubric of maintaining law and order.

IV. The Faces of Christ in Movements of Liberation

Both Bonhoeffer and Romero were able to recognize the viciousness of the criminal injustice that had dominated their governments. They were resolved to defend the weakest and most helpless of their victimized people in the name of Jesus Christ and of Jesus' oneness with the least of his brothers and sisters. In all faith, Bonhoeffer insisted, one had to recognize the image of God, Christ, in the other, regardless of his or her nationality or religion. In the same ecumenical conference in which he condemned the contempt for one's neighbor that the idolatry of national security promoted, Bonhoeffer reminds us that "Christ encounters us in our brother and sister, in the English, the French, the German. . . ."[28] To the church delegates representing those nationalities, Bonhoeffer's words jogged their memories of the great war of their recent past and aroused their awareness of the continuing distrust between their countries.

At the deeper level, however, Bonhoeffer was attempting to promote a more Christ-like attitude among the nations through their church leaders. He persuaded the ecumenical delegates to agitate for the changes in outlook necessary if they were to prevent the hate mongering with which the Nazi government tormented the Jewish underclass of Germany. It was the church alone, he felt, that had the power to thwart those who sow terror among the most defenseless of the people. According to Bonhoeffer, the churches had the mandate to forbid war, to snatch the weapons from their children, and to proclaim "the peace of Christ against the raging world." This peace "must be dared. It is the great venture."[29] The churches were, however, timid and lacking in the will to commit themselves to such a risky cause. They were, as Bonhoeffer put it in one of his letters from prison, too self-centered, caring only for their own interests because they lacked "personal faith in Christ."[30]

Just prior to his imprisonment, Bonhoeffer urged his fellow conspirators to do what the churches had failed to do. He asked them to tie together the Christian concerns that had permeated their resistance to Hitler with the gospel test of one's claim to be Christian. "We are not Christ," he wrote, "but if we want to be Christians, we must have some share in Christ's large-heartedness by acting with responsibility and in freedom when the hour of danger comes, and by showing a real sympathy that springs, not from fear, but from the liberating and redeeming love of Christ for all who suffer. Mere waiting and looking on is not Christian behavior. The Christian is called to sympathy and action . . . by the sufferings of his brothers and sisters for whose sake Christ suffered."[31] The extension of Christ's compassionate love to all who suffer depends, in turn, on the way Christians and their churches respond to the disturbing challenge expressed in Bonhoeffer's letter from prison of April 30, 1944: "What is bothering me incessantly is the question what Christianity really is, or indeed who Christ really is, for us today."[32] For Bonhoeffer the answer to that question could be seen in the long lines of Jews herded to their death in the extermination camps, in the tortured limbs and haggard faces of those who dared criticize the criminal regime, and in the bodies of the innocent victims of Nazism's fantasies of bloody conquest and military glory.

Bonhoeffer's search for the Christ crucified anew in the rubble, scaffolds, and gas chambers of a world at war had its counterpart in Romero's own challenge to those who called themselves Christian in his country. To the consternation of the corrupt and selfish, Romero linked the cause of the poor to Christ himself. It was time, he said, to admit that, "the Salvadoran people has been subjected to attack. Its human rights have been trodden underfoot—and protection of these rights falls under the church's responsibility. It is the church's belief that this persecution [of the poor] affects Christ himself: what touches any Christian touches Christ, because he is in personal union with all Christians—especially in anything that involves the poorest of society."[33] It was not lost on the rich landowners that these words were addressed as much against them, as to the exploited poor.

Like Bonhoeffer, Romero asked his people, both the oppressed and their oppressors, to see the face of Christ where they might least expect to find him. This face of Christ, Romero proclaimed, is seen in

> the faces of young children, struck down by poverty before they are born . . . and of the vagrant children in our cities who are so often exploited, products of poverty and the moral disorganization of the family; the faces of the indigenous peoples, and frequently of the Afro-Americans as well; living marginalized lives in inhuman situations, they can be considered the poorest of the poor; the faces of the peasants; as a social group, they live as outcasts almost everywhere on our continent, deprived of land, caught in a situation of internal and external dependence, and subjected to systems of commercialization that exploit them; . . . the faces of marginalized and overcrowded urban dwellers, whose lack of material goods is matched by the ostentatious display of wealth of other segments of society. . . .[34]

In those observations from Romero's *Fourth Pastoral Letter,* we see a contemporary answer to Bonhoeffer's question, "who really is Jesus Christ for us today?"

Here, too, Romero captures the essence of the tragedy that had befallen his people: those in power were blind to the presence of Jesus Christ in the poorest of the poor of that nation. In the name of these poor, Romero demanded an end to all violence in El Salvador, but only on condition of the reform and change in that country's unjustly structured society. "I have to say it again: in order for repression to be eliminated the roots that feed the violence in the social sphere, and which thus provoke the temptation to further acts of violence, must be attacked."[35] He went on to enumerate instances of the institutional violence that was in effect a constant torment to the poor. "In less than three years over fifty priests have been attacked, threatened, calumniated," he told an audience at the University of Louvain, Belgium. He then gave this international gathering a sampling of the daily horrors of church life in El Salvador. "Six are already martyrs—they were murdered. Some have been tortured and others expelled. Nuns have also been persecuted. . . . If all this has happened to persons who are the most evident representatives of the church, you can guess what has happened to ordinary Christians, to the *campesinos,* catechists, lay ministers, and to the eccesial base communities. There have been threats, arrests, tortures, murders, numbering in the hundreds and thousands. As always, even in persecution, it has been the poor among the Christians who have suffered most."[36]

Indeed, it is one of the ironies of those perpetrating crimes of violence against the poor in El Salvador that these criminal deeds have been for the most part the acts of soldiers recruited into the security forces from among the ranks of the poor themselves. Hence Romero informed the world that the poor were being forced to kill their own people, first by being pressed into soldiery, and then by being "brainwashed" during their indoctrination sessions into regarding villagers from the rebel zones as sub-human communists menacing their faith and homelife. In his Sunday homily of March 23, 1980, Romero did what Bonhoeffer had urged church leaders to do in 1934. He went so far as to command those troops and their counterparts in the national guard to obey God's law and not the evil orders of their officers. "In the name of God, in the name of our tormented people who have suffered so much and whose laments cry out more loudly to heaven, I beg you, I beseech you, I order you in the name of God, stop the repression!"[37] The next day he was murdered.

V. The Cross of Christ and the Liberation of a People

Romero's rebuking of those responsible for the repression of his people recalls Bonhoeffer's own legacy to the churches nearly forty years earlier. It was Bonhoeffer's contention that the church's claim to be herald of God's love for the world was only a vain boast if its credibility was not grounded in solidarity with the oppressed and in its willingness even to endure the bloody cross of persecution for the sake of those it would deliver from evil. It is in keeping with his conviction about the sacrifices demanded of Christians in Nazi Germany that Bonhoeffer made this remarkable claim in *The Cost of Discipleship*: Christians may have to renounce even their own dignity in order to reach out in compassion to those in distress.

> They [Christians] have an irresistible love for the down-trodden, the sick, the wretched, the wronged, the outcast and all who are tortured with anxiety. They go out and seek all who are enmeshed in the toils of sin and guilt. . . . They will be found consorting with publicans and sinners, careless of the shame they incur thereby. In order that they may be merciful they cast away the most priceless treasure of human life, their personal dignity and honor. For the only honor and dignity they know is their Lord's own mercy, to which alone they owe their very lives.[38]

Bonhoeffer's words are particularly apropos of a nation that looks on any subversion of the status quo as treasonous. Both Bonhoeffer and Romero had to forsake the privileges of academy and altar in order to follow Christ in the path of peace and justice. Indeed, in Bonhoeffer's theological outlook, fidelity to one's Christian vocation entails the closest possible identity with the suffering Christ. Such is the "cost of discipleship" in which the shame of being called disloyal citizens is often the price Christians must pay to be truly followers of a crucified Lord. For Bonhoeffer, Christian faith was as much a call to self-sacrifice, and even death, as it was a call to life.

At the height of the German people's adulation of Hitler, therefore, Bonhoeffer invoked the reality of the cross of Jesus Christ in order to address more meaningfully the mission of Christians to inspire their communities with the counter cultural values of the gospel. If God's way of being with people is epitomized in the crucifixion of Jesus, then the Christian path to God means "sharing the suffering of Christ to the last and to the fullest extent."[39] For Bonhoeffer, God's love is shown paradoxically in the ever escalating demands God makes on the individual Christian and the Christian community. What should result is neither correct doctrine nor mindless attention to liturgical rubrics, the trademarks of the organized religion in which even Nazis were comfortable. "The gift of Christ is not the Christian religion," he wrote, "but the grace and love of God which culminate in the cross."[40] Bonhoeffer depicts Jesus as the revelation of God's power in "weakness." The suffering Jesus becomes Bonhoeffer's inspiration for a Christian outreach to those who are hurting most in this world and for a commitment to change one's society according to the patterns of Jesus' life and word.

Accordingly, in the prison letters Bonhoeffer's reference to Mark 15:34 stands out: "My God, my God, why have you forsaken me?" Bonhoeffer cites this passage not only to make sense out of his imprisonment and impending fate, but also to share with Eberhard Bethge his convictions on what conformity with Jesus Christ had come to mean. The cross of Jesus Christ was the touchstone of Bonhoeffer's faith, precisely because of its imposing this-worldly dimensions. The cry of abandonment from the cross signified to Bonhoeffer that Christ chose to participate fully in the human condition, even to the violent death exacted for such a total involvement. Not even Christ would avoid the human consequences of sacrificing oneself for the sake of others, immersed in one's ministry to people of every station in life. Like Christ himself, the Christian must drink the earthly cup to the dregs. Bonhoeffer's understanding of the meaning of God's power manifest in the weakness of the cross is that Christ did not behave like some *deus ex machina* come from on high, supremely distant and untouched by the sufferings of ordinary people. God did not send the twelve legions of angels to carve up the Roman soldiers and to frighten off Jesus' enemies. Nor does God offer a complete answer to the sufferings of God's people. God suffers with them.

In prison Bonhoeffer criticized those church leaders who had in their preaching presented a distorted picture of God as someone set apart in transcendent aloofness. This to him was certainly not the God who had freely bound the divine self to people in the person of Jesus Christ. Bonhoeffer insisted that God was not revealed so much in the power but in the very weakness of Christ. Christ was related to people in his sufferings, not as the easy answer to problems or as the powerful founder of a religion. Only in the suffering Christ could people see the true depths of God's kinship with them. God was not "beyond," but by the cross was related to people in the very midst of their troubled lives. This is the biblical picture of God in Christ which Bonhoeffer expressed in his calling Jesus "the man for others."[41]

Being for others, being for the shaping of the world in the image of Jesus Christ, and being in communion with the God who suffers for and in us are theological phrases that can aptly link the ministry of Dietrich Bonhoeffer with that of Archbishop Romero. The theology of the cross provided Bonhoeffer the impetus for his involvement in the murky world of the church struggle and the courage to endure the risks of conspiratorial resistance to Nazism. Both Bonhoeffer and Romero met their God in the world of conflict thrust upon them, a world where Christ crucified was their exemplar and the sustenance of their faith. Bonhoeffer's theology of the cross fills the pages of his collected writings and culminates in the passages of his prison letters where he confesses that God's weakness and powerlessness in the world are "precisely the way, the only way, in which God is with us and helps us."[42] Bonhoeffer's letters, with their emphasis on the paradoxical power of God in weakness, send an unmistakable warning to the powerful rulers of society who use their might to crush the lowly and pretend that they are merely the agents of God's power unleashed against the so-called evil forces of Marxist subversion.

Unlike Bonhoeffer, Archbishop Romero has left little in his writings that could constitute a full "theology of the cross." Rather, his "theology of the cross" is expressed more in the details of his having taken up the cause of those who had been denied their dignity and rights by a Nazi-like military dictatorship. In the life of Romero the cross of Jesus Christ was a daily reality. His martyrdom served to confirm the unwavering truth of his life and mission to the poor. Few tributes have captured the power of this aspect of Romero's witness to the cross of Christ so well as that of his Protestant Colleague, Jorge Lara Braud, Director of the Council on Theology and Culture of the Presbyterian Church in the United States:

> Remembering how he lived and died, I have dared to say: Together with thousands of Salvadorans I have seen Jesus. This time his name was Oscar Arnulfo Romero. His broken body is broken with the body of Jesus; his shed blood is shed with the blood of Jesus. And as with Jesus, so it is with Monseñor, he died for us so that we might live in freedom and in love and justice for one another. His resurrection is not a future event. It is a present reality. His is life for us now, and that is why we must defeat the forces of death in El Salvador and wherever Jesus continues to be crucified.[43]

Romero, like Bonhoeffer, depicts the suffering of Christ as the outcome of his solidarity with the poor and outcasts of his own time. Jesus' God was the Father of unbounded compassion who demanded mercy and obedience to God's word and not the lip service of correct sacramental behavior. This God was, to borrow Bonhoeffer's phrasing, the God of costly grace who would not abide the cheap grace of a religion devoid of compassion. Romero argues this most forcefully in his second pastoral letter. While so many of his fellow bishops and the papal nuncio had cajoled the military and ruling oligarchy, Romero described, instead, a Jesus who

> denounced a religion that was devoid of works of justice – as in the well-known parable of the good Samaritan (Luke 10:29–37). He also denounced all those who made of their power a means to keep the weak and powerless in a state of oppression, rather than using it to serve them. He accused the wealthy of not sharing their wealth, the priests of imposing intolerable burdens (Luke 11:46). . . . From the beginning of Jesus' public life, these denunciations brought in their train frequent attacks upon him (Matt. 2:1–2). They brought personal risk and even persecution. The persecution was to go on through the whole of his life until, at the end, he was accused of blasphemy (Mark 14:64) and of being an agitator among the masses. For these reasons he was condemned and executed.[44]

This dramatic moment of the pastoral is revealing for the way Romero ties in his understanding of the mission of Jesus Christ with what he himself had been moved to do in El Salvador.

With Bonhoeffer and Romero, as with contemporary liberation theology, moreover, this cross symbolized the terrible things that continue to be done to those with whom Jesus identifies in the modern world. Jesus is crucified anew on the Golgathas of 20th century injustice. And the mission of Christians is to put an end to it. Bonhoeffer and Romero looked on their ministry as that of helping to create a society in which no one will ever be rejected and harmed as Jesus was. They adopted as their own the same outrage that moved Jesus to confront the evil forces distorting the image of his Father and denying the dignity of all peoples created in the image of the God of justice and compassion.

This is a faith inspired by the cross and sustained by what from God's side of death is resurrection. It is not surprising, therefore, to read that Bonhoeffer's last recorded words before the court martial that condemned him contain the hope of life in death: "I believe in the principle of our universal Christian fellowship which rises above all national interest. This is the end, but for me, the beginning of life."[45] Such confidence also explains in part why Romero was undeterred by threats against his own life. As he said so matter-of-factly in an interview with José Calderón Salazar, Guatemalan correspondent of the Mexican newspaper *Excelsior,* two weeks before his death: "I have often been threatened with death. I must tell you, as a Christian, I do not believe in death without resurrection. If I am killed, I shall arise in the Salvadoran people. I say so without boasting, with the greatest humility. . . . Let my death, if it is accepted by God, be for my people's liberation and as a witness of hope in the future."[46] It seems in retrospect that the full freedom and justice which Bonhoeffer and Romero wished for their people would come only through their determination to stake their lives on their faith in the gospel. The only faith that could liberate their people was that that lived in the shadow of the cross and in the strength of God's own suffering in God's people.

VI. Conclusion: Bonhoeffer, Romero and Liberation Theology

If the label "liberation theologian" is restricted to those only who come from the ranks of the Latin American or Southern Hemispheric poor and whose theology is done directly out of the experience of the poor, then it can be considered a stretch to number Bonhoeffer and Romero among today's liberation theologians. Yet, in their lives, their writings, and in their public witness both achieved such a remarkable solidarity with the oppressed that they are recognized as among the most inspiring figures in today's liberation movements.

Despite the flaws he detects in Bonhoeffer's attempts to come to grips with the "world come of age," and the obvious limitations of Bonhoeffer's social analysis vis-à-vis the conflict between the underclass and the powers that dominate Latin America, Gustavo Gutierrez lauds Bonhoeffer for inspiring the radical rethinking that could betoken a new way of looking at people and gauging the societal forces that determine the lot of the poor of Latin America.[47] Bonhoeffer could not have foreseen the rampant exploitation of the poor by insensitive, greedy oligarchies in Latin America. Nonetheless, he led the way to the radical reshaping of church priorities in affirming the dignity of the downtrodden.

Since it is more proper to speak of theologies of liberation rather than one theology of liberation set in the experience of the Latin American poor, one can say of Bonhoeffer and Romero that their theologies "liberate," because they affirm life in the face of death and demand that reflection on God's word carry over into everyday life. Their theologies interpret Christian faith out of the sufferings of people, as they plead for liberation from classist hatred of the poor, the dissenters, and the outcasts. Their theologies have, too, a dimension of prophetic outrage that enables them to criticize both the ideological underpinnings of the unjust society and the self-serving practice of the churches and of Christians who support acts of aggression against the weakest people of a nation. Finally, their theologies conjoin concrete action for justice with the cross of Jesus Christ.

In this context, it is intriguing to note that the "this-worldliness" of Bonhoeffer is a forerunner of the concrete emphasis on praxis, or the promotion of a Christian life in the midst of the world, that is foundational for liberation theology's statements about the church's public mission. On more than one occasion, Bonhoeffer reminded people that the Christian vocation is not to religious separatism, but to life. In his essay, "Thy Kingdom Come," he claimed that Christ does not lead Christians "in a religious flight from this world to other worlds beyond; rather he gives them back to the earth as their loyal children."[48] That statement is of a piece with Bonhoeffer's acknowledgement in prison that he was "discovering right up to this moment that it is only by living completely in this world that one learns to have faith. . . . By this-worldliness I mean living unreservedly in life's duties, problems, successes and failures, experiences and perplexities. In so doing we throw ourselves completely into the arms of God, taking seriously, not our own sufferings, but those of God in the world. . . ."[49] Bonhoeffer's words are in tune with a fundamental claim of liberation theology, namely, that faith entails a commitment to affirm human dignity and to enter the struggle for justice. Poverty is not a fate decreed from on high by an imperious God; it is the result of human sin, the indifference of the powerful, and the connivance of the greedy. Theology reflects on this concrete situation and progresses to prayerful discernment on what must be done to counteract the evil.

Bonhoeffer's "this worldliness" is close to Romero's own explanation of why he had become embroiled in the political machinations of El Salvador. He was, in his own estimation, merely a concerned pastor willing to do something concrete to make the life of his people better. In his address at the University of Louvain less than two months before his assassination, he told the audience:

> I am going to speak to you simply as a pastor, as one who, together with his people, has been learning the beautiful but harsh truth that the Christian faith does not cut us off from the world but immerses us in it, that the church is not a fortress set apart from the city. The church follows Jesus who lived, worked, battled and died in the midst of a city, in the polis. It is in this sense that I should like to talk about the political dimension of the Christian faith: in the precise sense of the repercussions of the faith on the world, and also of the repercussions that being in the world has on the faith.[50]

Romero then went on to present in meticulous detail the outrages perpetrated against the people by the forces of national security and to reiterate the theme of his anti-government denunciations. Romero told the highly-educated audience that personally he had learned much from the illiterate poor, and through them he had come to reject the ecclesiastical paternalism that offered heaven without a renewed earth.[51]

Finally, the liberation theology of Bonhoeffer and Romero is strongly linked with their prophetic demand for concrete action. Compassion for their victimized brothers and sisters provided the grist for the severe criticisms by Bonhoeffer and Romero of their society and their church. The strength of liberation theology lies in the ability of its protagonists to analyze the social conflict and to direct heartfelt criticism against the sources of the rampant injustice—whether political, ecclesiastical, governmental or military. Bonhoeffer and Romero fulfilled that role aptly when they became the voice of the voiceless, Jew and peasant, condemning the denial of justice to a people crying out to be freed from their sufferings. Their lives and heroic witness to the mission of Jesus Christ among the oppressed of every age are as much a confession of faith as a challenge to Christians to stand with Christ against the social evils from which one's brothers and sisters in Christ continue to suffer. Liberation theology is a call to action. In Dietrich Bonhoeffer and Archbishop Oscar Romero, that call to action became not only convincingly articulated; their words took flesh in their inspiring example.

Notes

1. See Geffrey B. Kelly, *Liberating Faith: Bonhoeffer's Message for Today* (Minneapolis: Augsburg Publishing House, 1984), 158–9.
2. Archbishop Oscar Romero, "The Church's Mission Amid the National Crisis," *Voice of the Voiceless: The Four Pastoral Letters and Other Statements* (Maryknoll: Orbis Books, 1985), 138.
3. Dietrich Bonhoeffer, "Jesus Christ and the Essence of Christianity," in *A Testament to Freedom: The Essential Writings of Dietrich Bonhoeffer*, ed. Geffrey B. Kelly and F. Burton Nelson (San Francisco: Harper and Row, 1990), 54.
4. Dietrich Bonhoeffer, *Gesammelte Schriften*, vol. I, ed. Eberhard Bethge (Munich: Chr. Kaiser, 1965), 97.
5. *Gesammelte Schriften*, I, 98.
6. Wolf-Dieter Zimmermann, "Years in Berlin," in *I Knew Dietrich Bonhoeffer*, ed. Wolf-Dieter Zimmermann and Ronald Gregor Smith, trans. Käthe Gregor Smith (New York: Harper and Row, 1966), 64–5.
7. See *A Testament to Freedom*, 15–8, 132–40.
8. Dietrich Bonhoeffer, *Ethics* (New York: Macmillan, 1965), 114–5.
9. Romero, 125.
10. See *A Testament to Freedom*, 132–40.
11. Plácido Erdozaín, *Archbishop Romero: Martyr of Salvador*, trans. John McFadden

and Ruth Warner (Maryknoll: Orbis, 1981), 9–27; see also James R. Brockman, *Romero: A Life* (Maryknoll: Orbis, 1989), 52–79.
12. Dietrich Bonhoeffer, *Letters and Papers from Prison,* ed. Eberhard Bethge (New York: Macmillan, 1972), 17.
13. Romero, 182.
14. Romero, 169.
15. Romero, 175.
16. Dietrich Bonhoeffer, "The Gospel and the New Order," in *A Testament to Freedom,* 215.
17. *Ethics,* 135.
18. *Ethics,* 137.
19. *Letters and Papers,* 378.
20. *Letters and Papers,* 382–3.
21. Erdozain, 22–3.
22. Romero, 189.
23. Romero, 134–5, 143–4.
24. Romero, 129.
25. Dietrich Bonhoeffer, *No Rusty Swords* (New York: Harper & Row, 1965), 186–7.
26. Romero, 134–5.
27. *Ethics,* 197–200.
28. *No Rusty Swords,* 186–7.
29. Dietrich Bonhoeffer, "The Church and the People of the World," in *A Testament to Freedom,* 240–1.
30. *Letters and Papers,* 381.
31. *Letters and Papers,* 14.
32. *Letters and Papers,* 279.
33. Romero, 80.
34. Romero, 119–20.
35. Romero, 147–8.
36. Romero, 181–2.
37. Cited in Brockman, 242, translation slightly altered. For Bonhoeffer's sermon on the church's mission to forbid war, see *A Testament to Freedom,* 239–41.
38. Dietrich Bonhoeffer, *The Cost of Discipleship* (New York: Macmillan, 1961), 100–1.
39. *Cost of Discipleship,* 78.
40. *A Testament to Freedom,* 56.
41. Kelly, *Liberating Faith,* 49–50.
42. *Letters and Papers,* 360–1.
43. Cited in Erdozaín, xviii.
44. Romero, 72.
45. *A Testament to Freedom,* 46.
46. Cited in Brockman, 248.
47. Gustavo Gutierrez, *The Power of the Poor in History* (Maryknoll: Orbis, 1984), 228–33.
48. Dietrich Bonhoeffer, "Thy Kingdom Come: The Prayer of the Church for God's Kingdom on Earth," trans. John Godsey, in *Preface to Bonhoeffer* (Philadelphia: Fortress Press, 65), 28–9.
49. *Letters and Papers,* 369–70.
50. Romero, 178.
51. Romero, 185.

ETHICS AND MATERIALIST HERMENEUTICS

STEPHEN J. PLANT

In the English translation of Bonhoeffer's *Letters and Papers from Prison* the following paragraphs are appended to the 1942 essay "After Ten Years":

> There remains an experience of incomparable value. We have for once learnt to see the great events of history from below, from the perspective of the outcast, the suspects, the maltreated, the powerless, the oppressed, the reviled—in short from the perspective of those who suffer. . . This perspective from below must not become the particular possession of those who are eternally dissatisfied; rather, we must do justice to life in all its dimensions from a higher satisfaction, whose foundation is beyond any talk of 'from below' or 'from above.' This is the way in which we may affirm it.[1]

Bonhoeffer's remarks on perspectives on history provide a useful commentary on the viewpoint from which his *Ethics* were written. With fellow conspirators, Bonhoeffer claims to have learned to see things from below, and from this new standpoint urges that a 'higher satisfaction' be sought with foundations beyond all talk of above and below.

This paper addresses the question: Can a foundation of life, of ethics and of theology truly constitute a gospel of liberation for the poor, or is a gospel of liberation a message which neither desires, nor believes it possible, to stand anywhere other than unreservedly alongside the poor, seeking to view history from below. In particular, I wish to examine the relationship between Bonhoeffer's uses of the Bible in the *Ethics* and the bourgeois liberal class and its ideological commitments out of which his biblical hermeneutics flow.

Any critique of Bonhoeffer's theology treads on holy ground. Bonhoeffer's courage and integrity as an opponent of Nazism mark every page of the *Ethics*. Constrained by his participation in the resistance movement

107

to mystery and camouflage, Bonhoeffer's *Ethics* boldly condemn Nazism's iniquitous policies towards the mentally disabled, and demand Christian action on behalf of the Jews: "An expulsion of the Jews from the west must necessarily bring with it the expulsion of Christ. For Jesus Christ was a Jew."[2] Bonhoeffer's existential solidarity with victims of Nazism furnishes his voice with a radical authenticity amongst those who struggle for liberation. For example, James H. Cone, writing on Bonhoeffer's reputation for radical theology, states:

> [W]hat most white Protestant professors of theology overlook is that these are the words of a prisoner, a man who encountered the evils of Nazism and was killed in the encounter. Do whites really have the right to affirm God's death when they have actually enslaved men in God's name? It would seem that unless whites are willing to endure the pain of oppression, they cannot authentically speak of God.[3]

However, Bonhoeffer's existential commitment to liberation is not sufficient to establish the ideological foundations of his *Ethics*. In his *Biblical Hermeneutics and Black Theology in South Africa* Itumeleng J. Mosala rightly contends that:

> Existential commitments to the liberation struggles of the oppressed are inadequate because those who are committed in this way are still ideologically and theoretically enslaved to the dominant discourses in the society.[4]

Because Bonhoeffer's unique skills as a theologian are combined with his integrity as a member of the resistance, he is a formidable conversation partner for Mosala's attempt to liberate the Bible from its hermeneutical captivity to the ideological assumptions of white, patriarchal western society. Mosala makes "the historical-materialist method of analysis usually associated with the name of Karl Marx rather than the idealist framework that makes up the history of ideas—abstracted from concrete historical and social relationships—the focus of its analysis."[5] Mosala's materialist approach to biblical hermeneutics, based on methods associated with the names of Norman Gottwald, Marvin Chaney, Robert Coote and others, develops a search for weapons of liberation. A key category in this search is that of *struggle*, for this is the motivating force of all human society. For Mosala, the category of struggle becomes a factor at two crucial points in the hermeneutical process:

> [T]he search for biblical-hermeneutical weapons of struggle must take the form, first of all, of a critical interrogation of the history, culture, and ideologies of the readers/appropriators of the biblical texts.[6]

Thus, Mosala argues that the perspective from which one begins to read the biblical texts is a crucial determining factor in the hermeneutical process.

The second point where the category of struggle gains purchase is "in one's understanding of the history, nature, ideology, and agenda of the biblical texts"[7] themselves. Using the same tools with which the perspective of the reader is interrogated, a biblical hermeneutics of liberation addresses "the question of the material conditions that constitute the sites of the struggles that produced the biblical texts."[8] In practice, such an approach involves Mosala in exploring the ways in which the lives of the biblical peoples were affected by their relationship to the means of material production. Mosala penetrates the biblical texts by asking such questions as: In whose interest is this passage written? What material conditions are reflected in the texts as we receive them ? And how may this text now be related to our struggle for liberation, the struggle to liberate our productive forces? For liberation is not only moral and spiritual, but material as well.

Mosala's materialist approach makes a number of valuable hermeneutical gains. Firstly, Mosala "is deliberately oblivious to the notion of 'scriptural authority,' which is at the heart of traditional biblical scholarship."[9] For Mosala the Bible is both a site and a weapon of struggle; to accord to it an authority which may not be questioned is to allow its ideological presuppositions to go unchecked. Mosala argues that:

> The insistence on the Bible as the Word of God must be seen for what it is: an ideological maneuver [sic] whereby ruling class interests evident in the Bible are converted into a faith that transcends social, political, racial, sexual, and economic divisions. In this way the Bible becomes an ahistorical, interclassist document.[10]

A second hermeneutical gain made by Mosala arises out of this genuinely critical approach to biblical texts. By treating each text as a site of struggle, materialist hermeneutics denies the possibility of escapist textual selectivity. Mosala allocates a full chapter to a critique of black and liberation hermeneutics which treat the Bible as though it has been written from a single liberating perspective, ignoring texts which do not fit easily into the liberation mould. Mosala contends that:

> the only adequate and honest explanation is that not all of the Bible is on the side of human rights or of oppressed and exploited people . . . oppressive texts cannot be totally tamed or subverted into liberating texts.[11]

A biblical hermeneutic is not liberating merely because it is read in the context of a struggle for liberation. Black and liberation theologies must effect a theoretical break with dominant bourgeois/liberal hermeneutical assumptions.

Mosala's description of materialist black hermeneutics provides a basis for conversation with the ideological perspective and biblical hermeneutics of Bonhoeffer's *Ethics*. What may be said of the ideological standpoint from which Bonhoeffer approached the documents he wrote between the summer of 1940, and his arrest on the fifth of April 1943? Bonhoeffer's *Ethics* is a political text. As a text of the resistance, Bonhoeffer's *Ethics* struggle to provide a theoretical and theological basis for a reconstruction of a post-Nazi German state. Christoph Strohm and James P. Kelley's paper on *Church and Public Policy*[12] details the political influences on Bonhoeffer's formation. Drawing on research into the political perspectives of Gerhard Leibholz and Hans von Dohnanyi, Strohm and Kelley suggest that the resistance group of which Bonhoeffer was a part was based upon a rejection of Nazism, and a search for a non-collectivist democratic alternative. Strohm and Kelley suggest that this circle

> saw the decisive alternative between a collectivistic, pseudo-religious, "totalitarian state" and an "authoritarian state" which continued to respect the liberal heritage of the last centuries.[13]

Bonhoeffer saw the political task as essentially a restorative one, re-establishing liberal, yet still authoritarian structures of society. Larry Rasmussen perceptively sums up Bonhoeffer's position:

> Rule by elites is not of itself misrule for Bonhoeffer. He was totally opposed to totalitarian rule, insisted upon the rule of law, believed in a distribution of powers, and promoted the guarantee of certain rights. But he was not in principle opposed to all forms of strong government and he was not an un-qualified democrat. He probably was closest to a studied, morally responsible Prussian conservatism.[14]

The most significant consequences of Bonhoeffer's political viewpoint are embodied in his theology of the mandates, which Bonhoeffer drafted in the summer of 1940 in "Christ, Reality and the Good" and re-worked again in early 1943 in the chapter "The 'Ethical' and the 'Christian' as a Theme." Bonhoeffer understands by the term mandate:

> the concrete divine commission which has its foundation in the revelation of Christ and which is evidenced by Scripture; it is the legitimation and warrant for the execution of a definite divine commandment, the conferment of divine authority on an earthly agent. . . . The bearer of the mandate acts as a deputy in the place of Him who assigns him his commission.[15]

The mandates establish the human person "always in an earthly relation of authority, in a clearly defined order of superiority and inferiority."[16] For Bonhoeffer, there are qualitative differences between the relations established between the superior and the inferior within the divine mandates, and within merely earthly orders. The relations are regulated to prevent abuse by God who confers the commission, by the other mandates, and by the rights of the inferior party within the relationship. Simple examples of the relationship are offered, between Father and Son, master craftsman and apprentice. In his final draft Bonhoeffer lists as mandates church, marriage and family, culture and government.

For Bonhoeffer the mandates are to be viewed from the standpoint of their foundation in Christ. Doubtless, Bonhoeffer's attempt to re-work Luther's *zwei-Reich-lehre* is an improvement on the theology of orders proposed by Paul Althaus and by Emil Brunner's *The Divine Imperative*,[17] but it is surely not an ethic which allows for liberation from below. Bonhoeffer's mandates theology seeks to re-establish a tolerant authoritarianism which, while providing safeguards for the inferior, legitimates the retention by the superior of control and power. Karl Barth's comments on Bonhoeffer's *Mandatsbegriff* are extremely telling:

> Is it enough to say that these particular relationships of rank and degree occur with a certain regularity in the Bible, and that they can be more or less clearly related to Christ as the Lord of the world? Again, does the relationship always have to be one of superiority and inferiority? In Bonhoeffer's doctrine of the mandates, is there not just a suggestion of North German Patriarchalism? Is the notion of authority of some over others really more characteristic of the ethical event than that of the freedom of even the very lowest before the very highest?[18]

Bonhoeffer's claim to rest the mandates on a Scriptural foundation leads well into a materialist interrogation of the hermeneutical perspectives undergirding the *Ethics*. At a precociously early stage in his theological career, Bonhoeffer began to develop an original approach to biblical hermeneutics which departed significantly from the Ritschlian liberal school of theology in Berlin. In a 1925 essay for Reinhold Seeberg, Bonhoeffer argues for a radical distinction between historical and spiritual biblical hermeneutics: "Scripture is for History a source, for Spiritual Interpretation it is a witness."[19] This distinction was further developed in *Creation and Fall*. Here, encouraged by Barth's method in his commentary on Romans, Bonhoeffer developed an interpretation of the Bible as the book of the church. Thus writes Bonhoeffer,

> When Genesis says 'Yahweh,' historically or psychologically it means nothing but Yahweh. Theologically, however, i.e., from the Church's point of view, it is speaking of God. God is the one God of the whole of holy scripture: the Church and theological study stand and fall with this faith.[20]

Bonhoeffer's allegiance to the Bible as the Word of God allows no critical questioning of the perspectives from which individual texts are written.

At Finkenwalde in a paper on "The presentation of New Testament Texts," Bonhoeffer clarified the relation between the Word of God, and the Word of God in Scripture:

> The norm for the Word of God in Scripture is the Word of God itself, and what we possess, reason, conscience, experience, are the materials to which this norm seeks to be applied. We too may say that the Word of God and the word of man are joined in Holy Scripture; but they are joined in such a way that God himself says where his Word is, and he says it through the word of man.[21]

Bonhoeffer's finely nuanced position is not antagonistic to criticism *per se*. In a fascinating letter to Rüdiger Schleicher, Bonhoeffer distinguishes the Bible from other books, for in the Bible it is God who speaks.

> Naturally, one can also read the Bible like any other book—from the perspective of textual criticism, for instance. There is nothing to be said against that. But that will only reveal the surface of the Bible, not what is within. . . . This is how I read the Bible now. I ask of each passage: What is God saying to us here ? And I ask God that he would help us hear what he wants to say. . . . Does this somehow help you understand why I am prepared for a *sacrificium intellectus*—just in these matters, and only in these matters, with respect to the one, true God![22]

Bonhoeffer's approach to biblical interpretation is not without points of contact with Mosala's materialist hermeneutics. Both approaches avoid the escapism of textual selectivity. In the theological climate of his day, Bonhoeffer was unusual in according to the Old Testament equal canonicity with the New. Bonhoeffer's deep dissatisfaction with the ability of liberal biblical hermeneutics to furnish an adequate theological response to Nazi ideology also resonates with materialist hermeneutics' attempt to allow the Bible to speak to the present age. In this limited sense, the Bible is for Bonhoeffer a weapon of liberation. Yet the biblical texts themselves cannot, with Bonhoeffer's hermeneutical presuppositions about the Bible as the Word of God, be treated as themselves sites of struggle. Outside the *Ethics* the classic example is Bonhoeffer's study on the books of Ezra and Nehemiah,[23] through which he authorizes the anathematization of the theologically impure German Christians. Because the Bible is perceived as witness to the Word of God, Bonhoeffer does not have the critical framework with which to critique these two books, and to discern in them precisely the same racist ideology as he is struggling to oppose in Nazism.

Bonhoeffer's *Ethics* are a richly diverse collection of essays comprised of incomplete and various entry points to his subject matter. Begging the question of how Bonhoeffer intended each new entry point to relate to that which preceded it, what we are left with is a plurality of approaches to ethics, a plurality of motifs characterizing the ethical life, and a plurality of approaches to biblical hermeneutics resting on the common hermeneutical assumptions I have outlined.

The editors of the new edition of Bonhoeffer's *Ethics* divide the manuscripts into five working periods. Using this chronological sequence as the basis of my reading of the *Ethics*, and taking the third working period on 'History and the Good' as belonging thematically with the motif of the first working period, I discern four motifs, or approaches to ethics within the manuscripts. In the first approach, characterised by the phrase 'Ethics as formation,' Bonhoeffer proposes that the reader be conformed to the 'Gestalt Jesu Christi.' The term 'Gestalt,' which has usually been translated as 'form' may also carry the sense of 'character.' Guided by this insight, I suggest that Bonhoeffer's approach in this method has much in common with the notions of character formation advocated by the proponents of narrative theology. In the second approach to ethics, characterised by the term 'Ultimate and penultimate things,' Bonhoeffer offers the only sustained engagement in the *Ethics* with micro-ethics, or with issues of concrete morality; abortion, suicide, and euthanasia. This motif, deeply influenced by the conversations with Roman Catholic theologians at the Ettal monastery where Bonhoeffer worked during this period, places the biblical, final word of justification alongside his penultimate struggle with concrete moral issues. However one enters the moral maze, the final word is the word of forgiveness spoken by God. The third approach in the *Ethics* begins with Nietzsche's direction to ethics to step 'beyond good and evil,' and relates the Bible to the ethical life by means of the motif of 'Proving the will of God.' The final motif concerns 'ethics as command' and develops an approach to ethics in the light of Bonhoeffer's reading of Karl Barth's *Church Dogmatics* II/2, returning at many significant points to the perspective of *The Cost of Discipleship.*

One of the most striking features of Bonhoeffer's *Ethics* is the manner in which these various motifs describing the ethical life co-exist without mutually contradicting one another. It is as if each motif characterising ethics represents a fresh metaphorical construal of the nature of ethics. Such plurality proves extremely resilient against any approach to biblical hermeneutics using a single category, such as Mosala's historical materialism. A rigorously materialist approach to biblical hermeneutics is not without difficulties; it is not only in Bonhoeffer that liberal reserve runs deep. In notes towards an unfinished section of the *Ethics*, Bonhoeffer writes, "Self assertiveness and an excess of zeal are uncultured."[24] In the first place, there is always a danger with any theological method dominated by a single defining approach that the prefix overrides theology itself. Thus feminist theology or black theology, liberation theology or narrative theology, methodist theology or Bonhoefferian theology become so wrapped up in being feminist or black, liberation or narrative, methodist or

Bonhoefferian, that theology is denied to any who approach it without bearing the password of their own particular talismanic shibboleth. And perhaps in the end that is all Bonhoeffer was warning against in inviting us to move beyond any single perspective and viewpoint. The plurality of motifs, of metaphors for the ethical life in Bonhoeffer's *Ethics* provide a liberating diversity in ethics and in theology.

Mosala's materialist method entails a number of crucial hermeneutical gains absent in Bonhoeffer's hermeneutics. Yet the plurality of Bonhoeffer's approaches to ethics allow a theological richness which is lacking in Mosala, dominated as he is by the category of struggle. Sure enough, interrogating the relation of a biblical text to the means of production yields important insights, but the variety of biblical genre is not all oriented around this single important category. There is a political dimension to all of the biblical literature, to law and poetry, myth and parable, as well as to history, prophecy, gospel and New Testament letter. But other categories are required to release anything like the full depth and variety of meanings which biblical texts offer. These reflections in no way undermine Gutierrez's judgment that "The protest movements of the poor . . . find no place in Bonhoeffer's historical focus."[25] Mosala writes his theology as a black South African. Bonhoeffer had not the advantage (or the burden) of all the nexus of experiences which that entails. But the plurality of Bonhoeffer's methods, and the authenticity of his existential witness, uniquely qualify Bonhoeffer as a bridge builder between his own privileged perspective, and that of those, like Mosala, who truly speak with the experience and zeal of the oppressed.

At the end of E. M. Forster's *A Passage to India*, Fielding, ambivalent representative of the oppressive British Raj, goes on a ride with Dr. Aziz, player and victim of the tragic misunderstanding which constitutes the plot of the book. Aziz looks forward to the day when the British shall be driven into the sea, for then the two shall truly be friends. They stretch out their hands, but, as if prevented from becoming one by the history of oppression between them, their horses stumble on the rocky ground and swerve apart. India in its hundred voices say "'no, not yet,'" and the sky says "'no, not there.'"[26] There is a huge gap between the perspectives from below, and from above. Perhaps, in addition to really hearing the voices from below, we also need theologians like Bonhoeffer to reach out their hands across the rocky ground ahead.

Notes

1. Dietrich Bonhoeffer, *Letters and Papers From Prison* (London: SCM Press, 1984), 17.
2. Dietrich Bonhoeffer, *Ethics* (London: SCM Press, 1985), 70.
3. James H. Cone, *Black Theology and Black Power* (New York: Seabury Press, 1969), 99.
4. Itumeleng J. Mosala, *Biblical Hermeneutics and Black Theology in South Africa* (Grand Rapids: Wm. B. Eerdmans, 1989), 4.
5. Mosala, 4.
6. Mosala, 8.
7. Mosala, 9.
8. Mosala, 9.
9. Mosala, 11.
10. Mosala, 18.
11. Mosala, 30.
12. James P. Kelley and Christoph Strohm, "Church and Public Policy: Bonhoeffer's Early Critique of Nazi Policy," an unpublished paper presented at the American Academy of Religion, 1987.
13. Kelly, 8.
14. Larry Rasmussen, *Dietrich Bonhoeffer: His Significance for North Americans* (Minneapolis: Augsburg Fortress, 1990), 47.
15. Dietrich Bonhoeffer, *Ethics* (New York: Macmillan, 1965), 254.
16. *Ethics*, 255.
17. Emil Brunner, *The Divine Imperative* (London: Lutterworth, 1937).
18. Karl Barth, *Church Dogmatics III/4* (Edinburgh: T. & T. Clark, 1990), 22.
19. Dietrich Bonhoeffer, *Jugend und Studium 1918–1927* (Munich: Chr. Kaiser, 1986), 320, my translation.
20. Dietrich Bonhoeffer, *Creation and Fall* (London: SCM Press, 1959), 8.
21. Dietrich Bonhoeffer, *No Rusty Swords* (London: Collins Fontana, 1977), 309.
22. Dietrich Bonhoeffer, *Meditating on the Word* (Cambridge, MA: Cowley, 1986), 44–6.
23. Dietrich Bonhoeffer, "Der Wiederaufbau Jerusalems nach Esra und Nehemia" in *Predigten, Auslegungen, Meditationen*, 2 vols. (1935–1945) (Munich: Chr. Kaiser, 1985), 216–30.
24. *Ethics*, 160.
25. Gustavo Gutierrez, *The Power of the Poor in History* (London: SCM Press, 1983), 229.
26. E. M. Forster, *A Passage to India* (Middlesex: Penguin, 1978), 316.

BONHOEFFER, MODERNITY
AND LIBERATION THEOLOGY

CLIFFORD GREEN

One impetus for re-examining Bonhoeffer's attitude to modernity is the interpretation of his theology by liberation theologians. In particular, Gustavo Gutierrez began using Bonhoeffer to interpret and critique modern theology in the 1970's, and continues to mention him in more recent writings.[1] The first section of this essay will set forth Gutierrez' interpretation of modern theology and Bonhoeffer's role in it.[2] The second will present my analysis of Bonhoeffer's theory of modernity as found chiefly in his *Letters and Papers from Prison*. The third will conclude with some critical evaluation.

I. Gutierrez on Bonhoeffer's Role in Modern Theology

For Gutierrez, all theology has a social location in a particular social class which serves as its 'inter-locutor,' the people who define the questions and set the agenda. If 'traditional (Catholic) theology' is rooted in feudalism, its successor, 'modern theology,' is based in the bourgeois revolution whose ideology is liberalism. Predominantly a Protestant phenomenon, modern theology really has three stages. Without being uncritical of the modern age, Kant, Hegel and Schleiermacher are nevertheless "altogether comfortable and at home in the modern, new 'world come of age,'"[3] i.e., the world of bourgeois revolutions. In the person of Ritschl (and presumably Harnack and their British and American disciples), "liberal Protestant theology became the theology of a self-assured, middle-class Christianity";[4] as Barth put it, Ritschl was "the very epitome of the national-liberal

German bourgeois of the age of Bismarck."[5] We may call this first group bourgeois modernists.

For them and their successors the interlocutor of modern theology is the modern spirit of the bourgeois class with its liberal ideology.[6] This modern person, says Gutierrez, is typically a rationalist, a skeptic, a secular person, or an atheist. In other words, 'modern theology' has a very specific agenda, rooted in the needs and interests of a middle class educated in the rationalism and skepticism of the Enlightenment. That agenda is to deal with issues of religion, with problems of belief and unbelief, that arise when traditional Christian beliefs clash with modern views emerging from the natural sciences, historical studies and other disciplines. Tillich and Bultmann quickly come to mind as working at that agenda—though I would not agree that this is all they were doing. In short, modern Protestant theology has focused on the intellectual reworking of tradition, dealing with the religious issue of belief and unbelief. This agenda reflects the interests of a relatively secure middle class concerned to modernize its faith.

The second of Gutierrez' stages is represented by Barth, Bultmann and Tillich, who may be called critical modernists. If, as Bonhoeffer said, "the weakness of liberal theology was that it conceded to the world the right to determine Christ's place in the world,"[7] each of these theologians criticized that accommodation (under various headings such as dialectical theology, theology of crisis, and existentialist theology). But Bonhoeffer, in the letter under review, is critical of this theological trinity—of Tillich for trying to interpret the world religiously, of Bultmann for the liberal reductionism of his demythologizing, and of Barth whom he notoriously charged—or slandered!—with *Offenbarungspositivismus*, 'positivism of revelation.' For Gutierrez, Bonhoeffer functions as a critic of the critics of modern theology, thereby pointing out their "limitations."

Bonhoeffer thus initiates the third stage (later to be represented by Moltmann and Metz) which Gutierrez himself calls progressive (modern) theology. More than a critic of his predecessors, Bonhoeffer is also a forerunner of liberation theology. The interlocutor of this theology is not the rationalist or sceptic of the modern West. Liberation theology is not concerned with the non-believer, but with what Gutierrez calls the "non-person,"[8] the "non-human," that is, those whom society has marginalized and exploited. Such persons, living in a *barrio* of Lima or an American slum, are hardly concerned with a Bultmann's demythologizing or a Tillich's symbolic existentialist ontology, but with economic survival and social justice.

In what sense might Bonhoeffer be seen as a forerunner of liberation theology? In Gutierrez' view:

no one else, perhaps, has appreciated the challenge of modernity as profoundly as has Bonhoeffer. The very depth of his posing of the question grasps the thinking of the spirit of modernity by its stalk and its roots start cracking.[9]

In this and related passages Gutierrez clearly suggests that Bonhoeffer is uprooting modern theology, that its time is over, and that its place will be taken by liberation theology. Why, according to Gutierrez, is Bonhoeffer's response to modernity so profound? There are several reasons.[10]

(1) Bonhoeffer puts aside the question of religion. This Gutierrez takes to mean the question of "whether the human being is or is not capable of believing in God," i.e., the question of modern theology.

(2) Bonhoeffer instead raises "the more important question" posed by the "modern world," namely, "a question concerning God himself."[11] The God-question for Gutierrez is simultaneously the question of injustice, the question of the contradiction of wealthy classes and nations in a world of poverty, the question of the suffering of millions of poor, marginalized and exploited people. "The question is not how we are to talk about God in a world come of age, but how we are to tell people who are scarcely human that God is love and that God's love makes us one family."[12] That is the God-question.

(3) When Bonhoeffer sharpens the God-question christologically to ask "Who is Jesus Christ for us today?"[13] he simultaneously answers it. "The God of the Christian faith is the God who suffers in Jesus Christ." A 'non-religious' interpretation of God is a *theologia crucis*, portraying the "weak and suffering God of the Bible."[14] If "God lets himself be pushed out of the world and on to the cross," then living the Christian life is to "share in the sufferings of God at the hands of a godless world."[15]

(4) This means that the church, the christian life and theology begins with the poor and suffering of the world. Here Gutierrez quotes Bonhoeffer's well-known remarks on "the view from below" from "After Ten Years."

> We have for once learnt to see the great events of world history from below, from the perspective of the outcast, the suspects, the maltreated, the powerless, the oppressed, the reviled—in short, from the perspective of those who suffer.[16]

So Bonhoeffer is a theological Moses who leads the way to the promised land of liberation theology. But Gutierrez does not let him enter, and that for two related reasons: first, Bonhoeffer lacks an adequate social analysis, alert to issues of class; and, second, he lacks an awareness of the human cost of the bourgeoisie's coming-of-age.[17] I will return to these points in my final section.

Reading essays of Gutierrez from 1977-79, one concludes as follows. With

Bonhoeffer modern theology cancels itself dialectically (recall the 'up-rooting' metaphor). Begun as a bourgeois project which came to comple-tion with Ritschl, it generated its own critics in the twentieth century in Barth, Bultmann, and Tillich. As the critic of those critics Bonhoeffer marked the end of modern theology, and stood on the brink of liberation theology. But he did not pass into the promised land because, Gutierrez argues, "no one ever vanquished the modern, bourgeois mentality while remaining at its heart."[18]

In the writings of Gutierrez from the 1980's, however, we find a different story. In the 1986 essay, "The Truth Shall Make You Free," having stated the obligation of liberation theology to the 'nonpersons,' Gutierrez continues:

> Those addressed in modern theology are different, and it is only right to take this fact into account. Modern theology is called upon to answer the ques-tions raised by the modern consciousness and perceptively expressed by the Enlightenment. For if theology is done in the service of evangelization, then it must first find the language needed for the Christian message to be effec-tively present in the modern world, the world in which the church, too, is living. Modern theology is therefore a necessary theology that has to meet the challenges of unbelievers and counteract the secularizing influences these challenges exert in the Christian world.[19]

And in *The God of Life* he presents an explicitly *contextual* approach. After summarizing modern theology and liberation theology, Gutierrez comments:

> The mystery of God cannot be captured by any one of the approaches I have summarily described. Each of them represents certain values and reveals to us aspects of a reality that is ineffable; the framework they supply enables us to grasp the complexity of the mystery we are approaching.[20]

Gutierrez appears to have moved, then, from the view that liberation theology *supplants* modern theology, to the view that these theologies each have legitimate roles relative to their particular social and historical contexts.

II. Bonhoeffer's Theory of Modernity

In the *Letters and Papers from Prison*, Bonhoeffer's assertion of the 'coming-of-age of humanity'[21] leads him to sharpen his long-standing critique of religion (initially adopted from Barth) and to sketch his proposal for a 'non-religious Christianity.' If *Mündigkeit*, becoming adult, suggests an interpreta-tion of 'modernity as maturity,' Bonhoeffer's previous interpretation should be considered first; this interpretation, found in the *Ethics*, some early prison letters, and in the prison fiction,[22] is 'modernity as decay.'

In the section of *Ethics* entitled "Inheritance and Decay,"[23] the argument focuses much more on decay than heritage. Bonhoeffer was surely reflecting on the historical roots of National Socialism, and argues as follows. The unity of the West in Jesus Christ is sundered by the Reformation. Secularization, which Bonhoeffer here traces to a misinterpretation of the Lutheran doctrine of the two kingdoms,[24] sets in along the line separating church and state, church and world. "Government, reason, economics and culture claim for themselves a right to autonomy. . . . The Reformation is celebrated as the emancipation of human conscience, reason and culture and as the justification of the secular [*Weltlichen*] as such."[25] Bonhoeffer has quite positive things to say about emancipated reason (*befreite ratio*), its science and technology, and its fruit in the "Declaration of Human Rights." But the *befreite Mensch, der neue Mensch* of the French Revolution, is a deformed and horrible figure. The Renaissance and the Enlightenment are not even mentioned explicitly here; rather, the French Revolution – in Bonhoeffer's reading of it – looms ominously over this whole section. It creates the new unity of modern Europe, namely western godlessness, the crisis of which is to be seen in Bolshevism, National Socialism and other forms. *Der neue Mensch* is the god of Western godlessness; its gospel is nihilism, and its end the void (*das Nichts,* the Nihil).[26] Largely neglected (except for Raymond Mengus' very critical discussion of it),[27] this section of *Ethics* is complex, and Bonhoeffer's attitude is ambivalent, rather than simply negative.[28] But enough has been summarized here to heighten the contrast with what he wrote in Tegel four years later.[29]

Bonhoeffer's second approach to modernity, modernity as maturity, is summed up in his key metaphor, *Mündigkeit*. The metaphor of coming-of-age, attaining adulthood, was not new with Bonhoeffer. It was a popular idea in the German Enlightenment, being used by both Lessing and Kant. Lessing viewed human history in the three stages of childhood, adolescence, and adulthood. Kant's famous essay "What is Enlightenment?" said that Enlightenment is the liberation of humanity from its self-incurred immaturity, its dependence on kings and priests who do their thinking for them. For Kant, therefore, the motto of the Enlightenment was "*Sapere aude!*" ("Have courage to use your own reason!"). The Enlightenment thus marked for him a turning point in Western consciousness, a transition in self-understanding from dependency to independence, autonomy and self-confidence – at least for the intelligentsia and privileged class.

Bonhoeffer's theory of modernity used the coming-of-age metaphor just like Kant and Lessing. Like many others, Gutierrez supposes that Bonhoeffer was inspired by Kant.[30] The real and indubitable source, however, was Wilhelm Dilthey. Bonhoeffer reports reading three of Dilthey's books in prison, the most influential being *Weltanschauung und Analyse des Menschen seit Renaissance und Reformation*, published in 1913. Ernst Feil and Christian Gremmels have shown how formative was Dilthey's influence on Bonhoeffer's theory of modernity.[31] Though the influence of Dilthey has largely been ignored in English language scholarship, it is hardly exaggerating to say that, on this point, Bonhoeffer swallowed Dilthey whole.[32]

First, the coming-of-age metaphor on which Bonhoeffer hangs his theory of modernity is taken from Dilthey; in *Weltanschauung und Analyse* Dilthey employs the term right at the beginning of the book. Secondly, all the philosophers, scientists, jurists and political theorists named by Bonhoeffer as he traces the historical process of coming-of-age in Europe are found in Dilthey's book.[33] Third, Dilthey was also the source for the phrase deriving from Hugo Grotius which Bonhoeffer made famous, *etsi deus non daretur*, as if God were not given. For Bonhoeffer this phrase summed up the methods of modern, secular thinking. "God as working hypothesis in morals, politics, or science, has been surmounted and abolished; and the same thing has happened in philosophy and religion (Feuerbach!)."[34] Fourth, the definition of religion as "metaphysics and inwardness"—which has never seemed to me an adequate summary of Bonhoeffer's concept of religion—is another borrowing from Dilthey.[35]

Even more significant than his appropriation of these names and terms is Bonhoeffer's adoption of Dilthey's whole interpretation of intellectual history and the emergence of the modern spirit from the late Middle Ages through the Renaissance and the Enlightenment. "There is one great development that leads to the world's autonomy," wrote Bonhoeffer in the well-known letter of July 16, 1944;[36] he was referring, in fact, to what he had read in Dilthey, who had written that

> humanity moved out of the theological metaphysics of the Middle Ages and towards the work of the seventeenth century with the help of the spiritual processes of the sixteenth century [i.e., the Reformation]. [And the work of the seventeenth century was this]: the establishment of human dominion over nature, the autonomy of human knowledge and action, the formation of natural systems in the fields of law, politics, art, morality and ethics.[37]

This statement shows that a secular naturalism was a leading characteristic of the modern mentality for Dilthey; Bonhoeffer adopted this view wholesale.

Concomitant with this naturalism, Dilthey saw in the development from the Middle Ages to the modern world a shift of orientation from otherworldliness to world affirmation. Between the fourteenth and seventeenth centuries, Dilthey wrote,

> there was a complete shift of interest . . . in otherworldly matters to this-worldly self-knowledge. People were now interested in learning about human beings, in the study of nature, the recognition of the independent value of reality, the value of work for them in their vocation; they were interested in uniform, worldly education and in the blessedness and happiness of life in the midst of the orders of reality.[38]

Bonhoeffer also affirmed, on his own theological grounds, this characterization of the modern attitude.

> It is not with the beyond that we are concerned, but with this world as created and preserved, subjected to laws, reconciled and restored. What is above this world is, in the gospel, intended to exist *for* this world; I mean that . . . in the biblical sense of the creation and of the incarnation, crucifixion and resurrection of Jesus Christ.[39]

Likewise, Bonhoeffer argued that the Old Testament referred to *"historical* redemptions, i.e., on *this* side of the boundary of death. . . ."[40] He interpreted the New Testament consistently.

> The Christian hope of resurrection, in contrast to the mythological, sends a person back to life on the earth in a completely new way—this is even more sharply defined than in the Old Testament. Christians . . . must, like Christ, totally give themselves to earthly life, and only in so doing are they crucified and resurrected with Christ. Earthly life may not be prematurely written off; in this the New and Old Testaments agree.[41]

Thus far, Bonhoeffer's theory of modernity appropriates two major themes from Dilthey: affirmation of human life in the world, and a naturalistic or secular rationality as the instrument for organizing life in the world. The latter gives rise to increasing knowledge of the world, from biology to astronomy, and to industry and technology which harnesses this knowledge through increasing power and control over natural processes. In medicine and agriculture, to give but two examples, people of the modern era have a degree of control over nature which is historically unprecedented.

Society, as well as nature, is also the field for the exercise of modern rationality in analysis, planning and organization. Bonhoeffer mentions insurance[42] as one example of rational analysis and planning designed to make social life more secure. He could easily have instanced other efforts at rational social analysis and organization, such as population control, economic planning, and world government.

Corresponding to these attitudes to the world and to organizing life in society is a new psychic posture; this is what the coming-of-age metaphor especially tries to express in Bonhoeffer's usage. Those who are the beneficiaries of these intellectual and social developments have a greater sense of autonomy, of security, of confidence – in short, of being at home in the world – than most of humanity has previously enjoyed. That is why the strategy of religion in appealing to childish human dependence is psychologically bankrupt; more importantly, it is also theologically bankrupt.

III. Assessing Bonhoeffer's Theory of Modernity

The first comment to be made is one that sharply separates Bonhoeffer from many other earlier theorists of modernity. The metaphor of *Mündigkeit* in Bonhoeffer's hands is not a doctrine of human ethical progress or an optimistic doctrine of history; he was no social Darwinist. The same prison letters which theologically affirm this coming-of-age are full of criticism of contemporary life and society. Bonhoeffer was, after all, painfully aware of the brutalities of the Nazi regime in whose prison he wrote. We can insure against all contingencies, he wrote, but that does not protect us from human evil. Modern organization, through its concentrations of power, multiplies the opportunities for destruction.[43] Efficiency experts, demigods and lunatics know nothing about human relationships; for many the experience of the *humanum* is unknown, and people are merely things.[44] Irrational forces have great power in the world, as evidenced in the world war.[45] Cities are often places of death; bureaucracy invades people's proper privacy, and huge organizations frustrate the need for personal relationships in manageable communities.[46] Culture is generally impoverished, and a shallow, banal secularism knows nothing of faith or discipline.[47] Envy, greed, suspicion, fear, and hate continue their evil deeds as of old.[48] In short, if coming-of-age means a marked increase of human power, control of the world, and even self-confidence, it has not abolished sin. Accordingly, Bonhoeffer speaks of the Christian life as "sharing the sufferings of God at the hands of a godless world."[49]

A second comment concerns the social location of Bonhoeffer's reflection on modernity. With bold self-confidence Bonhoeffer generalizes about the coming-of-age of "humanity" and "the world." But precisely whom is he speaking about?[50] As Gutierrez might ask: which people are the 'historical subject' of this social, cultural, and psychic development? As it is obvious that this is not a judgment about world history and all people, it is equally clear that it refers to a certain class of people who have been shaped by the Western historical development Dilthey and Bonhoeffer are describing.

A 'modern' person[51] is chiefly found in the contemporary West in Europe and America. 'Moderns' are those whose social and psychic life has been decisively shaped by the intellectual tradition of the Renaissance and the Enlightenment, and their practical consequences in science, technology, and social organization. A 'modern' is a person whose thought embraces the scientific view of the cosmos and history, whose science understands nature and whose technology controls it; and whose social organization gives people security and confidence in the world. 'Modern' people have much more knowledge, power and control over their lives and destiny than medieval or ancient people – and, indeed, most people living today.

'Modern' people, in other words, are members of that educated and economically successful social class to which Dietrich Bonhoeffer and his family and friends belonged. (Elsewhere I have analyzed the autobiographical aspect of Bonhoeffer's theology, including the affirmation of coming-of-age, for his own identity and family relations.[52]) Eberhard Bethge also pointed to this particular class when he wrote that Bonhoeffer's experience in the resistance movement with "liberal brothers and friends" was the *Sitz im Leben* for his non-religious Christianity.[53]

Bonhoeffer lacks an adequate methodology of social analysis in his theory of 'modernity as maturity.' It is suggestive that Bonhoeffer's metaphor of *Mündigkeit* and the category 'autonomy' are essentially psychological rather than socio-political. Here it is worth recalling, as Gremmels pointed out, that there was a distinct psychological cast to Dilthey's thought. He believed that historical epochs were disclosed in their great personalities, and held that biography was "the most philosophical form of history."[54]

To criticize Bonhoeffer for inadequate social analysis is *not* to argue that a Marxist class analysis is its only form. But it is to insist that one must always ask the question, when evaluating a particular theory or policy, 'Whose social interests benefit?' (This question applies not only to social class, but also to categories such as race, gender, and religion.) Here Gutierrez' sharp words are pertinent. At no point, he argues, does Bonhoeffer "suggest that the historical agent of modern society and ideology will be the bourgeois class." His analysis of humanity's coming-of-age moves in the realm of thought, technology and social organization ("the mastery of nature and society by reason"), but he does not focus on "the fact that one social class has wrested economic and political power from the grasp of more traditional sectors, and inaugurated a mode of production that is generating new forms of exploitation. . . ." More forcefully: Bonhoeffer did not see humanity (read: the bourgeoisie) "attaining its majority by trampling underfoot the writhing mass of the poor and the despoiled." He neglects both the protest movements of poor people since the late Middle Ages and the modern labor movement, focusing, rather, on the development of autonomy through the ways reason has mastered nature and society.[55]

While Bonhoeffer was quite aware of social class as a reality, and made personal efforts to transcend the limits of his own experience (for example, in the working class parish of Berlin-Wedding), nevertheless class categories were not a central part of his social-historical reflection. (To argue, as some do, that his 'modernity as decay' approach shows a marked suspicion of the lower classes and populist movements is hardly to prove that he had an adequate social analysis.) So I agree with Gutierrez' critique here, and contend that no theory of modernity can ignore the advent of capitalism or the conflict of capital and labor as a central characteristic of the modern age. While Bonhoeffer was inevitably and appropriately preoccupied with National Socialism and the plight of the Jews, the issue of capital and labor, after all, has been the dominant ideological and geo-political issue of the twentieth century. Marx had put it on the intellectual and social agenda already in 1867, and many of Bonhoeffer's partners in the resistance movement and Hitler's victims were partisans of labor and socialism, e.g. Karl Barth.

A second critical absence from Bonhoeffer's theory is any discussion of colonialism. Though popular images treat Columbus as a proto-modern figure, some recent fascinating research reveals a man imbued with thoroughly medieval ideas about the struggle of the Christian West with Islam.[56] In the context of the Columbus quincentennial, Columbus may signal colonialism as another hallmark of the modern age; it extends from the sixteenth century to the breakup of the great European empires in Africa and Asia after World War II. Bonhoeffer completely ignores colonialism as a characteristic of the modern age. Nor does Gutierrez' critique of Bonhoeffer raise this issue, which is the external counterpart to the internal issue of class and labor. Just as the upper classes benefited from the labor of the working class in Britain, Europe and North America (here, from slaves also, as well as from the land of the indigenous population), so colonizing nations benefited from their exploitation of colonies. To what extent did the wealth and other resources derived from colonies contribute to the process Dilthey and Bonhoeffer called coming-of-age? Bonhoeffer did not address this issue. It is not one that can be ignored in the postcolonial age.

The absence of capitalism and colonialism already point to major limitations in Bonhoeffer's theory of modernity in the *Letters*. What else might we expect to find in a comprehensive theory of modernity? We *do* find discussion of autonomous, secular reason; affirmation of the world; growth of power through technology and organization; and a psychic posture of competence and confidence among those who have benefited from these developments. What other characteristics of the modern age might Bonhoeffer have considered in a more comprehensive theory?

Here I can only make the sketchiest suggestions about leading characteristics of the modern era. I have already discussed economic and political life in relation to capitalism and colonialism. In intellectual life, critical rationality is probably more descriptive than Bonhoeffer's category of autonomy. Closely related to this is reductionism; this can be seen in particular figures like Marx and Freud and, on a broader front, it results from the dominance of the natural sciences from the 17th to the 20th century in defining reality, knowledge and truth. The technological application of the natural sciences, and its marriage to capitalism, has given birth to several industrial revolutions. The triumph of historical consciousness, both in the study of the past and projections of the future, is another expression of critical rationality. The 'turn to the subject' is another of its corollaries.

In social and political life individualism, closely allied with liberalism, is surely a characteristic of the modern age. The French Revolution's "Declaration of the Rights of Man" is a classical statement: "Every man is free to use his physical strength, his industry, and his capital as shall seem to himself to be good and useful. He may produce what he pleases and produce it as he sees fit."[57] Other expressions of liberalism include the doctrine of the market as regulator of free economic activity, the doctrine of society as based on free association (social contract), and Western interpretations of the meaning of democracy. Utilitarianism is the ruling social ethic of the liberal state. Reactions against Western individualism and liberalism in the form of communism and collectivism also seem to qualify dialectically as characteristics of modernity in some societies. In national and international politics nationalism is another dominant characteristic of the modern age.

Few of these subjects appear in Bonhoeffer's *Letters,* and we must conclude that his interpretation of modernity there is very partial and incomplete. It may seem unfair to characterize several pages of correspondence as a "theory" of modernity. But Bonhoeffer was evaluating the whole course of contemporary theology in light of his analysis of modernity, and proposing a new theological project on this basis. So his argument should be examined seriously, and not just excused.

I conclude, therefore, that the Diltheyan discussion of coming-of-age in the prison letters does not, by itself, reflect an adequate theory of modernity nor theological critique of modernity. However, when we consider that this theory in the *Letters and Papers from Prison* is one of two quite different perspectives, a more complex picture emerges. Sketchy, incomplete and inadequate though Bonhoeffer's two theories of modernity are, we may nevertheless see in them his awareness of the profound ambiguities of the modern age. They reflect its destructiveness and its glories, its contradictions and its promises, its injustices and its freedoms.

For more helpful reflections on issues of modernity we have to turn to the whole corpus of Bonhoeffer's writings, rather than focusing on the *Mündigkeit* catchword of the prison letters. Elsewhere I have argued that Bonhoeffer's theology as a whole is best understood as a theology of sociality.[58] At the center of this theology is a Christology of incarnation, cross and resurrection. Its theological anthropology is one in which individual person and community exist in relations of mutual reciprocity, nurturing ethical personhood through the encounters of independent, responsible wills. It issues in an ethic of responsibility which, as Bonhoeffer's life attests, is as public as it is personal.[59]

Finally, I would contend that the value of Bonhoeffer's *theological* proposal in the *Letters* for a non-religious Christianity is not vitiated by weaknesses in his theory of modernity. That Christian faith does not depend on the sort of religious dependence and regression which Freud discussed so suggestively is not contingent on a historical or sociological survey, but on our understanding of the gospel. Extremely important, particularly in light of liberation theology, is Bonhoeffer's critique of the 'power God' of religion. For such an image of God is not only psychologically destructive; but equally, speaking of God's power as if it were a projection of profane, worldly power allows it to be manipulated to legitimate unjust, profane power in the world. The Christology of the *Letters* subverts such abuse. This Christology, not a theory of *Mündigkeit*, is the real basis for the affirmation of the human subject as a free and responsible agent. Here Bonhoeffer and Gutierrez stand together on the same ground. Speaking anthropologically, Gutierrez put it this way:

> The project of creating a new and different society includes the creation of new human persons . . . who must be progressively liberated from whatever enslaves them, from whatever prevents them from acting as the agents of their own lot in history.[60]

Bonhoeffer, speaking Christologically, put it this way:

> Encounter with Jesus Christ. The experience that a transformation of all human life is given only in Jesus' 'being for others.' Jesus' 'being for others' is the experience of transcendence! In freedom from self, in 'being for others,' is grounded omnipotence, omniscience and omnipresence. Faith is participating in this being of Jesus—incarnation, cross, resurrection.[61]

Notes

1. See especially Gustavo Gutierrez, "The Limitations of Modern Theology: On a Letter of Dietrich Bonhoeffer" and "Theology from the Underside of History," in *The Power of the Poor in History* (Maryknoll: Orbis Books, 1983), 222–234, 169–221; the original Spanish articles were written in 1979 and 1977, respectively.
2. For my reading of Gutierrez' overall position see "Gustavo Gutierrez and James Cone: Liberation Theology," in Roger A. Johnson et al., *Critical Issues in Modern Religion* (Englewood Cliffs: Prentice-Hall, 1990), 271–308.
3. Gutierrez, *Power of the Poor*, 222.
4. Gutierrez, *Power of the Poor*, 223.
5. Karl Barth, *From Rousseau to Ritschl* (London: SCM Press, 1959), 392, cited in Gutierrez, *Power of the Poor*, 223.
6. Gutierrez, *Power of the Poor*, 212.
7. Dietrich Bonhoeffer, *Letters and Papers from Prison* (New York: Macmillan, 1972), 327, cited in Gutierrez, *Power of the Poor*, 223.
8. Gutierrez, *Power of the Poor*, 193.
9. Gutierrez, *Power of the Poor*, 181; see also 224 and 231.
10. Gutierrez, *Power of the Poor*, 180. For a different reading of the problem of religion in Bonhoeffer see Clifford Green, *The Sociality of Christ and Humanity* (Missoula: Scholars Press, 1975), chapter 6.
11. Gutierrez, *Power of the Poor*, 180.
12. In Sergio Torres and Virginia Fabella, eds., *The Emergent Gospel* (Maryknoll: Orbis, 1978), 241; cf. also Gutierrez, *Power of the Poor*, 193 and, more recently, Gustavo Gutierrez, *The Truth Shall Make You Free* (Maryknoll: Orbis, 1990), 7.
13. Gutierrez, *Power of the Poor*, 180, citing *Letters and Papers*, 279.
14. Gutierrez, *Power of the Poor*, 180f., citing *Letters and Papers*, 360 (letter of July 16, 1944); cf. Gutierrez, *Power of the Poor*, 230.
15. *Letters and Papers*, 361; cf. 369f.
16. *Letters and Papers*, 17, cited in Gutierrez, *Power of the Poor*, 231.
17. Gutierrez sees Bonhoeffer as so preoccupied with "the fascist enemy and its attacks on liberal society from the rear . . . [that he was] less sensitive to the world of injustice on which that society was built," see Gutierrez, *Power of the Poor*, 229.
18. Gutierrez, *Power of the Poor*, 223.
19. Gutierrez, *The Truth Shall Make You Free*, 113f.; cf. 24 where he says that modern theology "legitimately tries to answer the questions of the modern mind" but it should be critical of "new forms of domination."
20. Gustavo Gutierrez, *The God of Life* (Maryknoll: Orbis, 1991), xv.
21. Sometimes 'world' is used instead of 'humanity'; the latter is, by the way, Bonhoeffer's term (*Mensch*=human being), not the 'man' of English translations.
22. Dietrich Bonhoeffer, *Fiction from Prison* (Philadelphia: Fortress, 1981).
23. Dietrich Bonhoeffer, *Ethics* (New York: Macmillan, 1965), 88–109. Interestingly, the adulthood metaphor also appears in this section (100), but only as a passing term, not a central category.
24. See this same comment in the 1939 report, "Protestantism Without Reformation," in Dietrich Bonhoeffer, *No Rusty Swords* (New York: HarperCollins, 1965),

108, cited in Ernst Feil, *The Theology of Dietrich Bonhoeffer* (Philadelphia: Fortress, 1985), 191.

25. *Ethics*, 96, translation altered.
26. *Ethics*, 103, 106.
27. Raymond Mengus, "Bonhoeffer and the French Revolution: Loss or Gain?," in G. Carter et al., eds., *Bonhoeffer's Ethics: Old Europe and New Frontiers* (Kampen, Netherlands: Kok Pharos, 1991), 131–41.
28. See, for example, the theme of 'promising godlessness,' *Ethics*, 103.
29. As the new edition of the *Ethik* (Munich: Chr. Kaiser, 1992) shows, one of the influences behind this section is Karl Jaspers, *Die geistige Situation der Zeit* (Berlin: Göschen, 1932, 4th ed.; written 1930, first published 1931); see *Man in the Modern Age* (Garden City, NY: Doubleday, 1951; first English translation 1933). Note that a similar approach to modernity as decay is to be found in his Reformation Day letter (October 31, 1943) about the consequences of the Reformation (*Letters and Papers*, 123; cf. Ernst Feil, *The Theology of Dietrich Bonhoeffer*, 154f.), and is also probably in the background of *Fiction from Prison*; see also Feil, *Theology*, 185, 237 n. 211.
30. See Gutierrez, *Power of the Poor*, 228, and 172 where he cites Kant's essay.
31. Ernst Feil, *Die Theologie Dietrich Bonhoeffers* (Munich: Chr. Kaiser, 1971), 355–368; *Theology*, 178–185. Independently of Feil, Christian Gremmels also discovered Dilthey's influence; see Christian Gremmels, "Mündigkeit–Geschichte und Entfaltung eines Begriffs," *Die Mitarbeit* 18 (1969): 360–72.
32. While Feil documents heavy dependence, he also points out Bonhoeffer's disagreement with Dilthey on important points, namely inwardness, religion, and theological method. More critical examination of Dilthey is needed, not just as a source, but above all in terms of his social ethics and his political commitments: what sort of social philosophy was Bonhoeffer buying into in his appropriation of Dilthey?
33. Lord Herbert of Cherbury, Montaigne, Bodin, Machiavelli, Grotius, Descartes, Spinoza, Nicholas of Cusa, Giordano Bruno; cited in Feil, 180; cf. *Letters and Papers*, 359.
34. *Letters and Papers*, 360. Related to the term 'working hypothesis' are Bonhoeffer's references to God as 'stop gap' and '*deus ex machina.*'
35. *Letters and Papers*, 280; cf. Feil, *Theology*, 179, 183.
36. *Letters and Papers*, 359. The phrase "the autonomy of humanity and the world" in this same letter is equivalent to "*die Mündigkeit der Welt und des Menschen*" in the July 8, 1944 letter: *Widerstand und Ergebung* (Munich: Chr. Kaiser, 1971), 379; cf. *Letters and Papers*, 346. These phrases indicate that when he speaks of "the *world* come of age" Bonhoeffer is making an anthropological, not a cosmological, statement. See also the equivalence of "*menschliche Autonomie*" and "mündig gewordenen Welt," *Widerstand und Ergebung*, 356f.; *Letters and Papers*, 325f.
37. Dilthey, *Weltanschauung*, 41, cited in Feil, *Theology*, 181.
38. Dilthey, *Weltanschauung*, 322, cited in Feil, *Theology*, 182.
39. *Letters and Papers*, 286. Consequently, Bonhoeffer can also call his project of "non-religious interpretation of biblical and theological concepts" a project to "reinterpret in a 'worldly' sense–in the sense of the Old Testament and John 1:14–the concepts of repentance, faith, justification, rebirth, and sanctification" (286f.).

40. *Widerstand und Ergebung*, 368; *Letters and Papers*, 336, translation altered.
41. *Widerstand und Ergebung*, 369; *Letters and Papers*, 336f., translation altered.
42. *Letters and Papers*, 380.
43. *Letters and Papers*, 380.
44. *Letters and Papers*, 386.
45. *Letters and Papers*, 298.
46. *Letters and Papers*, 296; cf. 299, 380.
47. *Letters and Papers*, 369.
48. *Letters and Papers*, 390.
49. *Letters and Papers*, 361; cf. 370.
50. When Feil (*Theology*, 186) says that *Mündigkeit* "is not a category primarily of individual maturation but one of epochal social emancipation," he fails to ask which social class participates in this 'emancipation' and at what cost.
51. While 'adulthood' and 'come of age' are key metaphors for Bonhoeffer, it is interesting that the actual term 'modern' appears to play little role in his thinking.
52. Green, *Sociality*, chapter 6, esp. 309; also Green, "Bonhoeffer in the Context of Erikson's Luther Study," in Roger A. Johnson, ed., *Psychohistory and Religion: The Case of Young Man Luther* (Philadelphia: Fortress, 1977). See also Charles West, *The Power to be Human: Toward a Secular Theology* (New York: Macmillan, 1971), 262f.: "His nonreligious man in the 'world come of age' was precisely this bourgeois humanist, as he knew him in his father, his relatives, his friends, and his co-conspirators in the plot to assassinate Hitler. . ."
53. Bethge, "Turning Points in Bonhoeffer's Life and Thought," *Union Seminary Quarterly Review* XXIII (Fall, 1967), 19; also in P. Vorkink, ed., *Bonhoeffer in a World Come of Age* (Philadelphia: Fortress, 1968). Bethge's judgment is consistent with my later contention that the discussion of "Church and World" in *Ethics* (the old chapter two) points to the resistance movement as the *Sitz im Leben* of the religionless Christianity project of the *Letters*; see my "'Church and World' and 'Religionless Christianity'" in Guy Carter et al., eds., *Bonhoeffer's Ethics: Old Europe and New Frontiers* (Kampen: Kok Pharos, 1991), 42f.
54. Gremmels, 365.
55. Gutierrez, *Power of the Poor*, 228f.
56. See Roger A. Johnson, "Inter-Religious Conflict and the Voyages of Columbus," *The Muslim World* 83 (January 1993): 1–19.
57. Cited in Gutierrez, *Power of the Poor*, 174.
58. See note 10 above.
59. See Wolfgang Huber's essay in this volume, "Bonhoeffer and Modernity," for a creative engagement between such themes of Bonhoeffer and his own analysis of the ambiguity of modernity, especially as seen in recent European history.
60. Gutierrez, *Power of the Poor*, 192; cf. *God of Life*, xv.
61. *Widerstand und Ergebung*, 414; *Letters and Papers*, 381, translation altered.

Part III:

Refiguring Community

BONHOEFFER'S HERMENEUTICAL
MODEL OF COMMUNITY

LUCA D'ISANTO

Introduction

Dietrich Bonhoeffer has bequeathed us one of the most intriguing concepts in the history of theology, namely the hiddenness of God in the
world come of age. This radical concept is best expressed in Grotius's
words, cited by Bonhoeffer in the letters from Tegel: "We have to live in
the world *etsi deus non daretur,* as if God did not exist."[1] The aim of this
paper is to discuss the question of God's hiddenness in the world with
a view to Bonhoeffer's theological hermeneutics. In order to do so, I link
the question of God's hiddenness in the world with the theological axiom
of the early Bonhoeffer, that is "Christ existing as community" (*Christus
als Gemeinde Existierend*). In fact, the early Bonhoeffer was preoccupied
with the problem of how the divine reality—revealed in the historical life,
death and resurrection of Jesus of Nazareth—could still show itself in the
mode of *Gemeinde,* the community. Thus I argue that the promise of
Bonhoeffer lies in the hermeneutical effectiveness of the concept of God's
hiddenness in the world, and that of Christ as community.

The link between these two concepts was explored in the context of historical dogmatics by the German theologian Carl Heinz Ratschow. However, Ratschow did not develop a hermeneutical model of community,
and ignored the fact that Bonhoeffer had already consistently bridged
those two concepts. Indeed, in his conclusion, Ratschow turns against
contemporary hermeneutics and the significance of the process of
secularization. On the contrary, I show that Bonhoeffer's twin preoccupation in *Act and Being* with the *continuity of being,* on the one hand, and the

exteriority of God's *act* of *self-revelation*, on the other, is resolved in the *Ethics* and the *Letters and Papers from Prison*. His solution is the link between the secularization of the Western world and God's presence in the *Gemeinde*, that is to say, the development of an authentic herme-neutical model of community.[2] Thus in my construal of Bonhoeffer's posi-tion, I part radically from Ratschow's theological conclusions.

I. The Doctrine of Providence in the History of Dogmatics

Ratschow has formulated a compelling exposition of the question of the hiddenness of God by placing it under the rubric of the classical doctrine of providence. To what extent is the doctrine of providence related to the question of a theological hermeneutics? Ratschow notes that "faith in the providence of God does not ask about God's finite 'completion' goals. Rather it asks about the ways that the *impenetrable here-and-now of worldly existence in nature and history can be connected with, or is even compatible with, the God who is the 'object' of the Christian message.*"[3]

The hermeneutical problem described in this passage consists in the demand to provide an ontological mediation between God and world. In fact, Ratschow contends that faith in providence "forms the mediation between the human being and the world that has been estranged from him and subjected to time."[4] The question of providence arises only when the consciousness of estrangement from nature penetrates the human mind. Such an estrangement is portrayed as a loss of the sense of security in the world in the presence of natural calamities. The appeal to the provi-dential action of the gods is accompanied by a restoration of self-confidence and security, and by the meaningful reordering of the scat-tered events of nature and history. The feeling of estrangement from nature and history is overcome through the gods' providence. The quest for providence has, therefore, an ontological intention. Such an intention becomes clear in the formulation of the doctrine of providence in the theology of Thomas Aquinas and the Protestant reformers.

In the history of theology, the quest for an ontological mediation between God and world has been carried out under the rubric of *analogia entis*, the analogy of being. The reformers objected to the use of the *analogia entis* for developing a theological ontology, because it led to an ontological skepticism. Against the *analogia entis*, the reformers turned to the doctrine of providence with a view to carrying out an ontological mediation of a different type. In so doing, the Protestant reformers agreed with the *intention* of the *analogia entis* to develop a theological ontology.

The intention of the *analogia entis* was to find a continuity of being in nature and history. However, not enough emphasis was put on God's contingent act of self-revelation. The problem of the reformers, and of all Protestant theology since, was to correlate ontological continuity with God's overagainstness in the sovereign act of self-revelation. In the following sections, I will show that the reformers sought both ontological continuity and the exteriority of God's act of self-revelation through the doctrine of providence. I begin first with Aquinas's model of analogy.

The problem of analogy was addressed in medieval literature with respect to the question of whether it was possible to attain a natural knowledge of God. In his monograph on Barth and Aquinas, Henry Chavanne argues that the expression *analogia entis* never appears in Aquinas's texts[5], and was first employed by Cajetan.[6] The Protestant tradition has tended to see in Aquinas's model of analogy the danger of obscuring the *necessity* of God's self-revelation by putting God and world on the same level. However, Chavanne has shown that such is not the case in Aquinas's theology. He writes:

> It is not possible to say that God's being as such shares being in general, or an idea of being in which we also participate, so that the difference between God and us were just a difference of degree of a same reality. Theology cannot legitimately treat God and humankind as two comparable realities. There is no common measure (grandeur) between God's being and our being. How could God's being be satisfied with sharing in what we call "being in general" and become a being similar to us?[7]

Aquinas's approach is not based on the analogy of resemblance between God and world, but of proportionality. In fact, there is a rupture between divine being and worldly being: "The divine being, which is its own substance, is not being in general. It is a being who is distinct from all other beings. It follows that God's being differs in its being from all other beings."[8] Since there is no resemblance between God and world, a natural knowledge of God's essence is to be excluded. However, ontological judgments with respect to God's *effects* in the world are still possible. Since every effect resembles its cause, the creature resembles its creator. Thus we can know God only on the basis of God's effects. The ontological mediation between God and world is thought out in terms of causality.

In Aquinas's theology, the ontological mediation between God and world is also discussed in the context of the doctrine of providence. Aquinas adopts Aristotle's model of prudence, according to which all things are said to be ordered towards an end. Thus "all things which have being in any way are ordained by God toward an end."[9] The *teleological* orientation is evident. Aquinas begins with the insight that "every agent acts on account of an end." God, who is the *primum agens* (prime agent), extends his causality to the creature. Providence in this case accounts for the teleological ordering of actuality. Everything that participates in being must necessarily be ordered towards an end, namely the good—towards perfection.

However, the teleological model does not specify how the ontological mediation is carried out in the here-and-now of nature and history. The mediation is located in the historical future, in the form of the fulfillment of all things.[10] Such a mediation has become extremely problematic with the collapse of the major tenets of modernity, among them the idea that history is moving towards emancipation and freedom.[11]

Another attempt to connect God and world is made by the Protestant reformers. This second formulation of the doctrine of providence is provided by the Swiss reformer, Ulrich Zwingli, who deduces God's providence from the doctrine of God.[12] In a sermon preached in Marburg in 1529, Zwingli contends that *"Ist ein Gott-so muss auch ein Fürsichtigkeit sein"*[13] ("If there is a God, then there must also be a providence"). Zwingli's understanding of providence is quite similar to Aquinas's in the sense that both derive the belief in providence from God as the highest Good. However, Zwingli's model allows the estrangement of existence here-and-now to play a role in the doctrine of providence. Aquinas' teleology, to the contrary, had made it impossible to account for the condition of estrangement, which overwhelm human existence and the world as nature and history. The novelty of Zwingli's discussion lies in the place he grants to human fallibility, which enables him to question whether God's plan may have failed at the decisive juncture.[14] The connection between God and the world as nature and history is endangered by the condition of fallibility, by the presence of sin. Zwingli attempts to provide such a connection by grounding the doctrine of providence in the doctrine of election.[15] I now return to the main question of an ontological mediation between God and the world as nature and history, and of this topic's treatment in the theological literature.

Calvin provides an exposition of the doctrine of providence in the first book of the *Institutes of the Christian Religion* of 1559. The novelty of Calvin's exposition lies in the fact that he discusses the question of providence in connection with the doctrine of creation. The God of providence is the Creator God. However, Calvin does not move much further than others in expanding the doctrine, for "providence consists in a hidden counsel of God."[16] The consequence of this theological position is that the doctrine of providence becomes incommensurable and impenetrable. The novelty of Calvin lies in connecting the doctrine of providence and creation with the experience of faith. The conditions of estrangement to which the human being and the world as nature and history are subject are a testing for the Christian faith. Such faith has to stand up in the face of the appearance of chaos and fragmentation, believing that the God who created the world will reverse that chaos and fulfill God's plan of salvation.

Although Luther does not specifically deal with the doctrine of providence, he articulates concepts related to it. Like Calvin, Luther focuses on the connection between the doctrine of creation and the Christian faith in God's impenetrable plan of salvation. The belief in God as creator of the world is the basis for "God's inscrutable governing of the world today." Before the vicissitudes of life, faith instills the belief that "[God] did not create the world as a carpenter, who builds a house and then departs, leaving it stand as it is; rather, He stays there and sustains everything as he made it, otherwise it could neither stand nor remain."[17]

The point of convergence between the reformers and Aquinas lies in the central place they grant either the doctrine of creation or teleology in the form of the fulfillment of God's plan of salvation. While the reformers take their point of departure from the doctrine of creation, they do not adopt Aquinas's *analogia entis*. In Aquinas, God and world connect because all beings participate in the teleological ordering of all things toward an end. The ontological mediation is secured by the Aristotelian model of prudence, according to which all beings naturally attain their specific goal, namely some kind of good. Aquinas's understanding of "being" is linked to a hierarchical teleological scheme. The reformers opposed the Thomistic *analogia entis* but were in danger of reducing God's activity to the act of creation. By opposing the ontological continuity of Aquinas'model, they were only able to connect God and world either in the moment of creation or in the teleological moment of fulfillment. In other words, they were in danger of slipping into actualism. However, the intention behind the formulation of the doctrine of providence was to find a sort of mediation similar to the *analogia entis*.

The following section examines Bonhoeffer's attempt to provide a mediation between God and world by correlating the concept of God's hiddenness in, and to, the world with the concept of God's existence in, and as, *Gemeinde*.

II. The Church as Bonhoeffer's Hermeneutical Mediation

Bonhoeffer discusses the problem of the *continuity of being* and of the exteriority of God's act of *self-revelation* in his early theological writings.[18] In the later writings, he seems to depart from those questions to turn towards a concrete theology of history. Some scholars have noted a connection between Bonhoeffer's fragmentary theology of history and the doctrine of providence. For instance, John W. de Gruchy writes, "Indeed, like Augustine and Luther, Bonhoeffer had a doctrine of providence that informs all his thinking on history, and his views on providence 'are rooted in the concreteness of history, not in speculation or in metaphysics.'"[19]

In the *Letters and Papers from Prison* Bonhoeffer expresses his skepticism towards the modern attempt to provide a univocal interpretation of history. With respect to the problem of the *visibility* or interpretability of God's historical action in the world, the most important passage is to be found in the letter from Tegel dated July 16, 1944. Bonhoeffer argues here that God's hiddenness in the world is not only a result of modern consciousness, but that it is the constitutive element of God's self-revelation. He notes:

> And we cannot be honest unless we recognize that we have to live in the world *etsi deus non daretur* — and this is what we recognize — before God! God himself compels us to recognize it. So our coming of age leads us to a recognition of our situation before God who would have us know that we must live as humans who manage our lives without him. The God who is with us is the God who forsakes us (Mark 15:34). The God who lets us live in the world without the working hypothesis of God is the God before whom we stand continually. Before God and with God we live without God. God lets himself be pushed out of the world on to the cross. He is weak and powerless in the world, and that is precisely the way, the only way, in which he is with us and helps us.[20]

Bonhoeffer's insight that we have to live in the world as if God did not exist has to be taken as a theological statement, which is meant to explode the alternative of presence and absence. In light of Bonhoeffer's statement, history cannot be interpreted on the basis of either the "visibility" or interpretability of God's action in the world, or the visibility of the *ground*, if any, of history. For Bonhoeffer, God's action is hidden to the world. This reasoning, however, does not give in to hermeneutical skepticism. On the contrary, it guides hermeneutical reflection on a path which moves away from the univocal interpretations of history offered throughout modernity. For Bonhoeffer, this path is specifically theological in the sense that it has been traced by the death of Jesus of Nazareth upon the cross. The hermeneutical direction away from modernity is prepared by way of an *interpretation of the cross*. Bonhoeffer does not seek an understanding of history in the transmundane scheme of teleology, but in the historical manifestation of God's love for the world in the life, death and resurrection of Jesus of Nazareth. In fact, the meaning of history is hidden in the Christ-event.[21]

In the *Ethics* Bonhoeffer offers an *interpretation* of the doctrine of providence in the concept of *Stellvertretung* (deputyship), namely the representative nature of the Church with respect to Christ. The here-and-how of nature and history has to be connected to God by way of the representative action of the community of believers. Whereas God's action is invisible and hidden to the world, the action of the community is visible to the world. The ontological mediation is concretely carried out in two fields: the kerygmatic and the ontological space of the Church.

The kerygmatic locus of God's hidden action in the world is the *proclamation* of the gospel. The ontological space of the mediation is made specific, particular, in the ethical mandates or orders of preservation, namely the concrete spaces in which the Church is called to live out its divine mandate. Although there are serious questions about the continuities and discontinuities between Bonhoeffer and Luther, it is clear that they both agree on the localization of the spaces in which the church has to flesh out God's love for the world.[22] The particularity of Bonhoeffer's argument in favor of the Church's responsible action in the orders of preservation is that the ethical mandates have to be upheld in order to resist the decay and fragmentation of all values, i.e., the threat of the void. He writes, "The absence of anything lasting means the collapse of the foundation of historical life, of confidence in all its forms. Since there is no confidence in truth, the place of truth is usurped by sophistic propaganda. Since there is no confidence in justice, whatever is useful is declared just."[23]

In his *Christology* and in the *Ethics*, Bonhoeffer endeavors to develop an ontology of temporality and historicity[24] with a view to locating God's being in the *Gemeinde*. Bonhoeffer wants to understand God present in the historical and cultural locus of the "here and now."[25] God is "present" in the *Gestalt* (form or structure) of the word, the sacrament and the church. This triadic *Gestalt* of God's presence articulates polyphonically God's entrance into the historical dimension. The category of the Word is understood as *Anrede*, as address. By address, Bonhoeffer means the communicative nature of God's self-revelation. The fact that the Word is proclaimed *to* the community discloses its dialogical nature. The presence of Christ *in* and *as* the sacramental reality is an enhancement and empowerment of reality. The Christ preached by the Word and revealed as sacramental reality is *"der Geschichtliche und der Gekreuzigte, der Auferstandene und zum Himmel Gefahrene*" ("the one who is historical and who was crucified, who is resurrected and ascended to heaven").[26] However, the mediated character of God's presence is completed only with the disclosure of the being of Christ in and as *Gemeinde,* as the community of the Church:

> The Church is the body of Christ. Her body is not only a symbol. The Church is the body of Christ, it does not signify the body of Christ. When applied to the Church, the concept of body is not only a concept of function, which refers to the members of this body. It is a comprehensive and central concept of the mode of existence of the one who is present in his exaltation and humiliation.[27]

In his *Ethics,* Bonhoeffer contends that the concrete action of the church (*Gemeinde*) is the "mediation" of God's action in the world. The static notion of church as *Gestalt,* form, is injected with the more diachronic tension of *Stellvertretung,* the representative nature of the church, which opens the church towards the world. Indeed, the concept of *Stellvertretung* unfolds within a dialectic of dependence and responsibility. By *Stellvertretung,* Bonhoeffer means that kind of action which is effected by a father vis-à-vis his children, or a citizen vis-à-vis her country. The father or mother acts for her children, interceding for them, fighting and suffering for them. The father or mother is the deputy or representative of his or her children. "A matter of deputyship is demonstrated most clearly in those circumstances in which a [human being] is directly obliged to act in the place of other [human beings], for example as a father, as a statesman or as a teacher."[28] *Stellvertretung,* deputyship, involves every person's "limited" field of responsibilities. Responsibility means, therefore, that "the totality of life is pledged and that our action becomes a matter of life and death."[29]

Bonhoeffer applies this concept of representative responsibility christologically and ecclesiologically. He identifies Jesus Christ as the ideal example of *Stellvertreter,* namely the deputy *par excellence.* He writes:

> Jesus' life, our life, lived in deputyship for us as the incarnate son of God, and that is why through Him all human life is in essence a life of deputyship. Jesus was not the individual, desiring to achieve a perfection of his own, but He lived only as the one who has taken up into himself and who bears within Himself the selves of all men. All His living, His action and His dying was deputyship. In Him there is fulfilled what the living, the action and the suffering of men ought to be. In this real deputyship which constitutes His human existence He is the responsible person *par excellence.*[30]

The christological definition of deputyship is applied to the living space of the community: the church is the *Gestalt* of Christ. As *Gestalt,* the church mediates God's action on earth. "The Church can be called the Body of Christ because in Christ's body man is really taken up by him, and so, too, therefore are all mankind. The Church, then, bears the form which is in truth the proper form of all humanity."[31]

The identification of Christ with the Church does not mean a dissolution of christology into ecclesiology. What prevents a "dissolution" or a loss of a christological center in Bonhoeffer is his hermeneutical perspective. The proposition "Christ exists as Church" can be understood hermeneutically as the way in which the mediation between "God's action" and the world is carried out. In other words, the proposition is meant to locate the place in which the divine reality, which showed itself in the life, death and resurrection of Jesus of Nazareth, can still show itself today.

We can now see how the community functions as the ontological mediation between God and world. Is the community the *hypostatization* of God's being, namely does it make being absolute? Is the mediation to be taken in "strong" onto-theological terms as the localization of God's being? In my view, the community cannot be the mediation understood by the onto-theological tradition. In fact, when speaking of Luther's interpretation of the Lord's Supper, Bonhoeffer objects that his explanations are "impossible" metaphysical hypostatizations, because, as he says, "in each, an element of reality has been isolated and elevated into a system."[32]

Leaving aside the question of Bonhoeffer's interpretation of Luther, his main criticism is on the ontological level; namely that no part of reality can be raised into a system or rendered absolute. In light of this criterion, it is evident that the concept of community as ontological mediation cannot be intended as rendering absolute one part of reality. In what sense is, then, the ontological mediation to be understood? Bonhoeffer himself provides the key for interpreting his own concept. When speaking of christology's main task, Bonhoeffer argues that "it is not a question of the possibility of connecting humanity and divinity, but rather of the *hiddenness of the God-Man* present in his humiliation. God is revealed in the flesh, but hidden in the scandal."[33]

The mode of God's presence in the world is the mode of hiddenness.[34] This insight is strengthened in the *Christology*, where Bonhoeffer affirms that Christ cannot become a *doctrine* or a universal truth. "He is not only doctrine or idea, but nature and history. God has dressed himself with the insufficiency of nature and history."[35] Bonhoeffer also writes that "nature does not signify Christ."[36] The community *per se* does not signify Christ in the sense of being the hypostatization of divine reality. Rather, it is the form of God's hiddenness in the world.

In discussing the spatio-temporal location of Christ, Bonhoeffer notes that Christ lives at the *center* of reality as the "mediation" between old and new being. For "the essence of the person of Christ consists in his being at the center in the spatio-temporal sense."[37] The Christ who is present in the Word, in the community, in the sacrament is at the center of human existence, of history and of nature. "Christ is the mediator (*Vermittler*) to the extent that he lives *pro me*."[38]

The theme of "Christ at the center of life" points to how theological thought can move beyond the teleological aspects of modernity: the center of history is hidden to the world. Bonhoeffer insists that this centrality must not be demonstrated objectively, or become the epistemological foundation of a philosophical system.[39] This position is grounded in the hermeneutical nature of Bonhoeffer's notion of community. If the community were intended as the ontological mediation in the onto-theological sense, one could provide epistemological grounds to demonstrate its superiority before the world. This is not Bonhoeffer's intention.

On the contrary, Bonhoeffer provides a definition of the community that summarizes the essence of the hermeneutical event *par excellence:* "the Word is also itself Church, in so far as the Church itself is revelation, and the Word wishes to have the form of created body."[40] The identification of community with its language, with the proclaimed Word, shows an authentic hermeneutical model. The Church is not just the community of believers who interpret Scripture; rather, the community is itself the *interpretation*, the linguistic *Ueberlieferung*, form of delivery, in which God is *Ueberliefert*, transmitted, revealed. Only in this light can one understand Bonhoffer's preceding statement.

For Bonhoeffer, the community is the historical *Gestalt* of God's hidden presence in the world come of age, and the actions of the community have to be understood as the way in which God acts in the world today. God's action in the world is not visible or interpretable outside the community, because God lives in the form of hiddenness. The representative nature of the community, therefore, signifies also the possibility of proclaiming to the world the actuality of its invisible center of history. The community, however, cannot proclaim this belief as if in possession of privileged knowledge, or superior insights about reality. Rather, Bonhoeffer sees the community as finding the Lord of history only in the *interpretation* of the cross, in the humiliation of Jesus of Nazareth. The community itself does not escape the humiliation of the cross, but finds its self-understanding in the identification with the cross. In a speech given to the World League in Gland in 1932, Bonhoeffer wrote:

> No visible city of God can be erected in this world . . . . Everything which is done by the church is temporary, and has as its aim only to preserve the orders of the world in ruin, to prevent their collapse into chaos. This action of the church is indispensable, but a new order, a new society, a community

is not the Order of the kingdom. All the Orders and all communities will pass away, when God will create again his world, and will come back to its Lord Christ, to judge the old world, and institute the new world.[41]

This "eschatological tension" seems to prevent any claim of ultimacy on the part of the church, which can only understand itself as the community of the crucified. Any claim to absoluteness is put in question by the temporality of the Church. This eschatological tension shows that the community is not the hypostatization of God's being, but the historical, temporal *Ereignis* (event), happening. No community can aspire to be God's kingdom on earth, or God's representative on earth. Every community is the historical manifestation of "the invisible center of history," that is, of Christ.

Thus the model of community developed by Bonhoeffer does not find any parallel with the onto-theological tradition. The community is "weakened" by "the God who is coming"[42] and by its own historicity. The "movement" of the God who is coming preserves the *exteriority* of revelation. At the same time, this eschatological movement does not contradict God's presence in and as *Gemeinde*. There is not a contradiction, for Bonhoeffer, because his ontological discussion is not to be understood metaphysically or onto-theologically. If the identification of God's being with the *Gemeinde* were meant as a metaphysical hyposthatization, then Bonhoeffer's theological assertions would be contradictory. This is not Bonhoeffer's intention. The originality of Bonhoeffer's theological model with respect to historical dogmatics lies in his ability to connect God and world without lapsing into teleology or actualism. The "connection or mediation" is not hypostatized metaphysically. On the contrary, it is fleshed out in the historical praxis of the *Gemeinde,* and as such corresponds to the manifestation of the *crucified Lord.*

If the Church does not have a special privilege or knowledge about the process of history, how is history related to its invisible center? Bonhoeffer's response in one of the first fragments of the *Ethics* is that *"Geschichte entsteht durch das Wahrnehmen der Verantwortlichkeit für andere Menschen, bezw. für ganze gemeinschaften"*[43] ("History has its origin in the assumption of responsibility for others, namely, for whole communities"). History is no longer intended teleologically as the onto-theological tradition does, but in a dialectic of dependence and responsibility. The hidden meaning of history is indissolubly linked with the ethical *decision to respond to the call of an Other.* This decision has a hermeneutical feature in the sense that it is made towards the concrete Other, but it also includes one's own attitude towards the past. This concept of history should not be understood individualistically. Recall Bonhoeffer's concept of "heritage" in the *Ethics,* according to which the church should appropriate the invisible ground of the West, namely the humiliation of the cross. It is only by taking over, by handing over the past to itself that the church can function as the onto-logical mediation between God and world.

> The church as the bearer of historical *inheritance* is bound by an obligation to the historical future. Her vision of the end of all things must not hinder her in the fulfillment of her historical responsibility. She must not only leave the end to God's decision but also the possibility of the continuum of history.[44]

This hermeneutical relation to history is made possible by the *hiddenness* of its ground, that is of God. The true response of the church consists in rendering the *hidden* God *visible* and *interpretable* in the ecclesial *praxis* of contemporary individuals. In this sense, one can say that hermeneutics and ethics are intertwined in Bonhoeffer's model of mediation, because no interpretation of God's being can be authentically validated without moving into action. Yet, action cannot repose in the *security* of the teleological scheme of the onto-theological tradition. Rather, it has to be grounded in the *certainty* of faith in the God who is hidden to the world, but present in and as the church.

> We must confront fate—to me the neuter gender of the word 'fate' (*Schicksal*) is significant—as resolutely as we submit to it at the right time. One can speak of 'guidance' only on the other side of that two-fold process, with God meeting us no longer as 'Thou,' but also 'disguised' in the 'It'; so in the last resort my question is how we are to find the 'Thou' in this 'It' (i.e. fate), or, in other words, how does 'fate' really become 'guidance?' It is therefore impossible to define the boundary between resistance and submission on abstract principles; both of them must exist, and both must be practised. Faith demands this elasticity of behaviour. Only so can we stand our ground in each situation as it arises, and turn it to gain.[45]

This is Bonhoeffer's response to the "crisis of modernity", and his demand to flesh out an "ethics of concreteness" has to be intended as the actualizing of his theological hermeneutic. Bonhoeffer's position (and the best conclusion to this paper's discussion) can be summed up by the following passage in the letter from Tegel dated May 1944:

> We have spent too much time in thinking, supposing that if we weigh in advance the possibilities of any action, it will happen automatically. We have learnt, rather too late, that action comes, not from thought, but from a *readiness for responsibility*.[46]

Notes

1. Dietrich Bonhoeffer, *Letters and Papers from Prison* (New York: Macmillan, 1972), 360.

2. The link between Bonhoeffer's theology, contemporary hermeneutics and the process of secularizaton has been emphasized by Luca Bagetto, *Decisione ed Effettivita: La via ermeneutica di Dietrich Bonhoeffer* (Genova: Marietti, 1991), 124ff.

3. Carl Heinz Ratschow, "God's Action in Salvation and in the World: Thoughts on Shaping the Doctrine of Faith in Providence in Protestant Dogmatics," 60, from an unpublished translation by Robert Scharlemann of "Das Heilshandeln und das Welthandeln Gottes: Gedanken zur Lehrgestaltung des Providentia-Glaubens in der evangelischen Dogmatik," in Christel Keller-Wentorf and Martin Rapp, eds., *Von den Weindlungen Gottes: Beiträge zur Systematische Theologie zum Geburstag Carl Heinz Ratschow* (Berlin: W. de Gruyter, 1986).

4. Ratschow.

5. Henri Chavanne, *L'Analogie entre Dieu et le Monde selon Saint Thomas D'Aquin et selon Karl Barth* (Paris: Éditions du Cerf, 1969).

6. Thomas de Vio Cajetan, *De l'Analogie et du Concept d'Etre*, trans. Hyacinthe-Marie Robillard (Montreal: Presses L'Université de Montreal, 1963).

7. Chavanne, 217.

8. Thomas Aquinas, *De Potentia*, 7,2; cited in Chavanne, 218.

9. Ratschow, 191.

10. Ratschow, 194.

11. See Gianni Vattimo, *The End of Modernity* (Baltimore: John Hopkins University Press, 1988); *The Transparent Society* (Baltimore: John Hopkins University Press, 1992).

12. Ratschow, 195.

13. Ulrich Zwingli, *Zwingli Hauptschriften*, vol. III, ed. F. Blank et al. (Zurich, 1940), 193.

14. Ratschow, 194.

15. Otto Ritschl, *Dogmengeschichte des Protestantismus*, 3 (Göttingen: Vandenhoeck & Ruprecht, 1927), 60ff.

16. Ratschow, 194.

17. Martin Luther, *On Romans*, 12, 33–36; cited in Ratschow, 200.

18. On the ontological significance of Bonhoeffer's early works, see Charles Marsh, "Bonhoeffer on Heidegger and Togetherness," *Modern Theology* 8 (July 1992): 272ff.; and Luca Bagetto, 74ff.

19. John de Gruchy, *Bonhoeffer and South Africa: Theology in Dialogue* (Grand Rapids: Wm. B. Eerdmans, 1984), 52.

20. Dietrich Bonhoeffer, *Letters and Papers from Prison* (New York: Macmillan, 1972), 360.

21. See Dietrich Bonhoeffer, *Christology* (London: Collins, 1964), 62.

22. On this see Christian Gremmels, ed., *Zur Sozialgestalt des Luthertums in der Moderne* (Munich: Chr. Kaiser, 1983); and Jürgen Moltmann, *Herschaft Christi und soziale Wirklichkeit nach Dietrich Bonhoeffer* (Munich: Chr. Kaiser, 1959).

23. Dietrich Bonhoeffer, *Ethics* (London: Collins, 1964), 107.

24. Alexandre Dumas, *Dietrich Bonhoeffer: Theologian of Reality* (London: SCM Press, 1971).

25. *Christology*, 43.

26. Dietrich Bonhoeffer, *Christologie, Gesammelte Schriften*, III, ed. Eberhard Bethge (Munich: Chr. Kaiser, 1966), 188.

27. *Christology*, author's emphasis.

28. *Ethics*, 224.

29. *Ethics,* 222.

30. *Ethics,* 225.

31. *Ethics,* 83.

32. *Christology,* 56.

33. *Christology,* 35, emphasis added.

34. On the concept of God's hiddenness in history, see Geffrey B. Kelly, "Bon-hoeffer's Theology of History and Revelation," in A. J. Klassen, ed., *A Bonhoeffer Legacy: Essays in Understanding* (Grand Rapids, MI: Wm. B. Eerdmans, 1981).

35. Kelly, 34.

36. Kelly, 34.

37. *Christology,* 56.

38. *Christology,* 58.

39. *Christology,* 61.

40. *Christology,* 59.

41. Dietrich Bonhoeffer, "Ansprache in Gland," *Gesammelte Schriften,* II, ed. Eberhard Bethge (Munich: Chr. Kaiser, 1965), 169ff.

42. See Eberhard Jüngel.

43. Dietrich Bonhoeffer, "Die Geschichte und das Gute," in *Gesammelte Schriften,* III (1966), 456.

44. *Ethics,* 109.

45. *Letters and Papers,* 217.

46. *Letters and Papers,* 298.

THE COST OF FORGIVENESS: GRACE, CHRISTIAN COMMUNITY AND THE POLITICS OF WORLDLY DISCIPLESHIP

L. Gregory Jones

Some aspects of Bonhoeffer's theology are not only well known but have become well-worn. Perhaps the best example of this is Bonhoeffer's famous polemic against "cheap grace" in *The Cost of Discipleship*. Yet despite the notion's familiarity, comparatively little critical attention has been paid to situating such a theme as "cheap grace" within the larger context of Bonhoeffer's theology and life. The tendency has been to see *The Cost of Discipleship* and *Life Together*, the other book Bonhoeffer wrote during the Finkenwalde period of the mid-1930s, either as outstanding devotional books not essentially related to Bonhoeffer's "mature" theology or as reflecting a "sectarian" period which he later rejected by becoming a member of the Resistance and by writing the fragments of his *Ethics* and *Letters and Papers from Prison*.

Neither of these approaches is adequate. Bonhoeffer's arguments in *The Cost of Discipleship* and *Life Together* are theologically important. Further, as I will show, they present themes which precede those books, can be found in other writings and sermons of that same period, and continue to be presumed, as well as developed, in his later thought and life.

Indeed Bonhoeffer's polemic against "cheap grace," for example, is closely related to other prominent themes in his theology and life such as "judgment," "repentance," "confession," "guilt," and the "disciplines of Christian community." Further, analyzing such themes helps to illumine, and at times complicate, an understanding of Bonhoeffer's views on such topics as ecclesiology, eschatology, and the enigmatic "arcane discipline."

I will show how and why this is the case by using as a prism Bonhoeffer's understanding of "the cost of forgiveness." My argument is developed in three sections. In the first section, I explicate Bonhoeffer's understanding of the centrality of God's forgiveness for the shape of Christian community. In the second section, I explicate Bonhoeffer's account of the possibilities and limits of Christian forgiveness in relation to politics and the "world." Finally, in the third section, I briefly develop a critique of one aspect of Bonhoeffer's account, in order to point toward a more adequate conception of the cost of forgiveness.

I. God's Forgiveness and Christian Community

Christology and, more particularly, Bonhoeffer's understanding of the relation between Christ and Christian community underlie his account of forgiveness. This ought to be clear given Bonhoeffer's own abiding concern with the centrality of Christ and the question of who Christ is for us today.[1] Even so, I cannot attempt in this paper to develop a full account of Bonhoeffer's christology or its relation to Christian community. A brief sketch of Bonhoeffer's argument relating Christ to Christian community, however, is necessary in order to indicate the contours of Bonhoeffer's account of forgiveness in and through Christian community.[2]

Most fundamentally, Jesus Christ forgives sins through his person and work. This is accomplished *extra nos,* and, as such, human beings are freed from sin for new life in Christ. As Bonhoeffer puts it in *Christ the Center,*

> Only if I know who does the work can I have access to the work of Christ. Here everything depends upon knowing the person in order to recognize the work. If he was an idealistic founder of a religion, I can be elevated by his work and stimulated to follow his example. But my sin is not forgiven, God remains angry and I am still in the power of death. But if Jesus is the Christ, the Word of God, then I am not primarily called to do the things that he does; I am met in his work as one who cannot possibly do the work he does. It is through his work that I recognize the gracious God. My sin is forgiven, I am no longer in death, but in life.[3]

Christ's work is accomplished *extra nos;* but it is also inextricably *pro me.* Thus the work of Christ addresses people in their particularity, and confronts them with the truth about themselves. The content of the addressing Word, Bonhoeffer claims,

> is not the uncovering of hidden truths, nor the imparting of a new concept of God, nor a new moral teaching. It is far more concerned with the personal appeal of God to men to assume responsibility. Man in his being and existence

is placed in the truth. Christ becomes the address of forgiveness and command. It does not matter whether the command is old or new—it can be either old or new—but what matters is that it happens. And also that forgiveness happens. But both forgiveness and command happen because the Word of God is the person of Christ.[4]

Further, Christ is also *in nobis*. The addressing Word does not come to isolated individuals; it comes to the community. The Word's "character as address requires the community. The character of truth in this addressing word is such that it seeks community, in order to face it with the truth."[5] Christ is present in preaching and the sacraments, and that presence brings both judgment and forgiveness: "He is the one judging and forgiving Christ, who is the Word, in both [preaching and the sacraments]."[6]

Throughout, Bonhoeffer insists both on the theological primacy of christology *and* its essentially practical significance. He has no place for general or abstract christologies which are not inextricably linked to the formation and sustenance of Christian communities and, more specifically, Christian discipleship.

Thus far, Bonhoeffer's argument seems to fit into familiar patterns of christological reflection. Yet Bonhoeffer also develops important implications of that argument. I want to highlight four interrelated and inseparable implications that bear on Bonhoeffer's understanding of forgiveness: the inescapable, though carefully nuanced, emphasis on judgment; the significance of repentance; the pivotal importance of confession in relation to truth and community; and the question of how we ought to relate to those unwilling to acknowledge the truth.

Bonhoeffer attacks in numerous places, most notably in his famous polemic against "cheap grace," an understanding of Christ's work that presumes—among other things—forgiveness without judgment or repentance. It justifies the sin instead of the sinner. Such a presumption proclaims the forgiveness of sins as a general truth, and promises that "my only duty as a Christian is to leave the world for an hour or so on a Sunday morning and go to church to be assured that my sins are all forgiven."[7]

By contrast, costly grace recognizes that sin must be confronted and judged before forgiveness can occur. That is, sin must not be overlooked or forgotten. As Bonhoeffer describes it with reference to baptism, "The old man and his sin are judged and condemned, but out of this judgement a new man arises, who has died to the world and to sin."[8]

Yet there would seem to be a problem. Matthew 7:1 specifically indicates "Judge not, lest ye be judged," a passage Bonhoeffer knew well.[9] How can we reconcile that passage with Bonhoeffer's comments about the judgment which is crucial to forgiveness?

The key comes in the nature of Christ's judgment. In order to understand that judgment, however, it is important first to understand Bonhoeffer's critique of the judgment human beings tend to exercise. The prohibition of judgment in Matthew 7:1, according to Bonhoeffer, is a blow directed at sinful humanity which presumes to play the role of God.

> For man in the state of disunion good consists in passing judgement, and the ultimate criterion is man himself. Knowing good and evil, man is essentially a judge. As a judge he is like God, except that every judgement he delivers falls back upon himself. In attacking man as a judge Jesus is demanding the conversion of his entire being, and He shows that precisely in the extreme realization of his good he is ungodly and a sinner.

Thus, Bonhoeffer continues, "'Judging' is not a special vice or wickedness of the disunited man; it is his essence, manifesting itself in his speech, his action and his sentiment."[10] Such judgment is closely related to the attempts at "self-justification" which Bonhoeffer repeatedly condemns.[11]

Even so, there is also another judgment which, Bonhoeffer notes, is the "true activity" of humanity. It is a judgment which "springs from the achievement of union with the origin, with Jesus Christ." This union is accomplished through the work of Christ, the judge whose judgment does not condemn but brings salvation. God

> does not permit us to classify men and the world according to our own standards and to set ourselves up as judges over them. He leads us *ad absurdum* by Himself becoming a real man and a companion of sinners and thereby compelling us to become the judges of God. God sides with the real man and with the real world against all their accusers. Together with men and with the world He comes before the judges, so that the judges are now made the accused.[12]

As a result of Christ's work of reconciliation, we are enabled to understand the pattern of judgment's relation to forgiveness. It is "a judgment of reconciliation and not of disunion, a judgment by not judging, a judgment which is the act of reconciling."[13]

Christ's judgment is real. Our sin is forgiven only because it is confronted and judged. But that judgment is wholly in the service of mercy, reconciliation, and new life. "God binds elements together in the breaking, creates community in the separation, grants grace through judgment."[14]

Christ's judgment is also eschatological. Christ not only has judged and is judging; Christ also will judge. "He who was poor and weak among us, will in the end pass judgment on all the world. . . . No one is his own judge. Christ is the judge of humankind." Yet even that eschatological judgment ought not cause us to be afraid. "Christ judges; that means, grace is the judge, forgiveness, and love."[15]

In order to live in the judgment of reconciliation wrought by Christ, however, we must repent of our sin – more specifically, repent of the judgment by which sinful humanity lives. Such judging precludes our ability to see things rightly and to act well. The verses which follow Matthew 7:1 indicate a crucial problem: we so easily judge others while refusing to see our own sin. As Bonhoeffer puts it in a sermon on the parable of the unforgiving servant, "That is the whole lesson: the sins of others you see, but your own sin you fail to see. In repentance, recognize God's mercy toward you; in this way alone will you be able to forgive."[16]

Repentance is necessary because of the inescapability of Christ's judgment, even though that judgment is ultimately in the service of (a costly) grace. Without repentance, we are caught in the trap of cheap grace: "the preaching of forgiveness without requiring repentance, baptism without church discipline, Communion without confession, absolution without personal confession."[17] Cheap grace seeks a quick, easy path to God's forgiveness and the assurance of salvation. Yet Bonhoeffer recognizes the costliness of grace which requires repentance. Indeed he thinks there is a mutually reinforcing connection between repentance and forgiveness. In one sense repentance prepares us to receive God's grace, but in another, more profound sense we discover through our repentance that God's grace has already found us.

Moreover, the aim of repentance, as is the case with grace, is to lead people into community. The Body of Christ is created through the dynamic interrelations of repentance and forgiveness. So, in reference to Acts 2, Bonhoeffer contends that Peter "proclaims the full, free grace of God which calls men to action, to repentance, to new life. 'Repent,' in other words, 'Let yourselves be called to the church.' Through grace, on the strength of the call of God, take the step to the community of those who have been visited with grace, the community which has been called out of darkness."[18] Once called to the church, we become a part of that community which worships together and engages in ongoing practices of confession, forgiveness, and church discipline.

Bonhoeffer thinks confession, seen not as self-flagellation but as grace, is at the heart of Christian community.[19] Indeed confession occasions what Bonhoeffer calls "a breakthrough to community,"[20] because it is "the God-given remedy for self deception and self-indulgence." Through confession Christians are "conformed to the death of Christ."[21] Confession is "a conversion and a call to discipleship."[22]

Hence, Bonhoeffer is troubled both by the loss of confession within Protestantism and by the reliance on psychotherapy as a secular offshoot once confession was lost as an ecclesiastical institution. Both of those undermine the centrality of confession for the forgiveness of sin and new life in Christ.

> The most experienced observer of humanity knows less of the human heart than the Christian who lives at the foot of the cross of Christ. No psychology knows that people perish only through sin and are saved only through the cross of Christ. Anyone who has seen the meaning of the cross for but a moment is shocked by the godlessness of the world and by the awesomeness of his own sins; he will no longer be shocked by the sins of his sisters and brothers in Christ. The spirit of judgment is cut off at the roots.[23]

Thus, as those who have been forgiven by Christ's work *extra nos*, and who have appropriated that work *pro me*, we are enabled to embody—as people marked by forgivenness—Christ *in nobis*.

In this context we can see more clearly the connections Bonhoeffer draws between the work of Christ, repentance, forgiveness, confession, and community. The One who is the Truth addresses humanity in its sinfulness with the judgment of grace. Thus through repentance, forgiveness, and confession, people are enabled to recognize the Truth and to learn to embody truthfulness.

> Complete truthfulness is only possible where sin has been uncovered, and forgiven by Jesus. Only those who are in a state of truthfulness through the confession of their sin to Jesus are not ashamed to tell the truth wherever it must be told.[24]

This truthfulness also is crucial to the new life of discipleship. As Bonhoeffer summarizes the grace of the Gospel, "The message is liberation through truth."[25]

Even so, the question might be asked—and indeed was asked of Bonhoeffer—why must confession be communal? Isn't confession to God enough? Bonhoeffer responds that while there is confession to God alone, we also need to bring secret sins to light either now or at the last day. Confession to a brother or sister who also lives by Christ's forgiveness lessens the danger of the last judgment.[26]

Even more strongly, Bonhoeffer indicates that the certainty of confession and forgiveness occurs only when it is spoken by a fellow believer: "As the open confession of my sins to a brother insures me against self-deception, so, too, the assurance of forgiveness becomes fully certain to me only when it is spoken by a brother in the name of God. Mutual, brotherly confession is given to us by God in order that we may be sure of divine forgiveness."[27] In our brother or sister, "we find grace before the seat of judgment."[28] Even so, Bonhoeffer also stresses the crucial point that only those who have been forgiven, only those who "stand under the cross," are capable of hearing confession in the spirit of Christian community.[29]

Finally, Bonhoeffer thinks confession to another person is important in order to break the individual of pride, which according to Bonhoeffer—at least in *Spiritual Care* and in *Life Together*—is the root of all sin. This may be important for forgiveness in some cases, but it is dangerous to presume that all people need "knocking down" in order to be able to appropriate God's forgiveness as new life in Christ—a point which Bonhoeffer recognizes in *Ethics* and the *Letters and Papers from Prison*.[30]

Even so, while Bonhoeffer thinks it is important to confess not only to God but also to a brother or sister, he does not think it is the business of the whole community—nor does he think a "general confession of sins" can suffice. Bonhoeffer stresses the importance of one-to-one confession which respects the secrecy of the confessional seal—which is, Bonhoeffer insists, a "divine commandment." Otherwise, he fears two different sorts of problems. On the one hand, the "act of confession can easily turn into exhibitionism." On the other hand, "Gossip is usually the worst evil in a congregation."

But Bonhoeffer thinks a general confession of sins cannot suffice, for it is too disconnected from the obedience of discipleship. One of two things happens when we rely on general confessions: either we despair of genuine forgiveness, and so try to substitute forgiveness of ourselves for God's forgiveness; or we feel too secure in the confident knowledge and presumption that "God forgives because that is God's business."[31] As would be expected given Bonhoeffer's polemic against cheap grace, he notes that the second, the temptation to feeling too secure, is by far the more dangerous tendency.

Repentance and confession must be particular and concrete if they are to result in that truthfulness which empowers us for faithful discipleship of Jesus Christ. That is why Bonhoeffer stresses the importance of church discipline, and why he insists that forgiveness cannot be unconditional. "In other words the preaching of forgiveness must always go hand-in-hand with the preaching of repentance, the preaching of the gospel with the preaching of the law."[32] Bonhoeffer stresses that the Church must exercise ecclesiastical discipline if it is to walk in a manner worthy of the Gospel.

Such discipline means that for contingent reasons it may not be possible to forgive and be reconciled with other brothers or sisters. In such cases, where others are unwilling to repent and engage in practices of confession, forgiveness and reconciliation, fellowship may need to be temporarily suspended and sin retained—but always "in such a manner that the spirit may be saved in the day of the Lord Jesus (I Cor. 5:5)."[33] The aim remains repentance and reconciliation.

That is, Bonhoeffer stresses that even where forgiveness and reconcilia-

tion are not contingently possible, we still must love those who are—and/or
have become—"enemies" of the cross of Christ. To be sure, there are
important differences between those who have been temporarily excluded
from Christian fellowship and those who are determinatively opposed to
the cross of Christ. Not least among such differences is Bonhoeffer's clear
recognition that even those who have been excluded from Christian
fellowship remain part of the community of the baptized.[34]

Bonhoeffer insists both that we ought to acknowledge that, in this time
between the times, Christians will have enemies, and that nonetheless we
ought to pray for them and love them. In a sermon preached at Finkenwalde in 1937, he observes:

> So Satan hardens the hearts of those who have to serve him in his struggle
> against God's kingdom and Word. They are no longer able to hear or obey.
> However, because their ears are deaf to the grace of God, their mouths are
> also mute to the righteousness of God. They are enemies of God and his
> church. David, Christ, and the church of God recognize them as such.[35]

Even more significant, however, is the sentence that immediately follows
this observation: "This realization leads us into prayer."

For what do we pray? "We pray in fervent supplication that God may
bring all our enemies under the cross of Christ and grant them mercy. We
pray with burning desire that the day may soon come when Christ will
visibly triumph over all his enemies and establish his kingdom."[36] In so
doing, we also plead to God for the sake of those enemies.[37]

Why should we pray for, and actually love, our enemies? We do so in
the imitation of God's action in Christ. For at "a time when I was God's
enemy because of his commandments, He treated me like a friend." We
also know that God loves *our* enemies—"the cross tells us that." Or more
strongly, "Christ made peace with us while we were yet enemies. He made
peace with all our enemies too, on the cross. Let us bear witness to this
peace to all."[38]

Prayer is also important in helping give us the strength to love our
enemies. As Bonhoeffer notes,

> The spirit assents when Jesus bids us love our enemies, but flesh and blood
> are too strong and prevent our carrying it out. Therefore we have to practise
> strictest daily discipline; only so can the flesh learn the painful lesson that
> it has no rights of its own. Regular daily prayer is a great help here, and so
> is daily meditation on the Word of God, and every kind of bodily discipline
> and asceticism.[39]

Whereas from the standpoint of forgiveness and reconciliation the love
of enemies is the minimum we do, Bonhoeffer also recognizes the difficult

task that is entailed therein. It requires us to give up desires for vengeance in service even to our enemies.

Thus our discipleship as forgiven sinners requires us also to love our enemies. As Bonhoeffer puts it in *The Cost of Discipleship*, "The love for our enemies takes us along the way of the cross and into fellowship with the Crucified."[40] Conversely, "He who seeks vengeance on another person thwarts Christ's death, he sins against the blood of the reconciliation. . . ."[41]

Throughout his writings on Christian community, Bonhoeffer identifies and explicates a costly forgiveness which acknowledges the importance of judgment, repentance, confession, and the love of enemies in the context of truthful Christian community marked by God's action in Christ. Bonhoeffer identifies such community as a community of the Spirit rather than a community of spirit. That is, Bonhoeffer thinks a Christian community's truthfulness, confession, forgiveness, and love of enemies distinguishes it from illusory communities based on fellow-feeling.[42]

Further, Bonhoeffer is convinced that those who are summoned to follow Christ in the life of grace, the life of forgivenness and forgivingness, will be faithful disciples witnessing to God's kingdom. That is, through confession and forgiveness we are found in a new community and liberated for service to, and more importantly among, the lowly and needy.[43]

Bonhoeffer also recognizes, however, that such a path of discipleship marked by costly forgiveness will not be widely trodden. As he puts it, "To confess and testify to the truth as it is in Jesus, and at the same time to love the enemies of that truth, his enemies and ours, and to love them with the infinite love of Jesus Christ, is indeed a narrow way."[44] It would no doubt seem even more narrow to Bonhoeffer as he observed the collapse of any coherent witness against Hitler, lamented the lack of any legitimate sense of ecclesiastical discipline,[45] and embarked on the resistance which eventually cost him his life.

At the same time, however, Bonhoeffer never lost his commitment to the centrality of God's forgiveness discovered in and through the practices and friendships of Christian community. Bonhoeffer's fiance, Maria von Wedemeyer, has reported that in prison he indicated to her that the only book "of concern to him at that moment was *Life Together*."[46] Further, the concerns identified above can be found from the earliest to his latest writings.

Even so, as Bonhoeffer moved into that phase of his life which Eberhard Bethge describes as "Sharing Germany's Destiny," and into that phase of his thought where he was concerned more with issues of "the world," there were shifts and developments in Bonhoeffer's account of forgiveness and related themes. Thus I turn now to an exploration of those shifts and developments.

II. Ultimate Forgiveness and Penultimate Responsibility

The shifts and developments in Bonhoeffer's understanding of forgiveness are directly related to his thinking about christology. That is, as Bonhoeffer became increasingly concerned with a "Christian understanding of the world" in and through Jesus Christ, so also Bonhoeffer became increasingly concerned with questions of the relevance of such notions as "forgiveness" (and related themes) to the world.

I cannot in this context give a detailed explanation of Bonhoeffer's christological reflections about "the world."[47] But those reflections underlie his understanding of three themes which do need to be developed with regard to their relevance to Bonhoeffer's understanding of forgiveness in relation to "the world": expanded conceptions of guilt, confession, and repentance; the crucial role of eschatology and, more specifically, the relations between the "ultimate" and the "penultimate"; and the enigmatic significance of the "arcane discipline" in its connection to worldly discipleship.

In *Ethics* Bonhoeffer emphasizes the importance of the confession of sin and guilt. But here, as Bonhoeffer expressly concerns himself with the world and, more specifically, the "form of Christ" taking form among us, he stresses that confession is concerned *both* with personal sin *and* with our complicity in the world's sinfulness. More particularly, he stresses our complicity in "the apostasy of the western world from Jesus Christ."[48] Bonhoeffer sees it as the task of the Church in the midst of Nazi Germany both to confess its guilt and, in the imitation of Christ, to bear the burden of it.

Such confession of guilt leads, Bonhoeffer suggests, to the "re-attainment of the form of Jesus Christ who bore the sin of the world."[49] Through submitting to, and re-attaining, the form of Jesus Christ, the Church is justified and renewed. On the other hand, however, the Western world is only "justified and renewed" indirectly through the faith of the Church. As a result, the Church experiences forgiveness and new life, whereas the nations can only hope for a healing of wounds:

> The Church experiences in faith the forgiveness of all her sins and a new beginning through grace. For the nations there is only a healing of the wound, a cicatrization of guilt, in the return to order, to justice, to peace, and to the granting of free passage to the Church's proclamation of Jesus Christ. Thus the nations bear the inheritance of their guilt.[50]

The nations' guilt is not justified, removed, or forgiven; it is maintained. Bonhoeffer asks whether it is even accurate to say that the wounds are in fact "healed." He indicates that in the internal and external political struggle of the nations, "there is something in the nature of forgiveness, though it be only a faint shadow of the forgiveness which Jesus Christ vouchsafes to faith."[51]

Bonhoeffer terms this a "forgiveness within history." The possibility of such forgiveness ought not be denied, but neither should it be over-emphasized as if forgiveness is an ongoing reality among the nations—particularly in the midst of Nazi Germany.

> This forgiveness within history can come only when the wound of guilt is healed, when violence has become justice, lawlessness has become order, and war has become peace. If this is not achieved, if wrong still rules unhindered and still inflicts new wounds, then, of course, there can be no question of this kind of forgiveness and man's first concern must be to resist injustice and to call the offenders to account for their guilt.[52]

Hence in Bonhoeffer's view "forgiveness" can only become relevant to the life of the nations and, more particularly, the Western world when "justice, order and peace are in one way or another restored, when past guilt is thereby 'forgiven,' when it is no longer imagined that what has been done can be undone by means of punitive measures and reprisals, and when the Church of Jesus Christ, as the fountain-head of all forgiveness, justification and renewal, is given room to do her work among the nations."[53]

In one sense, Bonhoeffer's argument seems simply to mark a shift in emphasis from a concern for forgiveness within Christian community to questions of guilt, confession, and forgiveness between church and world. But there is a deeper logic involved, one that can be adequately understood only from the perspective of Bonhoeffer's eschatology and, more specifically, his understanding of the relations between the "ultimate" and the "penultimate."

In particular social and political circumstances, Christians must discern whether, and to what extent, it is possible to proclaim the ultimate word of forgiveness rather than live in the penultimate realm of preparing the way—perhaps in silence.[54] Insofar as the latter ought to be done, Christians are called to acts of repentance which, for example, "resist injustice." Such actions would be necessary to prepare the way so that, at some point, "forgiveness within history" might be possible again.

In either case, however, the definitively ultimate word of God's forgiveness in Christian community is presupposed as crucial to either the eschatologically ultimate or the contemporary penultimate. Indeed, as I will suggest below in the discussion of the "arcane discipline," it would not be too strong to suggest that the larger horizons of Bonhoeffer's thought require such Christian community for the ongoing discernment of ways to live in the tensions of the ultimate and the penultimate.

Before turning to the "arcane discipline," however, it is important to make one further step in unpacking Bonhoeffer's thought. Bonhoeffer believes that, because of the predicament posed by Nazi Germany, there are times of "extraordinary necessity" in which it is unclear what ought, or even can, be done. In such situations, the "ultimate question remains open and must be kept open, for in either case man becomes guilty and in either case he can live only by the grace of God and by forgiveness."[55]

Even when justified by necessity, however, the Christian is not freed from his or her relation to, and need for, the ultimate word—both definitively and temporally—of God's forgiveness.

> Before other men the man of free responsibility is justified by necessity; before himself he is acquitted by his conscience; but before God he hopes only for mercy.[56]

It is important to recognize that Bonhoeffer indicates the person "hopes" for God's mercy; he or she cannot "presume" it. If it becomes a presumption rather than something which must be hoped and prayed for under God's judgment, then the action loses its quality of repentance and becomes a cheap and venal grace.

Thus even in the midst of situations of "extraordinary necessity" where "responsible action" is required, there still remains the guiding significance of Bonhoeffer's account of God's forgiveness and Christian community. Such terms as "confession," "repentance," and even "forgiveness" have been extended, and in some sense revised or transformed, but they continue to structure the overall shape of Bonhoeffer's argument.

This is even more the case in Bonhoeffer's enigmatic references to the "arcane discipline" in *Letters and Papers from Prison*. The significance of the term far exceeds the two brief references to it in the *Letters*.[57] Most generally, it refers to that practice in the early church whereby the "*mysteries* of the Christian faith" were "protected against profanation."[58] The aim of a recovery of this discipline would be to provide the space for, and to enable, the Christian formation and discernment necessary for appropriate action in the world.

Bonhoeffer links the arcane discipline to his distinction between the ultimate and the penultimate. Such a discipline would provide communal worship and life that preserves both the definitively and the temporally ultimate word of forgiveness, thereby forming and sustaining Christian disciples. Even so, its focus would be to discern the content of, and to enable the embodiment of, worldly discipleship made possible by God's forgiveness—thereby preserving the world's maturity.

Even more important, however, is the way in which a conception of the "arcane discipline" should change the ways in which we use theological language. Bonhoeffer thinks that too much of our language has become cheapened, trivialized, and/or made so abstract that it no longer has force or meaning in the world. A famous passage from *Letters and Papers from Prison* is worth quoting at length:

> Reconciliation and redemption, regeneration and the Holy Spirit, love of our enemies, cross and resurrection, life in Christ and Christian discipleship – all these things are so difficult and so remote that we hardly venture any more to speak of them. In the traditional words and acts we suspect that there may be something quite new and revolutionary, though we cannot as yet grasp or express it. That is our own fault. Our church, which has been fighting in these years only for its self-preservation, as though that were an end in itself, is incapable of taking the word of reconciliation and redemption to mankind and the world. Our earlier words are therefore bound to lose their force and cease, and our being Christians today will be limited to two things: prayer and righteous action among men . . . It is not for us to prophesy the day (though the day will come) when men will once more be called so to utter the word of God that the world will be changed and renewed by it. It will be a new language, perhaps quite non-religious, but liberating and redeeming – as was Jesus' language; it will shock people and yet overcome them by its power; it will be the language of a new righteousness and truth, proclaiming God's peace with men and the coming of his kingdom. 'They shall fear and tremble because of all the good and all the prosperity I provide for it' (Jer. 33:9). Till then the Christian cause will be a silent and hidden affair, but there will be those who pray and do right and wait for God's own time.[59]

This passage is as provocative as it is enigmatic. I cannot here attempt a full analysis of the passage, but four points are important for my purposes.

First, Bonhoeffer thinks many traditional Christian notions have lost their force in the world today. Hence Christians need to discover which ones are still meaningful and to preserve them from profanation by turning to the "silence" and "hiddenness" of the "arcane discipline." As far as the world is concerned, Bonhoeffer seems to be suggesting that an appropriately Christian "silence" is better than the repetition of words and notions that have become either meaningless or distorted beyond recognition.[60]

A specific example of Bonhoeffer's view is offered in a letter where he reflects on the fact that "confession" is not important to the other prisoners. Bonhoeffer writes,

> Again, the desire for confession is something quite different. I think it's infrequent here, because people are not primarily concerned here, either subjectively or objectively, about 'sin.' You may perhaps have noticed that in the prayers that I sent you the request for forgiveness of sins doesn't occupy the central place; I should consider it a complete mistake, both from a pastoral and from a practical point of view, to proceed on 'methodist' lines here.[61]

From Bonhoeffer's perspective the traditional Christian notion of "the confession of sin" is not particularly important to people in, or perhaps even intelligible in, "the world." As such, we should live in the penultimate while believing in, and having our lives formed by, the ultimate.

Second, we need to read Bonhoeffer's reference to "prayer" in the letter in expansive rather than restrictive terms. Prayer seems to be a reference to the practices of the worshipping community. Given the rest of Bonhoeffer's thought, as well as other references throughout the *Letters*, it is difficult to imagine that Bonhoeffer did not include the sacraments and (some sense of) proclamation and Bible study in his reference to "prayer."[62]

Thirdly, however, it is also the case that Bonhoeffer relativizes the significance of some practices of Christian community such as the confession of sin. This occurs primarily because of Bonhoeffer's altered conception of the problem of sin.[63] In the *Letters* Bonhoeffer no longer thinks people necessarily need to confess the sin of pride. Rather, he focuses on the new life to which people are called. As Bonhoeffer puts it, "When Jesus blessed sinners, they were real sinners, but Jesus did not make everyone a sinner first. He called them away from their sin, not into their sin. . . . Jesus claims for himself and the Kingdom of God the whole of human life in all its manifestations."[64] Or, as Bonhoeffer puts it even more strongly,

> It is not the religious act that makes the Christian, but participation in the sufferings of God in the secular life. That is *metanoia:* not in the first place thinking about one's own needs, problems, sins, and fears, but allowing oneself to be caught up into the way of Jesus Christ, into the messianic event, thus fulfilling Isa. 53.[65]

Bonhoeffer goes on to mention some of that variety: among others, there is the act of the woman who was a sinner in Luke 7–an act, Bonhoeffer notes, which she performed "without any confession of sin"; and there is also the centurion of Capernaum, held up as a model of faith even though he "makes no confession of sin." The only thing these diverse forms of discipleship have in common is "their sharing in the suffering of God in Christ."[66] Bonhoeffer here suggests that repentance occurs not so much through confession as through discipleship.

In this light, is there a place for "confession" in Bonhoeffer's later thought? It might be suggested that Bonhoeffer simply wants to displace the confession of sin from its narcissistic and individualistic tendencies (note Bonhoeffer's consistent and polemical critiques of psychotherapy), relocating the emphasis in the new life of discipleship.[67] That is, in this scenario the problem with the confession of sin, even within the Christian community of the arcane discipline, is that it is too "methodical" and insufficiently attentive to the social and political circumstances of people's lives.

Hence, a truly personal yet communal confession of sin along the lines of *Life Together* (though with a transformed conception of the sin that needs to be confessed) might still be important in enabling the life of discipleship. However, as I suggested above, it is not insignificant that in *Life Together* Bonhoeffer discusses several other practices of Christian community before turning to confession. In this light, Bonhoeffer's critical comments in the *Letters* about confession may also have been an indictment of the impoverished practices of Christian community; it may also evidence a fear that the adoption of corporate confession without such correlative practices would occasion destruction (because it would invite self-righteous judgment), rather than truthful community.

On the other hand, it might also be the case that Bonhoeffer thinks the day has passed when the language of "confession of sin" has meaning for people's lives. That is, it may be that when the day arrives when people will be called once again, in the language of the *Letters*, "so to utter the word of God that the world will be changed and renewed by it," an entirely "new language" will be required in order to provide a liberating and redeeming speech capable of "proclaiming God's peace with men and the coming of his kingdom."[68]

I am not persuaded that this is the best way to read that part of the passage in Bonhoeffer's letter quoted above. Hence my fourth point is that I doubt the language that can change and renew the world with the word of God would be—even on Bonhoeffer's terms—completely new. His language, even in the closing letters, is thoroughly theological and biblical— even in the letter calling for a "new language." My own suspicion is that Bonhoeffer's conception of the "new language" is not so radically new as some of the theologians of the 1960s thought; rather it is a language radically *purified and re-newed* through the silence and hiddenness of the arcane discipline. It seems to me that throughout his life Bonhoeffer thought confession was sufficiently important to Christian community that a purified and re-newed conception of confession would remain a crucial part of the arcane discipline.

Overall, it seems that Bonhoeffer thinks the arcane discipline, if it were practiced, would serve a crucial role in enabling worldly discipleship. It would provide the primary means for learning, among other things, the cost of forgiveness. It would also enable people to be conformed to Christ so they could believe in, and embody, the ultimate while living in the penultimate. It would preserve the mysteries of the faith from profanation, purifying the Church's language so it could once again communicate the costly grace of God's forgiveness and enable Christians to learn to see the world "from the perspective of those who suffer," or as he also puts it, "from below."[69]

III. *Toward a Trinitarian Conception of The Cost of Forgiveness*

Bonhoeffer's account of the cost of forgiveness, both in relation to the shape of Christian community and to its possibilities and limits in the world, is rich and provocative. Trying to weave together Bonhoeffer's various reflections bearing on forgiveness is important, not least because those reflections were—given his own commitments and involvements—necessarily developed on an *ad hoc* basis. Even more, weaving them together not only illumines the significance of Bonhoeffer's argument, it also provides an important contribution toward a more adequate theological understanding of the issues for our own time.

In addition, articulating the full-range of Bonhoeffer's argument reveals the inadequacies of some standard criticisms of Bonhoeffer. For example, I have already suggested why criticisms that suggest Bonhoeffer was insufficiently eschatological miss the mark. Further, I have sought to show how Bonhoeffer's arguments in such books as *The Cost of Discipleship* and *Life Together* are integrally related to both his earlier and later theological reflections.

My argument also shows why, with specific reference to Bonhoeffer's account of forgiveness, it is at best a vast oversimplification to criticize him for being too "individualistic" and/or "private" in such books as The *Cost of Discipleship* and *Life Together*. At the same time, however, I think there are important ways in which Bonhoeffer's account of forgiveness needs to be clarified, supplemented, challenged, and criticized. I want briefly to develop one such criticism.

Bonhoeffer's account of forgiveness draws together a number of topics that are often treated separately. That is one of its real strengths. Even so, he does not adequately develop a doctrine of the Holy Spirit which would show the ways in which those topics and practices are integrally interrelated.

In one sense, his lack of an adequate pneumatology is not surprising. At least since Hegel, and in many ways even before, Christian theology has paid inadequate attention to pneumatology—a problem that certainly continued to beset German theology during Bonhoeffer's life.

But Bonhoeffer's lack of attention to pneumatology weakens his argument in at least three ways. First, in Christian theology the Holy Spirit is to serve as both judge and comforter in guiding the Christian community in its ongoing deliberations about how to discern—and embody—the significance of Christ's forgiveness. This is an ongoing reminder that Christian life entails both judgment and grace, thus contextualizing Bonhoeffer's polemic against cheap grace in a pneumatology which embraces the whole range of Christian living.

Hence an adequate pneumatology is important both to the shaping of Christian community and to an appropriate discernment of the ways in which, in our various particular social and political circumstances, the relations between the ultimate and the penultimate ought to be configured. Bonhoeffer's account of such notions as "responsible action" offers few resources for such discernment.

That is, Bonhoeffer's account of "responsibility" focuses primarily on individual, rather than communal, discernment. This is understandable given the social circumstances in which he was writing, but a doctrine of the Holy Spirit would clarify what guidance and, more importantly, under whose judgment and grace "responsible action" is to be undertaken. Further, if "acts of repentance" are to prepare the way for the coming of Christ, then a more coherent account of the Holy Spirit is necessary to show how the work of the Spirit (in guiding such acts) is related to the work accomplished in the first advent of Jesus Christ.

Further, this ambiguity about the relations between the two advents is directly related to an ambiguity in Bonhoeffer's understanding of forgiveness. It is at times unclear whether Bonhoeffer thinks forgiveness is primarily restorative or re-creative. In his discussion of "forgiveness within history," Bonhoeffer uses the language of restoration. But the work of the Spirit in enabling forgiveness and new life ought to be understood as an eschatological act of re-creation, not simply restoration. This points to complex issues in trinitarian theology, but they are necessary for an adequate explication of the themes with which Bonhoeffer was so rightly concerned.

Second, and closely related, an adequate doctrine of the Holy Spirit would show more clearly how these various christological, ecclesiological, and ethical/political themes are related to the doctrine of the triune God. There is a temptation in reading Bonhoeffer, particularly *The Cost of Discipleship* and *Life Together,* to focus so intently on discipleship and Christian community that we fail—both in our practices and in our theological reflection—adequately to identify the God who is enabling that discipleship and sustaining that community. This becomes even more important with Bonhoeffer's emphasis on "worldly" discipleship in *Ethics* and *Letters and Papers from Prison.*

Third, Bonhoeffer's inadequate pneumatology can be seen in language such as "Christ existing as the church" and the church attaining "the form of Jesus Christ in the midst of the world." Such formulations fail to stress the theological importance of Christ's transcendence over-against both the world and the church. A more adequate pneumatology would have enabled Bonhoeffer to stress *both* the transcendence and the immanence of the triune God — specifically, by theorizing the Spirit's work in judging, guiding, forming and re-forming the church.

At his best, Bonhoeffer's account of the cost of forgiveness holds crucial themes together: judgment and grace, confession and thanksgiving, communal discipline and worldly discipleship, the eschatological ultimate and the worldly penultimate.[70] That is why it is disappointing that Bonhoeffer fails adequately to theorize the ways in which these themes ought to be held together in a doctrine of God that holds together the relations among Father, Son, and Spirit.

It would, however, be somewhat churlish to end on such a note. For Bonhoeffer not only pointed toward a more adequate conception of forgiveness in his theological reflection. He also embodied the cost of forgiveness in his life and in his death. It is not difficult to discern which contribution is more important to God, and hence which ought to be more important to us.[71]

Notes

1. For further documentation of this point, see Ernst Feil, *The Theology of Dietrich Bonhoeffer*, trans. Martin Rumscheidt (Philadelphia: Fortress Press, 1985), 59–96, esp. 95–6.
2. Further comments about the shape of Bonhoeffer's christology, specifically in relation to Christ's work in "the world," will be made below in Section II.
3. Dietrich Bonhoeffer, *Christ the Center*, trans. E. H. Robertson (New York: Harper and Row, 1978), 38.
4. *Christ the Center*, 51.
5. *Christ the Center*, 50.
6. *Christ the Center*, 57.
7. Dietrich Bonhoeffer, *The Cost of Discipleship*, trans. R. H. Fuller (New York: Macmillan, 1963), 54. See also 45 for the indictment of forgiveness proclaimed as a general truth.
8. *The Cost of Discipleship*, 257. On the importance of not overlooking or forgetting sin, see 258.
9. See Dietrich Bonhoeffer, *Ethics*, ed. Eberhard Bethge, trans. N. H. Smith (New York: Macmillan, 1965), 30. The translation of Mt. 7:1 offered here is the one Bonhoeffer cites.
10. *Ethics*, 30, 31. See also, on 31, Bonhoeffer's criticism of Nietzsche on this point.
11. See Bonhoeffer's comments in Dietrich Bonhoeffer, *Life Together*, trans. J. W. Doberstein (New York: Harper and Row, 1954), 91: "Self-justification and judging others go together, as justification by grace and serving others go together."
12. *Ethics*, 71.
13. *Ethics*, 31.

14. *Life Together,* 108.
15. Dietrich Bonhoeffer, "On Repentance," in *A Testament to Freedom,* ed. G. B. Kelly and F. B. Nelson (San Francisco: HarperCollins, 1990), 229–30.
16. Dietrich Bonhoeffer, "On Forgiveness," in *A Testament to Freedom,* 277. See also *The Cost of Discipleship,* 206: "By judging others we blind ourselves to our own evil and to the grace which others are just as entitled to as we are."
17. *The Cost of Discipleship,* 47.
18. Dietrich Bonhoeffer, *The Way to Freedom,* ed. E. H. Robertson, trans. E. H. Robertson and J. Bowden (New York: Harper and Row, 1966), 47.
19. For the notion that confession *is* grace, see Dietrich Bonhoeffer, *Spiritual Care,* trans. Jay C. Rochelle (Philadelphia: Fortress Press, 1985), 60. The centrality of confession for Bonhoeffer's understanding of Christian community can be seen by the extensive treatment he gives the topic in *Life Together* and *Spiritual Care,* as well as in numerous references in the other writings. Even so, there are some enigmatic passages in *Letters and Papers from Prison* which seem to relativize the significance of confession. See my discussion in Section II, below, 161ff.
20. See *Life Together,* 112.
21. *Cost of Discipleship,* 325. See also *Spiritual Care,* 63: "Confession of sin before another person is an act of discipleship to the cross."
22. *Spiritual Care,* 63. See also my discussion below, Section II, of how Bonhoeffer develops and changes his views on confession in *Letters and Papers from Prison.*
23. *Spiritual Care,* 62.
24. *Cost of Discipleship,* 155.
25. *Life Together,* 112.
26. See *Spiritual Care,* 62–3; *Life Together,* 116.
27. *Life Together,* 116–7.
28. *Cost of Discipleship,* 146.
29. See *Life Together,* 118.
30. See *Ethics,* 61; *Letters and Papers from Prison,* ed. Eberhard Bethge, trans. R. Fuller, F. Clark, et al. (New York: Macmillan, 1971), 341, 345.
31. *Spiritual Care,* 43. The quotation is from Voltaire.
32. *The Cost of Discipleship,* 324.
33. *Ethics,* 33. Bonhoeffer points further to texts such as Galatians 6 and Matthew 18:15ff. for support of this point. See also his discussions in *Cost of Discipleship,* 324ff., and "The Power of the Keys and Church Discipline in the New Testament," in *The Way to Freedom,* 149–60.
34. See "The Power of the Keys," 152: ". . . community discipline cannot be exclusion from the community of the baptised; it must always be only from the fellowship of the community of the baptised."
35. Dietrich Bonhoeffer, "Vengeance and Deliverance," in *A Testament to Freedom,* 295.
36. "Vengeance and Deliverance," 298.
37. See *Cost of Discipleship,* 166: "Through the medium of prayer we go to our enemy, stand by his side, and plead for him to God."
38. Dietrich Bonhoeffer, "Christ's Love and Our Enemies," in *A Testament to Freedom,* 299, 300, 302.
39. *The Cost of Discipleship,* 189.
40. *The Cost of Discipleship,* 166.
41. "Christ's Love and Our Enemies," in *A Testament to Freedom,* 302.

42. See *Life Together*, 31ff. Even so, I will suggest in Section III that Bonhoeffer never adequately theorizes the Holy Spirit's work in and through such community.

43. See *Life Together*, 94: "The proud throne of the judge no longer lures [the one who has experienced God's mercy]; he wants to be down below with the lowly and the needy, because that is where God found him." See also Bonhoeffer's more pointed reflection on this theme in "After Ten Years," in *Letters and Papers*, 7. Gustavo Gutierrez has commented on the significance of Bonhoeffer's argument for Latin American liberation theologies in "The Limitations of Modern Theology: On a Letter of Dietrich Bonhoeffer," in *The Power of the Poor in History*, trans. R. R. Barr (Maryknoll, NY: Orbis, 1983) 222–34.

44. *Cost of Discipleship*, 211.

45. See *Ethics*, 302.

46. Cited in *Letters and Papers*, 416.

47. For extensive discussion of this issue, see Feil, *Theology, passim*.

48. *Ethics*, 111.

49. *Ethics*, 116.

50. *Ethics*, 117.

51. *Ethics*, 118.

52. *Ethics*, 118–119.

53. *Ethics*, 119.

54. As I suggest in the final section, Bonhoeffer's lack of an adequate pneumatology precludes him from articulating more clearly the nature and context of such discernment.

55. *Ethics*, 240.

56. *Ethics*, 248.

57. See *Letters and Papers*, 281, 286.

58. *Letters and Papers*, 286.

59. *Letters and Papers*, 299–300.

60. A similar point is made by Geffrey Kelly, "Freedom and Discipline: Rhythms of a Christocentric Spirituality," in *Ethical Responsibility: Bonhoeffer's Legacy to the Churches*, ed. J. D. Godsey and G. B. Kelly (New York: Edwin Mellen, 1981), 314. See also Bethge, *Dietrich Bonhoeffer*, 783ff.

61. *Letters and Papers*, 213.

62. See Bethge's comment in *Dietrich Bonhoeffer*, 785: "The discipline of prayer, meditation, worship and coming together ('in genuine worship') is as essential—though of course, reformable—as daily food and drink. But it is also as much an 'arcane' affair as the central events of life, which are not amenable to a missionary demonstration."

63. See also above, 156, for a discussion of this altered conception in Bonhoeffer's thought.

64. *Letters and Papers*, 341–2; see also 345–6.

65. *Letters and Papers*, 361–2.

66. *Letters and Papers*, 361–2. In such cases as Bonhoeffer adduces here, as in Luke's Gospel more generally, it is discipleship that occasions repentance.

67. Although Bonhoeffer is certainly right to criticize many aspects of psychology, therapy, and psychotherapy, his polemic is overdrawn and fails to grapple with the more important contributions of psychotherapy. Hence his critique of the confession of sin might well also be overdrawn. For an instructive treatment

of Bonhoeffer's views on psychotherapy, see Clifford Green, "Two Bonhoeffers on Psychoanalysis," in A. J. Klassen, ed., *A Bonhoeffer Legacy* (Grand Rapids, MI: Wm. B. Eerdmans, 1981) 58–75.

68. *Letters and Papers*, 298–300.
69. See *Letters and Papers*, 17.
70. In addition, Stephen Fowl and I have provided a reading of Bonhoeffer that shows how he sought to hold in tension his readings of Scripture and his readings of the world. See Chapter 6 of our *Reading in Communion* (London: SPCK, and Grand Rapids, MI: Wm. B. Eerdmans, 1991).
71. I am indebted to Jim Buckley, Michael Cartwright, Jean Bethke Elshtain, Stephen Fowl, Charles Marsh, Ralph Wood, and participants at the Sixth International Bonhoeffer Conference for their criticisms of earlier drafts of this essay.

CHURCH AND NATIONHOOD:
A REFLECTION ON
THE 'NATIONAL CHURCH'

VIGEN GUROIAN

Few theologians of this century understood better than did Dietrich Bonhoeffer what it means for the Christian churches to face realistically a post-Christendom world. Bonhoeffer called this phenomenon a "world-come-of-age." His criticism of the churches in light of a world-come-of-age today seems ever more prescient. Bonhoeffer saw that for large numbers of people living in the nations which made up Christendom God was no longer experienced in the old religious sense. In this cultural environment, the churches of a national and establishmentarian character were becoming fossils of a by-gone world. They were failing to bring the gospel to modern people. Early in his career, Bonhoeffer began a life-long reflection on the fate of the national church and alternatives to historic formations of Christian existence.

Bonhoeffer believed that with the passing of Christendom the churches had been given a special opportunity. The churches might now lay hold of their true freedom which through the long history of Christendom (Roman Catholic and Protestant) had been compromised. The collaboration of the German national church with Nazism came as no real surprise to Bonhoeffer. Nevertheless, it was devastating proof of where the conservative and accommodationist proclivities of this historic type of church could lead. In the face of this, Bonhoeffer insisted that the true freedom of the church is not something gained by sacralizing the temporal order, nor a privilege granted by the state. The true freedom of the church is not even freedom from state interference, as Anglo-American Christianity thought. "The freedom of the church is not where it has possibilities, but only where the Gospel really and in its own power makes room for itself on earth, even and precisely when no such possibilities are offered."[1]

In the last year of his life, as his hopes for release from a Nazi prison faded, Dietrich Bonhoeffer's thoughts about the future of the church increased. Six months before his death he wrote a sermon for the occasion of the baptism of his infant nephew and name-sake Dietrich Wilhelm Rudiger Bethge. In it Bonhoeffer spoke as if he were anticipating the possibility of what happened after the war. He hoped and expected that the German "church, which has been fighting these years only for its self-preservation, as though that were an end in itself," would change greatly by the time his nephew was grown up. He warned, however, that much yet needed to be corrected. "[A]ny attempt to help the church prematurely to a new expansion of its organization will merely delay its conversion and purification."[2]

It has been said that the greatest tragedy for the German church which came of Dietrich Bonhoeffer's death was his absence after the war. For immediately following the war, Bonhoeffer's fears came to pass. The Western allies and conservative forces within Germany used the national church structure once again to service the German state. Church leaders rushed "to secure their privileges in the shell of the same old state church."[3] Similarly, today the churches of formerly Soviet lands enter the world scene with a propensity and drive to reclaim lost privilege and power. They show little understanding of the challenges of post-Christendom to their historic faith and ecclesial polity. Tragedies for Christian existence threaten as these churches grope their way toward freedom. Soviet imperialism muted their nationalism and phyletic tendencies and shielded them from religious and secular pluralism. For as long as seventy five years these churches were frozen in medieval establishmentarian attitudes. At the same time, many stood as the sole symbol of national pride and identity in their country. Now ecclesiastical leaders are seizing the opportunity to align their churches with new nation states. Thus Bonhoeffer's analysis of the national church, as well as his worst fears and best hopes for the church, shed crucial light upon the church and state situation in Eastern Europe, Russia and the Caucasus.

The Armenian Church, with its deep history and strong national flavor, is especially apt for study in this Bonhoefferian light. There is much at stake in what this church will become for Armenians and for all others among whom it has been dispersed by the genocide of 1915. The Armenian church is behaving presently as if nothing has changed since the genocide and the long soviet captivity. Its conservative apologists argue that

Armenian culture and national identity are the special achievements of the church. They do not distinguish between what might have been in medieval Armenian Christendom, or what was in the latter centuries of the Ottoman Empire, from what has come to pass after the genocide and seventy years of soviet history. Yet Bonhoeffer's assessment of the church's situation in a world-come-of-age demands that the church conscientiously practice discernment, self-criticism and a public witness to the true freedom in Christ. In this essay I write for the sake of my church in Armenia, but also for all other churches whose faithfulness to the gospel of Jesus Christ is under trial as a new world order emerges. I look consciously and with appreciation to Dietrich Bonhoffer as a witness to the church's mission in these unusual times.

I. Old Habits and New Realities

In the late 1970's, during the bleak and repressive twilight of the Breznev era, the religious dissident Michael Meerson-Aksenov contributed a powerful piece of samizdat literature which analyzed the character of the national churches under Soviet domination. Strikingly reminiscent of Bonhoeffer's writings on the national church, Meerson-Aksenov sounded a keynote of admonition and hope for the post-Soviet life of the church. He wrote:

> A local national Church, torn away from other Churches and therefore from any ecumenical position, cannot be free. Depending on how much authority it has and on internal political conditions it can conclude more or less advantageous concordats with the State and can even transform the social order into a theocracy, but all this is a far cry from real freedom . . . .
> A national Church must inevitably share the fundamental political views of its government and place the objectives of the State's foreign policy above the interests of love among the churches . . . .
> Only the Ecumenical Church can be free [because it is] transnational, is spread everywhere, and no strictly homogeneously organized society has enough power to fully subordinate it.[4]

Meerson-Aksenov insisted that a new vision of the church would need to supplant the old forms which belonged to a by-gone sacral order. Though having followed a different path than Western societies, communism also altered permanently the future of Christian faith. Meerson-Aksenov emphasized this fact. He argued that when the system of official atheism was finally lifted, the church would be forced to come to terms with a new secular, pluralistic order filled with people of a variety of religious and non-religious persuasions. "The Russian Church, . . . [which had] inherited the cast consciousness of the clergy and the inert psychology of a dependent State establishment"[5] would be tested in its ability to preach the gospel and serve people in new and unfamiliar ways. "The fifteen hundred year era of the Christian empire has come to an end," declared Meerson-Aksenov, "and former Christian societies everywhere are hurrying to remove their priestly vestments. The Christian no longer lives in an environment of co-religionists."[6] Ultimately, even in once Holy Russia the world of the old national and establishmentarian-minded church would pass. But would this same church know this, admit this and respond appropriately?

In the initial phases of transition from soviet to free societies, the national churches (and other "independent" churches which have grown into the same mentality) have followed form in their efforts to reclaim old power and influence. The Armenian Church is an example. Even as a new, autonomous, secular and more pluralistic society is emerging, the church continues to claim that Armenia is a Christian nation (a Christendom) of which the Armenian Church is mother and guardian. Every seven years at the historic center of the Armenian Church, the See of Holy Etchmiadzin, the Holy Chrism is consecrated and distributed to churches everywhere for the sacramental rituals. September of 1991 was the occasion for such a blessing. As is customary, His Holiness Vazken I, Catholicos of All Armenians, presided. The event coincided with the extraordinary moment of newly gained Armenian independence. The patriarch's sermon, which one might have expected to refer to that event, went much further. Vazken I inaugurated a new civil religion in which the church's role loomed large and unchanged from the pre-Soviet past. No longer restrained by Soviet dogma and threat, Vazken I asserted that the church would stand at the very center of the nation building process. He asked that the government grant the Armenian Church special privileges.

The patriarch declared: "Today, it is only just to acknowledge the Armenian church as the proto-witness, the forerunner, of our national independence."[7] He called upon the Armenian government to grant the Armenian Church *de jure* status as the established national church. This appeal was carefully set within the context of a powerful rhetorical rehearsal of the Armenian Church's historic struggle against absorption by the Byzantines and others—the "history of the Armenian Church . . . [in] heroic battle against the expansionist desires of foreign churches." Now this protector of the "souls of the Armenian people" is under siege of "proselytizing ('man hunting'), . . . churches [which have entered] the bosom of our nation," exclaimed the patriarch. Thus "after the proclamation of our independent republic, it is crucial to secure the spiritual independence of the Armenian Church, as the sole authentic church of the Armenian people, free from foreign religious centers . . . One of the foundations of our new independent government," insisted Vazken I, "is the freedom and self-determination of the Armenian Church."[8] The patriarch's dramatic remarks also betrayed the church's forgetfulness of what its true freedom is. He defined this freedom as a grant of the state.

The new government has bestowed upon the Armenian Church the legal status as the single church in Armenia. All other denominations remain under the description of religous communities and are explicitly prohibited from proselytizing. The Roman Catholics and Baptists have had an historic presence in soviet Armenia. Since the opening up of Armenia, Mormons, Seventh Day Adventists and Pentecostals have been extremely active. The Armenian Minister of Religous Affairs, Lugwig Khachadrian, in an interview granted during the fall of 1991, merely echoed the rationale given by the Cathlicos for the Armenian Church's priviliged position. Khachadrian stated that "considering the persecution of the Armenian Church . . . we have created special opportunities for the Armenian Church and have given certain privileges, so that the Church may recover what she lost." Yet Khachadrian saw no contradiction in also claming that "there is no difference between the Armenian Church and other churches or religious groups, because the legal system that we have adopted assumes that everybody is free to choose his religion or faith and is free to practice his religion"[9].

Khachadrian's comments echoed the new *Law of Armenia on Freedom of Conscience and Religious Organizations* promulgated in June of 1991. The document contains the same logical contradictions as Khachadrian's statements. The preamble declares "the Armenian Apostolic Church as the national church of the Armenian people and an important stronghold of its spiritual life and the preservation of the nation." Later under Article 7 of Section 6, "Relations Between Religious Organizations and the State," we read: "In the Republic of Armenia the church is separate from the state." Several senses in which this holds true are enumerated with respect to powers and limitations applying to church and state respectively. But the *Law* seems to want it both ways. There will be separation of church and state, and yet there is a national church with privileges normally associated with church establishment. The same article goes on to state that "the Armenian Apostolic Church [is] the national Church of the Armenians, which also operates outside the Republic, [and] shall enjoy the protection of the Republic of Armenia." Part 1, "General Principles," declares: "In the Armenian Republic the citizens' "[f]reedom of conscience and religion is guaranteed." However, under Part 3 "The Rights of Religious Organizations," Article 8, "proselytism—[literally translated "soul stealing"]—is prohibited on the territory of Armenia." The term is not defined any further, although the article goes on to say, "No action within the limits of the rights indicated in Article 7 . . . may be regarded as proselytizing." The most significant of these rights include: the conduct of religious services in a variety of places, freedom to provide religious education for members, freedom to train clergy, and the use of the media according to the established law. The term proselytism has a distinctly negative connotation in Armenia. It identifies religious antagonists bent upon stealing Armenians from the mother church. Many of the freedoms and activities protected in Section 4 under Article 7 would count for evangelization as that term is understood in Western democracies where religious freedom is guaranteed. How proselytism might be distinguished in practice from such evangelization is not explained in the *Law*. To further confuse matters, under Part 6, the draft speaks of "missions which are the privilege of the national church." These privileges of the Armenian Church include: the right "to freely confess and spread its belief throughout the territory of the Republic of Armenia," "to build new churches," and "to contribute in practice to the moral standards of the Armenian people."[10]

Even with all its contradictions and lack of clarity, *The Law on Freedom of Conscience and Religious Organization* leaves one distinct impression, that the Armenian Church has a special legal and moral status in Armenia. The reasons why the new Armenian democratic government would oblige the church's pleas for special favor range from the strong residual existence of an establishmentarian mentality among even non-religious people in Armenia to the more pragmatic, political calculation that the church remains for the time being a unifying symbol for the nation. While the patriarch has insisted on various occasions that in the political realm the church takes no sides, the fact remains that the church is well on its way to compromising itself severely *vis-à-vis* the secular authorities—this, tragically, in the name of the church's freedom.

On the ideological plane, Vazken I's civil theology leaves few resources to distinguish the freedom of the church from the *raison d'être* of the national state. The patriarch's sermon for the blessing of the Holy Chrism concluded with a peroration in which he drew together all the strong symbols of Armenian church, nation and peoplehood:

> On the foundations of our new independent government is the freedom and self-determination of the Armenian Church.
>   We profess the Creed: one free nation, one free government, one free national Church.
>   With this Creed, with this understanding, we proclaim this holy chrism, which has been blessed by the power of the Holy Spirit, as the "*Chrism of Independence* (my emphasis)."

Armenians, our spiritual children, with this Holy Chrism, unite! Be brothers! Become one will! One happiness! One suffering! One nation! One family! One strong oath! And beneath their eternal sight of biblical Ararat, with the blessings of Holy of Etchmiadzin, believe in this one patch of Armenian soil and its future.[11]

The partiarch thus wove strands of the Armenian "sacred history" and the belief in Armenia as a specially chosen people of God upon the warp of the Armenian struggle for national independence. This peroration was built upon remarks earlier in the sermon in which the patriarch reminded his listeners of St. Gregory the Illuminator who, "with his miraculous works, achieved the conversion and baptism of the Armenian King Dirtad." It was according to the vision of St. Gregory that the Armenian Church and the cathedral of Holy Etchmiadzin were established where "the only begotten son of God descended." The patriarch asserted that this revelation and act of founding forever mixed "the spirit of the Armenian nation . . . with Christ's Gospel. . . . The Armenian people were transfigured and became a creative nation . . . History is witness to the fact that through Christianity the Armenian nation became a universal phenomenon."[12] This rhetoric leaves the illusion of universalism. In fact, it draws near to national idolatry.

For most of this century, Armenians everywhere have listened to incessant preachments of this kind by hierarchs and clergy. The final message is that the Armenian Church belongs to the Armenian people and *is* in some mystical sense the nation. As the South African theologian John W. de Gruchy has rightly concluded about Afrikaner religious nationalism: "There is nothing wrong with the idea of a church for the people, but a major problem arises when 'the people' is confined to a particular race, class, or *volk*, . . . for then the church denies not only its universal or catholic identity, but also the gospel."[13]

At this moment in history, the Armenian people deserve a better church than the nationalistic one. In a time of great peril and bloody hostility with Azerbaijan over the Armenian enclave of Nagorno-Karabagh, the church, by identifying itself so closely with the *ethnos* and the state, is in jeopardy of rendering itself incapable of offering a voice of restraint at a time when Armenian nationalism, so largely a function of the nation's long festering sense of victimization, might become an actual threat to the nation's life and future.

II. The Enduring Message of Dietrich Bonhoeffer on the 'National Church'

Dietrich Bonhoeffer began to envision a new relation of church and nation early. In his doctoral dissertation, *Sanctorum Communio* (1927), he struck a keynote for all he had to say through changing times. "There is a moment," the young theologian declared, "when the church dare not continue to be a national church, and this moment has come when the national church can no longer see how it can win though it be a gathered church . . . , but on the contrary is moving into complete petrification and emptiness in the use of its forms, with evil effects on the living members as well."[14]

Drawing on Ernst Troeltsch's typological distinction between the churchly and sectarian varieties of ecclesial formation, Bonhoeffer distinguished between a "gathered church" in which the voluntary principle prevails and a *Volkskirche* (or national church) which relies almost exclusively upon forces of kinship and common national history. Bonhoeffer was not unappreciative of these cohesive organic and historic qualities of a national church. A national church "possesses greater firmness and lasting power than the voluntary association," he observed. "It is a divine grace that we have a church which is deeply rooted in the history of the nation, which makes the divine will for us, given through the power of the church's historicity, relatively independent of the momentary situation."[15]

Yet in *Sanctorum Communio* Bonhoeffer already had concluded that the German national church was not responding adequately to the new conditions of secular modernity. Characteristically, he reflected upon this matter in dialectical terms. "[W]e can affirm that the national church and the gathered [voluntary and evangelical] church belong together." But it was "all too obvious . . . that a national church, which is not continually pressing forward to be a confessing church is in the greatest of peril."[16] These suspicions and admonitions were confirmed by the disappointing conservatism of the German national church and the acquiescence of the German Christian (Deutsche Christen) movement to the Nazi program. The national church proved incapable of distinguishing the confession of Jesus Christ from even the most excessive forms of nationalism and chauvinism. In *The Cost of Discipleship* (1937) Bonhoeffer lamented, "We Lutherans have gathered like eagles round the carcass of cheap grace, and there we have drunk of the poison which has killed Christ." The church had clung to all the right doctrines through the centuries. But "a nation had become Christian and Lutheran, . . . at the cost of true discipleship. Cheap grace had won the day."[17]

Bonhoeffer's later statements on a confessing church, a "religionless Christianity" and a "world come of age" are largely consistent with his early views on the weaknesses and strengths of a national church. In *Sanctorum Communio* at the close of his discussion of the national church, Bonhoeffer wrote: "We have reached the point where such questions" of defining a different *modus vivendi* for the church, with renewal of prayer and worship and mission in the world "must be decided."[18] During the 1930's, he watched the rise of threatening nationalisms. Bonhoeffer became even more convinced that the time had come when the German national church could no longer persist in being what it had been while also remaining faithful to the Gospel of Jesus Christ. In 1935, Bonhoeffer warned: "Under the onslaught of new nationalism, the fact that the church of Christ does not stop at national and racial boundaries but reaches beyond them, so powerfully attested in the New Testament and in the confessional writings, has far too easily been forgotten and denied."[19]

A decade after his reflections on the national church in *Sanctorum Communio*, Bonhoeffer explored the origins of modern nationalism. This analysis in the *Ethics* bridges his early work with the loose and incomplete discussion of a religionless Christianity and a world come of age in the *Letters and Papers from Prison*. In the second and third chapters of the English translation of the sixth German edition (1963), Bonhoeffer describes the French Revolution as the distinctive moment of "the birth of modern nationalism. Whatever national consciousness existed earlier," he argues, "was essentially dynastic in character. . . . The revolutionary concept of the nation arose in opposition to an exaggerated dynastic absolutism."[20]

Bonhoeffer's thinking about nation and church drew increasingly upon the conviction that Christendom indeed had been shattered ideologically and geo-politically in the eighteenth and nineteenth century. The process began in the Renaissance and Reformation, but assumed fully modern characteristics only with the Enlightenment and French Revolution. "The people deemed that they had come of age, that they were now capable of taking in hand the direction of their internal and external history."[21] No longer did they need or want peoplehood and government to be defined under the sacred canopy of Christendom. In the nineteenth century, radical voices of anticlericalism and atheism arose, which angrily protested against Christendom. The vision of a unified Christendom was challenged and empirically shattered. Large and small fragments of Christendom, however, continued to live on within national cultures under the signs of nation state and national church.

In the twentieth century, Nazism and Communism were symptoms of, as well as contributing factors to, the break-up and final eclipse of Christendom. These outbursts of radical politics and totalitarianism were gestated from within national environments where traditional religious forms abided simultaneously and in contradiction with virulent anti-Christian forces. "Since the French Revolution," observed Bonhoeffer, "the west has come to be essentially hostile to the Church. . . . Yet the Churches lose remarkably few of their members, and this points to an important fact, namely the ambiguous character of the hostility to the Church."[22] As they entered the twentieth century, the masses remained under the sway of various forms of Christian pietism and religious introversion at one pole and religious, sometimes highly aggressive, nationalisms, at the opposite pole. Those who continued to identify with the church often found comfort in corrupted and anachronistic "religious" concepts of sacral nationhood. Bonhoeffer called this "the godlessness in religious and Christian clothing."[23] Yet for a time, this late corruption of Christian existence continued to provide symbols of legitimation for legal establishments of national churches in Europe.

Bonhoeffer believed that the break up of Christendom everywhere was a loss of serious consequence and ominous foreboding. "By the loss of the unity which is possessed through the form of Jesus Christ, the western world is brought to the brink of the void. The forces unleashed exhaust their fury in mutual destruction."[24] Modern nationalism and atheist ideologies substituted for the unifying power of Christendom. But these forces did not satisfactorily acknowledge the transcendent destiny of humanity, nor the this worldly rights and responsibilities humanity owes its own kind. In the face of this "void made god"[25] Bonhoeffer tried to envision what new worldly "formations" of faith in Jesus Christ might look like. This work was begun in the *Ethics* and was restated in his *Letters and Papers from Prison.*

While the project was never completed, in *Letters and Papers* we have hints of where Bonhoeffer was heading. He called these new formations of Christian faith a "religionless Christianity." Religionless Christianity is faith in Jesus Christ stripped of the religious culture which such faith once inspired, a culture which prospered for a millennium as Christendom, fragmented with the birth of modernity, and persisted for a much shorter time in so-called "Christian" nations. National churches were those indigenous churches which fashioned garments for themselves out of the pieces of the sectioned quilt of Christendom. Modern nationalisms, meanwhile, often used the loose religious concepts of a fragmented and eviscerated Christendom to promote their own ends. Increasingly, nationalist ideology supplanted or pushed into the recesses of private life the lingering religious categories of transcendence and spiritual world (already corrupted forms of biblical faith) and replaced these with immanentistic and vitalistic categories of ethnic identity, racial purity or national destiny.

In this analysis, the negative characteristics of national churches come to light. The nature of their compromise with secular ideology is evident. Their abandonment of the evangelical faith and an ecumenical vision is not to be overlooked. The positive organic qualities of kinship, common history and respect for tradition retain a value, but they threaten to contribute to reactionary forces within church and nation. Because of its very nature and history a national church finds it difficult to forge a new mode of ecclesial existence. As a primary carrier of reified and hollowed out forms of religion, a national church naturally resists the conclusion that the social and political body it once sanctified is no more. It has much to lose in privilege and influence if these new circumstances are acknowledged. Instead, deeply rooted habits of survivalism are triggered within a national church when doubts arise that it can go on being what it once was. The threatened national church embraces nationalistic stirrings in a people whose loyalty it fears it might lose. It tries to retain its privileges through ever more explicit and insistent identification of church with *ethnos* and nation.

The rise of Nazism, in which all these trends seemed to culminate, moved Bonhoeffer toward a broader definition of church and an intense examination of the meaning of the freedom of the church, its being and boundaries. As Larry Rasmussen has pointed out, for Bonhoeffer the 1930's were years in which "the tensions of being Christian and being German drew taut."[26] Bonhoeffer's decision in 1939 not to stay in the United States, but to return to Germany, was a conscious choice to commit himself to the particularity of Christian existence as a citizen of the German nation. He would enter the church struggle in Germany and try to secure integrity for the church. The Confessing Church had sought to resist "both the Aryanizing of the church and the totalitarian claims" of the Nazis.[27] Ultimately, involvement in this struggle for the integrity of the German church would have to take precedence over Bonhoeffer's ecumenical activities. But those activities already had provided him with a perspective from which to re-evaluate the relationship between faith, nationality and people of God. While Bonhoeffer would not wholly abandon the concept of a national church, he sharply condemned the heresy to which all modern national churches have been prone, the subordination of the ultimate communion of all the faithful in Christ to the penultimate reality of national identity.

III. The Course of Armenian Christendom and the Origins of the National Church

The sources of the national character of the Armenian Church run as deep and far back as perhaps any church. This history includes Armenian Christianity's early divorce in the sixth century from Greek Christianity over the christological issue. For centuries afterwards, a vastly larger and more powerful Byzantine Christendom was a threat to the Armenian Church. The Armenian Church's isolation and vulnerability were intensified by the Arab-Muslim invasions of the seventh century. The Armenian Church was not the only church in isolation. Other churches were similarly estranged, the Syrian and Coptic, for example. Five centuries of Ottoman domination completed the transformation of these churches into ethnic and national churches. The Armenian patriarch Karekin II, Catholicos of Cilicia, has summarized this long history.

> A decisive turning-point in the whole history of the Eastern churches, and more specifically in the realm of church-nation relationship, was the Arab-Muslim invasion of the seventh century, which had a strong impact on the development of their national character.
> . . . [T]he conquers allowed them [the churches] to exist as separate entities within the Muslim world. . . . [They] were given internal independence, an autonomous status, on the basis of . . . religion. . . . The Christian people themselves, after the loss of their political independence or after their emancipation from Byzantine rule, regarded the church as the only expression of their national heritage. So they clung to it, and recognized its head as the leader of the nation. Thus, "the national churches found themselves transformed into some kind of ecclesiastical state, where bishops wielded political as well as religious authority, and whose patriarchs blossomed into the political leaders of their flocks, naturally under the supremacy of the Khalifs."[28]

After the fall of Constantinople in 1453, the new Ottoman rulers recognized "two Patriarchates, the Greek and the Armenian, as the centres of the Chalcedonian and non-Chalcedonian Eastern churches, with full authority over their peoples in everything but political action."[29] Ironically, the Ottoman rulers did not abuse the churches of their establishmentarian attitude. The Greek Church carried this over from its partnership with the Byzantine state. The Armenian, Syrian and Egyptian churches had practiced the same within their own "small" Christendoms. The antinomy of church and world, necessary for the church and good for the world, lost its sharpness. When one speaks of the lost freedom of these churches under the Ottoman rulers and the increased identification by the people of church with *ethnos*, one must include also the loss of a sense of mission and a deepening survivalist mentality.

This description of these churches holds through the modern period, but with some important twists and turns along the way. The European Enlightenment, the French Revolution and nineteenth century liberal, romantic and nationalist movements caught the imagination of Greeks, Bulgarians, Armenians and others. The churches were bound to feel the effects. The nineteenth century is crucial. For in that century two contradictory forces co-existed within these national and church bodies. A traditional folk religion and a very conservative national church shared the same space with virulent anticlerical and anti-religious movements. Newly emerging secular intelligentsia and political parties competed with the church for the soul of the nation. At stake was a claim to the authentic voice for national aspirations. The story of this struggle is conspicuously absent from the narratives of contemporary church apologists. In the effort to justify a continued intimate association of church and nation, most of the church leadership constructs myth out of history.

The whole of this history cannot be told here. But at least a few aspects of it which influence the church's own self-understanding need to be said. The short of the matter is the following. While the Ottoman millet system persisted into the nineteenth century, it was being challenged by rising nationalisms within the various ethnic communities. This led to the final unraveling of the Ottoman Empire itself. Early in the nineteenth century, Greece became independent. This was followed by the break-away of the Balkan nations. Thus the empire earned the name "The Sick Man of Europe." The Armenians too were effected by these trends. By mid-century, nationalist fever was running through the Armenian millet. Because the vast majority of Armenians were situated right in the heart of Asia Minor, dreams of national renaissance tended to be tempered. They focused on reforms that would achieve greater freedom and autonomy short of independence.

This nationalism had a distinctively secular cast. It was not yet anointed or religionized by the Armenian Church. In fact, those who championed nationalism were inclined not to look favorably upon the church. They envied its power or openly criticized its conservatism. The new Armenian bourgeois class became discontented with the millet system, because that arrangement left virtually all community power in the hands of a feudal-minded church. This helps explain why anticlerical and atheist influences from Europe found fertile soil among Armenian intelligentsia and within the first Armenian political parties. These groups viewed the Armenian patriarch's close association with the Ottoman power structure as a source of corruption not serving the best interests of the Armenian populace.

The opportunity to change the arrangement arose in the 1850's as a result of the Crimean War. A weakened Sultan Abdul Medjid agreed to reform initiatives. Among these were general provisions to create assemblies among the minority communities. These assemblies would be made up of both clergy and laity. Thus, in 1863 the Ottoman Sublime Porte ratified a new Armenian National Constitution which forever altered the structure of power within the Armenian community. Now power was to be shared between the patriarch and the National Assembly. This lent impetus to powerful secular nationalist stirrings among the intelligentsia and the rise of autonomous political parties. However one judges the degree of corruption or conservatism within the Armenian Church at the time, the empirical and historical nineteenth century reality was that the church did not invent, and certainly did not lay sole or even primary claim to, early Armenian nationalism.

Many important Armenian voices of the mid-nineteenth century saw the work of national renewal as a secular and political task for which the church was not suited. These nationalists blamed the Armenian Church for the ill fate that had befallen the nation. They said that the church taught the people passivity and pacifism in the face of threats to national survival. As one historian of the modern period has observed: "The Armenian Nation, rather than God," became "the chief source of inspiration" for Armenian intellectuals and political writers.[30] The most influential Armenian novelist of this period, Hakob Melik-Hakobian (1833–1888), who went by the pen name Raffi, wrote this famous toast into his novel *Jellaledin*. It typifies the anti-clericalism of the time:

> O fathers! O fore-fathers! I drink this glass, but not as toast to your remains. Had you built fortresses, instead of monasteries with which our country is full; had you guns and ammunition, instead of squandering fortunes on Holy urns; had you burned gunpowder instead of perfumey incense at the Holy altars, our country would have been more fortunate. . . . From these very monasteries the doom of our country was sealed."[31]

Echoing Raffi, Grigor Artsouni, an Armenian nationalist and political writer who received a degree at Heidelberg University, proclaimed, "Yesterday we were an ecclesiastical community; tomorrow we shall be a nation of workers and thinkers."[32]

In her classic study *The Armenian Revolutionary Movement*, Louise Nalbandian observes that this anti-clericalism ran to extreme in the 1860's on the heels of the new Constitution. During that time, "the Armenian Church was under constant attack."[33] But by the last two decades of the century, intellectuals and political leaders began to change their minds about the church. They now saw the church as a useful focal point of Armenian life. It could be an instrument of the national ideal. Those holding otherwise radical political views now "looked with disfavor" upon the "idea of reform within" the church.[34] They wanted it to serve as a conserving and cementing force of ethnic identity. Now the church's purpose and role within the nation was being defined by these secular forces. The new intellectual and political leadership had won the preponderance of power within the community. They felt sufficiently secure with their position to permit the church to go on thinking it was at the center of Armenian life, thus using it for their own purposes. The church along with the nation had suffered under the Ottoman rule. There was no reason to support a continuation of the *status quo*.[35] Church leaders committed themselves to the nationalist ferment, though not without voices of restraint and even dissent.

As it entered the twentieth century, the Armenian Church generally embraced, frequently with great enthusiasm, the role of safeguarding Armenian identity prescribed for it by the secular founders of modern Armenian nationalism. The history of this coalescence of religion and nationalism, and the submission and compromise of the church to nationalist movements, has not been evaluated critically by Armenian Church historians and theologians. The undeniable objective events of genocide, a worldwide Armenian diaspora, and the Soviet subjugation of the last remnants of the historic homeland, instead, provided the Armenian Church with occasion and excuse to rationalize and justify its behavior.

IV. Archbishop Tiran Nersoyan: An Armenian Theological Critique of the Nationalistic Church

In the intervening eighty years since the genocide, the Armenian church hierarchy and clergy have constructed a religio-national myth out of these circumstances and this history. This myth places the origin of the present secularized nationalistic church back in the very founding acts of the Armenian Church of the fourth and fifth centuries. It is preached and argued in all sorts of public forums that the religionized nationalism which the church promotes is the very faith of the founders of the church and its martyred defenders through the centuries.

To my knowledge only one modern Armenian churchman has exposed this myth for what it is and has explained the danger it presents for the church and the disservice it does to the nation. Archbishop Tiran Nersoyan (1904–1989) was the most brilliant and influential Armenian clergyman of the twentieth century. Among the several diocesan posts in which he served as bishop was his election in 1944 as Primate of the Diocese of the Armenian Church in America. He was in that position for eleven years. Nersoyan was a scholar, ecumenist and translated many of the primary Armenian liturgical texts into English. As a young deacon and priest in Jerusalem during the 1920's and 1930's he commenced his career as a theologian with articles written for the publication *Sion*.

In 1928, Nersoyan penned an article entitled "Nationalism or Gospel." There he stated boldly that the role of preserving ethnic identity and promoting Armenian nationalism was not the church's *raison d'être*. He reminded his readers that among those who now were encouraging this behavior and this role for the church were the disciples of a generation who had condemned "the Church [as] the graveyard of the people [and] . . . championed the cause of atheism."[36] Nersoyan's message was twofold. On the one hand, he reminded the church that in its midst there were wolves in sheep's clothing cynically using the church as a conserving force of ethnic cohesion and as a tool of nationalism. On the other hand, Nersoyan was calling the church back to its true purpose as witness of Jesus Christ and servant to the Armenian people. He was drawing the distinction between an enlightened and *confessing national church*, fully engaged in the world and with other churches, and a *narrowly nationalistic church* whose hubris would continue to blind it to the illegitimate use being made of it by enemies of Christ. Thus, he warned:

> . . . because of the ignorance of some, the intentional distortion of acts by others, the indifference of still others who should be most watchful, a secondary benefit derived from our Church, i.e. the preservation of our ethnicity, is presented as her only purpose and calling. As this misunderstanding further spreads and gets rooted in people's minds, it obviously harms both the cause of Armenian nationhood and nationalism, and does even more harm to the true calling of the Armenian Church, which, alas truthfully, she is still far from understanding and accomplishing.[37]

Nersoyan explained that the view promulgated by the ecclesiastical powers, that the "Church [is] the same with our nation, [and is] . . . the only protector and sponsor of our national identity," was incorrect. If the church now carried a burden of preserving ethnic identity, that was "only a partial quality of . . . its national character" imposed by an accident of history, "a consequence of the circumstances . . . [of an] absence of a viable national institution . . . , i.e. we never had a strong government, a dominant culture, or a nation with a concentrated population."[38] The present situation should not be reified as a normative description of the church's being.

Furthermore, the "accented nationalism" of the Armenian Church had to be understood in the context of a larger phenomenon of the breakdown of the "moral and intellectual foundations"[39] of the western world. The "tremors" of this had been felt in the old Ottoman Empire. From a distinctively Armenian perspective, Nersoyan was touching upon the very themes of the European crisis theology of the time, forged by such people as Karl Barth, Emil Brunner and Dietrich Bonhoeffer. That theology cannot be understood apart from the context of the aftermath of World War I.

One need not speak at length about the utterly devastating genocidal consequences of World War I for the Armenian people. Although, Nersoyan certainly had this in mind when he addressed the sources and meaning of modern nationalism generally and Armenian nationalism in particular. By taking seriously this new context in which theology and ecclesial life had to be conducted, he performed an invaluable service for the church's own self-understanding vis-à-vis Armenian nationhood. "Every penetrating mind can see," he wrote, that "the leaders of mankind want to be armed against it—[this breakdown of order]—and want to take measures for self-defense. The consequence of this presentiment for self defense is the growth of the idea of nationalism." Nersoyan defined nationalism as expressing both positive and negative possibilities. At crucial moments in a nation's history, when the idea of nationalism runs through it, choices are made which determine whether nationalism provides the inspiration for national rehabilitation and health or becomes the source of self-harm and destructive acts. Nationalism, he observed, can lead to "continuous and persistent efforts to establish lasting good relations" among nations. But nationalism can also assume a ruinous "dominance" in the national life. This, he worried, was what was threatening to happen in Armenian national life.[40]

"Nationalism or Gospel" was written just a decade after the genocide and only five years after the soviet takeover of Armenia in 1922. Nersoyan sensed that with the tragedy of genocide, the dispersion of hundreds of thousands of remaining Armenians into Europe and North America, and the new Soviet republic of Armenia, the Armenian Church and its relation to the "nation," near and dispersed, could never be the same. Especially in the diaspora Armenian political and religious life was carried on in a strange disembodiment from the Armenian soil. Armenians, "motivated by the presentiment of destruction," were resorting to the use of nationalism as a "shelter." The nation, he observed, "wants to cling totally to this idea, and through it open for itself a path of light in this dark labyrinth where everyone is grouping." Yet, there was a danger in this passion for the ideology of nationalism. This presentiment of destruction was becoming an obsession. Fear and self-pity were threatening to overcome hope and a larger spirit. Thus the creation of institutions which might realize the highest aspirations of nationhood were being hampered. "We cannot keep step with modern civilization by creating a culture that is born out of sad recollections and very shallow and often mediocre and worthless works. . . . And now, to overcome all these sad realities we need a new vitality, courage, gentleness, inspiration, a new thinking."[41]

The church had a role to play in the redemption of a people. But it was not the role that others had been urging upon it or that the church was deflected toward by circumstance. The church should not permit herself to become a "tool to promote nationalism. . . . That is not her calling. . . . The virtue of our church's Armenian saints is in their zeal as Christians and not in their nationalism. . . . They strived and they sacrificed their lives to lift up Armenian human beings through the grace of Christ. . . . They were not nurtured by mediocre mentalities like 'preserving the nation.'" Other kinds of political and cultural institutions were far better suited to pursuing the nationalist idea and vision. To the contrary, "every time she [the church] has tried to champion the cause of nationalism, the cause itself has suffered."[42]

Nersoyan understood that modern civilization, especially in its present condition of "decay," was not Christendom. If Christendom had passed on, the virtues of its faith and moral character remained worthy of retrieval. The idea of Christendom lingered in Nersoyan's mind not as a romantic reminiscence but as a worthy memory from which the church might recall and rededicate itself to its only true vocation, that of being a mission of salvation in the world. He did not look back sentimentally to a past golden age to which the church might return. Armenian Christendom had been a happy outcome of the evangelical life of the church. But it was this evangelical activity which was most important. At one point in "Nationalism or Gospel," Nersoyan observes, "the accented nationalism of our church is the result of her failure, for various reasons, to embark on foreign missionary activities, which is her top-most Christian duty."[43] The church before all else is this mission to the world, not nation builder, not even Christian nation builder.

In the midst of this ecclesiology, Nersoyan strove to envision a new national life. Within this life autonomous political institutions would carry out the idea of nationhood as a secular goal. He wrote: "The Armenian nation must look for other sources to assure the perpetuity of its nationhood." The church does not recede into a private sphere of conscience or personal piety. Rather, it assumes a truly public role of forming Christ anew in the people. Nationalism may not be what the church's purpose is about, but peoplehood is. "A healthy character and a pure spirit must be nurtured in our people through Christ and the Gospel. We must express our repugnance of becoming an evil and morally bankrupt nation because such a nation would soon fall. The Armenian Church must be mindful of her calling and devote herself to it alone. That is the only way to revitalize the Armenian people. Our people must have a life, and Our Lord came so we may have life and have it abundantly."[44]

V. The Fate of the National Church

Like Bonhoeffer, Archbishop Tiran Nersoyan did not reject wholly the idea of a national church. He wanted to navigate the church back to its primary purpose of mission and forming Christ in a people. Nersoyan and Bonhoeffer understood that a national church which does not make critical adjustments to the new situation of autonomy and secularity after Christendom is in jeopardy of complete ossification and irrelevance. Perhaps worse still, in circumstances when nationalism reaches a fever, a national church of the old establishment mentality is especially tempted to acquiesce or even lend support to the destructive proclivities and outbursts of the nation state.

Archbishop Tiran Nersoyan's life ended just before the commencement of the next crucial stage in the history of his church and the nation. Nersoyan died in 1989, two years before the independence of Armenia. In conversations we had before his death he spoke frequently of the necessity for completely rethinking the relation of the church to the nation and the Armenian diaspora to the people of Armenia. Had he lived longer, he might have helped to envision a new role for the national church.

The jockeying for power by the Russian Church and the Roman Catholic Church in Poland, and the terrible tension between competing Ukrainian Orthodox and Catholic churches, testifies to the scope of this issue of the national church in the newly emerging international order. National churches are struggling for identity and purpose where the reality of post-Christendom no longer is camouflaged by the Soviet system. But for this reason also the external pluralistic world looks especially threatening. The behavior of the Armenian Church illustrates the powerful temptation of many of these national churches to take cover within the nation from outside forces. Just when the future of the new Armenian nation depends so heavily upon full participation in the community of nations, the

Armenian Church is yearning to return to its former comfortable institutional and ideological identification with the nation. Yet a genuinely ecumenical church would be of far greater service to the nation. This ecumenical church would have the perspective from which to be a witness to the nation of the larger universal vision of the Christian faith.

In his samizdat article cited at the start of this essay, Meerson-Aksenov proposes a *modus vivendi* for the Russian Church which combines total "outward" participation in the world with intense "inward" ecclesial formation. "The Christian today is called above all to be conscious witness of his faith, and departure from the world is far from the best means to testify to it."[45] He continues:

> Every age finds its own means of seeking God. The Apostles found God in a crowd, and the anchorites followed Him into the desert. The many voices of the world call out from all sides, showing us where His presence must be sought and where the light of faith which He has lit must be carried. . . .[46]

Meerson-Aksenov insists that today the light of faith must be carried in new desacralized, secular places. This forces "the Church out from all of its former comfortable positions, [but] also . . . to strive for the concentration of all its spiritual energies, all its activities, all of its vital powers." A rigorous exercise of a "worldly" Christianity achieves its mission only if there is a commensurate retrieval and renewal of ecclesial community and discipline. To accomplish this the church "must return to that organic state of unity of the faithful which prevailed in the first centuries . . . when all Christians were 'like living stones built in a spiritual house' (1 Peter 2:5). All participated in the sacraments instead of just being spectators. . . . All were part of the 'royal priesthood.'"[47] Meerson-Aksenov regards the revitalization of these organic, communal, sacramental and evangelical characteristics of the church as the work of a new lay movement in the line of the apostles and early monastics.

Bonhoeffer had spoken of the same. He called it the "arcane discipline." And like Bonhoeffer, Meerson-Aksenov looks to restoring the "inner" ecclesial community of prayer and worship as part of a dialectical movement of the church "outward" in service to the "other." Where might this convergence of ecclesiology in Bonhoeffer, Nersoyan and Meerson-Aksenov lead when doing theology and ethics? New possibilities for ecclesial formations challenge the options created by the birth of modernity. The choice between a national or established church verses a "free church" has been surpassed. I believe that Bonhoeffer understood this. He realized that the historical free churches were no less developments of the Reformation and the break up of Christendom than were the national churches. He was looking beyond into a different world-historical context.

CHURCH AND NATIONHOOD   191

Even in the early *Sanctorum Communio,* Bonhoeffer argued that a national church and a gathered (or voluntary) church are not necessarily opposites, though in their modern manifestations of church and sect they tend to appear so. Troeltsch himself had left the impression that these two types were virtually exclusive of one another.[48] Ironically, the [churchly] church which is a national church can save its catholic character only if it begins to embody the voluntary principle of the sect type church. Otherwise, the national church will become purely a reserve of antiquated national life and ossified theological and ecclesiastical forms. After Christendom it is crucial to affirm that "the national church and the gathered [voluntary] church belong together, and [even more important] that . . . a national church, which is not continually pressing forward to be a confessing church, is in the greatest inner peril."[49]

Franklin Littell has shown that through this scheme of analysis Bonhoeffer envisioned a confessing church that is an alternative to both church and sect types of Christianity. Both the old type of national church and the old pattern of free church were committed to formations of Christian life that were inadequate for addressing the gospel to the new person come of age. The first conceived an uninterrupted continuum of church and culture. The latter was a "fortress concept" of a band of disciples huddled together in opposition to the world. "Bonhoeffer's quest was for a new statement of the church, not in terms of static pattern–'continuum' or 'fortress'– but in terms of mission to the world."[50]

Littell regretted that Bonhoeffer was limited in his understanding to "the Pietistic, conventicle-type German 'free churches.'"[51] Had he been acquainted with other historic forms of the free church, Bonhoeffer might have concluded that the free church is not necessarily a fortress church. The British Baptist theologian Keith W. Clements has sought to clarify the Bonhoefferian dialectic in a fashion which challenges Littell's reservations. Clements argues that Bonhoeffer understood all too well that after Christendom the differences between state church, free church and Roman Catholic church no longer are what they once were. After Christendom "all [churches] become confessing churches-and equally all could be inhibited from becoming so, by blindness, fear or inertia."[52] Clements gives the contemporary example of the British free churches, so many of which have become havens from an inhospitable world for middle class people.

Clements maintains further that Bonhoeffer saw how even a "'free church' is subject to manipulation by extraneous and sometimes sinister forces, at precisely the point where it feels itself to be free from the godless world, just as the national church can complacently assume that by its very existence it is upholding the divine order in the world. In both cases the question of the gathered people, bound to the Lord and to one another, can become the choice to be a church on one's own terms, in order (consciously or otherwise), to serve one's own particular social, political — and religious — interests." The church ends up accommodating "to the society as it is, rather than providing a critique of it."[53] Bonhoeffer himself had commented upon what had become of the free church principle of freedom, not just in Germany but in America. The free act of word preached and deed performed had become confused by American Protestants with a gift granted by the state under the formal provisions of the "free exercise" clause and the separation of church and state. Once having historically understood their freedom as the command and commission of God to take the gospel everywhere, even free churches had accepted their "place" within a denominational society under the umbrella of the American Way.[54]

In recent times, South Africa and the Soviet Union have provided further examples of the accommodation identified by Bonhoeffer. With these historical lessons before us, Bonhoeffer's treatment of the national church question is that much more compelling. The particular circumstances of the national churches in post-Soviet societies differ in significant ways. But the Armenian and other post-Soviet church examples, interpreted in a Bonhoefferian light, do advance our understanding of a larger complex situation. We have seen that the question of the national church raises two distinct issues which must be confronted. The first is church establishment. Many of the former Soviet churches will want to regain this status in old and new forms. They must be denied. The dangers in granting such privileges have been mentioned throughout this essay. In addition to state establishment there is a second issue which is even less easily solved. This is the problem of a church which is ethnocentric and suspicious of those who are racially and religiously different. The problem is not restricted to national churches. Free churches too can be ethnocentric.

In conclusion, the indigenous character of the national churches will not soon be shed. The dangers of new and old religious nationalisms must be addressed with realism. Otherwise, the new opportunities for renewal of the formerly Soviet churches cannot be creatively exploited. Something of the character of a national church will remain. In most cases, however, the pre-modern folk church character will recede. Nearly half of the population of Armenia lives in the capital city of Yerevan and its environs. The traditional village religion may persist in some places but not among vast numbers of urban people. Due to past forces of ottomanization and sovietization the Armenian Church has also been gutted of much of its doctrinal conviction, and it cannot sustain any longer its hold on the imagination and hearts of people with old forms of sacrament and liturgy. The church, if it is to be anything more than a keeper of ancient temples and artifacts, will have to come to terms with these weaknesses. It will have to take on more of the characteristics of what Bonhoeffer called a confessing church. The voluntary principle of the free churches and the gospel call to witness must more and more define the existence and behavior of the Armenian Church. But this transformation will not come easily.

The Armenian Church is now in a stage of denial—denial of the loss of its old world. It, like other such churches, will likely have to be shaken out of its present state of mind. At the same time there are movements of ecclesial renewal in Armenia. The *K'tutyune* (literally translated "compassion") organization is an example. On the one hand, *K'tutyune* exhibits the character of a western style voluntary charitable group. Its cadres of volunteers visit homes of the sick and needy, distributing food, clothing and medical supplies throughout the country. On the other hand, *K'tutyune* is an evangelical faith movement, sometimes in tension with the church leadership. But its members regard themselves as faithful to the church. Indeed the *K'tutyune* membership overlaps with an even more broadly based church centered evangelical group *Yeghpayrutyune* (Brotherhood). This organization holds prayer meetings in homes. It sponsors large public rallies in which sermons are delivered by lay ministers. New hymns have been created. *Yeghpayrutyune*, which until 1990 was a para-church organization alienated from the institutional church, now has the official sanction of the church. Since independence and the new freedom of religious practice in Armenia, members of *Yeghpayrutyune* have assumed the lion's share of the burden for religious instruction in the parishes. Similar things, though not on the same scale, have happened from within the traditional structures of the Armenian Church. The most significant is a vital lay and youth movement encouraged by the Bishop of Yerevan, Karekin Nersissian in his diocesan church of St. Sarkis. *K'tutyune* and *Yeghpayrutyune* are significant manifestations of a new confessing and evangelical form of Christian community attuned to an Armenia coming of age. They are well ahead of most sectors of the Armenian Church. It remains to be seen, however, whether such movements will become a source of serious ecumenical consciousness and turn the Armenian Church toward a new and energetic life of witness to Jesus Christ.

There is no simple answer to what the future has in store for the national churches of former Soviet societies. Even the most favorable outcomes will not resolve wholly the division of the catholic and apostolic faith into a variety of cultural embodiments. In a world which the Father of Creation has salted with so many different peoples and cultures, it is not always easy to sort out what is sinful in the national church from that which is a function of human finitude and historicity. Nevertheless, Dietrich Bonhoeffer gave all the churches a theology which profoundly fathomed the complexities of Christian existence and the challenges the churches faced after Christendom. Through his life and death, this Lutheran pastor cast a light forward into our time which illumines for all churches a path of truth and faithful witness to Christ.

Notes

1. Dietrich Bonhoeffer, *No Rusty Swords* (New York: Harper and Row, 1965), 104.
2. Dietrich Bonhoeffer, *Letters and Papers from Prison* (New York: Macmillan, 1972), 300.
3. Thomas I. Day, "Conviviality and Common Sense: The Meaning of Christian Community for Dietrich Bonhoeffer," in *A Bonhoeffer Legacy: Essays in Understanding*, ed. A. J. Klassen (Grand Rapids, MI: Wm. B. Eerdmans, 1981), 22.
4. Michael Meerson-Aksenov, "The People of God and the Pastors," in *The Political, Social and Religious Thought of Russian "Samizdat"–An Anthology*, ed. Michael Meerson-Aksenov and Boris Shragin (Belmont, MA: Nordland, 1977), 524–5.
5. Meerson-Aksenov, 524–5.
6. Meerson-Aksenov, 534.
7. "One Free Nation, Free Government, Free National Church," Address of His Holiness Vazken I Catholicos of All Armenians on the Occasion of the Blessing of the Holy Chrism (September 29, 1991), *Window: View on the Armenian Church* 2/3 (1991): 30.
8. *Window*, 31.
9. *Window*, "Church and State in Armenia: An Interview with Ludwig Khachadrian," 4.
10. Foreign Brodcasting Information Service-USR-91-016, "Armenia," July 23, 1991, 14–6.
11. *Window*, 31.
12. *Window*, 30.
13. John W. de Gruchy, *Liberating Reformed Theology* (Grand Rapids, MI: Wm. B. Eerdmans, 1991), 24–5.
14. Dietrich Bonhoeffer, *The Communion of the Saints* (New York: Harper and Row, 1963), 189–90.
15. *Communion*, 187–8.
16. *Communion*, 189.
17. Dietrich Bonhoeffer, *The Cost of Disipleship* (London: SCM Press, 1959), 44–6.
18. *Communion*, 190.
19. *No Rusty Swords*, 326.
20. Dietrich Bonhoeffer, *Ethics* (New York: Macmillan, 1965), 100.
21. *Ethics*, 100.
22. *Ethics*, 103. Of course, since Bonhoeffer wrote these words the European churches have lost massively in numbers of communicants.
23. *Ethics*, 103.

24. *Ethics*, 103.
25. *Ethics*, 106.
26. Larry Rasmussen, *Dietrich Bonhoeffer: His Significance for North Americans* (Minneapolis: Fortress Press, 1990), 36.
27. Rasmussen, 36.
28. Karekin II, *In Search of Spiritual Life* (Antelias Lebanon, 1991), 257.
29. Karekin II, 257.
30. Quoted by Leonardo P. Alishan, "Crucifixion Without 'The Cross': The Impact of the Genocide on Armenian Literature," *The Armenian Review*, 38 (Spring 1985): 34.
31. Quoted by Sakris Atamian, *The Armenian Community* (New York: Philosophical Library, 1955), 79.
32. Quoted by Alishan, "Crucifixion," 33.
33. Louise Nalbandian, *The Armenian Revolutionary Movement* (Berkley: University of California Press, 1963), 57.
34. Nalbandian, 57.
35. John Meyendorff, *The Byzantine Legacy in the Orthodox Church* (Crestwood, NY: St. Vladimir's Seminary Press, 1982), 226-7.
36. Tiran Nersoyan, "Nationalism and Gospel," *Sion* (September, 1928). Republished in *The Armenian Reporter* [New York], (October 5, 1989): 3.
37. Nersoyan, 3.
38. Nersoyan, 3.
39. Nersoyan, 3.
40. Nersoyan, 3.
41. Nersoyan, 18. Nicholas Wolterstorff has analyzed nationalism similarly in *Until Justice amd Peace Embrace* (Grand Rapids, MI: Wm. B. Eerdmans, 1983), 105-11.
42. Nersoyan, 18.
43. Nersoyan, 3.
44. Nersoyan, 18.
45. Meerson-Aksenov, "People of God," 534.
46. Meerson-Aksenov, 535.
47. Meerson-Aksenov, 535.
48. *Sanctorum Communio*, 186.
49. *Sanctorum Communio*, 189.
50. Franklin Littel, "Bonhoeffer's History, Church, and World," in *The Place of Bonhoeffer* (New York: National Board of Young Men's Christian Association, Association Press, 1962), 36, 37.
51. Littell, 36.
52. Keith W. Clements, *What Freedom? The Persistent Challenge of Dietrich Bonhoeffer* (Birmingham: Church Enterprise Print, 1990), 105.
53. Clements, 103.
54. See, for example, Bonhoeffer, *No Rusty Swords*, 108-9, and *Ethics*, 104-5.

THE EXEMPLIFICATION OF DECISION IN DIETRICH BONHOEFFER[1]

Luca Bagetto

I. The Church as the Community of Decision

It is easy to argue that the concept of decision is central to Dietrich Bonhoeffer's work. This position arises from Bonhoeffer's constant conversation with Karl Barth's theology, in which the concept of decision under God's claim (*Anspruch*) and the importance of "beginning at the beginning" ("*mit dem Anfang anfangen*") are at stake. Moreover, the concept of decision was hotly debated in the cultural milieu of the post World War I Weimar Republic and in the aftermath of the Kierkegaard renaissance.

Bonhoeffer's theological beginnings were marked by a preoccupation with the historico-institutional "origin" of the decision of faith as a divine appeal. The *Sanctorum Communio* is the church intended as the community of decision—where one decides individually and communally. In the community the appeal is admittedly *ad personam,* but it is marked as well by a trans-individual and historical aspect. Revelation does not manifest itself only in the instant of evidence and in the punctuality of the individual's decision, but unfolds itself in the historical continuity of the community: the appeal creates a *habitus,*[2] a condition of which one *can* have knowledge, without objectifying revelation, and which makes possible the continuity between the old and the new.

I have the suspicion that the discussion in *Sanctorum Communio* and in *Act and Being* about the discontinuity of the decision of grace with respect to the normality of the 'natural' does not have its origin in Lutheran conceptions of the Christ as both gift (*donum*) and example (*exemplum*), but in the influence of Gerhard Leibholz and his study, "*Das Wesen der*

197

Repräsentation.'[3] In the course of the twenties Bonhoeffer may have drawn from talks with his childhood friend (and future brother-in-law) the knowledge of the juridical debate of the Weimar Republic, in which the figures of Carl Schmitt and Hans Kelsen dominated. Leibholz had borrowed the concept of 'representation' from Schmitt's work; in the latter, representation makes present the absentee and mediates between the transcendent legitimation of power and the immanent legality of continuous history.

Schmitt had come to the theological concept of representation by way of the concept of the visibility of the church. The visible church bears a double representation in that it historically represents the Christ, which in turn represents transcendence. In the visible church, the decision that represents transcendence confers unity to the historical continuity of the ecclesial order (*Ordnung*). For Schmitt, as a Catholic, the visible church is a historical mediation in which the transcendent unity of God takes on the form of a legal succession: an inheritance. Maybe Bonhoeffer's variation on the Barthian theme of the discontinuity of the divine appeal is to be found in this concept of historical continuity, through Leibholz's mediation. Thus, the issue of representation would also be the origin of the Catholic features many interpreters have detected in Bonhoeffer's *Sanctorum Communio*.

Notwithstanding any influence Leibholz may have had on Bonhoeffer, it is certain that the latter—already in his first university course in Berlin in 1931—used the concepts of the Lutheran tradition in order to place side by side the continuity of revelation and its character of discontinuous appeal. According to Luther, as it is well-known, the Christ *donum* signifies the gratuity and non-disposability of revelation, which constitutes a break with human works and thoughts. Jesus as *exemplum* is the historical model, the Protestant answer to the Catholic sense of continuity. The *exemplum* represents a model of hermeneutical transmission that unlike the Catholic notion of tradition does not dispose of its own origin.

The theme of Christ as *donum* (*Urbild*, present as gift but also as evidence) and Jesus as *exemplum* (*Vorbild*, present as exemplary life that one can continue) of the Protestant faith guided Schleiermacher in founding modern hermeneutics. The concept of "technical" interpretation translates the notion of '*donum*,' and that of "grammatical" interpretation translates the notion of '*exemplum*.' The discontinuity of the *donum* (the present as gift and as evidence) stands for the true-God Christ, and corresponds hermeneutically to the leap out of the historical continuity for 'divining' the individuality of the other. The continuity of the *exemplum* of the true-man Jesus corresponds to the historical exegesis of texts, which inquires into the immanent relationships between parts and wholes and which turns to historical exemplary authorities.

In comparison with Schleiermacher, for whom the *donum* (the present as gift and as evidence) manifests itself in the "feeling of absolute dependence," Bonhoeffer held the position of dialectical theology. Indeed, Bonhoeffer suggests that faith has nothing to do with feelings, but deals rather with the spoken Word of God. But Bonhoeffer also criticizes Barth for conceptualizing the "divine appeal from above" still in subjectivist terms, and argued that modern Kantian subjectivism should be delegitimated:

> Even in Barth . . . the individual is the subject of the knowledge of God. What one has to know (through revelation) becomes subjectivized. There is no possibility for participating with the Other, who can receive such a knowledge only from time to time from God.[4]

Thus Bonhoeffer wanted to overcome the subjectivistic intentionality of revelation by conceiving the "act" of faith in the event of 'always already being in the Church': "The act of entry in the community is the ground of faith, just as faith is the ground of that entry."[5] This is the theme of *Sanctorum Communio* and *Act and Being*.

Nevertheless, Bonhoeffer is unable to pursue the theological direction sought in the early writings because theology cannot reconcile the demands of transcendental philosophy with Heideggerian ontology. The result of the early writings was that the transcendental act (of faith) expresses the free and contingent character of revelation—which always already precedes *a priori* individual works—whereas being (the Church) signifies the historical continuity of revelation in which community members are always already situated. But since the contingent character of revelation is expressed by the transcendental act, the contingency merges with the subjective act of faith, conceived as a condition which enables the knowledge of revelation in its historical and communicative aspect. The act makes being possible and not vice versa: there cannot be any mutual conditioning between transcendentalism and ontology. Therefore, only the act of faith acknowledges and enables the being of the community.

During his years at Union Theological Seminary in 1930–31, Bonhoeffer turns away from the early impasse between Kant's transcendental philosophy and Heidegger's ontology by focusing on the primacy of revelation. The intentionality of the social gospel towards the whole person (*anthrōpos teleios*), towards the world and modernity, suggested that the 'now' of revelation is not the instant of the decision of faith. The conversation with the present time belongs to revelation insofar as revelation is handed over in time. Revelation makes a decisive break with history, but it wants to be interpreted according to place and time. If in *Act and Being* Bonhoeffer intended the expression "contingency is only in the present" in accordance with the meaning of immediacy and of the 'present' evidence, now he intends it in a hermeneutical sense as the 'present' of the *kairos*. The contingency of revelation is no longer founded by the non-disposability of the transcendental act, but by the eschatological dimension of the church in Bonhoeffer's lectures, "The Nature of the Church." The tension between the *Christus praesens* as community and the coming Christ of the parousia begins the hermeneutic movement of the Church towards its place and time, and its search for a trace of the promise.

In this hermeneutic turn (*Kehre*) Bonhoeffer went beyond the subjectivism of the religious act to the advantage of the communicative and hermeneutic character of the knowledge of revelation.

> Instead of seeking refuge in transcendental philosophy, it is necessary to form and keep an ecclesiastical theory of knowledge. Only in this way can we get round the danger of subjectivism.[6]

The *ekklesia* is the historical milieu in which revelation takes shape and makes itself present. In hermeneutic terms, interpretation always already "takes place" or is carried out in the context of a community. Thus Bonhoeffer asks in the 1930s: how do we carry out the appeal to the Church's historical situation? How do we proclaim the kerygma with the language of historical continuity? How do we reconcile the *donum* (the present) of faith with the concrete and historical *exemplum*? These questions raise the issue of how the relationship between the Church and the world has to be understood from the point of view of historicity. Is the historicity of the Church similar to that of the world? Does the Church have any privilege with respect to the world?

The aim to found the concreteness and the historicity of the Gospel's *donum* shapes Bonhoeffer's different positions up to the *Ethics*: from the elevation of the State which safeguards the secular community, to a form of the Kingdom in Bonhoeffer's lecture "Thy Kingdom Come," to the inclusion of the absolute beginning – the *donum* – in the middle of historical facticity in *Creation and Fall*; from the historical hiddenness of the christological *pro nobis* in his *Christology*, to the daily *exemplary* life pervaded by the faith's *donum* in *The Cost of Discipleship*. In all these solutions, Bonhoeffer kept the *tertius usus legis*: faith remains the condition for acknowledging 'true' history, 'true' secular continuity. The believing community is aware of the historical facticity.

My thesis is that Bonhoeffer challenged the Church's claim to privileged status (the privilege of the *peritomē*) in disclosing the real meaning of facticity:

In what way are we *ekklesia,* those who are called forth, not regarding ourselves from a religious point of view as specially favored, but rather as belonging wholly to the world?[7]

The discontinuity of the divine "appeal" and "calling" as *donum* takes place by taking on historical facticity without possessing a privileged, transcendental understanding of its real meaning. Bonhoeffer discloses this view of facticity only in the letters from prison.

II. Interpreting Existence "in the Middle" of History

Bonhoeffer begins to question the Church's privileged status in the world in the *Ethics,* by focusing on the Christological ground of reality as the reconciliation of norm and fact, of being and having to be. Ethics is the *Bildung* (formation) on the *Bild* (form) of Christ, who reconciles being and having to be and grounds the possibility of living Christianity in full fidelity to the earth. Here, in the *Ethics,* Bonhoeffer turns his attention away from the *tertius usus legis* to the *primus usus* of the law of the Hebrew Scriptures: the Christ-*donum* is 'present' in the *disciplina externa et honestas* ("external and honest discipline"). The worldly orders are brought back to the christological foundation, and the continuity of the law is brought back to its decisive origin. But if in the *Ethics* the church is the only order which knows this origin and shows it to the other mandates of the state, the family and work, in the prison letters, on the contrary, the full "this-worldliness" of the Christian discloses the meaning of historical facticity. Thus, Bethge's original title to the *Letters and Papers from Prison, Widerstand und Ergebung,* best exemplifies the issues raised by Bonhoeffer: the *Widerstand* (resistance) of the norm and the *Ergebung* (submission) of facticity must be composed in Christ. The letters, however, go a step further. On February 21st, 1944 Bonhoeffer writes: "So that in the last resort my question is how are we to find a 'thou' in 'It' (i.e. fate), or in other words, how does fate really becomes 'guidance'?"[8] How does the Christian decision emerge from historical continuity? How does the promise emerge from pure facticity? How are we church, namely "those who are called forth," without being religiously—i.e. transcendentally—privileged?

Bonhoeffer's perception of the empty and senseless time of his detention—his destiny—retrieves the nostalgia for historical continuity as the bourgeois expression of fidelity to the earth. The nostalgia *which listens to* time is already an interpretation, because it breaks the *unilinear* sense that is imposed on time. The place of "meaning" is thus located where one "listens" to time according to the mode of presence of Christ as *donum.*

The meaning is disclosed at "the center of the village," where one "listens" to and takes on the facts of destiny, instead of sanctioning them in conformity to a telos.[9] The acceptance of one's own destiny corresponds to the interpretation of "resurrection" in the Christian tradition of *caritas*. The critical awareness of living in the midst of historical continuity renders *actual* the *donum* of resurrection.

By contrast, religion is an effort to deny life in the midst of history by focusing on individualism, or transcendental privilege, to escape from facticity. Similarly, religion is the lack of mediation and interpretation—Barth's "postivitism of revelation"—the immediacy of a religious *a priori* of humanity whose decision is not made in accord with love for the world, but with an ideological commitment to keeping a place in the world. The concept of "unconscious Christianity" in Bonhoeffer's letter of July 27, 1944 seems to address the same issue of "being in the middle" of the *donum*, and to refute the comprehension "at a distance" typical of transcendental awareness. Similarly, the arcane discipline directs us towards the interpretation and the facticity of "being in the middle." In fact, the fundamental aspect of the Christian tradition is this, that truth is "in the middle."

III. Bonhoeffer and the Mirror of Modernity

Christ as the mediator is the image and the sensible form of the intelligible Father. Nevertheless, only the modern crisis of the Principle's intelligibility and the killing of the Father by the world "come of age" stressed the role of the mediation between humanity and truth. Since truth has become obscure, the mediation is no more a transparent lens through which one can see the light of the intelligible Principle. Mediation for modernity is a mirror reflecting the look, transforming what was an instrument to see into a *medium* which is an end in itself. Starting with the first "reflecting" elements of Kantian philosophy, mediation turns upon itself, and not upon what is to be seen. The mediation turned upon itself, unable to look beyond itself, is the "gaze" of modernity. Since mediation is no longer a transparent lens through which one could see the light of the intelligible principle, the truth remains obscured. But the mediation of transcendental schematism, which shows the intelligible concept—even though it founds itself upon the productive imagination and not upon the reproduction of what is already product and shows itself to be seen—applies still the christological mediation between the sensible and the intelligible.

In particular, Kant's notion of schema retrieves the Christian *exemplum*, but leaves the *donum* obscure. The essence of the unknowable experience

of freedom is *exemplifying*, and is founded upon the productive imagination, so that the noumenon is shown by a communicative and inter-
subjective relation: this, for example, is the truth. The universality of the
example is always a universal consensus, and is similar to a general truth.
Yet it is an undetermined, rather than a necessary one.

Heidegger highlighted the role of the schematism in Kant's philosophy.
In his interpretation, we *must not, rather than cannot, say anything* about
the thing-in-itself. Even better, we have to say "nothing." Since thought
is subordinated to the realm of the sensible, mediation is carried out only
in the middle of facticity. It is well known that Bonhoeffer draws on Heidegger's concept of the Being-already-in of care, that is, of mediation, as well
as his critique that modernity reduces thought to a medium as an end in
itself. In my opinion, Bonhoeffer belongs to the mainstream of modernity
in his according primacy to interpretation (mediation) over the text. The
truth's mediation attracts a vision upon itself by stressing interpretation
rather than the text. The mediation of modernity is an interpretation of
the Christian *exemplum,* that is, an interpretation of historical facticity. Thus,
Bonhoeffer refutes the immediacy of religious individualism by focusing
on the primacy of the mediation carried out by the history of interpretations. According to Bonhoeffer, this is also the communitarian and communicative, i.e., non-subjectivistic, aspect of the Christian faith. Bonhoeffer
refutes "immediacy" because it belongs to the demand for evidence carried
out by the metaphysics of subjectivity, which calls for the *imitation*, rather
than the *exemplification,* of the truth.

The difference between imitation and exemplification is that the former
does not derive from historical continuity, from facticity, but from the
"moment of evidence." Imitation prescribes a reductive verification, and
follows a logic of unmasking that Bonhoeffer detested. Thus, one can better
understand Bonhoeffer's refusal to articulate questions like: what really
happened in the historical event of Jesus of Nazareth? How can we hold
onto the effectiveness of Jesus of Nazareth upon each and every subjective *imitation*? Instead, Bonhoeffer thinks that the truth of Christianity is
not a universal, metahistorical idea imitated by a subjective, religious *a
priori*. "The Word is itself Church,"[10] and "the Word of God is the thing
itself."[11] This means that the *donum* lives from exemplifying historicity.

Yet, unlike the reflexivity characteristic of modernity, Bonhoeffer (refusing immediacy) does not obliterate the text to be mediated. The Christian
original image of mediation remains the "text" that must not be obscured.
Christ represents God, and therefore Christ is not only example but also
gift. This is the meaning of resurrection. For Bonhoeffer, the historical
mediation must remain transparent, and not reflective (it cannot turn upon

itself), in order to show what is "beyond." This is, for me, the essence of the witness and the martyrdom which Bonhoeffer offers to us as *exemplum* of the assumption of historical facticity. His death is a Christian exemplification of what is beyond. His death is a "showing" of the truth that is always mediated by an interpretation: it is an example.

Notes

1. I wish to thank Massimo Baldi for his aid in the translation, and Luca D'Isanto for his helpful discussion of the paper and for his choice of some terms.
2. Dietrich Bonhoeffer, *Gesammelte Schriften*, V (Munich: Chr. Kaiser, 1972), 340ff.
3. Gerhard Leibholz, *Das Wesen der Repräsentation unter besonderer Berücksichtigung des Repräsentativsystems* (Berlin-Leipzig: de Gruyter, 1929). The title of the 1973 edition is *Die Repräsentation in der Demokratie*.
4. Dietrich Bonhoeffer, *Das Wesen der Kirche* (Munich: Chr. Kaiser, 1969), 31, my translation.
5. Dietrich Bonhoeffer, *Sanctorum Communio* (Munich: Chr. Kaiser, 1969), 36; *The Communion of Saints*, trans. Ronald G. Smith et al. (New York: Harper & Row, 1963), 116, translation altered.
6. *Das Wesen der Kirche*, 31, my translation.
7. Dietrich Bonhoeffer, *Letters and Papers from Prison* (New York: Macmillan, 1972), 281.
8. *Letters and Papers*, 217.
9. "The church stands not at the boundaries where human powers give out, but in the middle of the village." Dietrich Bonhoeffer, *Letters and Papers*, 282.
10. Dietrich Bonhoeffer, *Christology* (London: Collins, 1964), 59.
11. Dietrich Bonhoeffer, *Gesammelte Schriften*, vol. IV (1965), 240.

Part IV:

Postmodern Perspectives

BONHOEFFER AND DECONSTRUCTION: TOWARD A THEOLOGY OF THE CRUCIFIED LOGOS

WALTER LOWE

It has been argued in recent years that we live in a period of cultural transition, a watershed period comparable to the Enlightenment in importance, but quite different from the Enlightenment in worldview. Key among the characteristics of this "postmodern" age are the dissolution of any unitary, "metaphysical" world picture, and the "deconstruction" of the human subject. This postmodern vision bears a *prima facie* similarity to Dietrich Bonhoeffer's account, half a century earlier, of a world which would have outgrown the temporary crutches of metaphysics and inwardness.

It is the initial purpose of this essay to probe these similarities, to see what may lie behind them. The more fundamental intent, however, is to enter into a "loving combat" with Bonhoeffer regarding the status of human reason. Accordingly, the essay will proceed in six sections. The first section describes one account of postmodernity, inspired by the French philosopher and critic, Jacques Derrida. The second section sketches an independent view of Derrida's thought, a sort of deconstructionist primer. The third section brings that view of deconstruction to bear upon the notion of postmodernity and upon Bonhoeffer's world come of age. In the second half of the essay, the issue of postmodernity recedes and the issue of reason comes to the fore. The fourth section formulates an implicit norm which seems to be operating in Bonhoeffer's thought. The fifth assesses Bonhoeffer's own theology in light of the norm. And the sixth draws a few implications regarding "the way Christ takes form among us here and now."[1]

I. Postmodernity

Within American reflection on religion, the most vigorous champion of the notion of postmodernity is undoubtedly Mark C. Taylor, author of *Deconstructing Theology, Erring* and *Alterity.*[2] In a manner reminiscent of "a world come of age," Taylor recalls Nietzsche's proclamation of "the death of God." To interpret this historical-cultural phenomenon, he embraces the deconstructionist thought of Jacques Derrida—indeed he speaks of deconstruction as "the 'hermeneutic' of the death of God." Deconstruction is of such pivotal cultural significance, Taylor believes, because it is uniquely suited to the task of interpreting, and indeed of radicalizing, carrying through, the epoch-making process of the death of God.

And what is this process? Minimally, it is the demise of ontotheology, the discrediting of the god of metaphysics. But that alone is by no means the entirety of the necessary demystification. What deconstruction helps one to recognize is that the secular humanism which has followed in the wake of traditional belief has simply enthroned a new god in the place of the old. The name of this new god is: the human subject. Taylor sees in western culture, as far back as Augustine's *Confessions,* a struggle for self-*presence,* which is thought to be attainable within a single privileged moment, the *present.* Viewing matters in light of this theme of presence, the deconstructionist finds it matters little whether what is postulated is the eternal present of God's self-presence or the temporal present of human, existentialist decision and authenticity. The logic remains the same: a resistance to real temporality, a reaction formation against mortality and death. Taylor's understanding of deconstruction as the hermeneutic of the death of God may thus be summarized in two points. First, deconstruction gives us in the notion of "presence" a way of thematizing that which is common to the two apparent adversaries, ontotheology and secular humanism. Secondly, deconstruction applies to the western fetish of presence a certain hermeneutic of suspicion, indicting it as a life-denying flight from finitude and mortality.

Even so brief a characterization of deconstruction and postmodernity points up *prima facie* connections with Bonhoeffer's "world come of age." In the much-quoted passage, Bonhoeffer envisioned a time when one would speak of God "without religion, i.e. without the temporally con-ditioned presuppositions of *metaphysics, inwardness* and so on."[3] Clearly, Bonhoeffer's rejection of metaphysics presses in the same direction as Taylor's repudiation of ontotheology. As for inwardness, we may read here a reference to Bonhoeffer's denial of the liberal conflation of religion and faith, a conflation which went hand in hand with a divinizing of the inwardness of the individual. In inwardness liberalism sought a timeless presence.

Most interestingly, there is yet a further point of correspondence. In his helpful account of "religion as a historically conditioned and transient form of expression" in Bonhoeffer's late thought, Ernst Feil speaks of the "distinct and limited time of religion" as having not two characteristics, but three — "metaphysics, inwardness, and *partiality*."[4] By "partiality" is meant the doomed effort to "clear a space for religion in the world or against the world."[5] This is precisely the sort of thing which deconstruction goes after when it dissolves, breaks down, deconstructs the walls of separation which define and defend some privileged space, some recess of presence.

So there is reason to think that something might be gained by a conversation between Bonhoeffer and deconstruction. For that to happen, however, we first need to clarify what is meant by such terms as "presence." Thus the following section, a primer in deconstruction.[6]

II. Deconstruction

Derrida's thought may be approached as a series of strategies for undercutting or "deconstructing" the twofold lure of metaphysical monism (which collapses difference into one) and metaphysical dualism (which dichotomizes difference, creating opposition.) Derrida deals with the threat of monism by critiquing, as we have already observed, a pervasive human desire for "*presence*." The term "presence" here refers to any reality which is taken to be autonomous and self-sufficient, and which is regarded as being at some point accessible in a direct, unmediated fashion.[7] Philosophical examples are as various as the empiricist's notion of "sense data" and the idealist's conception of the self. But it is important to observe that this critique of presence is only one side of Derrida. There is the second lure, that of dualism. Derrida speaks of a widespread penchant for *oppositional* structures of language and thought, and, related to this, a penchant for oppositional or adversarial ways of relating to the world at large.

The point of using these general terms, "presence" and the "oppositional," is to stress that they point to tendencies which are by no means confined to philosophy, tendencies far more pervasive than our initial references to "metaphysical monism" and "metaphysical dualism" might suggest. We have to do here with penchants and predilections which so permeate our language, character and thought that they are never definitively overcome. No one can step cleanly beyond these involvements and dependencies; and it is evidence of Derrida's rigor that he does not claim for himself a prophetic exemption from the quandaries and dilemmas he describes. In such a situation, one's method is never definitive, never more than a series of *ad hoc* devices for resisting the monist/dualist undertow. And that is what is meant by "deconstruction."

Having introduced the issues of presence and oppositionalism, we now need to attend to how the two play into one another. Let us take as our point of departure the observation which has become a commonplace in structuralist linguistics and anthropology, that human language and thought commonly proceed by way of various binary distinctions, such as left/right, stranger/friend, the cooked and the raw. Such distinctions may seem innocent enough. But time and again they become invidious. We know that to "discriminate" may mean simply to distinguish, but it may also mean a great deal more. Distinction transmutes into hierarchy —"one of the two terms governs the other (axiologically, logically, etc.), or has the upper hand"— and hierarchy brings with it the temptation to attempt to banish the disdained reality altogether.[8] The implicit goal, in such a case, is to establish a pure linguistic domain predicated solely upon the acceptable terms, whether defined socially as acceptable speech, or philosophically as well-founded categories. And it is Derrida's contention that in each such case the various terms will circulate around a central term or set of terms which itself is regarded as stable, self-evident. The center is regarded, that is to say, as a "presence."

Thus we see how, despite the apparent contradiction, a certain dualism issues in an attempted monism. Accordingly, deconstruction of oppositional thinking must go hand-in-hand with critique of presence. Similarly, an analogous point may be made by beginning at the other end, with critique of presence. For when one encounters a term which has acquired such power as to define a linguistic domain, the effect is, for those within that domain, as if the terms are self-explanatory, immediately comprehensible. But closer inspection may reveal that the defining term is in fact dependent, dependent in its very meaning, upon a whole network of associations, and particularly upon certain contrast-terms. Indeed —and this is perhaps the distinctively Derridean turn— one is apt to find that the original term draws upon the other terms not just negatively, by way of contrast, but *positively*, i.e. to supplement its meaning and its authority. Derrida never tires of tracing these subtle processes of supplementation as a way of demonstrating that the various presence terms actually lack the serene self-sufficiency which has been attributed to them. The threads of unacknowledged dependence then become the point of entry for a linguistic and conceptual deconstruction, in the sense of a careful, textual relativization of the avowed opposition or dichotomy.[9]

An example treated at length in *Of Grammatology* is the primacy accorded by Western thought to the immediacy of spoken language over the written. The author shows how those who have sought to affirm the primacy of the spoken word have had frequent recourse to metaphors which actually draw upon the peculiar character of *written* language.[10] To complete our thumbnail introduction to deconstruction, we may consider an example of theological supplementation, as suggested by a somewhat styllized example. We are often advised that the classical Christian tradition is hopelessly wedded to a "static" conception of God, and that what is required in the contemporary world is a thoroughly "dynamic" conception of deity. Clearly this is a proposal to center a linguistic domain upon one set of terms, while resolutely excluding another. But suppose one were to ask, half seriously, "Tell me more about this dynamic character of God. Is it something that comes upon God occasionally, like a fever?" The response, somewhat offended perhaps, would be to this effect: "You have not begun to understand the dynamic character of God if you can imagine it to be episodic. No, God is *permanently* dynamic." The banished vocabulary of unchangeability is thus reintroduced as clarification or supplement at the very center of the purportedly purified domain.

Wayne Floyd has observed that Bonhoeffer was wary of his cultural milieu, in which "pseudo mysticism, voelkism, neo-romanticism, *Lebensphilosophie* and popular irrationalism all called increasingly for 'immediacy,' the conjuring of '*presence*.' . . ."[11] As for oppositionalism, it is well known that Bonhoeffer had no patience with "thinking in terms of two spheres." We thus have reason to hope that there may be an affinity of spirit between Bonhoeffer and deconstruction.

III. Partiality

Let us return now to the issue of postmodernity. Taylor's argument rests (in part) upon a three-part story: first there was theism; then (making due allowances for transitions and overlappings) there was secular humanism; and finally postmodernity.[12] This history matters because the entire thrust of Taylor's argument is toward the third moment, in which, with the help of deconstruction, the meaning of the whole becomes clear. Returning to Taylor with our own somewhat independent understanding of deconstruction, we may be struck that Taylor's own position seems to privilege one particular historical time, namely the present (or the emerging present), the time of postmodernity. Moreover, this privileged period just happens to be the period in which we ourselves live. Here Taylor needs to remember that suspicion is a two-edged sword. The all too felicitous conjunction privileging our own historical moment cries out for deconstruction. Taylor has claimed deconstruction as the "'hermeneutic' of the death of God," and thus as the mode of thought appropriate to the unique, present time. But the *effect* of this mode of thought is *to undercut the very notion of* such a unique, present time.

This line of criticism can be further developed by attending to the way in which deconstruction questions our natural impulse to enclose time within a linear narrative. For all its acknowledgment of temporality, the well wrought story serves to contain history within reassuring shape. Like children at bedtime, we, confronting mortality, take comfort in familiar tales, each with its beginning, middle and end.[13] To summarize, Taylor's argument consists of two elements, postmodernity and post-structuralism, with the latter as the hermeneutic of the former. But ultimately, it seems, one must choose *between* the two, as to which will "inscribe" the other. Will the notion of a privileged postmodern period be allowed to *contain* the practice of deconstruction? Or will the notion of our own distinctiveness be, itself, submitted to deconstruction—letting the chips fall where they may regarding one's notion of postmodernity? My own conviction is that if critical reflection is to be *self*-critical, it has to follow the latter course. Accordingly, henceforth in this essay we will treat the notion of postmodernity with reserve; we will rely on our own reading of deconstruction; and we will treat Taylor much less, and Bonhoeffer much more.

Of Bonhoeffer's three cardinal themes—metaphysics, inwardness and partiality—we may be struck, in light of the foregoing, by the importance of the critique of partiality. By partiality Bonhoeffer means the effort to "clear a space for religion in the world or against the world."[14] As I read him, Bonhoeffer is not speaking solely of partiality promulgated explicitly on behalf of religion, as if other forms of partiality would escape critique. Rather, "religion" here stands *pars pro toto* for *every* effort to privilege a particular space. For indeed every such effort does eventuate in the space's being regarded as quasi-sacred. This larger point is articulated in Bonhoeffer's repudiation of "thinking in terms of two spheres." But it is most evident in a conceptual move which is virtually his trademark, namely the critique of various notions as lacking concreteness —i.e. as being "abstractions" which have forgotten that they are but abstractions.[15]

Read as a rejection of partiality *per se*, Bonhoeffer's third theme presses reflection to a level beyond that of the other two. And in doing so it performs a gesture very much like that of Derridean deconstruction. For one can be against "metaphysics" and yet interpret that term in a particular way (e.g. as static thought) such that one has the reassuring sense of being

oneself beyond metaphysics (e.g. simply by virtue of thinking dynami-
cally.) Similarly, one can be against "inwardness" and yet interpret that
term in a particular way (e.g. as a form of individualism) such that one
has the sense of being safely beyond the fetishizing of inwardness (e.g.
simply by virtue of thinking sociologically.) In contrast, things proceed quite
differently if one is determined to reject partiality as such. For that gesture
would require that one not rest content with some privileged base beyond
metaphysics, beyond inwardness or beyond whatever. It would require that
we get beyond needing to think of ourselves as "beyond."[16] Might it not
be that with the issue of partiality Bonhoeffer meant to articulate the fallacy
common to metaphysics and inwardness? Might it not be that the third
issue is a meta-statement about the other two?

IV. Contextualization

Thinking Bonhoeffer this way has implications not only for the "world
come of age," but for his theology at large. The approach is consonant,
for example, with his characteristic appeal to concepts such as "totality"
and "reality." Conversely it suggests the extent to which such concepts do
not refer to entitites (namely, entities on the largest scale) but function rather
as critical *principles*.[17] In the *Ethics* one finds an example of Bonhoeffer's
critique of partiality which might have been penned by a deconstructionist.
Bonhoeffer is critiquing an ethic based on motives. "For what right have
we to stop short at the immediate motive and to regard this as the ultimate
ethical phenomenon, refusing to take into account the fact that a 'good'
motive may spring from a very dark background of human consciousness
and unconsciousness . . . ?" But the critique goes further, for just as an
ethic based on motives becomes "lost in the inexplicable complexities of
the past," so too an ethic based on consequences becomes lost "in the mists
of the future." "On both sides," Bonhoeffer concludes, "there are no fixed
frontiers and nothing justifies us in calling a halt at some point which we
ourselves have arbitrarily determined so that we may at last form a definitive judgment."[18] Bonhoeffer's clear implication is that it is not enough to
say, "Well, of course the unconscious plays a part, but it is secondary,"
or "What is involuntary is outside the sphere of moral responsibility." What
real grounds have we for saying it is secondary? or for delimiting our
responsibility?

This is an instance of the critique of partiality. Boundaries melt. The
responsibility and darkness interpenetrate. In Derridean language, we

confront the reality—the centrality— of that which we constantly seek to marginalize: the phenomenon of "undecidability."

I dwell on this example from Bonhoeffer because it is precisely when *Derrida* makes this kind of move that he is charged with nihilism and irrationalism. A traditional ethicist, particularly one skeptical of religion, might level the same charge of nihilism and irrationalism against Bonhoeffer. So we need to ask how this passage does in fact function. No portion of the *Ethics* is more crucial than the pages in which this passage appears. It is the early section on "The Concept of Reality," in which Bonhoeffer ousts the question "How can I be good?" in favor of "What is the will of God?" Any other question remains "occupied by the antithesis of 'should be' and 'is' . . . ," as in the dilemma of whether an action is to be judged by its intent or by its results.[19] Imported into theology, the ill-framed question "tears asunder what by its origin and essence forms a unity, namely, the good and the real, man and his work."[20] It is in the context of this discussion that Bonhoeffer asks, "For what right have we to stop at the immediate motive . . . " and proceeds to enter into reflection of ever more encompassing contexts (a legitimate rational demand); but contexts which also prove ever more *elusive* (whence the potential charge of irrationalism).

Bonhoeffer is not negating reason, but he *is* trying to render reason concrete. To use terms which are my own, but with which I believe Bonhoeffer would agree, he locates human reflection within a context which it cannot comprehend, but *within which* it *can* make decisions and can make sense. This disturbing but crucial conceptual move is nicely articulated by Theodor Adorno, who affirms that "to happiness the same applies as to truth: one does not have it, but is in it. Indeed, happiness is nothing other than being encompassed, an after-image of the original shelter within the mother."[21] Truth is often imaged as a matter of grasping, subsuming, comprehending. Here it is affirmed that one knows truth only by being *in the truth*, by being comprehended. Reflection is precisely located, placed, within a context which it cannot comprehend, but within which it can nevertheless make sense. For this distinctive process, it would be useful to have a distinctive term. I propose to speak of *"contextualization"* —not in the routine sense, in which reason contextualizes some particular reality, thereby remaining in control; but in a radical sense, in which reason itself is contextualized. (Paraphrasing Derrida, one might speak of contextualization "without reserve.") The notion highlights a central issue with which Bonhoeffer wrestles in *Communion of Saints* and *Act and Being* —how are the implicitly absolutist pretensions of the reflective Ego to be countered and relativized? The question presides over the presentation of the I-Thou encounter in *Communion of Saints*; it constitutes the test of the various philosophical options in *Act and Being*. And, as we have seen, it is not a merely academic theme confined to the early works. For in the *Ethics* Bonhoeffer pits himself against a pervasive idealism which is simply the most explicit, most self-aware expression of the original sin of modern western culture, the deification of subjectivity.[22]

In these passages and others like them contextualization is Bonhoeffer's guiding question; and as guiding question, it is also a *norm*. Subjectivity *ought* to be contextualized. Now, with this norm in mind, I propose to address two issues. In the section which follows I will conduct an immanent critique of Bonhoeffer, asking whether there are points where his own theology fails to accomplish this intended goal. Then in the final section I will ask in a more affirmative vein, "Given that this norm does play an important albeit often implicit role in Bonhoeffer's thought, what are the impications of his use of such a norm? And how might a recognition of those implications contribute to the ongoing effort to think Bonhoeffer anew?"

V. Oppositionalism

It could be said that the norm of contextualization is simply a more positive, reflective formulation of Bonhoeffer's rejection of partiality. And in most respects Bonhoeffer is, of all theologians, the least given to partiality: even "the realm or space of the devil is always only beneath the feet of Jesus Christ."[23] Yet when this most philosophic of confessional theologians speaks of *reason,* something odd occurs. The phenomenon is most evident in the opening pages of the Christology lectures. Here, as in the *Ethics*, Bonhoeffer is intent upon displacing the customary question, in this case displacing "How?" with "Who?" "The question 'Who?' is the question of transcendence. The question 'How?' is the question of immanence."[24] But "transcendence," "immanence," and the one question pitted against the other—is this not "thinking in terms of two worlds"?

Succinctly put, the confrontation is between "man's immanent Logos" and "Christ himself, the Word, the Logos." But by virtue of this confrontation, Christ the Logos becomes Anti-Logos; for Christ is "the death of the human Logos."[25] What, then, is the offense deserving of death? Bonhoeffer's answer: it is that the human Logos insists on the question "How?" And why does it so insist? Answer: because of "the need for classification."[26]

A need for classification—which is deserving of death. Surely something is slipping here. If the need is an inherent and necessary need of human reason *per se*, if human reason cannot possibly do anything else, does it truly deserve to be condemned to death? Conversely, if reason *can* in principle do otherwise, is it really *reason* which chooses not to? Is not choice rather the work of the human will, or more inclusively the human subject?

One way of pinpointing the fallacy is to say that in the phrase "human Logos" Bonhoeffer too closely identifies human reason with the human subject. Another way is to say that Bonhoeffer has taken "instrumental reason" to be the entirety of reason, allowing it to become definitive of reason *per se*.[27] Thus Bonhoeffer begins by saying, "All *scientific* questions can be reduced to two"; but when the two are reduced in turn to one, namely the question of classification, he proceeds to draw conclusions regarding the "human Logos" *per se*.[28] Feil notes that Bonhoeffer parted with Barth over Barth's tendency to speak of religion in an abstract and ahistorical manner. Ironically, Bonhoeffer displays a similarly ahistorical penchant with regard to reason. Moreover, the parallel tendencies are no accident. In the one case as in the other, the distortion (the fastening upon abstractions which have forgotten that they are but abstractions) springs from a too-fixed determination to set Christ in contrast, nay, in opposition, to another reality.

The result is, in my quasi-deconstructionist language, a situation of oppositionalism. The result is that, as in any such contest, Bonhoeffer winds up mirroring his opponent. Bonhoeffer circulates without question instrumental reason's own self-aggrandizing conviction that it is, in and of itself, definitive of the whole of reason. And this is debilitating; for having ceded so much, Bonhoeffer is left without a more comprehensive ground within reason from which to launch a properly internal critique. Hence his hasty resort to revelation. In like manner, Bonhoeffer yields too much to instrumental reason's complacent assumption that it itself is monolithic, internally consistent —thus depriving theology of the uniquely effective tactic of undermining the pretensions of instrumental reason from within.

An approach more consistent with the norm of contextualization would be to subject instrumental reason to what one might call a geneological hermeneutic of suspicion. So viewed, instrumental reason's own self-understanding is no longer definitive; one senses within it the marks of reaction formation (cf. Kierkegaard's dialectical analysis of the System.) Bonhoeffer speaks of the need to set barriers to subjectivity. But erecting walls of exclusion is more properly the business of instrumental reason; and there it generally functions as a defensive response to the threatening realities of human finitude and mortality.

But a defensive response to certain realities betrays an implicit *awareness* of those realities. Reason is capable of this awareness; indeed I would argue that reason per se is not capable of *not* having this awareness. It is contextualized by it. Its pretensions notwithstanding, instrumental reason operates with an implicit awareness that it is not in fact in control. That awareness is, in part at least, an operation of reason; it arises from within the citadel.

From this interior chamber, the way lies open for deconstructionist critique.

VI. Logology

The effects of Bonhoeffer's oppositionalist stance toward reason are debilitating. Yet, as we have just begun to see, there are presuppositions within this thought which point in a different direction. When in *Act and Being* Bonhoeffer declares, "it simply is not true that concrete man . . . is in full possession of the mind," is this not an appeal *to reason*—namely an appeal to reason to recognize that the assumption that "man . . . is in full possession of the mind" is just that, an assumption? He goes on to write: "only when existence . . . is said not to be able to understand itself (*or only to understand that it does not understand itself*) is the true sense of *the act* expressed. . . ."[29] In parentheses, at the margin, as it were, Bonhoeffer —sensing perhaps the requirements of his own assertion— acknowledges reason's own marginal capacity to "understand that it does not understand itself."

It will be objected that I am placing too much stock in human capacity. Bonhoeffer warned in the Inaugural lecture that "the concept of possibility has no place in theology and therefore in theological anthropology."[30] I concur with the warning, and I concur with the wariness regarding human capacity. But here we must be ask, *where is it written that reason is "a human capacity"*? Isn't that the ultimate triumph of a narrow, anthropocentric instrumental reason—reducing reason to a passive tool, utterly under the thumb of *homo faber*? In a similar fashion, one speaks of language as a human capacity: how clever of the human being to "create symbols" and fashion words. But deconstruction has taught us that it is at least as legitimate to say that human being is a capacity of language; or that in more Bonhoefferian terms human subjectivity is "a historically conditioned and transient form of expression." Surely a theology with any adherence to the concept of Logos, in whom and through whom all things are, must similarly be prepared to say that the human creature is a capacity of reason.

The reversal is disorienting, admittedly. But no more so than Bonhoeffer's own reversal when he insists on replacing the question of "How?" with "Who?" Moreover, I think that unless Bonhoeffer's reversal of question is in fact accompanied by a similar move regarding reason, the first reversal cannot be sustained. For the reversal of question in the Christology lectures is but another form of the effort which was made in *Communion of Saints* to erect a "barrier" to the subject by means of the I-Thou.[31] The "Who?" of the Christology echoes the Thou of the *Communio*; both are based on the distinctiveness of "address." But Floyd in his penetrating study of the early works shows that Bonhoeffer's appeal to the I-Thou in *Communion of Saints* remained equivocal, and that Bonhoeffer carried into the epistemological reflections of *Act and Being* a sense of problems unresolved.[32] *Communion of Saints* oscillates between conceiving the I-Thou in the manner of Buber, as the immediacy of a "between" whence both I and Thou arise; and conceiving the Thou as absolute barrier, mediated by the ethical. In effect, Bonhoeffer sensed that there lay on the one side the danger of presence; and on the other, oppositionalism.

The equivocation stands unresolved because Bonhoeffer wanted to set a limit, but he did not want a theology of boundary situations. What was needed was precisely a limit at the center. But that is what is provided by an internal critique of reason, such as that which Bonhoeffer undertook in Part One of *Act and Being*; and such as is carried forward, in a rather similar spirit, by deconstruction.

What would a non-oppositional limit at the center look like? Bonhoeffer was right, I believe, to seek it in ethics, understood as reflection on the concrete, responsible agent; but he was misguided insofar as he may have sought under the heading of ethics to pit "practical" against "theoretical" reason. In a remarkable study of the categorical imperative, Jean-Luc Nancy, one of the French philosophers most closely associated with Derrida, reads the imperative as an "injunction," By an injunction Nancy intends something which is simultaneously less and more than an order. It is less in that "it does not threaten, it does not compel action — and the imperative as such is totally deprived of the power to carry out."[33] A still, small voice, it threatens no punishment, offers no reward.[34] Yet at the same time, because it is categorical and not contingent or hypothetical, the imperative is also *more* than an order. It "humbles" reason, it "imposes itself the way a *fact* imposes itself. . . ." Nancy even goes so far as to liken Kant to Nietzsche in that the imperative presents itself as a given, like a constraint of nature (83). Yet even at so distant a point we cannot accuse it of heteronomy; while it is indeed a sort of fact, it is a *"factum rationis*, a fact of reason."[35]

It will be objected that I betray Bonhoeffer in this sudden lurch toward Kant, for Bonhoeffer warned against the pride of conscience. By way of response, it may be possible to turn to Kant's favor a criticism which is often made of him. For it is often said that Kant's ethic is hopelessly formalistic; it provides no sure direction regarding concrete cases. One could hardly ask for better testimony that the unhelpful Kant does *not* do what Bonhoeffer says that conscience does, namely to give us regarding our concrete acts a "knowledge of good and evil." For his part, Bonhoeffer was aware that the primary task of theology was not to be "helpful" but to attest to what is real. And what Kant is talking about, it seems to me, is precisely the concrete person living in a situation of "undecidability," yet having to make decisions; unable *not* to use both "practical" and "theoretical" reason, yet torn by the tension between them; asking "Who am I?", wondering whether the deepest source of his or her own actions is good, yet finding the self no more given to immediate knowledge than is God or the totality of the World. Even the god of human subjectivity is effectively out of the picture. "The person, however, cannot be known by us, but only by God."[36] Such a situation meets even Taylor's standards for living "etsi Deus non daretur." Yet it is the situation of us all.[37]

It is in this situation that Christ encounters us. But now the notion of "encounter" can no longer be elucidated by opposing a living, personal (cf. spoken!) Logos against a classificatory and "immanent" Logos (which is by analogy dead/deserving of death —written.) For that mesmerizing contrast is not just an incidental trapping. It is the very contrast which has presided over the entire western metaphysical tradition. And its formidable rhetorical power is evidence that in our thinking, and even in our spontenous ethical instincts, metaphysics continues to exercise its spell. Nancy's accomplishment is to have delineated an "injunction" which would decenter the human subject without recourse to heteronomy. It is without heteronomy, remember, because it is a given, a fact, *of reason*. Precisely because it is reason, and reason at full stretch, no longer confined to prudential counsel, it threatens no punishment and offers no reward. As reason—reason without reserve, reason perusing a sort of Kantian disinterestedness—it transcends the self-interested calculations which Bonhoeffer associates specifically with religion.

Interestingly, Barth, that other critic of religion, says something similar about the Gospel. "The Gospel does not expound or recommend itself. It does not negotiate or plead, threaten, or make promises. It withdraws itself when it is not listened to for its own sake."[38] The Gospel behaves in this manner because it is only by such "indirectness" (Kierkegaard again) that it can witness to Christ, and him crucified. If, finally, there is that about reason which behaves similarly, perhaps we may take that as invitation to consider what would be the implications, in our own time, of a theology of the crucified Logos. For: "Christology is *logology*."[39]

Notes

1. Dietrich Bonhoeffer, *Ethics*, ed. Eberhard Bethge (New York: Macmillan, 1962), 23. It is a pleasure to acknowledge the debt I owe to Wayne Whitson Floyd, Jr., for the direction he has provided both personally and through his book, *Theology and the Dialectics of Otherness: On Reading Bonhoeffer and Adorno* (Lanham, MD: University Press of America, 1988).
2. Mark C. Taylor, *Deconstructing Theology* (New York: Crossroad, 1982); *Erring* (Chicago: University of Chicago Press, 1984); *Alterity* (Chicago: University of Chicago Press, 1987).
3. Dietrich Bonhoeffer, *Letters and Papers from Prison* (New York: Macmillan, 1971), 280, emphases mine; quoted in Ernst Feil, *The Theology of Dietrich Bonhoeffer* (Philadelphia: Fortress Press, 1985), 173.
4. Feil, *Theology*, 172, 174; emphasis mine.
5. Feil, *Theology*, 174; cf. Bonhoeffer, *Letters and Papers*, 328.
6. The following section is drawn from chapter 1 of my *Theology and Difference: The Wound of Reason* (Bloomington: Indiana University Press, 1993).
7. Jacques Derrida, *Positions* (Chicago: University of Chicago Press, 1981), 26.
8. Derrida, *Positions*, 41. Note, however, that the dismantling of hierarchy is not to become an end in itself (42).
9. "Thus one could reconsider all the pairs of opposites on which philosophy is constructed and on which our discourse lives, not in order to see opposition erase itself but to see what indicates that each of the terms must appear as the *différance* of the other, as the other different and deferred in the economy of the same. . . ." Derrida, *Margins of Philosophy* (Chicago: University of Chicago Press, 1982), 17. Here as elsewhere there are striking parallels between Derrida and the later Wittgenstein; see Harry Staten, *Wittgenstein and Derrida* (Lincoln: University of Nebraska Press, 1984).
10. Derrida, *Of Grammatology* (Baltimore: Johns Hopkins University Press, 1974), 1–26; cf. Derrida, *Dissemination* (Chicago: University of Chicago Press, 1981), 84–94.
11. Floyd, *Theology and the Dialectics of Otherness*, 115; emphasis mine.
12. Certainly this view of history is not the sole warrant for Taylor's affirmation of postmodernity; but neither is it incidental.
13. Taylor himself develops this criticism in *Erring*, chapters 4 and 8.
14. *Letters and Papers*, 328.
15. *Ethics*, 62. "All so-called data, all laws and standards, are mere abstractions so long as there is no belief in God as the ultimate reality," 56. Cf., with appropriate reservations, Whitehead's "fallacy of misplaced concreteness."
16. It has become a theological tic to say that theologian X "goes beyond" theologian Y simply because Y does something *different* from X; as if every subsequent assertion were ipso facto an advance.

17. Cf. Martin Jay, *Marxism and Totality: The Adventures of a Concept from Lukacs to Habermas* (Boston: Little, Brown and Co., 1973).

18. *Ethics*, 59.

19. *Ethics*, 55, 57, 58.

20. *Ethics*, 58.

21. Theodor Adorno, *Minima Moralia: Reflections from Damaged Life* (London: NLB, 1974), 112.

22. In a similar vein, Derrida contends that time and again the ideologies of our time betray the tacit presence of Hegel. "[M]isconstrued, treated lightly, Hegelianism only extends its historical domination . . ." *Writing and Difference*, (Chicago: University of Chicago Press, 1978), 251.

23. *Ethics*, 62, 70.

24. *Ethics*, 30.

25. *Ethics*, 30.

26. *Ethics*, 29.

27. The term "instrumental reason" is borrowed from the Frankfurt School; see, for example, Max Horkheimer, *Critique of Instrumental Reason* (New York: Seabury Press, 1974).

28. Dietrich Bonhoeffer, *Christ the Center* (New York: Harper and Row, 1966), 28–9; emphasis mine.

29. Bonhoeffer, *Act and Being* (New York: Harper and Row, 1961), 28.

30. Dietrich Bonhoeffer, *No Rusty Swords: Letters, Lectures and Notes 1928–1936* (New York: Harper and Row, 1965), 64.

31. Dietrich Bonhoeffer, *Communion of Saints: A Dogmatic Inquiry into the Sociology of the Church* (New York: Harper and Row, 1963), 29, 32–7 and *passim*.

32. See Floyd, *Theology and the Dialectics of Otherness*, 117–42.

33. Jean-Luc Nancy, *L'impératif catégorique* (Paris: Flammarion, 1983), 20.

34. Nancy, 17.

35. Nancy, 21.

36. *Christ the Center*, 38. This is the point made earlier by Bonhoeffer's "deconstructive" invocation of the unconscious.

37. "Such action is not blind and irrational but something that one dares to go into and that leads into the uncertain. This distinguishes genuine responsible action from ideological self-justifying action." Feil, *Theology*, 50, referring to Bonhoeffer, *Ethics*, 234. The point is treated at some length in Lowe, *Theology and Difference*, chapter 5: "The Otherness of the Ethical."

38. Karl Barth, *The Epistle to the Romans*, trans. Edwyn C. Hoskyns (London: Oxford University Press, 1960), 38–9; the passage raises serious questions regarding the common view of Barth as oppositionalist.

39. *Christ the Center*, 28.

ETHICS AND THE PROBLEM
OF METAPHYSICS

Hans D. van Hoogstraten

Who am I?
Who am I? They often tell me
I would step from my cell's confinement
calmly, cheerfully, firmly,
like a squire from his country-house.

Who am I? They often tell me
I would talk to my warders
freely and friendly and clearly,
as though it were mine to command.

Who am I? They also tell me
I would bear the days of misfortune
equably, smilingly, proudly,
like one accustomed to win.

Am I then really all that which other men tell of?
Or am I only what I know of myself,
restless and longing and sick, like a bird in a cage, struggling for breath,
    as though hands were compressing my throat,
yearning for colours, for flowers, for voices of birds,
thirsting for words of kindness, for neighbourliness,
trembling with anger at despotisms and petty humiliation,

223

tossing in expectation of great events,
powerlessly trembling for friends at an infinite distance,
weary and empty at praying, at thinking, at making,
faint, and ready to say farewell to it all?

Who am I? This or the other?
Am I one person today, and tomorrow another?
Am I both at once? A hypocrite before others,
and before myself a contemptably woebegone weakling?
Or is something within me still like a beaten army,
fleeing in disorder from victory already achieved?

Who am I? They mock me, these lonely questions of mine.
Whoever I am, thou knowest, O God, I am thine.[1]

In this poem Bonhoeffer shows the ambiguous character of his behaviour and feelings. Against this background, I will, *first* of all, try
to clarify the importance of Bonhoeffer's anti-metaphysical pronounce-
ments in *Letters and Papers from Prison*, using these statements as the
structure of interpretation of the poem. *Second*, I will pay attention to
Bonhoeffer's focus on modern humanity, particularly the way he pro-
nounces the end of its great expectations. Having understood this, we will
better understand Bonhoeffers anti-metaphysical attitude. To strengthen
my remarks, I use some central themes in Alasdair MacIntyre's moral
philosophy.[2] *Third*, I will show why it is a necessity for theology to follow
his attitude such that metaphysical dualism is left behind and the liberating
theological accent of the existential and social relation of God and humanity
(and its being *in* and *for* the world) comes to light. *Finally*, consideration
will be given to the post-modern critique of metaphysics as formulated
by Richard Rorty[3] and Gianni Vattimo[4] and its importance for theology.
The Western post-modern condition should not encourage us to fall back
on Aristotle (like MacIntyre seems to do); rather we should take up
Nietzsche's, Heidegger's and Freud's challenge as advocated by Rorty and
Vattimo.

I

The poem deals with *self*-knowledge: *who am I?* Everything is concentrated on Bonhoeffer's own feelings; no consideration is given to a wider

context. There are only two reference points: himself and the others with whom he has contact in prison. The poem focuses on the way other people see him and he sees himself, on what he chooses to reveal and what he prefers to keep hidden. What is the truth? What he shows is his super-iority and his control of the situation. He is squire, Lord of the guards, conquerer; but at the same time he has his insecurities and fear. In utmost concentration Bonhoeffer acknowledges the impossible division: at the same time a strong character before others and before himself a 'con-temptibly woebegone weakling.'

In prison, Bonhoeffer still behaves as a bourgeois but he doesn't suc-ceed in controling his feelings, like a bourgeois should. His *objective* position as a member of the bourgeois must give priority to his *subjective* experience. But what is working is his super-ego; that's why he looks at himself as a 'contemptibly woebegone weakling.' He recognizes the fact that he no longer has a will to live, that he is 'flying like a beaten army, from victory already achieved.'

In this uncertainty concerning the classical questions *"who am I"* and *"what can I know,"* he changes the focus and order: "whoever I am, Thou knowest, O God, I am thine." Objectivity is attacked from all sides; nothing remains but the outside behaviour. No culture, no education, no commu-nity; only 'these lonely questions which mock him.' In this extreme distress, Bonhoeffer knows that he is known and owned by God.

Looking at the meaning of these words in the broader context of the letters, we can't possibly speak of a typical religious attitude. Bonhoeffer condemns religion as escape. Criticizing the religious attitude, he criticizes metaphysics at the same time. His understanding of faith leads him to say NO to the religious relation between God and humanity, because, in his understanding, it is defined by individualism and metaphysics. Bonhoeffer advocates a relation to God which is neither a final fixed ground of being nor the redemption of our individual souls.

God is pushed out of the world on the cross. So we cannot, *at the same time,* claim his presence in a metaphysical way. Only by an extreme iden-tification with Christ is one able to know God:

> The Christian, unlike the devotees of redemption myths has no last line of escape available from earthly tasks and difficulties into the eternal, but, like Christ himself ('my God, why hast Thou forsaken me?'), he must drink the earthly cup to the dregs, and only in his doing so is the crucified and risen Lord with him and he crucified and risen with Christ.[5]

The escape motive is central. Neither God's omnipotence nor metaphysical concepts do justice to the meaning of God as the incarnate, the one who entered into a relation with humanity. Bonhoeffer puts this very clearly in *Outline for a Book:*

> God in human form – not, as in oriental religions, in animal form, monstrous, chaotic, remote, and terrifying, nor in the conceptual forms of the absolute, metaphysical, infinite, etc., nor yet in the Greek divine-human form of 'man in himself,' but 'the man for others,' and therefore the Crucified, the man who lives out of the transcendent.[6]

This quotation contains a sharp indication of the danger of a wrong interpretation of God's incarnation, of God becoming a human being. In this wrong way people will be slaves of their own projections. What Bonhoeffer has in mind is an active, historical, this-worldly relation of God and humanity. In *this* relation the question of God has to be put in all sharpness. Just preceding the above quote, Bonhoeffer writes:

> Who is God? Not in the first place an abstract belief in God, in his omnipotence etc. That is not a genuine experience of God, but a partial extension of the world. Encounter with Jesus Christ. The experience that a transformation of all human life is given in the fact that 'Jesus is there only for others.' His 'being there for others' is the experience of transcendence.[7]

Here Bonhoeffer is warning against 'a partial extension of the world' the metaphysical prolongued world. Metaphysics in a religious sense always means a presupposition for being able to speak about God in our human terms. Thus, elsewhere Bonhoeffer wonders:

> How do we speak of God without religion, i.e. without the temporally conditioned presuppositions of metaphysics, inwardness, and so on? How do we speak (or perhaps we cannot now even 'speak' as we used to) in a 'secular' way about 'God'? In what way are we 'religionless-secular' Christians, in what way are we the ek-klesia, those who are called forth, not regarding ourselves from a religious point of view as specially favoured, but rather as belonging wholly to the world?[8]

Metaphysics appears here in the linguistic sphere in the role of keeping human beings from the real encounter with Christ – from a real relation with God. It expresses a false meaning of the essence of faith and life. It deals with the perception of God and human existence, in close connection. Bonhoeffer is trying to say that faith, not metaphysics, constitutes the knowledge of the *self*. The poem *Who am I?* shows this to be the truth at the ultimate moment. Masks fell off and so the metaphysical certainty becomes a false security. In order to understand Bonhoeffer here we might compare his ambivalence to MacIntyre's remarks on 'characters.' But we first have to listen to the way Bonhoeffer characterizes modern humanity.

II

I consider one of the most important issues of the Enlightenment to be its contributing legitimation and justification of the free human subject. This subject is always more or less a communicative subject. That we find, for example, already in John Locke's writings on property.[9] As God's public authority decreases, the influence and prestige of human rationality increases. Against this background, I think, Bonhoeffer draws a picture of Enlightenment humanity (den Aufklärungsmensch) as autonomous subject, living in a world come of age. (Bonhoeffer mostly speaks of the 'world's autonomy' or autonomy of man and the world'[10]). It concerns the strong side of the human being, not open to pastoral twaddle and meddlesomeness. Human strength must be challenged by the biblical message, not its weakness (cf. Bonhoeffer's remarks on existentialist philosophy and psychotherapy in the letters[11]). Approaching human beings as slavish, sinful or weak, engenders totally different consequences than the one Bonhoeffer has in mind. That's why it is so important to take Enlightenment-humanity seriously.

We should not, however, over-estimate human autonomy. Rationality surmounted old metaphysics, but now ideologies and metaphysics have the opportunity to fill the vacuum. One has to be protected against oneself. Bonhoeffer sketches the situation in his *Outline for a book:*

> The coming of age of mankind (as already indicated). The safeguarding of life against 'accidents' and 'blows of fate'; even if these cannot be eliminated, the danger can be reduced. Insurance (which, although it lives on accidents,' seeks to mitigate their effects) as a western problem. The aim: to be independent of nature. Nature was formerly conquered by spiritual means, with us by technical organization of all kinds. Our immediate environment is not nature, as formerly, but organization . . . The question is: What protects us against the menace of organization. Man is again thrown back on himself. He has managed to deal with everything, only not with himself. He can insure against everything, only not against man. In the last resort it all turns on man.[12]

Here we see the reason why the transcendence of Christ as 'the man-for-others' is so important. It is better to live with risks than avoid them, to look after transcendence than metaphysics. Bonhoeffer criticizes modern, autonomous humanity by accepting modernity and at the same time pronouncing its end, as far as the *free* subject is concerned. Modernity's stress on progress easily leads to the avoidance of things that make human life human. Technical autonomy tends to abandon tradition, in order to overcome[13] all kinds of threats and possible origins of danger. One of the external effects of organization and technique is the loss of being free. There is no protection against human power which is practiced by technical means.

According to Bonhoeffer, we have to get rid of metaphysical ideas, including abstract catalogues of virtues. For even morality, coming to light in a doctrine of virtues, can be used as means to power. In Bonhoeffer's thought, *justice* is the most central biblical virtue, but it can only be practiced by representing Christ's powerlessness, not by the representation of his heavenly power! If we don't engage ourselves in the messianic movement, we play roles—like those indicated in the poem *Who am I?* These kind of roles are supported by a moral and metaphysical approach to reality.

What do these statements by Bonhoeffer mean to us, almost fifty years later? I suggest that the way Alasdair MacIntyre uses Max Weber's 'characters' or 'types' can make clear the practical meaning of Bonhoeffer's opposition to a false, metaphysical approach to reality.

First, a few things about MacIntyre's main point. The way the modern so-called autonomous human subject behaves is best described in terms of *emotivism*.

> Emotivism is the doctrine that all evaluative judgments and more specifically all moral judgments are *nothing but* expressions of preference, expressions of attitude or feeling, insofar as they are moral or evaluative in character.[14]

The growing impact of this doctrine runs parallel with the disappearance of objective truth and meaning. Emotivism is a subjective matter and deals with moral elements in a judgment. But, according to MacIntyre, in modern moral debates, participants try to persuade each other: the sense is that you have to see things my way and join my conviction. As a result, endless diversification threatens. Because subject-oriented preferences dominate the ethical field, a subjectivity constituted by duty or moral order is diminishing. Still people need an image, a standard in order to test their ethics. In modern society 'characters' get influence by claiming support. This MacIntyre calls 'the social content of emotivism.' The key to the social content of emotivism, according to him, is the fact that emotivism involves the obliteration of all genuine distinctions between "manipulative and non-manipulative social relations." One finds here an evident difference from Kantian ethics.

> For Kant—and a parallel point could be made about many earlier moral philosophers—the difference between human relationship uninformed by morality and one so informed is precisely the difference between one in which each person treats the other primarily as a means to his or her ends and one in which each treats the other as an end.[15]

For emotivism, something like standards of a normative rationality do not exist:

> The generalizations of the sociology and psychology of persuasion are what I shall need to guide me . . . evaluative utterance can in the end have no point or use but the expression of my own feelings and attitudes and the transformation of feelings and attitudes of others. I cannot genuinely appeal to impersonal criteria, for there are no impersonal criteria.[16]

To show what the social world is like, MacIntyre presents three characters, typical for our time: the *rich aesthete*, the *manager*, and the *therapist*. They are the kings of 'organization.' And exactly here, metaphysics comes in. We have 'incorporated moral and metaphysical theories and claims,' a kind of secularized *incarnation*. MacIntyre observes that, on the one hand, such characters are not able to participate in a moral debate because they are technicians, but on the other hand, they represent the Self-evident and the Good. In this respect they are moral metaphors.[17] But this representation is false, because a generally accepted realm of morality doesn't exist anymore, so it can't be represented. (To this problem of representation we will return later.) MacIntyre stresses the role his characters play in the organization of the social system. It is their duty to make technical functioning possible and acceptable; this means the manipulation of taste (the aesthete), wealth (the manager) and health (the therapist).

Ultimately, MacIntyre pleads for a return to virtue.[18] What he has in mind are principles like honesty and justice.[19] He thus pretends to annihilate the hidden metaphysical-moral claim proceding from the *characters* and to terminate the ultimate manipulation of the free subject. As far as I see, he finally pretends to make the world 'come of age.'

Here we encounter a problem: in order to perform virtues and to make them acceptable, we need a *concept of community*. This is precisely what is lacking in our type of society. So the question is whether MacIntyre does not end up with a new type of metaphysics. According to his logic, our society needs common sense about life-controling virtues. But he doesn't indicate how and under which conditions this could be achieved. Because this is lacking, he seems to need a new kind of metaphysics, a reality apart from the everyday life-world, providing orders 'from outside.' In my view we have here an argument for a dominating structure, which neglects the development of modern time.

III

We have to ask ourselves what the acceptance of modernity means for our language and for our concepts of God, history and humanity. Not only the form but also the content is concerned. Only after having explored this question thoroughly can we say something about a new way of human, social and religious communication. As we shall see, we have to become students of such thinkers as Nietzsche (as was Bonhoeffer) and Freud. If we are not ready for this, we'll have to surrender to the dualism and metaphysics of the 'New Age melting pot.'

If we want to conquer dualism, social selfishness and existential loneliness, we should first explore their origins and actual working. This might also be important for the exploration of the possibilities of a new kind of community. As a Bonhoeffer scholar I have in mind the urgently needed communities which differ from the well-known dualistic-spiritual communities, which are so attractive to so many people today. The refusal to join and support *non*-political spiritual movements might be a consequence of Bonhoeffer's claim of a *worldly* interpretation of faith.

Highlighting the way Bonhoeffer connects the end of religion and metaphysics with the rise of the autonomous subject, we are speaking of Western humanity leaving the *selbst-verschuldete Unmündigkeit* (the immaturity described by Kant, for which one has to blame oneself).[20] This concept throws human beings back to rationality. There is nothing but one's own thought and conscience that binds one (cf. the concept of 'emotivism'). And this causes an opposition between human being and the reality from which it originates: the subject-object dualism. This happens as well in epistemological as in existential, moral and social respect. Philosophers like Kant and Hegel and their offspring respond affirmatively to the question whether or not the emancipated Western citizen finds himself or herself in some kind of order. This order can be the moral scheme of things, the progress of history or culture (depending on the personal philosophical preference); in any case it serves as a context for the rational-autonomous subject—an entirely metaphysical context, I should say.

The problem I see, generally speaking, concerning the *theological* reception of Western culture and thought is the inclination to consider these idealistic philosophers as theological guides—while, for example, Nietzsche's profound analysis of nihilism and the death of God is rejected as atheism. The fragility of the above idealistic concepts however is very clear. It can be illustrated in Bonhoeffer's personal position; he is, so to speak, the incarnation of Western sophisticated humanity. The bourgeois is able to behave in an autonomous and superior manner, because he lives according to moral law (Kant), and because he is ready to bear historical responsibility (Hegel). He is in control of himself, but at the same time there is a continuing danger of loosing himself, falling into nothingness. It is in this situation that Bonhoeffer reflects the Christian tradition.

We can distinguish two aspects of the same theme in Bonhoeffer's thought: the notion that God has faded away from public life and that metaphysics doesn't offer much solace meets its counterpart in the (autonomous) overburdened subject. This character can insure itself against many things and avoid many risks, but against humanity and against the *self* there is hardly any defense possible (to repeat Bonhoeffer's words). It is a matter of power and powerlessness; at the same time one sees oneself as a strong person *and* as a weakling. Everything depends on context and faith.

IV

A dedicated fighter of metaphysics is the well-known American philosopher Richard Rorty. He repudiates all kinds of concepts which presume to establish a foundation of existence; he even opposes 'objectivity' in general. Rorty agrees with MacIntyre's criticism of moral discussion:

> MacIntyre is, I think, right in saying that contemporary moral discourse is a confusing and inconsistent blend of notions that make sense only in an Aristotelian view of the world (e.g., 'reason,' 'human nature,' 'natural rights') with mechanistic, anti-Aristotelian notions that implicitly repudiate such a view.[21]

But MacIntyre is wrong when he assumes the possibility of a generally accepted realm of virtue. Rorty opposes objectivity with solidarity and opts for the latter.[22] This results from a re-thinking of the autonomous subject.

In his essay on Freud and moral reflection,[23] Rorty shows that MacIntyre's characters of the rich esthete, the manager and the therapist fit well into his concept of solidarity. The only condition is *not* to describe them as representatives of *metaphysical* characters. In Rorty's view, the autonomous subject has to be approached as a machine. Defending his mechanical approach of human beings, he admonishes us "to be Baconian" about ourselves. For such an attitude "lets one see oneself as a Rube Goldberg machine that requires much tinkering, rather than a substance with a precious essence to be discovered and cherished."[24] The subject is decentered and it doesn't represent any higher reality—no worship of being, no essentialism. According to Rorty, this discovery was made by Freud who "helped us (to) become increasingly ironic, playful, free, and inventive in our choice of self-descriptions." Rorty continues:

> This has been an important factor in our ability to slough off the idea that we have a true self, one shared with all other humans. . . . It has helped us think of moral reflection and sophistication as a matter of self-creation rather than self-knowledge. Freud made the paradigm of self-knowledge the discovery of the fortuitous materials out of which we must construct ourselves rather than the discovery of the principles to which we must conform. He thus made the desire for purification seem more self-deceptive, and the quest for self-enlargement more promising.[25]

Rorty advocates a post-modern, mechanistic approach of human being. His interpretation of Freud is based on this presupposition. The *self* is not a representative of archetypes or other concepts/symbols of wholeness. We'd better say that it is disrupted and that different persons and voices are part of our being. As such, the presupposition for the 'tinkering' is to become acquainted with unfamiliar persons in the unconscious, 'if only as a first step toward killing them off.'[26] A helpful method to accomplish this job is psychoanalysis. We should try to tell our own story as an episode within larger historical narratives.

> [These] . . . narratives that help one identify oneself with communal movements engender a sense of being a machine geared into a larger machine. This is a sense worth having. For it helps reconcile an existentialist sense of contingency and mortality with a Romantic sense of grandeur. It helps us realize that the best way of tinkering with ourselves is to tinker with something else – a mechanist way of saying that only he who loses his soul will save it.[27]

If we want to understand and to evaluate these anti-metaphysical assertions, we have to view them in a broader context of post-modern thinking. The concept of 'post-modernity' should make us careful. Jean-Francois Lyotard, one of the godfathers of this concept, warns of over-emphasizing it and using it as a new kind of thought. He stresses that postmodern thought is all about modernity and therefore he prefers to speak of re-writing certain modern themes.[28]

This *réécrire la modernité* is beautifully accomplished by Gianni Vattimo in his book *The End of Modernity*.[29] This author pays serious attention to some central characteristics of modernity. As his chief witnesses he uses Nietzsche and Heidegger. But before all other things he wants to stress the role of Christianity in the concept of 'the new':

> Only modernity, in developing and elaborating in strictly worldly and secular terms the Judaeo-Christian heritage – the idea of history as the history of salvation, articulated in terms of creation, sin, redemption and waiting for the last

Judgement—gives ontological weight to history and a determining sense to our position within it.[30]

Modernity elaborates this 'ontological weight of history' in a secular, 'worldly' manner in the sense of progress. Vattimo writes as follows:

> From the point of view of Nietzsche and Heidegger, which we may consider to be a mutually held one in spite of the considerable differences between the two philosophers, modernity is in fact dominated by the idea that the history of thought is a progressive 'enlightenment' which develops through an ever more complete appropriation and reappropriation of its own 'foundations.' These are often also understood to be 'origins,' and thus the theoretical and practical revolutions of Western history are presented and legitimated for the most part as 'recoveries,' rebirths, or returns. The idea of 'overcoming,' which is so important in all modern philosophy, politics and economics, understands the course of thought as being a progressive development in which the new is identified with value through the mediation of the recovery and appropriation of the foundation-origin. However, precisely the notions of foundation, and of thought both as foundation and means of access to a foundation, are radically interrogated by Nietzsche and Heidegger. Both philosophers find themselves obliged, on the one hand, to take up a critical distance from Western thought in so far as it is foundational; on the other hand, however, they find themselves unable to criticize Western thought in the name of another, and truer, foundation. It is this that rightly allows us to consider them to be the philosophers of post-modernity. . . . It involves the negation of stable structures of Being, to which thought must necessarily have recourse if it is to 'found' itself upon solid certainties.[31]

So Vattimo draws a central antagonism and tension of modernity: the *re*-thinking, *re*covery, *re*presentation of the past, of the origin and at the same time the *over*coming of it, the very fast renewing of things and opinions and meanings, which are considered as old. In Vattimo's words:

> Whether we understand reappropriation in the form of the defence of a zone free of exchange-value, or in the more ambitious form (which unites Marxism and phenomenology at a theoretical level) of a 'refoundation' of existence in a horizon focused on use-value and beyond the reach of exchange-value, the perspective of reappropriation has been used up. . . . In fact, the perspective of reappropriation has lost its meaning as an ideal norm; like Nietzsche's God, such a perspective reveals itself in the end to be superfluous. In Nietzsche's philosophy, God dies precisely because knowledge no longer needs to arrive at ultimate causes, humanity no longer needs to believe in an immortal soul, etc. . . . It is here, in this emphasis on the superfluity of the highest values, that the roots of an accomplished nihilism may be found.[32]

Explaining Nietzsche's 'philosophy of morning,' Vattimo shows that here arises a kind of thought that is oriented towards proximity rather than towards origin or foundation.[33] It concerns a proximity of things immediately around us and inside of us:

The insignificance of the origin increases when the origin becomes known, and, as a consequence, 'the nearest reality, that which is around us and inside of us, little by little starts to display colour and beauty and enigma and wealth of meaning–things which earlier men never dreamed of.'[34]

Stressing the essence of Nietzsche"s 'philosophy of morning' which is 'nothing other than the very errancy of metaphysics, but seen from a different point of view, that of the man of good temperament, who posesses a firm, mild, and, at the bottom, cheerful soul,' Vattimo comes close to Rorty's ideal type of the free, joyful subject.

V

I think this kind of non-metaphysical re-writing of the concept of the 'autonomous' subject is more promising than giving re-birth to the Aristo-telian virtues according to MacIntyre's scheme. However, the condition of the former is the de-centering of the subject. Rorty explains, "Freud thought of himself as part of the same 'decentering' movement of thought to which Copernicus and Darwin belonged."[35] The same could be said about Marx and Nietzsche.

I would like to put forward this thesis: *If we accept the proposal to re-write the modern concept of the autonomous human subject, and thus grant that this subject is decentered inasmuch as there no longer exists metaphysical foundations, then we have to give up the claim of (all kinds of metaphysical) representation.*

What I have in mind is such a thing as the representation of truth, justice and God. Keeping in mind Bonhoeffer's approach to reality as a whole, we should not primarily consider the problem of representation as a *theoretical* problem. Bonhoeffer's remarks on the transcendence of Jesus' 'being there for others' are equally practical in character as are Rorty's and Vattimo's on the de-centered subject. Speaking in Carl Schmitt's terms,[36] the dangerous political context of Bonhoeffer's practice had to do with a 'situation of exception' (*Ausnahmezustand*) in which a 'strong man' had come to power again. This strong man claimed to represent the *Volk*, the *race*, *nationalist feelings* (the *Deutschtum*) and even *God himself*.

We, in our phase of history, should be very careful and guard democracy with all our strength. To be sure, I do agree with those thinkers who try to exterminate old and new metaphysics. But Rorty's concept of solidar-ity, I think, is too liberal and too self-evident. The playful, free, ironic per-son as postulated by Rorty (and Nietzsche), is also a person with interests and desires. In a culture where the concept of representation is declining in the public sphere, we must keep asking what kind of things are represented in a hidden way by people bearing public responsibility, making policy in the political field and/or defending moral and economical values.

What we can learn from Bonhoeffer's poem *Who am I?* and from the kind of 'post-modern' philosophers we are focusing upon here is that we should not exclude *ourselves*. Putting it in a Bonhoefferian-theological way, we should give up the personal or institutional claim of the representation of Jesus as heavenly king, son of God etc.; we only have to follow him in being there for others. This is transcendence-in-proximity, leaving behind the order of things we consider as normal and necessary and instead practicing a new and redescribed human possibility. This is political practice.

The condition for the possibility I am describing is the de-centered subject, who considers his social context as a polis, a community. But it can not be a kind of Aristotelian polis, where slavery, war and commerce are the central constituents of the metaphysical order and the free Greek citizen the absolute center. Neither should we advocate a modern metaphysical order of virtues like Adam Smith in his *Theory of moral sentiments*, constituting and protecting capitalist relations.[37]

Existing for others, however, still contains a certain kind of representation – but in a different sense from the above criticized one. It means the representation of those people who are the victims of the system, speaking in the context of their narrative. This might be the most profound understanding of Bonhoeffer's decentering himself as a subject. I'm thine, O God. This might also be the 'considerable improvement' Rorty acknowledges 'on cultures dominated by, for example, the Warrior and the Priest' (Rorty 1991–2, 161).

Finally, I wish to make a very practical concluding remark. As I have learned from people in the former East-Block who are now free to travel to Western Europe, a strong desire exists for proximity, solidarity and recognition. It is within the reach of Western power to abolish the still existing dichotomy between East and West. This means in fact to *share* power, knowhow, money and a good philosophy of life. Much more should be done in this respect than is happening now. For Bonhoeffer scholars and theologians, this means *decentering* the power of persons and of the collective Western subject, which in fact *is* governing the world. This is not only a personal, but primarily an economic and a political task, which, however, cannot be carried out without personal courage. And this means dispensing with every possibility of metaphysical escape and deciding for life-together.

Notes

1. Dietrich Bonhoeffer, *Letters and Papers from Prison* (New York: Macmillan, 1972), 347f.
2. Alasdair MacIntyre, *After Virtue: A Study in Moral Theory* (London: Duckworth, 1985).
3. Richard Rorty, "Solidarity or Objectivity?," in *Objectivity, Relativism and Truth*, Philosophical Papers 1 (Cambridge: Cambridge University Press, 1990) and "Freud and Moral Reflection," in *Essays on Heidegger and Others*, Philosophical Papers 2 (Cambridge: Cambridge University Press, 1991).
4. Gianni Vattimo, *The End of Modernity* (Baltimore: Johns Hopkins University Press, 1988).
5. *Letters and Papers*, 337.
6. *Letters and Papers*, 381.
7. *Letters and Papers*, 381.
8. *Letters and Papers*, 280f.
9. John Locke, *The Second Treatise of Government*, ed. Richard H. Cox (Arlington Heights, IL: H. Davidson, 1982) [1690]; see chapter V: "Of Property" and chapter IX: "Of the Ends of Political Society and Government."
10. *Letters and Papers*, 359, e.g.
11. *Letters and Papers*, 326, 341, 346.
12. *Letters and Papers*, 380.
13. The idea of 'overcoming' is important in post-modern thinking; cf. Vattimo and part IV of this essay.
14. MacIntyre, 11f.
15. MacIntyre, 23.
16. MacIntyre, 24.
17. MacIntyre, 28–32.
18. Cf. MacIntyre, chapter 18: "Nietzsche or Aristotle."
19. MacIntyre, chapter 14: "The Nature of the Virtues."
20. Immanuel Kant, the first sentence of his 1784 essay, "Was ist Aufklärung?"; see "What is Enlightenment?," in *On History*, trans. and ed. Louis White Beck (Indianapolis: Bobbs-Merrill, 1963), 3–10.
21. Rorty, *Essays on Heidegger and Others*, 159.
22. Rorty, *Essays on Heidegger and Others*, 21–35.
23. Rorty, *Essays on Heidegger and Others*, 143–63.
24. Rorty, *Essays on Heidegger and Others*, 152.
25. Rorty, *Essays on Heidegger and Others*, 155.
26. Rorty, *Essays on Heidegger and Others*, 148.
27. Rorty, *Essays on Heidegger and Others*, 163.
28. Jean-Francois Lyotard, "Réécrire la Modernité," in *L'inhumain: causeries sur le temps* (Paris: Éditions Galilee, 1988).
29. See n. 4 above.
30. Vattimo, 4.
31. Vattimo, 2f.
32. Vattimo, 24.
33. Vattimo, 169.
34. Vattimo, 169.

35. Vattimo, 143.
36. Carl Schmitt, *Political Theology: Four Chapters on the Concept of Sovereignty,* trans. George Schwab (Cambridge, MA: MIT Press, 1985 [1922, 1934]).
37. Adam Smith, *The Theory of Moral Sentiments,* ed. D. D. Raphael and A. L. Mac-fie (Oxford: Clarendon Press, 1979 [1759, 1761]; about the meaning of Smith's doctrine of virtues for his dealing with economics in *The Wealth of Nations* (New York: Knopf, 1991 [1776]), see Arend Th. van Leeuwen, *De nacht van het Kapitaal* (Nijmegen: SUN, 1984).

STYLE AND THE CRITIQUE
OF METAPHYSICS: THE LETTER AS FORM
IN BONHOEFFER AND ADORNO

WAYNE WHITSON FLOYD, JR.

> In the fields with which we are concerned, knowledge exists only in light-
> ning flashes. The text is the thunder rolling long afterward.
> Walter Benjamin

Dietrich Bonhoeffer—theologian and victim of Nazism—almost certainly would not be remembered so widely, nor be read in the present with more than historical interest, were it not for the letters which he wrote from prison. Yet there has been no sustained exploration of the significance for Bonhoeffer's theological project of the fact that he most characteristically expressed himself in precisely this form—the letter and kindred shorter writings. Indeed, the general assumption about Bonhoeffer's letters has been that they were composed out of the exigencies of history, rather than as a manifestation of a particular style of critical thought.

Heinrich Ott in his *Wirklichkeit und Glaube* (1966) was one of the first to reflect on the significance of "letter-writing as a style of thought," partic-ularly when one is inquiring into the "especial importance [that] has been won for Bonhoeffer's imprisonment letters for the general interpretation of his work."[1] More recently, the late Jörg Rades (1988) urged an inquiry into this matter of form and style, arguing that "to introduce some kind of literary criticism into Bonhoeffer research seems to be unavoidable since we have to deal with a writer who expressed himself not only in theo-logical tractates but also in speeches, poems, plays and not to forget the letters."[2] Still, in the interim between Ott and Rades virtually no one has taken as a guiding clue to the *substance* of Bonhoeffer's theology the literary *form* of the letter itself—and by extension the essays, sermons, lectures, poems, outlines, rough-drafts and other so-called 'occasional' pieces which make up the bulk of Bonhoeffer's written legacy. Care must be taken not to gloss over the differences between letters and other shorter forms of written discourse, for example regarding the matter of their intended audiences. However, I propose that letters share more with essays, for example, than they differ from them. We see this especially when we notice the essay's—and the letter's—ability to enact certain linguistic and cognitive strategies by means of which the skillful writer can resist and criticize the prevalent system-building propensities of western philosophy and theology.[3]

Having sketched in the first section below the clear evidence of the dominance of what I call the letter/essay form in Bonhoeffer's corpus, I then will clarify the methodological significance of this form in which Bonhoeffer wrote most of his theology. For this task I will employ as dialogue partner the short work of the critical theorist, Theodor Adorno, "The Essay as Form," from his *Noten zur Literatur*. Finally, in the light of both Bonhoeffer's early work, *Act and Being*, and his final written meditations, the *Letters and Papers from Prison*, I will sketch the role of the letter/essay form in the enduring contribution of Bonhoeffer to constructive theology. In particular I will argue that his anti-systematic or anti-metaphysical style of thinking points towards what I will call a polyphonic form of theological practice, best enacted through the interventions and interruptions of the literary form of letter and essay.

I. Bonhoeffer and Form: Letters, Essays and Fragments

There is no small irony in the fact that, on the one hand, if it *weren't* for the letters and essays which Bonhoeffer wrote, we probably wouldn't remember him at all; yet, on the other hand, since it is precisely for these fragmentary, unsystematic works that we *do* remember him, posterity has taken Bonhoeffer less seriously as a philosophical theologian. Inspirational as he may have been, the fact that he produced no "systematic" theological opus has allowed him to be disregarded as a thinker to reckon with.

I would propose to the contrary that the future of Dietrich Bonhoeffer's theology may well lie in a critical appreciation of the very *style* of his theological thought—and its expression in a certain fragmentary *form*. I argue that it is precisely the fragmentariness of the written form of his theology which, in the words of his own letter to Bethge in 1944, may enable his own thought to "move out again into the open air of intellectual discussion with the world, and risk saying controversial things."[4] It almost begs the obvious to note that with the exception of his two dissertations, Bonhoeffer wrote only one other book-length manuscript, *Nachfolge* [*The Cost of Discipleship*]. The rest of his writings were in the form of letters, sermons, essays, and lecture notes and speeches, such as those collected in the *Gesammelte Schriften* or in the recently published volumes nine and ten of the *Dietrich Bonhoeffer Werke*[5]; or they took the form of short, though densely packed, lectures published at the request of students, such as *Schöpfung und Fall* [*Creation and Fall*]; or they were in lecture-style, such as the posthumously published reconstructions of student notes, for example, Bethge's version of the *Christologie* lectures [*Christ the Center*] or the more recently published *Hegel-Seminar* notes of Ferenc Lehel, edited by Ilse Tödt; or they took the form of brief, occasional pieces, such as *Gemeinsames Leben* [*Life Together*], written for the Finkenwalde seminarians. Even those works for which he is best known are but edited fragments: the *Ethik* [*Ethics*] is a reconstruction of several unfinished drafts for a book; and *Widerstand und Ergebung* [*Letters and Papers from Prison*] is Bethge's edited release of a significant portion, but not all, of the letters Bonhoeffer wrote from prison in the last years of his life.

Altogether his literary legacy is a rich but fragmentary array, of which it is difficult to make a coherent, much less a complete, whole. Thus we today inherit the challenge to make of his fragments more than a pastiche of "eminently quotable but egregiously misconstruable"[6] aphorisms. It is our task to turn them back into riddles, fragments, and traces which can then be brought into productive, if not final, trial combinations and constellations of theological insight, as Bonhoeffer himself was prone to do. The lightning flashes of Bonhoeffer's fragments need to claim our attention, rather than the attempt to systematize the thunder rolling afterwards.[7]

II. Adorno: "The Essay as Form"

Just as Adolf von Harnack had lived just across Berlin from the great Jewish philosopher Leo Baeck, without evidently having commerce with him at all, Dietrich Bonhoeffer in the 1920's lived in the same Berlin as did the Jewish intellectuals Gershom Scholem, Walter Benjamin, and the often-visiting Theodor Adorno. And he, too, appears to have been oblivious to his neighbors' highly original critiques of Weimar culture—even those with strong similarities to his own. In a brief post-war writing, "The Essay as Form," Theodor Adorno—who was himself often in Berlin during the time that Bonhoeffer was writing *Akt und Sein*—meditated upon the nature of the much neglected, and oft-disparaged, form of the essay itself. What he says there about the form and the significance of the essay sheds light, I will argue, on the broader significance of Bonhoeffer's letters and occasional writings. A brief detour into Adorno here may help to bring to thematic attention the qualities of the letter and essay which were to make them the most desirable, not merely the most necessary, forms of writing through which to bring to life Bonhoeffer's own theological concerns.

Scorning the specificity of the historical occasion for most essays, not to mention letters, "the academic guild," Adorno wrote, "accepts as philosophy only what is clothed in the dignity of the universal and the enduring" (3). Whereas western philosophy has prided itself in the development of a variety of systems of metaphysics, the essay has no such pretense. "Its concepts are not derived from a first principle, nor do they fill out to become ultimate principles" (4). However, Adorno argued, it is no deficiency, but the essay's very glory, that "in the realm of thought it is virtually the essay alone that has successfully raised doubts about the absolute privilege of method. [For] the essay allows for the consciousness of nonidentity, without expressing it directly" (9). Whereas philosophy's systems, particularly in idealism, have striven to comprehend their object, to render it transparent to the power of the system of reason, the essay as form, "in its accentuation of the partial against the total, in its fragmentary character," (9) finds its *raison d'être* in "the critique of system" (9). Adorno concludes: The brief, sometimes heretical, always incomplete essay is "the critical form par excellence" (18).

To what Adorno terms "the customary objection that the essay is fragmentary and contingent," and thus of less value than the eternal verities of metaphysical systems, Adorno responds that this very seeming "weakness bears witness to the very nonidentity it had to express" (11). The essay "thinks in fragments, just as reality is fragmentary, and finds its unity in and through the breaks and not by glossing them over. . . . Discontinuity is essential to the essay . . ." (16). Adorno says, "In particular, it rebels against the doctrine, deeply rooted since Plato, that what is transient and ephemeral is unworthy of philosophy—that old injustice done to the transitory, whereby it is condemned again in the concept. . . . Hence the essay challenges the notion that what has been produced historically is not a fit object of theory" (10). And this would seem especially true, Adorno argued, when what has been produced historically is the deep rupture of reality we so feebly label Shoah, or Holocaust.

The very reason, Adorno realized, that "the essay arouses resistance" is "because it evokes intellectual freedom" (3). Thus, he infers, "the essay's innermost formal law is heresy. Through violations of the orthodoxy of thought, something in the object becomes visible which it is orthodoxy's secret and objective aim to keep invisible" (23). The essay subverts the very formation and power of ideology.

It is somewhat surprising to discover that such trenchant social criticism as Adorno's is couched in a certain 'aesthetic', particularly 'musical', style of thought.[8] For example, a philosophical interpretation of the legacy of western rationality, according to Adorno, should evoke in the reader the sort of participation exemplified, for example, in Schönberg's early compositions. This music, beyond the expected orthodoxies of tonality, "requires the listener spontaneously to compose its inner movement and demands of him not mere contemplation but praxis."[9] The listener is not 'given' a tonal totality, toward which the appropriate stance is that of the spectator. Rather the listener is given an unexpected, experimentally non-tonal riddle, whose 'meaning' cannot be imputed to the 'intention' of the composer. As Martin Jay has commented, "instead of being complicitous with the growing facade of universalism, the false totality that Adorno and his colleagues saw as dominating contemporary consciousness," Schönberg's music was "truly progressive," just as philosophy was called to be. It sustained itself precisely by attending to the fragmentary, unintentional clues given it by a broken society.[10]

The participatory composition of the inner movement of Schönberg's music by the listener was, in Adorno's opinion, just that sort of experimentation, or trial interpretation, which could bring to light the unintentional meaning of the music. Adorno's style of philosophy wished to evoke the same performative practice in the reader as had the a-tonal music of Schönberg in the listener. To conceive of thinking as having a musical style meant for Adorno to emphasize the ultimate impossibility of reducing reality to transparent conceptuality.[11] Whereas the totality of a philosophical system "is essentially conceptual and thus threatens to dominate the non-identical and heterogeneous particulars subsumed under it," the totality of the musical composition "is non-conceptual and thus less inclined to eliminate otherness." Music is both given to and constituted by the listener as well as the composer.[12] Likewise, the essayist and her reader, the letter-writer and his correspondent, the word and the hearer of the word, engage in a dialogical subversion of all pretense to totality, all metaphysical nostalgia for the lost, or unattainable, "comprehensiveness" of systematic thought.

The essay provided Adorno with a strategy with which to confront "the same paradox which beset Nietzsche, namely, how to present or ground a philosophy or point of view when the aim of that philosophy is to criticize reality or society altogether and thus the prevailing norms of philosophical or sociological discourse as well."[13] This was a particularly acute methodological issue for Adorno, as for Bonhoeffer, because early in his own career Adorno, too, was searching for a means by which to undertake a critique of the total cultural structure being promulgated by Nazi ideology. Essay- or letter-writing was one of those strategies by which thought could transcend the limits of a totally ideological culture, resisting National Socialism's attempt to collapse the distance between ideology and reality so completely that immanent critique was no longer possible. The essay/letter form, understood as a heretical-subversive style, provided the Archimedean point from which a critique of a totalizing system could be made.[14]

For Adorno, criticism must be undertaken in the face of an ideologically determined culture. And "the dialectical critic of culture" must be able to think and to write in a manner which can be said "both [to] participate in culture and not participate."[15] Such critical rationality for Adorno was by no means an abstraction, but required the responsible practice of criticism itself. "The essay," Adorno wrote, "is concerned with what is blind in its objects. It wants to use concepts to pry open the aspect of its objects that cannot be accommodated by concepts, the aspect that reveals, through the contradictions in which concepts become entangled, that the net of their objectivity is a merely subjective arrangement" (23). Such radical critique required stratagems such as the essay—and in Bonhoeffer, the letter. For these were forms which accomplished in practice what systematic thought directly could not.

III. Bonhoeffer's Theology: Anti-Systematic Thinking

From the perspective of theology, we well might mark the advent of *modernity* with transcendental, particularly Kantian, philosophy's renunciation of the metaphysical Other [*Theos*]. As a result of the demise of the 'availability' of the noumenal realm, the metaphysically chastened, Hegelian phenomenal Self [*logos*] was all that appeared to remain certain. In the wake of Hegel, the *telos* of 'modern' philosophy, and theology as well, has been aptly described as the triumph of subjectivity.[16] Thus, the very notion of *post-modernity* often is defined precisely as the subversion, or the transcendence, of the subject—a movement beyond any such idealistic logocentrism. This much has become a commonplace of our own current methodological discussions.

What is unexpected is to find this problematic status of post-modern theological thinking already described by Bonhoeffer in just such terms in his *Habilitationsschrift*, published in 1931. At least from the time of *Act and Being*, Bonhoeffer had pursued theology's need for a non-metaphysical, anti-systematic way of thinking. This book is best read in the anti-idealist spirit of Kierkegaard, Marx, or best of all, Nietzsche, who wrote: "I mistrust all systematizers and I avoid them. The will to a system is a lack of integrity."[17] Thus *Act and Being* inveighs against any "system of pure self-transcendence on the part of thinking" (32), against the "secret power" of the system that breeds the sort of philosophy which, as Kierkegaard complained, "obviously forgets that we exist" (33), that obscures the mystery of humanity's embeddedness in the contingencies of time. "System" and "metaphysics" come to be synonymous in *Act and Being* with "the philosophical reflection of idealism" (44)—a "phantom movement within [the] self-contained repose" (44) of the power of the thinking subject. The system of idealism is defined by its very grasp or com-prehension of its object, taking all otherness into the self's power to make otherness transparently intelligible.

Contrary to such a "system of reason" (48), Bonhoeffer's theology would resist all forms of foundationalism—whether founded upon the 'act' of the thinking subject or the 'being' of thought's object—precisely on the basis of the contingency, that is to say, the temporality, of the Christian revelation in Christ. A genuine philosophical theology, Bonhoeffer claimed, must remain aware that "theology and philosophy [both] are executed in reflection, into which God does not enter." The essential difference between systematic philosophy and genuine theological thinking is that while the former "essentially remains in reflection... theology at least knows of an act of God, which tears man out of this reflection. . . ."[18] This act occurs in time, as incarnation.

The promise of such an encounter of theological thinking with the contingency of revelation in history is that "if the logos really surrenders its claim, it abandons its system of immanence." However, Bonhoeffer the theologian distrusts reason's power to surrender its own hegemony. "The question," he concludes, "is whether the logos *per se* can possibly carry this out." For he was aware, as was Hegel, that "there is also a cunning of logos, by which it can give itself up only to recover in greater strength" (54). The "will to have a system" nurtures "the mastery of being by the knowing I," which Bonhoeffer views as no less than the subject's "claim to divinity" (61). "Metaphysics" is the name for these pretensions of reason to be "comprehensible through itself"—to acquire an illusory "access to God" (70).

Bonhoeffer's conversation with the transcendental tradition remains continually aware that "thinking, including theological thinking, will always be 'systematic' by nature and can, therefore, never grasp the living person of Christ into itself."[19] Even so, theology must learn that "yet there is obedient and there is disobedient thinking."[20] Thinking is obedient to the historical, contingent event of revelation insofar as it refuses to "become a system confined in the I, a system in which the I understands itself through itself and can place itself into the truth."[21] But the system of metaphysics is disobedient to anything 'other' than its power to comprehend, to grasp, reality in a unity upon which it tries to erect a theology.

Bonhoeffer was well aware in *Act and Being* that the challenge for theology is not somehow to escape the act-being framework of western metaphysics. Thus, towards the end of that work he warned that "the objection that categories of a general metaphysical kind also have been employed in these proceedings overlooks the necessity of a certain formal 'preunderstanding,' on the basis of which alone questions—even if wrong ones—can be raised, whose answer is then surrendered by revelation, together with a fundamental correction of the question."[22] The challenge for theology is not to step outside metaphysics; it is that of "adequately interpreting the idea of revelation from the standpoint of the act-being problem."[23] "The idea of revelation must therefore yield an epistemology of its own,"[24] one which is non-systematic, and capable of sustaining theology's own language of the encounter in revelation with the living Christ.

IV. Bonhoeffer's Style: Polyphonic Theology

In the *Letters and Papers from Prison* Bonhoeffer often reflected on the fragmentariness of life, a theme with obvious personal significance. To speak of fragmentariness is, on one level, to speak of loss—academic careers left unfulfilled, engagements left pending, letters left unfinished (one has only to remember the litany in the letters, "I must break off for today.")[25] From this perspective Bonhoeffer could understandably lament that "the man who allows himself to be torn into fragments by events and by questions has not passed the test for the present and the future."[26]

But Bonhoeffer also took the theme of fragmentariness to a deeper level of inquiry, as when he wrote that "this very fragmentariness may, in fact, point towards a fulfillment beyond the limits of human achievement. . . ."[27] Then three days later Bonhoeffer wrote the following remarkable letter:

> The important thing today is that we should be able to discern from the fragment of our life how the whole was arranged and planned, and what material it consists of. For really, there are some fragments that are only worth throwing into the dustbin (even a decent 'hell' is too good for them), and others whose

STYLE AND THE CRITIQUE OF METAPHYSICS 247

importance lasts for centuries, because their completion can only be a matter for God, and so they are fragments that must be fragments. . . . If our life is but the remotest reflection of such a fragment, if we accumulate, at least for a short time, a wealth of themes and weld them into a harmony in which the great counterpoint is maintained from start to finish . . . , we will not bemoan the fragmentariness of our life, but rather rejoice in it.[28]

Now does this appeal to 'wholeness' vis-à-vis the fragmentation of his life simply represent Bonhoeffer's own final longing for a metaphysical-theological system? Or does the musical imagery lead us to the brink of a non-metaphysical style of theological thinking?

One of Bonhoeffer's favorite images in the *Letters and Papers* was the musical metaphor of what he called "life's polyphony" and its effect on theology. Even in prison, he celebrated the fact that "life isn't pushed back into a single dimension, but is kept multi-dimensional and polyphonous. What a deliverance it is to be able to *think*," he wrote, "and thereby remain multi-dimensional."[29] Adorno, too, in "The Essay as Form" had remarked that "the essay approaches the logic of music . . ." (22). Multi-voiced, contrapuntal, weaving together many strands whose goal is nothing more than their harmonic diversity, music—and by extension the essay and the letter—at times achieves what Adorno described as "something that eludes official thought—a moment of something inextinguishable, of indelible color" (17). It is precisely in sustaining their protest against the system that the essay—and the letter—retain their power to keep in play the diversity of themes, which the metaphysical system would feel compelled to weave into a totality, or choose among—discarding some, retaining others.

The fragmentariness of the letter, the essay, the contrapuntal voice of music, all subvert the pretensions of the system; they keep open space for what Bonhoeffer termed "the concept of contingency, as the occurrence which comes to us from outside,"[30] which the Christian theologian names "revelation." And this "beyond" which transcends the system is in *Act and Being* conceived not with a spatial analogy, but with a temporal one. Whereas "in the system the present is determined by the past," by means of the reflection of the subject on what already exits, to the contrary "in the concept of contingency, as the occurrence which comes to us from outside, the present is determined by the future."[31]

Future means: the definition of being by something outside 'yet to come'; there is a genuine future only through Christ and the reality, created anew by him, of the neighbor and creation. Estranged from Christ, the world is enclosed in the I, which is to say, already the past. In it life is reflection. What is 'yet to come' demands immediate acceptance or rejection, and reflection signifies refusal. As the one absolutely yet to come, Christ demands faith directed towards him without reflection.[32]

Bonhoeffer does not say faith without *thinking*, but faith that can be conceived as shattering the closed *system* of metaphysical thinking. It is the future of Christ, not the potentiality and possibility of the thinking subject, which, according to Bonhoeffer, comes out of the future, dissolving the bonds of totalizing reason, redeeming each of life's fragments as worthwhile in itself, not because it fits into some larger 'whole'.

> To let oneself be defined by means of the future is the eschatological possibility of the child. The child, full of anxiety and bliss, sees itself in the power of what 'future things' will bring, and for that reason it can live only in the present. However, one who is mature, who desires to be defined by the present, falls subject to the past, to themselves, death and guilt. It is only out of the future that the present can be lived.[33]

It is only the 'outside', the 'future' of revelation, that can turn the *cor curvum in se*, the heart turned in upon itself, beyond itself into the future of its this-worldly responsibilities. "It is the new creation of those who no longer look back upon themselves, but only away from themselves to God's revelation, to Christ. It is the new creation of those born from out of the world's confines into the wideness of heaven, becoming what they were or never were, a creature of God, a child."[34] 'Beyond' being for oneself in the present lies the 'childlike' eschatological possibility of an authentic human future: being for others.

The fragmentariness of the letters from prison provided Bonhoeffer with the most appropriate vehicle by which to return to this theme of living out of the future, encountered by "the man for others," who is none other than "the Crucified, the man who lives out of the transcendent."[35] The contingency of the letter was the form best suited to express the contingency of revelation – and the historicality of the encounter with one's neighbors. It is in the fragmentariness of this literary form that Bonhoeffer comes closest to being able to let the future speak in the present, to interrupt the voice of the logos, and yet to make that transient, seemingly ephemeral encounter-from-'beyond' intelligible –"of some help for the church's future," as he put it in the fragment entitled, "Outline for a Book."[36]

We must never forget that Bonhoeffer the pastor, the participant in resistance, and the prisoner never ceased being Bonhoeffer the thinker and theologian. Hanfried Müller, whatever final evaluation history itself forces us to make of his larger theological interpretation of Bonhoeffer, bordered on the prophetic when he said:

> I believe that the right way to follow Bonhoeffer is to take up his development, his path, his intention and the tendency of his work: to follow him rather than stifle his vigor and vitality with a system. I think that [an] understanding of the whole Bonhoeffer will come about not by systematizing everything he

thought as though it were all on the same level, and thus relativizing it, but rather by taking up the movement of his thought in its entirety as the thing which can lead us further.[37]

The texts of Bonhoeffer, beyond the confines of his time, have truly become what Walter Benjamin called a "thunder rolling long afterward." Yet we must not forget that Bonhoeffer's texts come to us not complete, but only in the "lightning flashes" of radical theological insight, which themselves must be seen against the horror of the dark night of Nazism. Bonhoeffer himself had put it this way in one of his drafts for an *Ethics:* "Instead of the uniform greyness of the rainy day we now have the black storm-cloud and the brilliant lightning-flash. The outlines stand out with exaggerated sharpness. Reality lays itself bare. Shakespeare's characters walk in our midst."[38]

Still, it is the style of the movement of his thought, and the characteristically fragmentary form in which it was expressed—rather than merely those dramatic topics and themes about which he wrote—which may be his greatest and most enduring gifts to contemporary philosophical theology. The anti-systematic, and anti-metaphysical, style of the interventions and interruptions of the literary forms of letter and essay may illuminate theology's tasks even long after his great, rolling thunder has faded into historical memory.

Notes

1. Heinrich Ott, *Reality and Faith: The Theological Legacy of Dietrich Bonhoeffer,* trans. Alex A. Morrison (Philadelphia: Fortress Press, 1972), 93.
2. Jörg Rades, "Bonhoeffer and Hegel: From *Sanctorum Communio* to the Hegel Seminar, With some Perspectives for the Later Works," 10 n. 22. Unpublished manuscript, University of St. Andrews.
3. In this regard I agree with Gadamer, who saw the letter as an intensification of, not an exception to, the general hermeneutical problem. See Hans-Georg Gadamer, *Truth and Method,* trans. G. Barden and J. Cumming (New York: Seabury, 1975).
4. Dietrich Bonhoeffer, *Letters and Papers from Prison: The Enlarged Edition,* ed. Eberhard Bethge (New York: Macmillan, 1971), 378 (Letter of August 3, 1944).
5. *Dietrich Bonhoeffer Werke,* ed. Eberhard Bethge et al. vol. 9: *Jugend und Studium, 1918–1927* and 10: *Barcelona, Berlin, Amerika, 1928–1931* (Munich: Chr. Kaiser, 1986, 1992).
6. Gillian Rose, *The Melancholy Science: An Introduction to the Thought of Theodor W. Adorno* (New York: Columbia University Press, 1978), ix-x.
7. This is the difficulty faced by all attempts to date to systematize Bonhoeffer's corpus, such as Ernst Feil's *The Theology of Dietrich Bonhoeffer,* trans. H. Martin Rumscheidt (Philadelphia: Fortress Press, 1985).

8. See Theodor Adorno, *Aesthetic Theory*, "On the Concept of Style" (Boston: Routledge & Kegan Paul, 1984), 293–6. Also see Susan Buck-Morss, "Theory and Art: In Search of a Model," *The Origin of Negative Dialectics* (New York: The Free Press, 1977), 122–35, and Rüdiger Bubner, *Modern German Philosophy*, trans. Eric Matthews (Cambridge: Cambridge Univ. Press, 1981), 179–82 on "Adorno's Shift to Aesthetics."

9. Theodor Adorno, *Prisms*, trans. Samuel and Shierry Weber (Cambridge, MA: MIT Press, 1982), 149–50. See Martin Jay, *Marxism and Totality: The Adventures of a Concept from Lukacs to Habermas* (Berkeley: University of California Press, 1984), 252ff. As Jay points out, Adorno was attracted to the pre-1925 'free atonality' of Schoenberg's so-called expressionist phase, prior to the serial compositions using the 12–tone row, which Adorno saw as the ultimate triumph of 'system' even in Schoenberg. Cf. Buck-Morss, *The Origin of Negative Dialectics*, 15: "It seems clear that Schoenberg's revolution in music provided the inspiration for Adorno's own efforts in philosophy, the model for his major work on Husserl during the thirties. For just as Schoenberg had overthrown tonality, the decaying form of bourgeois music, so Adorno's Husserl study attempted to overthrow idealism, the decaying form of bourgeois philosophy."

10. Jay, *Marxism and Totality*, 254.

11. See Rose, *The Melancholy Science*, 11–26 on "The Search for Style."

12. Martin Jay, *Adorno* (Cambridge, MA: Harvard University Press, 1984), 142. On the persistence of the symphonic analogy in German academic thought in the late-nineteenth and early twentieth centuries, see Fritz K. Ringer, *The Decline of the German Mandarins: The German Academic Community 1890–1933* (Cambridge, MA: Harvard University Press, 1969), 108, 117, and 397: "The symphonic analogy, like the concept of wholeness, certainly did not originate in the 1920's. One might almost say that it was always implied in the German intellectual tradition. But it acquired a new popularity—and the status of a habit—during the crisis of learning. It almost always came into play when a German academic of this period discussed the relationship between an individual and the group to which he belonged."

13. Rose, *The Melancholy Science*, 18.

14. See Jay, *Adorno*, 117.

15. Adorno, *Prisms*, 33.

16. For example, see Fred Dallmayr, *Twilight of Subjectivity: Contributions to a Post-Individualist Theory of Politics* (Amherst: University of Massachusetts Press, 1981).

17. Friedrich Nietzsche, "Twilight of the Idols," in *The Portable Nietzsche*, ed. and trans. Walter Kaufman (New York: The Viking Press, 1968), 470.

18. Dietrich Bonhoeffer, "The Theology of Crisis and its Attitude Toward Philosophy and Science" in *Barcelona, Berlin, Amerika 1928–1931*, 448.

19. Dietrich Bonhoeffer, *Akt und Sein: Transcendentalphilosophie und Ontologie in der systematischen Theologie*, ed. Hans-Richard Weber (Munich: Chr. Kaiser, 1988), 130–31, trans. H. Martin Rumscheidt and Wayne Whitson Floyd, Jr.

20. *Akt und Sein*, 131.

21. *Akt und Sein*, 70–71.

22. *Akt und Sein*, 152.

23. *Akt und Sein*, 74, emphasis mine.

24. *Akt und Sein*, 26, emphases mine.

25. E.g., *Letters and Papers*, 281 (April 30, 1944).

26. *Letters and Papers*, 200 (January 29–30, 1944).
27. *Letters and Papers*, 200 (January 29–30, 1944).
28. *Letters*, 219 (February 23, 1944) and 297 ("Thought on the Day of the Baptism of Dietrich Wilhelm Rüdiger Bethge," May 1944).
29. *Letters and Papers*, 305, 311.
30. *Akt und Sein*, 107.
31. *Akt und Sein*, 107.
32. *Akt und Sein*, 157.
33. *Akt und Sein*, 159.
34. *Akt und Sein*, 161.
35. *Letters and Papers*, 382 ("Outline for a Book").
36. *Letters and Papers*, 383 ("Outline for a Book").
37. Hanfried Müller, "Concerning the Reception and Interpretation of Dietrich Bonhoeffer," trans. Antony Phillips and Ronald Gregor Smith, in *World Come of Age* (Philadelphia: Fortress Press, 1967), 183–4.
38. Bonhoeffer, *Ethics* (New York: Macmillan, 1965), 64.

AUTHENTICITY AND ENCOUNTER: BONHOEFFER'S APPROPRIATION OF ONTOLOGY

ROBERT P. SCHARLEMANN

In Protestant theology, Bonhoeffer, Bultmann, and Tillich represent three different appropriations of what we might call the ontological existentialism connected with Heidegger's raising the question of the meaning of being. Bultmann's appropriation was confined almost entirely to the question of self understanding, or the question of the nature of human existence in the world, and it depended upon seeing in Heidegger's concept of *uneigentliche* existence — inauthentic existence, or existence unowned by an "I" or a "you" — a philosophical expression of the fallenness of human being. Bonhoeffer's was an appropriation more directly concerned with the relationship between the ontological and the theological. Indeed, the stated purpose of his *Akt und Sein* was to work out a theological ontology different from the ontological ontology of Heidegger's *Being and Time.* This purpose might seem to place Bonhoeffer closer to the third of the three, Tillich, than to Bultmann — he was, after all, working in the field of systematic theology, like Tillich but unlike Bultmann. Tillich's appropriation of Heidegger, however, was considerably less direct than the other two because it was filtered through a total systematic conception that was in place before Tillich encountered Heidegger,[1] and it differed from Bonhoeffer's in being willing to regard existentialism as "the good luck" of Christian theology because it provided on its own grounds an analysis of human existence that corresponded with the one presupposed by Christian theology. Bonhoeffer appropriated but also attacked this same ontology in the name of a theological ontology, that is, in the name of a reading of ontology done not in the light of the idea of being but in the light of the idea of God or, more exactly, in the light of the revelation of God.

My interest here is not that of telling Bonhoeffer scholars things that they already know. It is, rather, a double one: that of examining what Bonhoeffer's sketch of a theological ontology in his *Habilitationsschrift* might still have to say, and that of interpreting the contrast between this ontology and Heidegger's by reference to its temporality. For Bonhoeffer seems to have been the only one among the theological interpreters of Heidegger to see the pervasive significance of the question of time in Heidegger's work, whose title did not have to do with existence and being but with being and *time*. One has to bear in mind, of course, the limits of any dissertation; and there is no denying the fact that many of the suggestions about a theological ontology made in this work of Bonhoeffer are more like stenographic suggestions than like elements of a clearly conceived whole. Nonetheless, the question which Bonhoeffer raised, and raised almost as a solitary voice in Protestantism, is still worthy of attention. It is the question whether there is such a thing as a theological ontology – Bonhoeffer at the time was Barthian enough to assume that *anything* could be treated theologically – and, if so, how it differs from ontology otherwise.

Initially, it would have to be said that the idea of a theological ontology is not itself clear. And there is no account in Bonhoeffer himself to indicate the difference in definition between an ontology as such (or an ontological ontology) and a theological ontology, except that the latter is one that comes from thinking in response to the revelation that has occurred and is the *echte Ontologie*. Nor can we, in Bonhoeffer's case, use his later works to shed light on what was germinating in the habilitation thesis; for there is little, if any, suggestion that Bonhoeffer in the dramatic years of 1933 and later gave much thought to the possibility of a theological ontology as such.

For introductory purposes, we can approximate a distinction between an ontological and a theological ontology by reference to the idea in the light of which the analysis is carried out. If we think in terms of the three unitary ideas – the idea of the self, the idea of the world, and the idea of the unconditioned – added to Bonhoeffer's distinction of the historical, the ontic, and the ontological, then we have a manageable list of conceptions with which to work. Historical concepts are those with which we say what has happened; ontic concepts are those with which we say what something is; and ontological concepts are those with which we say what the being of anything, whether a historical event or a natural entity, might be. We can ask what something is; we can ask what happened; and we can ask what the meaning of a thing or an event is in its being an event or thing at all. This last question involves ontological concepts.

But how are we to make a distinction between ontological concepts when they are only ontological and ontological concepts when they are theological? Bonhoeffer does not tell us in so many words, although he gives indications. The difference has to do with the idea in the light of which the ontological concepts are illuminated. First, an ontology illuminated from the idea of the self along Kantian lines would amount to one in which the meaning of the being of entities is provided by reference to the idea of freedom, the idea of that possibility which the human I exercises in its free acts and constructive powers. Along Heideggerian lines, it would be an ontology illuminated from the idea of care or anxiety that governs the way in which the self is in the world in its daily existence. Both of those are ontologies illuminated from the idea of the self. Second, an ontology illuminated by the idea of the world would amount to a conceptualization of the being of things by the way in which the concept of causality is explanatory of the meaning of the being of all things. Third, a theological ontology must, then, be an analysis of the concepts that grasp the being of events and things in the light of the idea of God. The idea of God for Bonhoeffer's analysis is, of course, not simply the idea of the unconditioned; it is, rather, the event in which the divine-human reality shows itself in the context of human history and makes real a possibility not there otherwise. The idea of the unconditioned is one that we can, as it were, always have. The idea that is the event of revelation is, by contrast, not at our disposal but accessible only to the extent that it makes itself known in the deed or event that is real as revelation. Explicating the differences in kinds of ontology in this way, by reference to the idea which illuminates them, goes considerably beyond anything that Bonhoeffer himself said about such distinctions. But it is a way of indicating how there might be differing ontologies corresponding to the three different ideas. In a Kantian lexicon, ideas are distinguished from concepts by being notions that can never be exhibited in any reality but are the light in which any reality is known, and they therefore provide three different kinds of ontology.

We should also bear in mind that Bonhoeffer's context is that of epistemology. To "be in"—*Sein in* or *In-sein*, as in Heidegger's "being in" the world—is to know; and the care, or *Sorge*, with which the self "is in" the world of the everyday involves a certain kind of knowledge of the world. Bonhoeffer adopts this conception.[2] Hence, being in the *Gemeinde*, the community or congregation—which in Bonhoeffer is set against just being in the world—designates not simply a societal or juridical place but also a kind of know-how or knowing. Being in the world is a knowledge that manifests itself in the language of everyday; to be in the world is to have a certain know-how, whose content is made manifest in everyday talk and is made explicit in existential concepts that interpret it. Being in the *Gemeinde* is a knowledge that manifests itself in connection with, and in response to, the reality called revelation; it is made explicit in theology. This parallel may not be precisely one that Bonhoeffer had in mind.[3] But it is useful for seeing the nature of his appropriating existential ontology. Being in the world is a mode of knowing the world, and the understanding of being that is connected with this knowledge is the one that is made explicit when we interpret the language of the everyday. Being in the *Gemeinde* is a mode of knowing the new reality of revelation; and the understanding — or shall we say "faith" here? — connected with this knowledge is made explicit by interpreting the language in which revelation is expressed.

What we have in both cases is a hermeneutical project, which involves interpreting a language that is already there by explicitly grasping its meaning. There is the talk of the everyday; it provides the language which Heidegger's *Sein und Zeit* interprets so as to make explicit the understanding of being that it implicitly expresses. There is also the kerygma; it provides the language which theology interprets so as to make explicit who is there and in what reality.[4] The talk about Christ is the way in which Christ is present. He is present in the kerygma, the talk in the *Gemeinde* in its preaching and sacrament. If it is possible to make explicit through ontological interpretation the understanding that is implicit in the talk about being in the world, then it is also possible to make explicit the theological understanding of being that is implicit in the way in which Christ is preached and celebrated in the church. We see a contrast almost immediately. The understanding of being implicit in the talk of the everyday is an understanding of being as *Sein zum Tode*. To be in the world is to be there as one who is called to answer for the simple possibility of being not; for what demarcates being in the world is the understanding of the possibility of being not. Every understanding of being is limited here by this simple possibility, the can "not-be" that defines the "there" of being there. That answerability for the not is what is expressed in the notion of the *Sein zum Tode*; it is the understanding of being implicit in the talk of the everyday, taken over as one's own in the talk of authenticity, and interpreted in existentialist concepts. It is not the expression of a kind of Romantic preoccupation with death but an ontological definition of what Kierkegaard described in a biblical allusion as the "sickness unto death." By contrast, being in the *Gemeinde* is to be present as one to whom a new possibility of being has been given. It is not a being toward death but a new being which, in some way still to be defined, has death behind it. If a theological ontology is possible, then being in the dead and resurrected

Christ is not merely a metaphor for something, but can be conceptually articulated, just as can the understanding of being that goes under the heading of *Sein zum Tode*. This is tantamount to saying that the self not only can be its own in being itself in the propriety hidden in the "everyone" of everyday existence but also can be something else in the "being met from outside" that represents existence in revelation.

Bonhoeffer's *Act and Being* undertook to work out the outlines of such an ontology. A theological ontology is not derived from nor implicit in the understanding that goes with *Dasein,* an understanding of being as defined by a can-always-not-be. It is, rather, a different understanding of being.[5] Can such an ontology be worked out with the same strictness and the same direct application as can an ontology of *Dasein* which expresses its understanding of being in the talk of the everyday? And, if so, can it be done in some fashion other than that of automatically reversing the ontological characteristics of Dasein? Bonhoeffer's project indicated an affirmative answer to both questions. A being in Christ is not the simple opposite of everyday being or authentic being; it cannot be defined by negating all of the characteristics that belong to Dasein as such. Rather, it needs to be worked out hermeneutically, by reference to the language that bespeaks this mode of being just as the everyday mode of being is expressed in the language of daily affairs. It is not a being there, *Da-sein*; it is, rather, a new being in which being in the church as a new self is parallel to being in the world as an authentic self.[6] Bonhoeffer saw this clearly, even if it did lead him to a couple of misplaced criticisms of Heidegger as well as of Tillich.[7] What I offer hereafter is an account of two ways in which this contention about Bonhoeffer's project can be supported. The first has to do with the question of the relation between the self and time; the second has to do with the difference between the self of ontological self-understanding and the self of theological understanding, of *Entscheidung,* or decision.

I. The Self and Time

We can treat the time of being in the world and the time of being in Christ from the standpoint of the epistemological sense of the phrase "being in." Bonhoeffer rightly saw that "being in" expresses more than a location; it expresses a way of knowing. What does one know when one "is in" the world? and what does one know when one "is in" Christ? One knows the temporality of one's being. As Heidegger put it, the soul does not "fall into" time but is the very temporalizing of being. We can consider this notion from the standpoint of three aspects of time: the flow of time that gives a sense of the now; the temporal differentiation within nonbeing that gives a sense of the past; and the expectation that gives a sense of the future.

For the experience of the flow of time we can take the familiar but still illuminating discussion that Augustine gives of the passing of time as measured by his recitation of a psalm. The present moment is nothing else than the perpetual transition from what has been recited toward what is yet to be recited. The past is represented by the portion of the psalm that has been already recited; and the future is measured by the portion which is yet to be recited. One can transfer this sense of time from the recitation of a psalm to the reading of any story that has a beginning and an end. If one knows the beginning and the end and how the story flows, then in the reading of the story one knows how far one is away from the beginning and toward the end by measuring how much has already been read through and how much there is still to read through. The *passing* of time is what is conveyed in these examples. To recite a verse is to be aware of the present moment as a continuing passage from what has been already done to what is yet to be done. Then one can, as Augustine suggested, expand the experience of the distended soul, which is stretched between past and future in the recitation, to the whole history of the whole world by reference to the divine view, in which what has already occurred in history is comparable to what has already been recited in a psalm.

This Augustinian depiction of time has to do with the awareness of the *passage* of time, and the experience of the present moment comes in as the experience of the perpetually vanishing now. In one sense the now is eternal because we are always in it as transition. But the now that is connected with the flow of time, rather than the now that is the symbol of eternity, is not the unity of the past and the future but rather the connecting point of the movement between the two, the restlessness of transition from what is gone to what is coming, from what has been done to what is still to be done, held together by the self distended in memory and expectation.

If Augustine's account of time in this example is the experience of the flowing of time, the now's perpetual moving on, then a second aspect of time has to do with its historical character indicated by the way in which things that now are can be not merely things that are present in our world with us but also signs of what was there or what happened in the past. We confront not only things that are there but also things that mean. We can not only say that certain objects before us are stones; we can also ask, "What mean these stones?" For the experience of time comes from there being among the objects of our world, not just those things that we can use and those that we can objectify and the other people with whom we can converse, but also things that are traces of what has gone. They exist as monuments. The past has not only gone away; it is also connected with present time by those things in the world that remain as monuments of what once was. This too is part of the experience of the temporality of being-in-the-world: things are there as traces left by what has passed and is no longer. The fact that we can distinguish between things that are there now to be used or objectified and things that are there now as pointers toward something that no longer is there because they are traces of the past is the aspect in our experience of time that gives us a sense of the historical past and enables us to distinguish between the nonbeing before we were and the nonbeing which is ahead of us. This is—if we may risk a pun—a monumental distinction. The "not" of not-being, undifferentiated as such, is differentiated within itself by this temporalizing. A monument of the past is different from the portion of a psalm that one has already recited because its connection with the past has nothing to do with one's own memory of oneself as having said or done something. Monuments therefore bring in that aspect of time which is the endurance of the past as past in the present moment, and the nonbeing they bear has the character of admonition or warning. They serve in the cosmic sphere the same purpose as the psychic sphere does in our memory of what we have done.

If the flow of time is expressed in the passage through a memorized verse and is connected with the past and future by means of the distention of the self; and if the historical past is peculiarly connected with those things in the world that have the signifying character of monuments, or traces, then the third dimension of time, the future, has a different connection, one that is suggested by the German word as well as one of the Latin words for future. The future is the *Zu-kunft*, the ad-vent. It is the coming to, or the coming toward. Monuments are pointers toward that away from which we are moving. They do not *come to* us from the past; they are *left over for us* from the past. What is there in the world that points toward what is coming to us and has the quality of the futurity—of the *Zukünftigkeit*, or adventivity—of time. In the recitation of a psalm or the telling of a story there is already some indication of the future. Augustine's account of the passage of time sees the future in the end of the recitation that arrives when the whole has been recited. The future in this sense has more to do with the reaching of a certain point than with a coming toward us of something. What does come to us? It is the self in its most radical potentiality. The "can-be" that peculiarly defines human existence as a whole is the potentiality of being not. And to the extent that what we understand by death, or the end of the I's possibilities, means the end of that experience connected with the personal center of the I, death represents the *Zu-kunft* that is radically *zukünftig* for the self as an I. As long as the I is an I in time, what is coming toward it is the end of its possibilities of being an I, namely, the not-be that I as I always *can* but never *do*. That is what radically delimits human existence in the form of the existence of the I and what, in existential ontology, makes the I-ness whole.[8] There is a difference between the possibility of nonbeing related to the I as it now is and the nonbeing that is in the objectivity of monuments. A monument is something that makes us think because it signifies what was, but is not, there. It always points in the direction of what has gone; the temporal movement of existence is away from that to which the monument points.

What is to be noted here, in connection with nonbeing, is that a monument shows a distinction within nonbeing. Nonbeing is not undifferentiated in its negativity. There is a difference in directionality between the "not" that is the nonbeing from which we are moving away and the "not" that is the nonbeing which is coming toward us. The monument is, in other words, the worldly object that has the peculiar characteristic of always pointing only in the direction of the nonbeing behind us. By contrast, the phenomenon of death, not in the physiological sense but in the ontological sense as the end of our being as I, always has the characteristic of coming toward us, so that facing the future means facing the I as it comes toward itself from out of the purely negative possibility indicated by the not-be that I (or you) always can, but never do, as I (or you).

II. The Self of Existence and the Self of Entscheidung

The ways outlined above are the ones in which the experience that the self has of its being in the world is connected with a temporalization in the direction of the past by means of monuments and in the direction of the future by means of awaiting the self in the possibility of its own not being. Now, the question which is raised in Bonhoeffer, and raised with respect to certain Pauline passages as well as with reference to being in the church (in contrast with being in the world), is the question whether the temporal experience of nonbeing as a movement from the future toward the past can be reversed, so that what is the future for the ordinary experience of the self can in reality or in truth be the past. It is the question, in other words, of being *new*, not of being here, of *neues Sein* rather than *Dasein*. Is it possible in literal, and not only in metaphoric or poetic terms, to conceive of the end that is existentially connected with our possibility of not being at all as a moment of time that already belongs to our past? Is it possible that the existential experience of time, which is defined by the coming to ourselves of ourselves in the form of the possibility of not being at all, can be supplanted by or transcended in an experience of the time in which we find ourselves as ones who have already ended, who have—in Pauline language—already died and who are therefore living not toward, but away from, nonbeing? Is it possible that the figure of death is not only an image of the can-be that is always coming toward the self most its own as I but also a monument of what the self can no longer be? This is the question raised by the Pauline language having to do with the declaration that Paul's audience is composed of those who have already died with Christ; and it is the question that Bonhoeffer sought to answer affirmatively in a theological ontology.

Theological ontology concerns a mode of existence, a mode of being there, of Dasein, which in Bonhoeffer's interpretation is illuminated not by reference to a self-understanding of Dasein but by reference to an *Entscheidung*, a decision, in the self-understanding of new being. Normally, our being in the world is interpreted explicitly when we work out the concepts that define the way in which the self understands itself as a unity of the particular and the universal in its existence in the world. "Self-understanding" is the way in which we connect the singularity of our own place in the world with the universality that is indicated by the subjectivity of I. It is given embodiment, a linguistic tangibility or perceptibility, in the language we speak and hear. The unity of our human existence is the unity of the I, which is not confined to one person's saying it and is universal in that sense, with the concreteness of time and place that remains the inalterable and unique location of the particular person who I am or you are. Self-understanding joins the self in that universality with the self in this indisposable or undiscardable particularity. It is expressed in the language in which we speak of our being in the world. Hence, an existentialist interpretation of the language which bespeaks being in the world is an interpretation that makes explicit the self-understanding through which the I is its own self in a location in the world of which it cannot divest itself. All of this would belong to the Heideggerian project of interpreting the being of human being that is implicitly contained in the language of the everyday and that is made explicit in the conception of a self-understanding. In the everyday, the self does not understand death as something that lies within the self's own possibility, as its extreme but negative form of can-be, but understands it rather as a power which comes to it from outside it. The self-understanding of the everyday is thus a disguise of the true character of the nonbeing that is the end of every self, coming to it in the form of a "can be" that for the I is never a "do be."

Now, what Bonhoeffer sets in opposition to both a daily and an authentic self-understanding is an understanding connected with *Entscheidung* made in an encounter with something from outside. The mode of being contained in revelation – being in the church or being in Christ or being in that reality which is presented in the proclamation – is a mode of being connected not with a self-understanding always there but with an *Entscheidung*. Decision has to do with the way in which existence is temporalized. When presented in the proclamation with the new reality, the self is timed by cutting off one of the possibilities of temporal ordering in favor of the other one. It cuts off the temporality related to the possibility of being not, the *Sein zum Tode*, in favor of the temporality that is beyond death. It cuts off the future most its own, in favor of the one given it. A decision is made between being in *Dasein*'s own possibility and being in the possibility presented in and as revelation. As Bonhoeffer put it, the place of self understanding is the church rather than *Dasein*'s own possibilities.[9] It is the church as the place where revelation happens, and being drawn into the event of revelation is conceived as *Sein in der Kirche*. To be in the church is the alternative to being within the context of the possibilities that are *Dasein*'s own. Here we can see the contrast clearly. The limit of *Dasein*'s own possibilities is marked by the one extreme possibility of being not at all. Being in the church is the sphere of reality as determined by the event of revelation. The limit of this sphere is determined by what becomes possible where revelation happens. The end possibility, in this sphere, is that of having put death into the past.

What mode of being can be ascribed to this reality? How is this reality real? In one word, the answer is "contingency," *Kontingenz*, a concept in which Bonhoeffer combines a Lutheran notion of sacramental presence with a Barthian notion of the actuality of the word. The church is constituted by the present proclamation of the death and resurrection of Christ in the *Gemeinde*, through the *Gemeinde*, and for the *Gemeinde*. So Bonhoeffer puts it.[10] This implies, on the one hand, that there is no separation between the proclamation and the reality proclaimed. To hear the proclamation is to become a part of the reality proclaimed. But the reality is purely contingent, always coming *von außen* and never becoming a unit in a network of causes and effects or actions and consequences. It is always tangent, always con-tingent. It always comes from outside the whole connection of causes and effects, temporal and spatial orderings, that constitute existence in the world. There is no system into which it can be fit; it is always present only contingently in the proclamation.

On the other hand, this mode of being has its own temporalizing structure. What that structure is we may need to extract from Bonhoeffer's words. But it involves the future of a past in the present. We might describe it by reference to the structure in the content and proclaiming of the kerygma. The content of the proclamation refers to one who did live and die and was raised; the coming of this one is always the coming of one who is to come; the is-to-come (future) of the one who did live and did die (past) is in the proclamation (present) itself. Proclamation presents — we should almost say: presentifies — the reality; it makes it present, and makes it present as having both the mode of past and future connected with it. The pastness lies in the content of the proclamation, which refers to one who did live and did die and was raised. The futurity is that the reality made present has the contingent form of both "coming to" those who participate in the reality by hearing as well as coming from outside everything that is an element in the structured world. The future is there as the *Zukünftigkeit* of the *Verkündigung*. The pastness is incorporated in the tenses that are used in the talk of the one who is proclaimed. They are tenses of past time. Jesus lived, died, was raised. The present is incorporated in the character of the kerygma as making present the very reality of which it speaks. The future is incorporated in the relation of the hearer to the reality; the reality *comes to* the hearer, it is *Zu-kunft* that never becomes an objective thing but remains in the *Zukünftigkeit*, the adventivity, of what is proclaimed. In the proclamation something comes to the listening self purely from outside, apart from all structured connections.[11] It *comes to* the self and is, thus, the voice of future. The content of what it says from the future in the present is a content told of as past.

Proclamation, together with the decision that constitutes its response, thus unites the modes of time in the reality of the proclamation itself. But it does more than unite the tenses of time; it also inverts them in a certain way by identifying the very hearing of the proclamation as a participation in the mode of existence made possible by the proclamation. This implies, in turn, something about language that Bonhoeffer did not discuss. It implies that language is not only the manifestation and formation of a self-understanding, whether that be the self-understanding of *Eigentlichkeit* or of faith; it implies that language is also the manifestation of a world that we can inhabit. Language not only manifests who the self is; it also is the way in which we can inhabit worlds, not only the world of everyday utility and known objects but also a world of which the only intuitions we can have are provided by the images evoked through the language itself. Bonhoeffer's theological ontology did not go this far. But it points in this direction, and it is sketched in enough detail to indicate that it is a theological ontology different from the better known ones of Bultmann and Tillich and also, I think, one still capable of being developed. Both its credibility and its intelligibility depend upon whether such an ontology can be so explicated as to show that our being indisposably here, the *Da* of *Sein*, is timed by a temporality that inverts the temporality of existence. The time of existence as such is structured by the difference in nonbeing that is indicated by the monumental past, which *Dasein* never can be, and the mortal future, which *Dasein* only can be.

Notes

1. In his autobiography, Tillich refers to the influence of Heidegger as that of showing the possibility of a theonomous philosophy. Paul Tillich, *On the Boundary* (New York: Scribners, 1936), 56.

2. A genuine ontology, Bonhoeffer remarks, would come into its own by defining "*Sein in* . . ." in such a way that the knowledge already there is always superseded (*sich aufhebt*) in the presence of the being of an entity and does not bring it under its own control. This would then be the basis of speaking theologically of man's knowledge of God and God's knowledge of man. Dietrich Bonhoeffer, *Akt und Sein* (Munich: Chr. Kaiser, 1956), 87; *Act and Being*, trans. Bernard Noble (New York: Harper & Row, 1961), 115.

3. It might be asked whether the parallel terms should be those of "being in the world" and "being in Christ" or rather those of "being in the world" and "being in the church." The parallel of being in the world with being in the church can be justified on the grounds that the church is nothing other than the form in which Christ currently exists. The only difficulty is that "in Christ" also characterizes a certain kind of subjectivity and, therefore, also suggests a contrast with being inauthentically (as but one example of *das Man*) or being authentically (as one's owning up to one's own subjectivity). The closest parallels seem to me to be these: being in the world (comparable with: being in the church, or the *Gemeinde*) and being either in *das Man* or authentically (comparable with: being in Christ). Since, for purposes of this essay, nothing of consequence depends upon deciding that question, I have mostly used "being in the church (or the *Gemeinde*)," and only occasionally used "being in Christ," in order to designate the alternative to being in the world.

4. "The question of the presence of the Christ in the sacrament cannot be answered from the question, 'How?' '*Who* is present in the sacrament?' is the only question to ask. . . . Is the one who is present in the sacrament different from the one who is present in the word? No!" Dietrich Bonhoeffer, *Christ the Center*, rev. trans. Edwin H. Robertson (San Francisco: Harper & Row, 1978), 57. "The question of *how* this can be must be changed into the question, '*Who* is this person who is thus present?'," 58.

5. Bonhoeffer does call this a new "understanding" of being.

6. That the two are distinct as ontological concepts does not mean, of course, that the church is not also in the world and the world in the church.

7. In *Akt und Sein*, 54 n. 89 (*Act and Being*, "Note," 73–6), he seems, for example, to

miss the point of Tillich's declaring that a distinction could not be made between a philosophical and a theological anthropology: it is not the question whether human existence is to be characterized by the concepts of "sin" and "grace" or by a concept like "being threatened unconditionally" but whether sin and grace are concepts at all.

8. Bonhoeffer's general criticism of Heidegger's interpretation of death seems to be misplaced. The criticism is that it draws this radical end that death is—the radical not-be of the I—into the dialectic of already being a self in the world. That, however, could scarcely be justified as an interpretation of the section in *Being and Time* in which Heidegger discusses the *Zukunft* that is the coming of the end of the self. What is characteristic of Heidegger is not that the sting of death is removed but rather that the phenomenon of death is put into onto-logical concepts and is defined as a mode of being which involves two charac-teristics. It is, first, the mode of being that is purely negative, of being not; it is not being something else than what one is, but simply being not at all. And, secondly, it is the mode of being which in worldly existence is always present only as a potentiality and never as an actuality. End, or not-be, comes into the experience of the self always in the form of what can be, of what the self as I can be, but never in the form of what the self as I, or thou, actually is or actually are or actually am. Hence, the difference between Bonhoeffer and Heidegger in the interpretation of mortality, or being in the world, in ontological terms should not be reduced to the difference between taking seriously and not taking seriously the end. The point is, rather, that the sense of the future as *Zukunft* is a reference to what is always coming to the self, what is so purely a future that it can never be converted into a present and placed into the past. That which is always only future and never present or past is the nonbeing which comes to us in the form of the possibility that I can always also not-be at all.

9. *Akt und Sein*, 88f.; *Act and Being*, 118f.

10. *Akt und Sein*, 89; *Act and Being*, 119.

11. "Zukunft heißt: die Bestimmtheit des Seins durch von außen 'Künftiges' . . . ," *Akt und Sein*, 136; "'Future' signifies the determination of being by something yet to come: something 'coming' from outside," *Act and Being*, 180.

Part V:

*Repentance and the Practice
of Responsibility*

FREEDOM AND RESPONSIBILITY IN A WORLD COME OF AGE

Jean Bethke Elshtain

Dachau, West Germany, June 23, 1981, an entry in my journal:

What astonished me was that this was a place with living people in it—a tidy, *real* town. Clean, bedecked with blooms and kempt gardens, sidewalk vegetable stands, and outdoor cafe. These were the directions: Take S-Bahn #2–Petershausen from München-To the Dachau stop. In front of the Dachau Bahnhof get on bus #3. I did. The bus traveled on what appeared to be the main street of town—a left turn, right, left: about one mile out of town we stopped at the Stadtwerke Dachau, the concentration camp. I got out, the only passenger for this particular stop. It was late, after four in the afternoon. I made my way in: my first thought was, well, this isn't *so* much, not like Auschwitz. The museum was closed. As I walked toward the monument opposite, a huge abstract metal sculpture that reminded me of Picasso's "Guernica," and saw both fresh and faded flowers at its base, I realized tears were flowing down my cheeks. The place wore me down. Through a reconstructed bunker: no human stench now, no crowding, illness, starvation. No palpable despair. But people slept in those tiny, hard rectangular wooden 'beds,' one after the other, separated only by a slat? Yes, and died in them, too. Past rows and rows where block houses once stood, numbers now, on the ground, an empty space inhabited only by the silent screams of those long buried. A sign: Toward the Krematoria? I had 'forgotten' they burned people at Dachau. No, not like Auschwitz after being gassed by the thousands—Dachau was a concentration camp, not a killing center, but burning was the most efficient way to get rid of the hundreds who died through starvation, illness, beatings, torture, shootings, if they tried to escape. The gate was closed. I peered in. A park. Green life; concrete death. The evangelical chapel was closed; so was the Jewish temple. But the Catholic chapel was open. Vestments and trappings of the priestly office preserved—testimony to the human spirit for these were fashioned stealthily from contraband materials by priest prisoners in Dachau.

269

Candles burned in the chapel. I collapsed on a pew. Then I moved slowly into the courtyard of the Carmelite Precious Blood Church, a place where the Carmelites dedicate themselves to vicarious atonement for the sins committed here. Out again into the greying day. The place weighing heavily. I headed along the gravel path nearest the exterior wall with its barbed wire and guard towers and found myself gathering wild flowers from an unmowed grassy area to the side of the path—a different flower for each of my children, and for my husband, and for the three dogs. For myself, I picked up a hard, black stone—so I would not forget the hardness of this place. I headed back to the bus stop knowing I has just passed through a symbol to and of the most salient political fact of our century: systematic, bureaucratized death. I pressed the flowers in a book I was carrying. They will go home. Life will go on.

The book into which those flowers were pressed, and where they remain today, was Eberhard Bethge's biography of his great and good friend, Dietrich Bonhoeffer. I had purchased the book rather by accident, the way many important discoveries are made. I was visiting a daughter, then a student at Earlham College in Indiana, and found in a little bookstore in a meeting house at the edge of the Earlham College campus, a fat paper-back with two names: "Dietrich Bonhoeffer" and "Eberhard Bethge." I knew a bit about Bonhoeffer, having picked up odds and ends over the years. I knew he was a twentieth-century martyr, a victim of Nazi repression. I knew nothing about Eberhard Bethge, but his last name was also my own, "Bethke," anglicized when my father's people emigrated to the United States, so I thought of him as kin. (I do not know if I am actually related to Eberhard Bethge, but I like to think so.) I bought the book and carried it about for awhile, intending to begin reading it. Always there were distrac-tions. Finally, making my first trip to Germany to deliver a paper at a conference at the University of Mannheim, I packed the Bethge biography at the last moment, figuring that reading it in Germany would be a good idea. It was. But I can not say that it contributed to my peace of mind. That is not what Dietrich Bonhoeffer is all about.

Upon my return, the flowers drying between the pages of the biography, I ordered Bonhoeffer's *Letters and Papers from Prison*. At that point, I was touched more by his life than by his thought. I do not think I was quite ready to appreciate his complexity. He writes with great lucidity but his thoughts are tough, uncompromising, difficult to grasp because he so per-sistently indicts a way of thinking that we so persistently cling to, whether we are officially "religious" or not. Bonhoeffer is making the most rigorous of all demands upon us: he is insisting that we be adults in a world come of age; that we accept the burden of free responsibility; that we enfold within a single frame obligation *with* freedom. Indeed, it is *only* the action of "the responsible man . . . performed in obligation which *alone* gives freedom, the obligation to God and to our neighbor as they confront us in Jesus Christ."[1]

But this obligation, this freedom is "performed wholly within the domain of relativity, wholly in the twilight which the historical situation spreads over good and evil; it is performed in the midst of the innumerable perspectives in which every given phenomenon appears."[2] These two sentences are dizzying in their complexity and their implications. Bonhoeffer is no "don't worry, be happy" kind of guy. He found intellectually vacuous and spiritually insulting American doctrines of harmonious convergence with the deity. Were we still blessed to have him among us, my hunch is his comments on our ongoing search for what makes us feel good about God would be even more scathing than they were during his visits to the United States in the 1920s and 1930s.

Listen, then, to *this* voice: "We Lutherans have gathered like eagles round the carcass of cheap grace, and there we have drunk of the poison which has killed the life of following Christ."[3] Or, again:

> Today there are once more villains and saints, and they are not hidden from public view. Instead of the uniform greyness of the rainy day we now have the black storm-cloud and the brilliant lightning-flash. The outlines stand out with exaggerated sharpness. Reality lays itself bare. Shakespeare's characters walk in our midst. But the villain and the saint have little or nothing to do with systematic ethical studies. They emerge from primeval depths and by their appearance they tear open the infernal or the divine abyss from which they come and enable us to see for a moment into mysteries of which we had never dreamed.[4]

Who is this man Bonhoeffer? Who is he for us today? He defies all our current political alternatives: he is neither an individualist nor a communitarian; neither an absolutist nor a relativist; neither a universalist nor a localist; neither an idealist nor a materialist; neither a liberal nor a conservative; neither a deontologist nor a situationalist; but simply and profoundly one who dared to be faithful to what he dared to call "the real." He is a preeminent performer of scripture.[5] But I jump ahead of my story. Let me begin, first, by letting you know "where I'm coming from," as we like to say these days. I share a few questions, if not a whole lot of answers, with Michel Foucault. In one of his many interviews he asked: "What is happening today? What is happening now? And what is the 'now' which we all inhabit, and which defines the present in which I am writing?"[6] Those are my questions too: How are things with us? Not—what *ought* we to be—but *how are we what we are*? We must press reality and try to live in it; we must explore its constraints and its possibilities and their inner connections.

My second way of beginning is with Bonhoeffer's question: "Who is Christ for us Today?," a twist on a question put by Jesus himself in Matthew 16:13, "Who do you say that I am?" Bonhoeffer insisted throughout his life and work that God and the world came together "in the babe in the crib and the man on the cross."[7] Thus "the question, 'Who?', expresses the strangeness and the otherness of the one encountered and, at the same time, it is shown to be the question concerning the very existence of the questioner."[8] Who/you speaks to an essential relational understanding of self and other. Thus it is with any genuine encounter with any 'other.' Jesus as the man for others was "the key to understanding, the *cantus firmus*, the underlying theme . . . Jesus as 'the man for others' now displaces God as the root metaphor, now takes the place of ontological priority," in the words of Paul Van Buren.[9]

For James Burtness, Bonhoeffer is one who refuses "to allow the words of Jesus to be detached from his person, set adrift in the abstractions of ethical discourse."[10] Burtness goes on, "He [Bonhoeffer] is not the proclaimer of a system of what would be good today and at all times. He teaches no abstract ethics. He did not, like a moralist, love a theory of the good. He was not, like a philosopher, interested in the 'universally valid,' but rather in that which was of help to the real and concrete human being."[11] When one makes Christ, or the categorical imperative, a principle, one winds up in absurdity, the absurdity of Immanuel Kant who, in Bonhoeffer's words, "draws the grotesque conclusion that I must even return an honest 'yes' to the enquiry of the murderer who breaks into my house and asks whether my friend whom he is pursuing has taken refuge there: in such a case self-righteousness of conscience has become outrageous presumption and blocks the path of responsible action."[12] This is contrary to the example of Jesus who died for sinners within the world of his own lifetime.

"Who is present and contemporaneous with us here?" Bonhoeffer asks. It is the Jesus who "chose to participate *fully* in the human condition even to the death exacted for such total involvement."[13] Jesus is for us today in those boundary situations of sin, failure, suffering, and death, yes, but also in the fullness of human life and strength. He wills us strength, not weakness, boldness, not cringing. This Jesus "does not allow Himself to be invoked as an arbiter."[14] He threatened the whole "system of dependence on legal initiative and authoritarian sanction of all actions."[15] He taught, not abstract ethics, but love of the real person. He leads us away from systems "towards a more concrete ethic. What can and must be said is not what is good once and for all, but the way in which Christ takes form among us here and now."[16] No more than a powerless Jesus, can we free ourselves from experiences, responsibilities and decisions save falsely, by an abstraction. With the incarnation, history becomes a serious matter; with Jesus' crucifixion the infinite and the historically instant become an unresolvable tension. We must live in and with that tension. To resolve it by a too-worldly relativism, or a too heavenly absolutism, is to play the life and death of Jesus false.

Jesus, the man for us, bids us in this way: "One man asks: what is to come? The other: what is right? And that is the difference between the free man and the slave." Doing ethics in this mode means one automatically gives up the assurance of "being right." Bonhoeffer writes: "Doestoevsky let the figure of Christ appear in Russian literature as the idiot. . . . He is laughed at and loved. He is the fool and the wise man. He bears everything and forgives everything. He is revolutionary and yet he conforms. He does not want to—but he does—call attention to himself just by his existence. Who are you? Idiot or Christ?"[17]

Who is this Jesus for us today? A man who blessed sinners but who called them away from their sin, not into it—to strength, not to weakness. How do we claim this Jesus in a world come of age? "We are certainly not Christ; we are not called on to redeem the world by our own deeds and sufferings, and we need not try to assume such an impossible burden." But we must share in Christ's large-heartedness "by acting with responsibility and in freedom when the hour of danger comes, and by showing a real sympathy that springs, not from fear, but from the liberating and redeeming love of Christ for all who suffer. Mere waiting and looking on is not Christian behavior."[18] Writes his friend, Bethge: "Bonhoeffer pointed to the Christ who undermined pre-accepted doctrines: the Christ who did not escape into a *deus-ex-machina* religion; the Christ who parted himself from the privileged ones and ate with the outcasts; the Christ who by his defenselessness freed man for his own responsibilities. . . ."[19] Who do you say that I am? A powerless God who paradoxically frees our power so that we might act responsibly. A God who does not make us slaves to principles nor to abstract metaphysical constructions. Not: What do you think of Christ? but How has Christ been understood? Who is he for us now? Bonhoeffer's answer is clear: Jesus, the Man for others, not the unambiguously omnipotent sovereign; God, not Almighty, but embattled and suffering.

Who is *Bonhoeffer* for us today, the man who put so many troubling questions to us in and through his life and his work—for one, "the life," cannot be separated from the other, "the work." It was only by living in reality and for others that Bonhoeffer found faith and found himself. Bonhoeffer deeply distrusted idealist illusions, the overly pure, the disembodied intellectual. Hegel, he complained, "wrote a philosophy of angels, but not of human existence. It simply is not true that concrete man (including even the philosopher) is in full possession of the mind."[20] He offers us, in life and death, the "will to refrain from a system, as a deliberate gesture of ethical modesty towards others. . . ."[21] There is no absolute, sovereign individual. This is an abstraction "with no corresponding reality."[22] We are located within a web. Pluck one part and all quivers and hums. This means that "the preaching of the Church is therefore necessarily political, i.e., it is directed at the order of politics in which man is engaged." It does not *dictate* to that realm but "points to the limits to the law, to order, to the State."[23] Christian ethics of this sort—pointing to the limits—need not imply an interposition or conclusion; rather, Christian ethics, for example, "refuses to give physical scientists the last word on environmental policy or to allow military strategists alone to determine defense policy. . . ."[24]

Bonhoeffer offers not a full-blown political philosophy, but a set of limits to what the state is permitted to do. He resists ideology. He would spell out, indeed act out, an alternative to ideology in a world come of age. He does not leave faithfulness to the earth to Nietzsche; he speaks of and celebrates our creatureliness and insists that ethical behavior is how we act "in the midst of the needs, the conflicts, the decisions of the immediate world around us, from which there is no escape into general ideals and principles."[25] We are beset by false absolutes. What *is*, he declares, effects what *ought* to be—thus overturning the assumptions of those ethicists who would derive *is* from *ought*. The world is a sphere of concrete responsibility in which "one's task is not to turn the world upside-down, but to do what is necessary at a given place and with a due consideration of reality."[26]

Bonhoeffer criticized Western Christianity for "its having inflicted on people a psychic posture of weakness and immature dependence." Religion pushes Christ to the margins of real life, "where fear of sin and death hold a tenacious grip over peoples' consciences and a military oath can contravene resistance to evil."[27] Thus the church, his church, "is guilty of the deaths of the weakest and most defenseless brothers of Jesus Christ."[28] Taking a cue from Nietzsche, Bonhoeffer remarked that Christ "does not lead man in a religious flight from this world to other worlds beyond; rather, he gives him back to the earth as its loyal son."[29] Bonhoeffer leaves us with the question: "What is the ground under our feet?" And he answers: Not "a system of ideas" but "the whole combination of human relations, including the traditions, the values, and the ways of living, which have been bred in us and which we find good."[30] Not the person of conscience who flees into a position of Hegel's Beautiful Soul; rather, the conscience set free in Christ is set free for service and relishes life. The moralist, the overburdened person of conscience, loses *hilaritas*, "a distaste for scrupulosity," and taking of life in stride, joy in life's polyphony.[31]

What were those human relations, those traditions, out of which Bonhoeffer sprung and to which he remained faithful? Here matters get more complex for us as we ask: Who is Bonhoeffer for us today? For the way of life which gave birth to him is gone forever – a world of high bourgeois culture; strong, extended familial networks; sets of parental expectations and actions embodying honor, duty, discipline, rectitude, a strong mother and a strong father. Can we adopt Bonhoeffer's way *into* reality if we have not shared his world? I do not feel sure-footed here. Certainly Bonhoeffer would not want himself, for us, to be an argument. His life was rooted in family and friendship. He was cultivated. A generalist. A music lover. Sweet and modest, yet authoritative. By contrast to our contemporary North American culture which knows no shame and parades everything before us in the harsh and dizzying glare of publicity, Bonhoeffer endorses shame, for the way we *must* live is between "covering and discovering, between self-concealment and self-revelation, between solitude and fellowship."[32] Shame is not weakness but is central to discipline. It is a way to unfetter our ability to be for others.

What sort of man? Consider the parents. Writing to an emigré colleague after the war, Karl Bonhoeffer, noting the deaths of his two sons-in-law and two sons, states that he and his bereaved wife are "proud of their attitude which has been consistent."[33] Do we have it within our cultural repertoire to praise in this way? To grieve in this way?

When his indomitable maternal grandmother died at age 94, Bonhoeffer delivered the eulogy.

> With her a world is buried, which we all in some way bear within us, and wish so to bear. The unbending authority of the right, the free vow of a free man, the binding power of a promise once made, clarity and moderation in speech, honor and simplicity in public and private life – this she cared for with all her heart. In this she lived. She had discovered in the course of her life that it costs trouble and effort to achieve these aims in one's own life. She did not flinch from this trouble and effort. She could not bear to see these aims despised, or to see human rights denied. Therefore, her last years were darkened by the distress she felt over the fate of the Jews in our country, for this she herself grieved and suffered. She belonged to a different age, to a different spiritual world – and this world shall not be buried with her. This inheritance, for which we must thank her, *puts us under obligation*.[34]

Are we similarly "put under obligation"? If we come from strong families where dignity and decency were honored fare, perhaps. But our task in this regard is more difficult than Bonhoeffer's. He was sustained by centuries of familial honor and tradition: *a strong story.* We must find ways to sustain ourselves through acts of appropriating tradition, hence obligation, in a world in which the ground on which we stand is shaky and constantly shifting. Is this possible? Yes, but not as a merely rationalistic act; not as the affirmation of abstract principle. Only by living fully in the present, as Bonhoeffer taught, can we make Bonhoeffer-for-us part of the ground on which we stand.

Listen to Bonhoeffer on "The Sense of Quality." Christianity's business today, he writes, is "to defend passionately human dignity and reserve. The misinterpretation that we are acting for our own interests, and the cheap insinuation that our attitude is anti-social, we shall simply have to put up with; they are the invariable protests of the rabble against decency and order."[35] Spoken like a true aristocrat, you might say, yes, but also spoken like a man surrounded by the depredations of a thuggish, vulgar politics. "Nobility," he continues, "arises from and exists by sacrifice, courage, and a clear sense of duty to oneself and society, by expecting due regard for itself as a matter of course; and it shows an equally natural regard for others."[36] Modesty, moderation, concentration. Amid the hectic pace of modern life, Bonhoeffer offers boldness. He *is* that person of whom he writes, one who brings out crucial questions and forms a clear opinion about them. The weak, by contrast, always "have to decide between alternatives that are not their own."[37] Modern culture expects us to be weak; it trains us for weakness, for slackness of thought. Bonhoeffer offers strength, not force, not brutality, not peremptoriness, but strength that accepts and acknowledges limits.

I have asked, "Who is Bonhoeffer for us today?" To answer we must consider the reality in which we are imbedded. Considering that reality requires the revelation of conflict. Sometimes the conflict really *is* as stark as Christianity or Germany. On this score, Bonhoeffer was clear: "I must live through this difficult period of our national history with the Christian people of Germany. I will have no right to participate in the reconstruction of life in Germany after the war if I do not share the trials of this time with my people. . . . We face the terrible alternative of either willing the defeat of our nation in order that Christian civilization may survive, or willing the victory of our nation and thereby destroying our civilization. . . . The question really is: Christianity or Germanism and the sooner the conflict is revealed in the clear light of day the better."[38] For the world in which we live, he reasoned, is a world come of age. A world "which does not think itself bound to leave the determining of its fate to anyone outside itself, and which has in fact an even greater mastery over what used in the past to be called 'the secrets of nature.' Man has learnt to deal with himself in all questions of importance without the recourse to the 'working hypothesis' called God."[39]

Retreating to that hypothesis, praying and waiting for bad things to pass, will not do when what is *really* at stake is, for example, a conflict between Christianity and one's country. To be *for* others requires our identification *with* their powerlessness and suffering, in and through our strength, a strength that enables us to act freely, hence responsibly. One acts to reestablish limits. One acts without a handy guidebook. One acts in such a way that future generations, hopefully, will not be presented with a conflict as harsh as that which drew Bonhoeffer into action. Perhaps they will *not* have to decide—Christianity or Germany. By being *un*faithful to a murderous regime, Bonhoeffer declared his faithfulness, his patriotic allegiance, to the Germany of the culture of his ancestors; the Germany of Luther; the Germany of Christian civilization.

A situation that requires extraordinary action and demands dirty hands should be rare, a "peripheral and abnormal event."[40] One then acts in full knowledge of guilt. One knows one cannot expiate the wrong one has committed. But one embraces forgiveness—what Hannah Arendt calls Christianity's greatest contribution to politics—as the only way we have to break cycles of vengeance. Guilty parties cannot restore everything "just as it was before." All who act decisively incur guilt. Only God's forgiveness justifies. Claims cast within, and dependent upon, an ethical system for justification fall short. For what brings one to act? A sound reading of the situation. Civil courage properly understood. A knowing risk of personal corruption. All systematizing abstract ethical systems must fail us here, for we live in what is finite, historical, concrete, and unique.

Here things get tricky. Let me slow down and build the argument piece by piece, relying on Bonhoeffer's *Ethics.* Jesus loved human beings as they are. He does not permit us to classify others and their world "according to our own standards and to set ourselves up as judges over them."[41] But we cannot simply be subservient to events. In the face of the unexpected, fear, desire, irresolution and brutality most often reveal themselves. Here Bonhoeffer's words are powerful:

> At such a time as this it is easy for the tyrannical despiser of men to exploit the baseness of the human heart, nurturing it and calling it by other names. Fear he calls responsibility. Desire he calls keenness. Irresolution becomes solidarity. Brutality becomes masterfulness. Human weaknesses are played upon with unchaste seductiveness. . . . The vilest contempt for mankind goes about its sinister business with the holiest of protestations of devotion to the human cause.[42]

Where is the man or woman for others? His or her freedom to act cannot be absolute for he or she must recognize the freedom of the other person. This recognition collides with one's own autonomy, "yet [one] must recognize it."[43] For freedom is a relationship between two persons. Being free means "being free for the other, because the other has bound me to him."[44] The Nazifiers of the church can never understand the real nature of freedom, because they have separated themselves from the attitude of Jesus, exemplified in the "stark cadences of his Sermon on the Mount."[45]

We need courage and strength to be involved in worldly tasks without recourse to "miraculous or extramundane solutions. . . . Put bluntly, would prayer alone be sufficient to remove the evil of Hitlerism and cause an end to the war?"[46] Bonhoeffer, the man for others, living in reality, insisted that answer had been revealed; that conflict made manifest. Retreat into private piety would not serve, would not constitute the freedom and obligation of the man for others. Violence, to be sure, must always and only be an extreme measure. Bonhoeffer deplored and experienced the pain of his own desertion of non-violence. Violence was never the norm. But it may be the last resort. For the sake of the ultimate, the penultimate, the here and now, must be preserved.

Action never loses its ambiguity. We take the world as it is, not as ideologists would have it, as it ought to be. We cannot break out of ties to the present moment. A call comes to us only in a concrete place of responsibility. We must begin in our own backyards. This concept of reality, and of acting in and with and from it, "needs to be defined more exactly," Bonhoeffer writes. Craven "correspondence with reality" is the contrary of responsibility. "Neither servility to the given, nor an abstractly principled revolt against it in the name of some higher reality, locate us in service to others."[47] Both extremes are very far removed from the essence of the matter. Action in accordance with Christ, hence with reality, is borne in one's own body and is spoken from the standpoint of one who has not fallen victim to ideology. "One's task is not to turn the world upside down but to do what is necessary at the given place and with a due consideration of reality. At the same time one must ask what are the actual possibilities; it is not always feasible to take the final step at once."[48] There is no shelter from the storm; no law to cover us when we embark upon a free venture, particularly one that requires breaking of the law in order to honor the law. The structure of responsible action is readiness to accept guilt and freedom. Responsibility presupposes freedom and freedom consists in responsibility.

To whom or what am I responsible? I am not to answer that question in a way that guarantees that I "wear myself out in impotent zeal against all wrong and all the misery that is in the world." But neither am I "entitled, in self-satisfied security, to let the wicked world run its course, so long as I cannot myself do anything to change it and so long as I have done my own work. What is the place and what are the limits of my responsibility?" Bonhoeffer leaves us with these questions. He leaves us with a concept of the living truth that eschews the "cynical concept of truth," that idol of the fanatical devotee of truth which leaves no allowance for human weaknesses. There is, finally, "too much talk." Words have become rootless and homeless. This erodes the condition for truth. Rooted, at home, but not relentlessly absorbed in one single order of being, we can move towards living in truth. "Thinking and acting for the sake of a coming generation, but being ready to go any day without fear or anxiety—that, in practice, is the spirit in which we are forced to live. It is not easy to be brave and keep that spirit alive, but it is imperative."[49] Banish illusions and fantasies, including the false pride that demands that we be independent in everything. In fact, what we owe to others belongs to and is part of our own lives.[50] We must live unreservedly in life's duties, problems, successes and failures, experiences, and perplexities.[51]

Human life, Bonhoeffer insisted, was pathologically overburdened by the ethical. "They [the professional idealists] seem to imagine that every human action has a clearly-lettered notice attached to it by some divine police authority, a notice which reads either 'permitted' or 'forbidden.' They assume that a man must continually be doing something decisive, fulfilling some higher purpose and discharging some ultimate duty. This represents a failure to understand that in historical human experience everything has its time (Ecclesiastes 3), eating, drinking, and sleeping as well as duty, play as well as earnest endeavor, joy as well as renunciation. The presumptuous misjudgment of this creaturely existence leads either to the most mendacious hypocrisy or else to madness. It turns the moralist into a dangerous tormentor, tyrant and clown, a figure of tragi-comedy."[52]

Who is Bonhoeffer for us today? The man who, peering into the future, prepared, with that "consistent" attitude his parents so much admired, for his own death. He wrote a poem, "The Death of Moses" (September 1944), from the Tegel Prison, which says:

Der die Sünde straft und gern vergibt,
Gott, ich habe dieser Volk geliebt.

Das ich seine Schmach und Lasten trug
und sein Heil geschaut—das ist genug.

Halte, fasse mich! Mir sinkt der Stab,
treuer Gott, bereite mir mein Grab.

"God, who punishes then forgives,
this people I have truly loved now lives.

It is enough that I have borne its sorrow
and now have seen the land of its tomorrow.

Hold me fast! − for fallen is my stave,
O faithful God, make ready now my grave."[53]

These are the most difficult thoughts of all in our death denying culture. One of Bonhoeffer's most important lessons is that a culture that denies death must deny life. He did not have us in mind but, thinking with Bonhoeffer, that is precisely where we, to our shame and our peril, belong.

Notes

1. Dietrich Bonhoeffer, *Ethics* (New York: MacMillan, 1965), 248.
2. *Ethics*, 248.
3. Dietrich Bonhoeffer, *The Cost of Discipleship* (New York: MacMillan, 1978), 57.
4. *Ethics*, 64.
5. See chapter 6 in Stephen E. Fowl and L. Gregory Jones, *Reading in Communion* (Grand Rapids: Wm. B. Eerdmans, 1991).
6. From "Kant on Enlightenment and Revolution," trans. Colin Gordon, *Economy and Society* 15 (February 1986), 80–96.
7. James H. Burtness, *Shaping the Future: The Ethics of Dietrich Bonhoeffer* (Philadephia: Fortress Press, 1985), 39–40.
8. Dietrich Bonhoeffer, *Christ the Center* (New York: Harper and Row, 1978), 30–31.
9. Paul M. Van Buren, "Bonhoeffer's Paradox: Living with God without God, a Hypothetical Investigation," in Peter Vorkink, ed., *Bonhoeffer in a World Come of Age* (Philadelphia: Fortress Press, 1968), 14.
10. Burtness, 34.
11. Burtness, 152.
12. Burtness, 152.
13. Geffrey B. Kelly, *Liberating Faith: Bonhoeffer's Message for Today* (Minneapolis: Augsburg Publishing House, 1984), 49.
14. *Ethics*, 29.
15. Kelly, 132.
16. *Ethics*, 84–5.
17. *Christ the Center*, 35.
18. Dietrich Bonhoeffer, *Letters and Papers from Prison* (New York: MacMillan, 1973), 37.
19. Eberhard Bethge, "Bonhoeffer's 'Christology' and his 'Religionless Christianity,'" *Union Seminary Quarterly Review* 23 (Fall 1967), 69.
20. Dietrich Bonhoeffer, *Act and Being* (New York: Harper & Row, 1961), 27–8.
21. *Act and Being*, 88–9.
22. *Act and Being*, 130.

23. René Marlé, *Bonhoeffer: The Man and His Work*, trans. Rosemary Sheed (London: Geoffrey Chapman, 1968), 67.

24. Robin W. Lovin, *Christian Faith and Public Choices: The Social Ethics of Barth, Brunner, and Bonhoeffer* (Philadelphia: Fortress Press, 1984), 172.

25. William J. Peck, ed., *New Studies in Bonhoeffer's Ethics* (Lewiston, New York: Edwin Mellen Press, 1987), 236-7.

26. Bonhoeffer, cited in Burtness, *Shaping the Future*, 42.

27. Kelly, 130-9.

28. Kelly, 124.

29. Kelly, 73.

30. Peck, 271.

31. Burtness, 104.

32. *Ethics*, 22.

33. Eberhard Bethge, Renate Bethge, and Christian Gremmels, eds., *Dietrich Bonhoeffer: A Life in Pictures* (Philadelphia: Fortress Press, 1986), 234.

34. Mary Bosanquet, *The Life and Death of Dietrich Bonhoeffer* (New York: Harper and Row, 1968), 172.

35. *Letters and Papers*, 35.

36. *Letters and Papers*, 35-6.

37. *Letters and Papers*, 206.

38. Dietrich Bonhoeffer, quoted in *Testament to Freedom: The Essential Writings of Dietrich Bonhoeffer*, ed. Geffrey B. Kelly and F. Burton Nelson (San Francisco: Harper San Francisco, 1990) 504, 442.

39. Marlé, 111.

40. Lovin, 146.

41. *Ethics*, 71.

42. *Ethics*, 72-3.

43. Dietrich Bonhoeffer, *Life Together*, trans. John W. Dokerstein (San Francisco: Harper and Row, 1954), 101.

44. Kelly, 62.

45. Kelly, 43.

46. Kelly, 131.

47. *Ethics*, 223.

48. *Ethics*, 233.

49. *Letters and Papers*, 38.

50. *Letters and Papers*, 102.

51. *Letters and Papers*, 202.

52. *Ethics*, 122.

53. Dietrich Bonhoeffer, "Der Tod des Mose," in *Gesammelte Schriften*, 4 (Munich: Chr. Kaiser, 1965), 620. Translated by Nancy Lukens in *Testament to Freedom*.

CHRISTIAN WITNESS IN SOUTH AFRICA
IN A TIME OF TRANSITION

JOHN W. DE GRUCHY

Doing theology in dialogue with Dietrich Bonhoeffer within the South African context has developed in relation to changing historical circumstances. Until recently, the most obvious and immediate point of correspondence has been the German *Kirchenkampf* and the church struggle against apartheid in South Africa.[1] During the past two years, however, South Africa has begun to move beyond apartheid as a legislated system of racial domination and oppression. This does not mean that apartheid is now something of the past, nor does it mean that there will be an easy ride into a future of non-racial and just democracy. Indeed, some apartheid legislation remains and probably will remain until there is an interim government and a new non-racial and democratic constitution. Moreover, the horrendous legacy of apartheid and its colonial precursors will be with us for generations as the vast gap between rich and poor and the present violence in the country bear frightful testimony.

Nonetheless, we are no longer in the same historical era of a few years ago. The situation is far more fluid; in fact, it is now fragile and tenuous, with as much reason for despair as for hope. Certainly it is no longer possible to provide a social analysis which is as clear-cut and unambiguous as previously. For this reason there is considerable debate about the role of the church and the nature of Christian witness at this time. In some ecclesial circles, however—notably within the South African Council of Churches and more progressive/prophetic Christian groups—the church struggle continues and will of necessity continue until the last vestiges of apartheid have been overcome. Even then, we may anticipate further issues which will require a bold confession and courageous action on the part

284   JOHN W. DE GRUCHY

of Christians and the church.[2] But newly emerging realities have begun to reshape the character of the church struggle in terms of the responsibility of the church in the process of the transition to democracy.

The major task now facing both the church, as well as the emerging but deeply divided new nation, is overcoming the legacy of apartheid—working towards national reconstruction. This suggests that the most appropriate point of dialogue between us in our context at this time and Bonhoeffer is his reflections on the future of Germany and a new world order in the post-war context, though we may well find it helpful to draw on other periods in his life and thought. It must be kept in mind, however, that there are too many contextual differences for the two situations to be equated simplistically. Bonhoeffer, for example, anticipated that the war would end decisively in favour of the Allies, and that Nazi power would be destroyed. In South Africa the end to apartheid rule is a sine qua non, but the transition to a workable democracy will of necessity require a series of compromises during which former enemies will somehow have to co-operate in order to ensure a workable future. For example, the present civil bureaucracy, the army, and police force, will not simply disappear but have to be integrated in some way into a new democratic and non-racial order. In many respects a more appropriate comparison would be that between contemporary South Africa and the developments which have recently taken place in eastern Europe with the collapse of totalitarian communist regimes.

Despite the differences between Bonhoeffer's situation and ours, there are at least five interrelated areas in which reflection on his theology and praxis is helpful in illuminating the task of Christian witness in South Africa during this time of painful transition. First, his witness to peace within a context of escalating violence; second, the way in which he perceived the relationship between the church and political movements engaged in the struggle for a democratic order; third, Bonhoeffer's concern to strengthen the relationship between the church and labour; fourth, Bonhoeffer's linking the need for a confession of guilt to deeds of restitution and reparation; and fifth, Bonhoeffer's recognition that the historic position of the church and Christianity can no longer be taken for granted in a society undergoing rapid secularization.

We need to raise conscious attention to each of these issues, suggesting possible ways in which dialogue with Bonhoeffer may help clarify the nature and content of Christian witness at this time of transition in South Africa. The key to such dialogue may be found in the question: what perspective would Bonhoeffer bring to the issues? As an overall response to that question we would highlight those oft quoted words which he wrote shortly before his arrest:

We have for once learnt to see the great events of world history from below, from the perspective of the outcast, the suspects, the maltreated, the powerless, the oppressed, the reviled—in short, from the perspective of those who suffer.[3]

I. The Interconnection of Justice and Peace

Previous discussion on violence within the context of the church struggle in South Africa had to do with the justification of the use of violence to overthrow an unjust regime. In that regard Bonhoeffer's participation in the conspiracy to assassinate Hitler provided a basis for reflection. With the unbanning of liberation movements, it is now accepted by most that the use of violence to transform South African society is no longer morally or practically justifiable. On the contrary, the violent struggles taking place in the country are counter-productive in the process of working towards an interim government and a non-racial democracy. Thus many of those who previously sought to provide Christian legitimation for a "just revolution" or the armed struggle now argue strongly against the recourse to violence as a means to achieve democracy. At the same time they recognize the need for mass action such as strikes, and some speak of the "Leipzig option," namely the need for escalating yet peaceful protest, which will finally topple the government from power as in the former German Democratic Republic.

The causes of the present violence are extremely complex. Undoubtedly they are the result of years of apartheid repression which have destroyed the fabric of black society within many townships and squatter camps. The government argues that much of the violence has to do with a power struggle taking place between rival political organizations, notably the Zulu-based Inkhàta Freedom Party (IFP) and the ANC. This is partly true, as the Goldstone Commission has indicated. But there is far more to this than simply a "black on black" power struggle. There is little doubt that the IFP, which is part of the ruling National Party's alliance, has also received support from the state security forces. Whether this support is from rogue elements within the security forces who wish to scuttle negotiations and who are, in effect, opposed to President de Klerk's reforms, or whether it has the tacit support of the government, is a matter of intense debate. The government, in any case, is ultimately responsible for maintaining law and order, and therefore responsible for allowing the violence to reach such alarming proportions.

Bonhoeffer was never a consistent pacifist. There was a period during the early 1930's when he came close to such a position, and if developments in Germany had been otherwise he might have remained such. But in the

end his *Grenzfall* (limit-case) ethics required that he participate in the conspiracy. Subsequently Bonhoeffer's example has often been used to support the argument for Christian participation in the violent overthrow of
an unjust regime. Whatever the justification for using Bonhoeffer's position in this way, there can be little doubt that this cannot be justified in
the present situation in South Africa. On the contrary, Bonhoeffer's equally
powerful testimony to the Christian responsibility of peace-making is not
only more appropriate but more essential. The immense suffering caused
by current violence has to end.

In his sermon at the ecumenical conference in Fanø on "The Church and
the People of the World"[4] Bonhoeffer made three points, which still are
of particular relevance for us in South Africa. The first is the fact that the
church in its own membership transcends the political, social and racial
boundaries which divide people and lead to enmity. Within South Africa,
in fact, the church is really the only institution which can be the mediator
of peace, precisely because its constituency embraces virtually all segments
of society.

Second, Bonhoeffer spoke about the costliness of peace-making. "For
peace must be dared. It is the great venture. It can never be safe. Peace
is the opposite of security." While the Church in South Africa must be the
peace-maker, it cannot play the role of an objective and neutral referee.
The peace to which the Church bears witness is a peace which arises out
of a commitment to justice. There can be no peace in South Africa unless
there is an end to apartheid, which is ultimately the cause of the violence.
At the same time there is no possibility that a transition to democracy can
take place as long as the present violence continues. Thus, while justice
is the basis for enduring peace, penultimate steps to secure peace now
are also the condition for working towards a just democracy.

Third, Bonhoeffer called on the ecumenical church to play a role in bringing about peace amongst the nations of the world. Likewise the ecumenical
church should take a lead now in helping to end the violence through support of international efforts established to achieve this end, and, moreover,
through bringing pressure to bear on their respective constituencies in
South Africa to do so as well. This leads us to the next critical issue, namely
the way in which the church relates to the political parties and movements
in South Africa at this time.

II. Not Neutrality but Critical Solidarity

Bonhoeffer, perhaps more than any other major theologian of the first
half of the twentieth century, stressed the need for the church and for

Christians to be politically committed. This derived from his insistence that Christian witness be concrete both at the level of proclamation and praxis. Such concreteness required his opposition to the abuse of the Lutheran doctrine of "the two kingdoms," which allowed the church to claim neutrality in the political sphere. There can be no neutrality, Bonhoeffer argued, in the face of evil. The church must take sides, and it must take sides with those who suffer. In his case this meant solidarity with the Jews and other victims of oppression. But this, in turn, meant involvement in the resistance, solidarity with secular people who had given up on the church in the struggle against evil.

In the long years of struggle against apartheid the prophetic Church in South Africa participated increasingly with other political organizations and movements which shared the same commitment to ending oppression. Indeed, since the beginning of the ANC's existence in 1912, Christians have played a major role in its leadership, and there remains a strong Christian presence within the liberation movement today. Progressive Christians have not hesitated to participate with non-Christians, whether they be people of other faiths, secularists, or Marxists, in the struggle for justice. They have, in other words, chosen sides with the victims of apartheid and have thus been in solidarity with the movement for political liberation. Solidarity with victims implies solidarity with those engaged in the struggle for liberation.

In his essay on "The Church and the World," subsequently published in the *Ethics*, Bonhoeffer argued strongly for such solidarity. He also argued that such solidarity is a witness to Christ, and that the struggle for justice, truth and freedom needs to be justified by Christ.[5] By this Bonhoeffer means that such values cannot be understood as ideals in themselves, but have to find their meaning in relation to the historical reality of Jesus Christ. Hence, on the one hand there is an affirmation of those who struggle for justice. "He that is not against us is for us," says Jesus. But on the other hand, justice, truth and freedom must be critically evaluated in relation to the crucified Christ. In other words, Christians are called to be in critical solidarity with those who struggle for justice, truth and freedom on behalf of, and together with, the victims of society, even against other Christians who support reactionary forces. "He that is not with me is against me." Thus solidarity means participation in the struggle for justice, while critical solidarity requires that within the struggle Christians continue to bear witness to the message of the cross. This has fundamental implications both for the way in which the struggle takes place and the way in which power is exercised beyond liberation.

III. The Church and the Working Class

Historically, the relationship between "mainline" Christianity and labor in South Africa, and particularly the black proletariat, has been neither strong nor good. There have been isolated clergy who have identified with workers through the years, and there are some attempts to relate the church more relevantly to labor issues and the trade unions today.[6] Even where the majority of members in a denomination are, in fact, from the black working class, which is frequently the case, this does not mean that the church takes their labor struggles particularly seriously or has much knowledge about them. Today the problem has been exacerbated by the massive rate of unemployment, which some estimate to be almost 50% of the working population. All of this may account for the popularity which the South African Communist Party presently seems to enjoy within the townships.

In prison Bonhoeffer noted that the witness of the Confessing Church had little impact upon the masses.[7] The church appealed largely to the upper and lower middle classes. Indeed, the proletariat in Germany had either turned to communism or had fallen prey to national socialism— both of which did take the worker and unemployment seriously. For Bonhoeffer this failure had to be understood in relation to the long history of Europe, during which its Christian inheritance had decayed.[8] Much of Bonhoeffer's ministry was an attempt to overcome this historical failure on the part of the church, to reach not only the secular people typified by those co-conspirators who had given up on the church on the grounds of reason, but also to reach the proletariat who had given up on the church because of its lack of concern about labor, unemployment and poverty. The alliance between "throne and altar" put the church on the side of those in power, those who controlled industry and capital.

If we are to take seriously "the perspective from below . . . the perspective of those who suffer," then the complaints of those who are badly paid or unemployed must become a priority for Christian witness. This means a far greater concern by the churches with regard to labor and trade union issues, as well as developing modes of ministry to the unemployed. Indeed, there is a need for the churches to take seriously the "theology of work" which is already present amongst Christian workers, and to respond with sensitivity and solidarity. The present situation is unacceptable, and there is no way that a just democracy can flourish in a context where the gap between rich and poor, and between the middle-class and the poor, is so great. The alternative is increasing poverty and violence, and, inevitably a turning to totalitarian forms of government, whether of the right or the left.[9]

IV. Confessing Guilt and Practicing Restitution

If we are to take seriously the gap between rich and poor, then we have to take seriously the historic reasons for that gap. One reason stands out clearly above all others, namely the way in which European colonial power, and subsequently white apartheid domination, has resulted in African dispossession of the land. Although the process began much earlier, the notorious Land Act of 1913, and subsequent amendations to it leading up to the Land Act of 1936, meant that only 13% of South Africa was allotted to the vast majority of the population. This led, in turn, to the uprooting of people, the destruction of family life, turning peasant farmers into poorly paid farm laborers and tenants, forcing people to seek labor elsewhere, and the destruction of the environment. This has resulted in the massive problem today of urban homelessness and sprawling squatter communities. There is no way whereby we can move towards a just democracy unless the fundamental, but extremely complex and thorny, issue of land restitution is tackled.

Bonhoeffer, as far as I am aware, did not address the problem of land redistribution, but he did write and speak about two issues which are fundamental to the problem. First, in discussing "The Freedom of Bodily Life" he attacked every attempt to deprive people of their basic needs, and argued that when this happens the whole order of society is undermined. The only way to restore order is through what he described as "a restoration of the rights of natural life."[10]

Second, Bonhoeffer's understanding of the "confession of guilt" provides considerable insight into both the nature of the problem and possible ways to deal with it, at least theologically. In the first instance Bonhoeffer acknowledged with considerable realism the impossibility of turning back the clock of history. "Not all the wounds inflicted can be healed," he writes. Furthermore, he cautioned that retribution can "only give rise to new disaster."[11] But he also argued with great force that the healing of society can take place only when there is a genuine confession of guilt which leads to justice. Furthermore the church has to take the initiative and confess her own guilt as a step towards national restitution and healing.

> The church confesses that she has desired security, peace and quiet, possession and honour, to which she had no right, and in that way she has not bridled the desires of men but has stimulated them further.[12]

At the well-publicised Rustenburg Conference held at the end of 1990, and at the World Council of Churches consultation in Cape Town a year later, the link between the church's confession of guilt—and, indeed, any white confession of guilt for apartheid—and the need for concrete acts of reparation was affirmed. It was further recognized that the key to such reparation would be the redistribution of wealth and a new and just land policy. Hence the Rustenburg resolution:

> The Church must examine its own land ownership and work for the return of all land expropriated from relocated communities to its original owners.[13]

Unless there is a confession of guilt by white South Africa, a confession in which the church should be at the forefront, and unless such a confession is embodied in the fundamental restructuring of the economy of the land and making significant reparation for past oppression, the country cannot be healed.

V. Christianity in a Post-Christian Context

Aware that the process of secularization in the West could not be halted, and that the war would hasten the demise of Christendom, Bonhoeffer's final thoughts as expressed in his prison letters focused on Christian faith and the church in a world come of age. Despite the resurgence of religion since the nineteen-sixties and its challenge to previously accepted theories of secularization, there can be no doubt that Christendom is now largely something of the past for much of the world where it was previously a reality.

In many respects, however, Christendom has remained a reality in South Africa. Although this may be anachronistic, the fact is that the vast majority of the population still regards itself as Christian, and the present constitution of the country is avowedly Christian. Indeed, one of the more intense public debates at the present time concerns the future role of religion in general, and Christianity in particular, within the anticipated non-racial democracy. Will South Africa remain constitutionally a Christian state or will it become a secular state? If the latter, what will be the public role of Christianity and religion within it? Such questions cut across the ideological and political divide. Just as the ruling National Party has sought Christian legitimation since its inception, and drafted the present constitution accordingly, so the African National Congress has had a close connection with the churches, and from its inception has had chaplains and a religious affairs desk.

At the same time the religious situation is undergoing profound changes. In the first place it is being widely recognized now that South Africa is far more of a religiously plural society than was previously acknowledged by Christians. In the second place the historical link between Christianity and colonialism, Christianity and apartheid, and Christianity and capitalism in South Africa has resulted in an increasing alienation of many people, mainly black but also white, from the church and Christian faith. In the third place, while there has been a strong prophetic and progressive Christian presence in South Africa that has stood against racism and oppression, many are now questioning its tendency towards a "confessing triumphalism" which assumed a favored status for the church and Christianity. In the fourth place, despite a powerful residue of religion, and a prevailing religious world view, the same historical forces which have led to the secularization of the western world have had an irrevocable impact on South Africa. The question thus faces us as to the future of Christianity in a South Africa beyond colonialism and apartheid, that is, beyond South Africa's own legacy of Christendom. Already far-reaching proposals are being made with regard to this and related questions.

As Bonhoeffer intimated in his prison correspondence, the church in Germany was responding in different ways to the "world come of age." Pietism, Lutheran Orthodoxy, and the Confessing Church each had its own agenda.[14] The same is true in South Africa today, except that the church situation is far more complex and diverse than it ever was in Bonhoeffer's Germany. Our concern is, however, primarily with Bonhoeffer's critique of the Confessing Church and therefore his challenge to confessing Christianity in South Africa, particularly as we move into a new era in which the presuppositions of Christendom will no longer apply as they have previously. For however radically pro-apartheid and anti-apartheid confessing theology were opposed to each other they both worked from within a Christendom paradigm.

Bonhoeffer remained appreciative of the fact that the Confessing Church carried on "the great concepts of Christian theology." He also acknowledged that it gave evidence of "elements of genuine prophecy" and worship. The temptation into which the Confessing Church was falling, however, was the attempt to preserve the church through "conservative restoration," instead of interpreting prophecy and worship in a way which related to the new social reality.[15] A similar temptation faces the church in South Africa after these years of struggle against apartheid. There are two opposite facets to this temptation, both of which must be resisted. The first is the danger of triumphalism in a post-Christian context, relating to public issues on the assumptions, and with the attitudes, of 'Christendom.' The second is the danger of withdrawal from the political arena now that the end to apartheid is in sight, leaving public issues in the hands of the politicians.

Bonhoeffer's critique has already been taken into account in South Africa with the development of "prophetic Christianity," as evidenced in *The Kairos Document* and the more recent *Road to Damascus* document. Indeed, instead of going along the path of a secular reinterpretation of the gospel, however, as was the case in Western Europe, prophetic South African theologians have sought to interpret the gospel in word and action from the perspective of the poor and the oppressed. In doing so they have not denied, but affirmed, the reality of religion. Yet they have done so as a means of empowerment for people engaged in the transformation of their social condition, rather than as an affirmation of human weakness dependent upon a *deus ex machina*.[16]

The problem remains, however, that increasing numbers regard religious faith as superfluous. So the challenge of secularization remains to be faced by the church in South Africa. Increasingly the church in South Africa will have to provide a reason for the faith which it confesses if it hopes to fulfil a significant role in society. But this cannot mean, as Bonhoeffer so rightly maintained, either reductionism or a failure to speak and act prophetically in the public arena. That is why Bonhoeffer's vision of a church which exists for others, and yet one which is sustained by the secret discipline of its own liturgical life and biblical reflection, remains so pertinent for our context.

Notes

1. See John W. de Gruchy, *Bonhoeffer and South Africa Theology in Dialogue* (Grand Rapids: Eerdmans, 1984).
2. See *The Road to Damascus: Kairos and Conversion*, A document signed by Third World Christians from seven nations (Johannesburg: Skotaville, 1989).
3. Dietrich Bonhoeffer, *Letters and Papers from Prison* (London: SCM Press, 1971), 17.
4. "The Church and the People of the World," August 28, 1934, in Geffrey B. Kelly and F. Burton Nelson, *A Testament to Freedom: The Essential Writings of Dietrich Bonhoeffer* (San Francisco: Harper, 1990), 239f.
5. Dietrich Bonhoeffer, *Ethics* (New York: Macmillan, 1965), 55f.
6. J. R. Cochrane and G. O. West, eds., *The Three-fold Cord: Theology, Work and Labour* (Pietermaritzburg: Cluster, 1991).
7. *Letters and Papers*, 381.
8. "Inheritance and Decay," in *Ethics*, 88f., esp. 100.
9. Cf. *Ethics*, 100.
10. *Ethics*, 186.
11. *Ethics*, 118.

12. *Ethics,* 115; see John W. de Gruchy, "Confessing Guilt in South Africa Today in Dialogue with Dietrich Bonhoeffer," *Journal of Theology for Southern Africa* 67 (June 1989): 37–45.
13. "The Rustenburg Declaration," Article 5.2, in Louw Alberts and Frank Chikane, eds., *The Road to Rustenburg: The Church Looking Forward to a New South Africa* (Cape Town: Struik, 1991), 284.
14. *Letters and Papers,* 381.
15. *Letters and Papers,* 328.
16. *Letters and Papers,* 282.

BONHOEFFER, THE CHURCHES, AND JEWISH-CHRISTIAN RELATIONS

CHRISTIAN GREMMELS

These reflections are meant to help us approach the three keywords of our topic. The three approaches are not similar to each other in their contents, but in their methodologies; all of them search for the pre-conditions and the assumptions that help create understanding. In other words, I attempt to "understand" understanding by reconstructing the pre-conditions of understanding.

I. Bonhoeffer

Within my first approach I have a certain question in mind: As one of the editors of *The Letters and Papers from Prison* within the new edition of the *Dietrich Bonhoeffer Werke,* I have studied during the last years the complete material related to this book, published or unpublished. By doing so I had to ask myself: How should we read these letters and papers *today,* with which I myself have lived a quarter of a century?

To begin to answer this question, I would like to ask you to join me on my trip to the cell in Berlin-Tegel where those letters and papers were written. It is the 5th of October 1944. On this day a report issued by the Oberkommando of the Wehrmacht announces: "Near the Belgian-Dutch border in the southwest of Arnheim . . . the fierce fights against the strengthened forces of Canadian and English troops are continuing. . . . In the region of the Donau-Bogen the fights against the progressing Soviet formations continue . . ."[1] October 5, 1944. On this day Bonhoeffer writes his poem entitled "Jona." Fourteen days before this day in October the discovery of documents by the Gestapo had made the situation worse for his family and for himself. The consequence Bonhoeffer draws from these new developments is to give up the plan of a prepared escape from the Tegel prison. It is the last decision he will be able to make for his life and by himself. Later others will decide his fate for him. In his poem "Jona" Bonhoeffer deals with the meaning of that decision. He sends the poem on the 5th of October to Maria von Wedemeyer whom he tells: "Please type up the poem and send it to Eberhard. He will know who wrote it, without anybody telling him. Maybe you won't understand – or maybe you will?"[2] This is what then happened to the poem, that all of you know. It reads:

> In fear of death they cried aloud and, clinging fast
> to wet ropes straining on the battered deck,
> they gazed in stricken terror at the sea
> that now, unchained in sudden fury, lashed the ship.
>
> 'O gods eternal, excellent, provoked to anger,
> help us, or give a sign, that we may know
> who has offended you by secret sin,
> by breach of oath, or heedless blasphemy, or murder,
>
> who brings us to disaster by misdeed still hidden,
> to make a paltry profit for his pride.'
> Thus they besought. And Jonah said, 'Behold,
> I sinned before the Lord of hosts. My life is forfeit.
>
> Cast me away! My guilt must bear the wrath of God;
> the righteous shall not perish with the sinner!'
> They trembled. But with hands that knew no weakness
> they cast the offender from their midst. The sea stood still.[3]

Adopting the Jonah-motif (the same goes for the poem "The Death of Moses") Bonhoeffer tries to understand his situation by looking at another historical figure, exchanging roles with a prophet from Israel. This is what we see. There, we have the prophet of the Bible to whom God spoke: "Arise, go to Nineveh, that great city, and cry against it; for their wickedness is come up before me," and Jonah, who heard the message "rose up to flee . . . from the presence of the Lord. . . ." Here, we have Bonhoeffer, who decides on October 5, 1944 not to flee, who does not flee, who now knows that he has to stay and that this means his death. There, is Jonah, the biblical prophet, who knows, that, in contrast to the false prophet, a true prophet is only a prophet if what he foresees becomes true (Deuteronomy 18:21–22). "Forty days more and Nineveh shall be overthrown." With

this message in mind Jonah faces a hopeless dilemma: Either to be identified as a true prophet after the citizens of Nineveh have died, or to be
identified as the false prophet in the case of their rescue. What an alternative, what a choice: When truth means death, when credibility means
the downfall of a city and the death of both the guilty as well as the innocent inhabitants. What an alternative, when, on the other hand, life and
rescue are possible only when God's prophets become false prophets,
when God himself becomes untrustworthy. How can the true and living
God possibly be proclaimed under these circumstances?[4] So much for the
Jonah-dilemma.

And Bonhoeffer? What is Bonhoeffer's dilemma? Being in this venerated
location, we should remember that Bonhoeffer—having escaped his
dilemma while being here in America—decided to face his dilemma:
"Christians in Germany will face the terrible alternative of either willing
the defeat of their nation in order that Christian civilization may survive,
or willing the victory of their nation and thereby destroying our civilization."[5] What Bonhoeffer had to face upon his return from America was
an ethical variant of this biographical dilemma. Back in Germany he faced
the question, "whether one is to be guilty for not doing anything, or guilty
in doing something which is not innocent but which must be done."[6] The
poem "Jona" expresses as well as solves the dilemma.

"The Sea stood still" —this is how Bonhoeffer's poem ends. The biblical
book of Jonah, meanwhile, continues in the following way: "But the Lord
provided a large fish to swallow up Jonah; and Jonah was in the belly of
the fish three days and three nights." After God had acted in this way, Jonah
acts as well, and starts to pray. This is the prayer of Jonah, prayed "from
the belly of the fish," "out of the belly of she'ol":

> You cast me into the deep,
> into the heart of the seas,
> and the flood surrounded me;
> all your waves and your billows passed over me.
> Then I said, I am driven away from your sight;
> how shall I look again upon your holy temple?
> The waters closed in over me;
> the deep surrounded me;
> weeds were wrapped around my head
> at the roots of the mountains
> I went down to the land
> yet you . . . (Jonah 2:3–6)

We know how often Bonhoeffer read the Old Testament while in Tegel.
Is it possible that he did not know this psalm of thanksgiving and that

he did not hope for himself to join in the hopeful words "yet you"? "Yet you brought up my life from the pit." Until the end he had hoped. "But should it be thy will once more to release us to life's enjoyment" are the words he uses in "Powers of Good,"[7] written in the prison cellar of the Prinz-Albrecht-Strasse, where he had been brought three days after finishing the Jonah-poem.

In order to give an answer to the question, "how are we to read the Bonhoeffer of the *Letters and Papers from Prison*," I think it necessary to re-read Bonhoeffer in the light of the Bible he read in prison. So, trying to understand "Stations on the Road to Freedom,"[8] I read the following story from the New Testament.

> . . . Herod the king stretched out his hand to harass some from the church. Then he killed James, the brother of John, with the sword. And he proceeded further to seize Peter also. Now it was during the Days of Unleavened Bread. So when he had apprehended him, he put him in prison, and delivered him to four squads of soldiers to keep him, intending to bring him before the people after Passover. . . . And when Herod was about to bring him out, that night Peter was sleeping, bound with two chains between two soldiers; and the guards before the door were keeping the prison. Now behold, an angel of the Lord stood by him, and a light shone in the prison; and he struck Peter on the side and raised him up, saying 'Arise quickly!' And his chains fell off his hands. Then the angel said to him: 'Gird yourself and tie on your sandals.' And so he did. And he said to him: 'Put on your garment and follow me.' So he went out and followed him, and did not know that what was done by the angel was real, but thought, he was seeing a vision. When they were past the first and the second guard posts, they came to the iron gate that leads to the city, which opened to them of its own accord; and they went out . . . (Acts 12:1-10)

Although we know that this is not what happened to Bonhoeffer at the end of his life, I believe, *ubi angeli latent* (when angels are absent) God himself will open the iron gate, inviting out all the victims of this century of the wolves.

II. Church

Bonhoeffer wrote from prison,

> the church is the church only when it exists for others. To make a start, it should give away all its property to those in need. The clergy must live solely on the free-will offerings of their congregations, or possibly engage in some secular calling. The church must share in the secular problems of ordinary human life, not dominating, but helping and serving. It must tell men of every calling what it means to live in Christ, to exist for others.[9]

With a glance at this famous passage, which generations of female and male theologians bear in mind while accommodating themselves to the church we have, I would like to stress that the phrase "church for others" has changed its meaning. A critical term of Bonhoeffer has become a legitimizing term for the church. Let me give you an example to make myself clear.

Christmas eve in a church in Kassel. Well dressed people. A pastor preaching in good Bonhoeffer tradition, and no word is used more often than "church for others." And still, something is wrong. And as I turn around I understand what it is. An atmosphere of German-Christmas-*Gemütlichkeit* (geniality) fills the church. And the sermon goes on and on, and the pastor continuously opens his mouth for those who have been silenced: the groups of refugees—those, who at that time came from Eritrea, in northern Ethiopia. And maybe it was here when I—at the verge of falling asleep—began to dream. I dreamt about one of those women from Eritrea, for whom this pastor (a very friendly man) stood there. This woman herself was not actually there—she, who could have been there; she, who could have spoken for herself, would one have given her the opportunity. Rather, I dreamed that one of those women from Eritrea would be there, would get up, would walk to the front of the church, would open her mouth, would tear her clothes into pieces, just like the women in her country do when they mourn. She would tell us, while weeping and lamenting at the same time, the story of her suffering, when hunger came and when the girl to whom she had given birth had died. If this would be possible, we would have the "church *with* others." We would have the other in our midst. There is a very subtle possibility in the concept of the "church *for* others," as it is often used nowadays, that actually it is used to keep others away.

Trying to reconstruct the "context" within which to understand the term "church for others," I would like to point out that Bonhoeffer's sentence, "The church is the church only when it exists for others," is the exact expression of Bonhoeffer's experiences of the *Kirchenkampf* (church-struggle). The sentence, when turned into the negative, makes this even clearer: The church was not Christ's church when it was not there for others, when it was not there for those who had become the other, when it, by being silent, estranged itself from the One who did not want to be, but to be there for others. Eleven years earlier Bonhoeffer had already described the church as existence for the sake of those who had become victims: "The church bears a responsibility towards the victims of any order of society, even if they are not part of the Christian community."[10] In Bonhoeffer's *Ethics* we can read that the purpose of the church is to be "itself just a tool."[11]

Therefore, "Church for others" is an immanent critique aimed at the one-sided legacy of "Barmen," according to which the purpose of the church is to remain a church. Therefore repentance is needed for the fact that the church *ceased* to be church by *remaining* church. While the *Ethics* contains the church's confession of sins, the thoughts expressed under the title "Outline for a Book" are close to being a form of atonement. Bonhoeffer demands that the church atone and formulates the following for the post-war-church: "I hope it may be of some help for the church's future" reads the last sentence of the conclusions reached by Bonhoeffer towards the end of his life. It must have seemed unthinkable to him, that the church after this war in Germany might have a future without repenting for its past, its silence, its cooperation and its self-denial.

I don't think it is necessary to stress the extent to which those reflections of Bonhoeffer in his "Outline for a Book" were formed by his experiences of the German *Kirchenkampf*. I would like to cite just one passage: "In particular, our own church will have to take the field against the vices of hybris, power-worship, envy, and humbug, as the roots of all evil. It will have to speak of moderation, purity, trust, loyalty, constancy, patience, discipline, humility, contentment, and modesty."[12] The experiences of the *Kirchenkampf* remain an important presupposition, even where theological reflection has blurred these experiences through its own logic. This is what I intended to make clear with my statement on the ecclesiological sentence: "The church is the church *only* when it exists for others." To leave out the tiny word *"only"* – and this is what happens, if we use the phrase "church for others" – means to leave out the center piece of what Bonhoeffer says about the church in his "Outline for a Book." "Only" means "sola" or – to say it in theological terms – this "only" is a continuation of "notae ecclesiae," the "signs of the Church," a continuation of what the "Augsburg Confession" means when it speaks of the "Gospel . . . taught purely" and the "sacraments rightly adminstered"[13] as the two main Protestant criteria that determine the substance of the church. These two traditional criteria are completed by Bonhoeffer's third one: "when it exists for others."[14] And this completion is so important because it touches upon a different dimension. The first two other criteria – the "Gospel taught purely" and the "sacraments rightly administered"– serve to define the purpose of the church as a church, and thus they are equivalent to the first phase of the Kirchenkampf, in which the slogan "church has to remain church" was dominant. Church "existing for others," meanwhile, was Bonhoeffer's understanding of his experiences from a later period of the Kirchenkampf.

To give you an example for these later experiences, I quote the "Denk-schrift an Hitler" ("Memorandum to Hitler")[15] of the Confessing Church in 1936, which was a first attempt to realize the "existence for others" of the church. With this memorandum, the church transgressed for the first time a border in its relationship to the National Socialist government. It surpassed "Barmen" by raising its voice for something the church had not yet raised its voice for, by addressing the insecurity of law ("Rechts-unsicherheit") within the "new Germany"–the concentration camps and the official politics of antisemitism. "Should the terms blood, race, nation-hood and honour, within the National-Socialist philosophy of life, receive the importance of eternal values, Protestants are forced to reject this philosophy through the authority of the First Commandment. Should the Aryan race be glorified, God's word stands as a witness for the sins of humankind. Should antisemitism, demanding the hate of Jews, be forced on Christians, then the Christian commandment of love of neighbor stands against that."[16]

I have been referring to the "Denkschrift an Hitler" as a first attempt to practice "existence for others" within the church. The title under which the memorandum was published after the war is correct: "Die Bekennende Kirche sagt Hitler die Wahrheit" ("The Confessing Church tells Hitler the Truth"). And still–for the sake of history–the book should have had a subtitle, informing the reader that this truth was told while excluding the public. Only three copies existed.

Since I have started telling this story I should finish it quickly. Since Hitler was silent and some assumed that the leadership of the Confessing Church might, satisfied with its own courage, be content now to remain in silence, two of Dietrich Bonhoeffer's students (Werner Koch and Ernst Tillich) decided to act. They took the copy from the legal adviser of the Confess-ing Church, which was Dr. Friedrich Weißler, made a new copy and smuggled it across the border, so that the "Basel Information Service" could publish the entire text. Only then was this "heroic but certainly useless gesture," which the Confessing Church had agreed upon, in the words of Emil Fackenheim, transformed into "an enormous political deed."[17] The echo from abroad was disruptive to the Summer Olympics. How disrup-tive this was became clear when the perpetrators of the deed were pun-ished. Dr Friedrich Weißler, a Christian of Jewish descent, was beaten to death in Sachsenhausen.

I hope you will excuse my extensive use of this example from church history of a first attempt to practice Pro-Existenz within the church. The speaking of the church here does not compare to its silence at other times.

The reason for emphasizing this seemingly minute detail is this: Sometimes hope for the future needs to find a small reason for its existence by looking into the past.

At the end of my second approach, I have to make a methodological remark concerning the term "church for others." In my opinion Bonhoeffer's legacy does not lie in the term itself—and the same goes for "this-worldliness," "world come of age," or "Mündigkeit."[18] Rather, it lies in the conjunction of such "words" and the "situation," which has a hermeneutical function for each of these terms.

III. Jewish-Christian Relations

My third approach is related to Jewish-Christian relations—not to that relation itself, but to the conditions and presuppositions which Christian theology has to revise in order to build up this relationship. As an example I have chosen Bonhoeffer's words about "God's powerlessness and suffering." The methodological issue I would like to raise in this context might be stated as follows: There is no grasping of an idea or conception without the effort to rethink the situation under which the conception received its meaning. Pondering the idea of "God's suffering," I wonder whether *this* is the situation that gives meaning to the idea of a suffering God. As Hans-Joachim Iwand said in a speech given during the "Woche der Brüderlichkeit" ("Week of Brotherhood") in 1958:

> Recall a scene, as reported by the German civil engineer Herrmann Gräbe, who happened to witness an execution in Volhynia. It happens within a pit; on a stairway that has been carved out of the mud wall, the victims—men, women and children—have to descend, totally naked, and lie down to be shot. The engineer describes the human being that is doing the executing: 'I looked at the rifleman: he, an SS man, sat on the narrow side of the pit on the ground, his legs hanging down into the pit, a gun on his knees, and smoked a cigarette.' The report continues: 'Nobody was crying, nobody was begging to stay alive.' However, the witness saw a father who held a perhaps 10-year old boy in his hands. 'The boy was fighting back his tears, the father was pointing towards heaven with his finger, and caressed the boy's head and seemed to explain something to him.'"[19]

One has to bear this "scene." By bearing I mean that it is unbearable to see how Christian theologians think they have to be helpful by giving quick interpretations. Theological interpretations of that kind are a specific form of "ignoring," through which a "second guilt" is committed, which Ralph Giordano has expressed so poignantly.[20] Since the great ideas of German culture, as well as the classic terms and systems of theology, have not been able to prevent what this "scene" stands for, how can one possibly assume to be able to use the same terms in order to give a sufficent theological interpretation of the Holocaust?

"God's own suffering." While Bonhoeffer was in prison, the extermination of the Jews was being executed. "Something happened that nobody had even imagined as being possible. Here a deep layer of connectedness between every human being was cut apart. The integrity of this layer till then, had been—despite all the natural bestialities of world history—assumed. A ribbon of naïveté was torn apart then—a naïveté that before had nurtured unquestioned traditions,"[21] entire theological fields and complex assumptions. "Auschwitz has happened" ("Auschwitz *war*," Theodor W. Adorno). The fact that *this* has happened means that the conditions of historical processes, including the theological interpretations of the world, have lost the innocence of historical identity. Therefore, the word Auschwitz stands not only for an event in history, but it has become the presupposition for any Christians who want to continue interpreting history. Are we going to use our classical terms without changing their frame-work?

Shortly before his death the former commander of Treblinka, Franz Stangl, was interviewed:

Q(uestion):   If you recall them now—do these horrible deeds of Treblinka make any sense to you?

F. Stangl: Yes, I am sure it was 'wanted' . . .

Q: When you are saying 'wanted'—do you mean 'wanted' by God?

F. Stangl: Yes.

Q: What is God? . . . Was God in Treblinka?

F. Stangl: Yes. How else could it have happened?[22]

In 1967 Milan Machovec, during a public discussion cited Adorno's famous sentence: "Poetry after Auschwitz does not exist any more."[23] Referring to that sentence, he then asked his audience whether there still could be prayers for us after Auschwitz? It was Johann Baptist Metz who gave the answer, the theological consequences of which we hardly are able to grasp yet: "We can pray *after* Auschwitz, because there was prayer *in* Auschwitz."[24] Of course it is true that this is the answer of a Christian, and since I have not yet had the chance to hear how this answer sounds to a Jew, I accept it as a theological answer only with reservations. Rabbi Greenberg says: "After the Holocaust, there should be no final solutions, not even theological ones."[25] I have interpreted this word to mean that the "leaving behind" of "final solutions" could also mean that the path should be cleared in order for us to think about a possible theological "solution" and what it could look like, in order that it would not—again—be a solution that exludes the Jews. So let me ask you, what could an "inclusive" solution look like?

Since it might not be appropriate to conclude my remarks with an open question, I would like to cite from Eberhard Bethge's attempt to formulate a "christological credo after Auschwitz": "I believe in Christ, who brings us closer to God and to life, who directs our thoughts and our hearts against false gods, while, at the same time, directing our thoughts and hearts towards the victims of those false gods."[26]

Notes

1. *Die Wehrmachtsberichte 1939-1945*, 3 (Cologne: Gesellschaft für Literatur und Bildung, 1989), 275f.
2. Dietrich Bonhoeffer to Maria von Wedemeyer. Letter of October 5, 1944. In Ruth-Alice von Bismarck and Ulrich Kabitz, eds., *Brautbriefe Zelle 92. Dietrich Bonhoeffer—Maria von Wedemeyer 1943-1945* (Munich: C. H. Beck, 1992), 206.
3. Dietrich Bonhoeffer, *Letters and Papers from Prison: The Enlarged Edition* (New York: Macmillan, 1971), 398-9. Cf. J. Henkys, *Dietrich Bonhoeffers Gefängnisgedichte: Beiträge zu ihrer Interpretation* (Munich: Chr. Kaiser, 1986), 51-6.
4. Cf. Jürgen Ebach, "Vom Untergang reden müssen: Jona, der Prophet, und die Stadt Ninive," in *Theologische Reden, mit denen man keinen Staat machen kann* (Bochum: Selbstverlag des Sozialwissenschaftlichen Instituts der EKD, 1989), 53ff.
5. Dietrich Bonhoeffer to Reinhold Niebuhr. Letter of June 1939. In *Gesammelte Schriften*, I (Munich: Chr. Kaiser, 1965), 320.
6. John W. de Gruchy, "Christus bekennen in Südafrika," in Christian Gremmels and I. Tödt, eds., *Die Präsenz des verdrängten Gottes: Glaube, Religionslosigkeit und Weltverantwortung nach Dietrich Bonhoeffer*. Internationales Bonhoeffer Forum, 7 (Munich: Chr. Kaiser, 1987), 133.
7. *Letters and Papers*, 400-1.
8. *Letters and Papers*, 370-1.
9. *Letters and Papers*, 382.
10. *Gesammelte Schriften*, II (Munich: Chr. Kaiser, 1965), 48.
11. *Dietrich Bonhoeffer Werke*, 6. *Ethik*, ed. I. Tödt, H. E. Tödt, E. Feil and C. Green (Munich: Chr. Kaiser, 1992), 408.
12. *Letters and Papers*, 382f.
13. *The Augsburg Confession*, commentary by Leif Grane, trans. John H. Rasmussen (Minneapolis: Augsburg, 1987), Article 7.
14. *Letters and Papers*, 382-3.
15. "Denkschrift der Vorläufigen Leitung der Deutschen Evangelischen Kirche an den Führer und Reichskanzler Adolf Hitler vom 28. Mai 1936," in Wilhelm Niemöller, *Die Bekennende Kirche sagt Hitler die Wahrheit. Die Geschichte der Denkschrift der Vorläufigen Leitung vom Mai 1936* (Bielefeld: Ludwig Bechauf, 1954), 9-18. Cf. Martin Greschat, ed., *Zwischen Widerspruch und Widerstand: Texte zur Denkschrift der Bekennenden Kirche an Hitler 1936* (Munich: Chr. Kaiser, 1987).
16. "Denkschrift," 14.

17. Emil L. Fackenheim, "Letter to Dr. Bethge" (Toronto, February 1979), in *Wie eine Flaschenpost: Ökumenische Briefe und Beiträge für Eberhard Bethge*, ed. H. E. Tödt in Zusammenarbeit mit H. Pfeifer, F. Schlingensiepen and I. Tödt (Munich: Chr. Kaiser, 1979), 331-2.

18. Cf. Jürgen Moltmann, *The Way of Jesus Christ* (San Francisco: Harper San Francisco, 1990), 64-5.

19. Hans-Joachim Iwand, *Umkehr und Wiedergeburt, Vortrag zur Woche der Brüderlichkeit in Düsseldorf am 9.März 1958*. Unpublished manuscript, 2.

20. Ralph Giordano, *Die zweite Schuld oder Von der Last Deutscher zu sein* (Hamburg: Rasch und Röhring, 1987).

21. Jürgen Habermas, *Die Moderne—ein unvollendetes Projekt: Philosophisch-politische Aufsätze, 1977-1990* (Leipzig: Reclam, 1990), 162.

22. "War Gott in Treblinka? Bekenntnisse eines Biedermanns—Franz Stangl gibt zu Protokoll," *Die Zeit* (Oct. 29, 1971): 10.

23. Theodore W. Adorno, *Prisms* (Cambridge: MIT Press, 1982), 34.

24. Johann Baptist Metz, *The Emergent Church* (New York: Crossroad, 1981), 19.

25. Irving Greenberg, "Cloud of Smoke, Pillar of Fire: Judaism, Christianity and Modernity after the Holocaust." Quoted by Larry Rasmussen in *Dietrich Bonhoeffer: His Significance for North Americans* (Minneapolis: Fortress Press, 1990), 116.

26. Eberhard Bethge, "Christologie und das erste Gebot," in *Erstes Gebot und Zeitgeschichte: Aufsätze und Reden. 1980-1990* (Munich: Chr. Kaiser, 1991), 70.

ABOUT THE CONTRIBUTORS

LUCA BAGETTO is a doctoral candidate in aesthetics at the University of Torino, Italy. He is the author of *Decisione ed effettivita: La via ermeneutica di Dietrich Bonhoeffer.*

LUCA D'ISANTO recently received his Ph.D. in philosophical theology from the University of Virginia, Charlottesville, Virginia.

JEAN BETHKE ELSHTAIN is Centennial Professor of Political Science and Professor of Philosophy at Vanderbilt University, Nashville, Tennessee. She is the author of *Public Man-Private Woman, Meditations on Modern Political Thought, Women and War,* and *Power Trips and Other Journeys.*

WAYNE WHITSON FLOYD, JR., is General Editor of the *Dietrich Bonhoeffer Works* Translation Project and visiting Professor of Theology at The Lutheran Theological Seminary at Philadelphia, Pennsylvania. He is the author of *Theology and the Dialectics of Otherness: On Reading Bonhoeffer and Adorno* and co-author with Clifford J. Green of *Bonhoeffer Bibliography: Primary Sources and Secondary Literature in English.*

CLIFFORD J. GREEN is Professor of Theology and Ethics and Director of the Public Policy Center at Hartford Seminary, Hartford, Connecticut. He is the author of *The Sociality of Christ and Humanity, Dietrich Bonhoeffer's Early Theology,* as well as other works on Bonhoeffer, including contributions to volumes in the *Dietrich Bonhoeffer Werke.*

CHRISTIAN GREMMELS is Professor of Systematic Theology at the University of Kassel, Germany. He is president of the Internationale Bonhoeffer Gesellschaft, Sektion Bundesrepublic Deutschland. He is co-author with Hans Pfeiffer of *Theologie und Biographie: Zum Beispiel Dietrich Bonhoeffer,* editor of *Bonhoeffer und Luther* and co-editor with Eberhard Bethge and Renate Bethge of *Dietrich Bonhoeffer: A Life in Pictures.*

JOHN W. DE GRUCHY is Professor of Christian Studies at the University of Cape Town, South Africa, and editor of the *Journal of Theology for Southern Africa.* He is the author of *Church Struggle in South Africa* and *Liberating Reformed Theology.*

VIGEN GUROIAN is Associate Professor of Theology and Ethics at Loyola College in Baltimore, Maryland. He is the author of *Faith, Church, Mission: Essays for Renewal in the Armenian Church* and the forthcoming *Ethics after Christendom: Toward an Ecclesial Christian Ethic.*

DOUGLAS JOHN HALL is Professor of Christian Theology in the Faculty of Religious Studies at McGill University, Montreal, Canada. His most recent book is *Professing the Faith: Christian Theology in a North American Context.*

BARRY A. HARVEY is a Lecturer in Theology in the Department of Religion at Baylor University, Waco, Texas. He is the author of the forthcoming *Politics of the Theological.*

HANS D. VAN HOOGSTRATEN is Professor of Theology and Social Ethics in the Department of Theology at the University of Nijmegen, The Netherlands. He recently published *Geld en geest: over milieu-ethiek* (*Money and Mind: On Environmental Ethics*).

WOLFGANG HUBER is Professor of Systematic Theology (Ethics) at the University of Heidelberg, Germany, and the recently elected Bishop of the Evangelical Church in Berlin-Brandenburg. Among his numerous books are *Unvollendete Auferstehung* and *Die tägliche Gewalt.*

L. GREGORY JONES is Assistant Professor of Theology at Loyola College in Baltimore, Maryland, and co-editor of the journal *Modern Theology.* His publications include *Transformed Judgment* and *Reading in Communion* (with Stephen Fowl).

GEFFREY B. KELLY is Professor of Systematic Theology in the Department of Religion at LaSalle University, Philadelphia, Pennsylvania. He is the president of the International Bonhoeffer Society, English Language Section. He is the author of *Liberating Faith: Bonhoeffer's Message for Today, A Testament to Freedom: The Essential Writings of Dietrich Bonhoeffer,* and *Karl Rahner: Theologian of the Graced Search for Meaning.*

WALTER LOWE is Professor of Systematic Theology at the School of Theology, Emory University, Atlanta, Georgia. His books include *Evil and the Unconscious* and *Theology and Difference: The Wound of Reason.*

OTTO A. MADURO is Associate Professor of Latin American Christianity at Drew University, Madison, New Jersey. He is the author of *Religion and Social Conflicts,* the editor of *Judaism, Christianity and Liberation* and with Marc Ellis edited *The Future of Liberation Theology.*

CHARLES MARSH is Assistant Professor of Theology at Loyola College in Baltimore, Maryland, and Director of Theological Horizons, a non-profit organization which supports theological research and education. He is the author of *Reclaiming Dietrich Bonhoeffer: The Promise of His Theology.*

STEVEN PLANT is currently completing his dissertation for the doctoral degree at Cambridge University, England. He serves as a Methodist Minister in central London.

ROBERT P. SCHARLEMANN is Commonwealth Professor in the Department of Religious Studies at the University of Virginia, Charlottesville, Virginia. His most recent book is *The Reason of Following: Christology and the Ecstatic I.*

STEVEN SCHROEDER teaches Philosophy and Liberal Studies at Roosevelt University, Chicago, Illinois. His most recent publications include *A Community and a Perspective: Lutheran Peace Fellowship and the Edge of the Church, 1941–1991.*

WORKS CITED

Adorno, Theodor. *Aesthetic Theory.* Boston: Routledge and Kegan Paul, 1984.

———. *Minima Moralia: Reflections from Damaged Life.* London: NLB, 1974.

Atamian, Sarkis. *The Armenian Community.* New York: Philosophical Library, 1955.

Bagetto, Luca. *Decisione ed Effettivita: La vis ermeneutica di Dietrich Bonhoeffer.* Genova: Marietti, 1991.

Barth, Karl. *Church Dogmatics,* III/4. Translated by A. T. Mackay et al. Edinburgh: T and T Clark, 1961.

———. *The Epistle to the Romans.* Translated by Edwyn C. Hoskyns. London: Oxford University Press, 1960.

Beck, Ulrich. *Gegengifte: Die Organisierte Unverantwortlichkeit.* Frankfurt: Suhrkamp, 1988.

Bellah, Robert N., et al. *The Good Society.* New York: Knopf, 1991.

———. *Habits of the Heart.* Berkeley: University of California Press, 1985.

Bethge, Eberhard. *Bonhoeffer: Exile and Martyr.* Edited by John W. de Gruchy. New York: Seabury Press, 1976.

———. *Dietrich Bonhoeffer: Theologian, Christian, Contemporary.* Translated by Eric Mosbacher et al. New York: Harper and Row, 1970.

Bonhoeffer, Dietrich. *Act and Being.* Translated by Bernard Noble. New York: Octagon Books, 1983. (*Akt und Sein.* Munich: Christian Kaiser Verlag, 1988.)

———. *Christ the Center.* Translated by Edwin H. Robertson. New York: Harper and Row, 1978.

———. *The Cost of Discipleship.* Translated by R. H. Fuller. New York: Macmillan, 1950. (*Nachfolge.* Munich: Christian Kaiser Verlag, 1985.)

———. *Creation and Fall.* Translated by John Fletcher. New York: Macmillan, 1959.

———. *Ethics.* Translated by N. H. Smith. New York: Macmillan, 1965. (*Ethik.* Edited by Eberhard Bethge. Munich: Christian Kaiser Verlag, 1985.)

———. *Gemeinsames Leben.* Edited by Gerhard Ludwig Müller and Albrecht Schönherr. Munich: Christian Kaiser Verlag, 1987.

———. *Gesammelte Schriften.* Volumes 1–5. Munich: Christian Kaiser Verlag, 1965.

———. *Jugend und Studium, 1918ffn%1927.* Edited by Hans Pfeifer, Clifford Green, and Carl-Jürgen Kaltenborn. Munich: Christian Kaiser Verlag, 1986.

———. *Letters and Papers from Prison.* Edited by Eberhard Bethge. New York: Collier Books, 1971. (*Widerstand und Ergebung.* Edited by Eberhard Bethge. Munich: Christian Kaiser Verlag, 1985.)

———. *Meditating on the Word.* Translated by David Gracie. Cambridge, Mass.: Cowley Publications, 1986.

———. *No Rusty Swords: Letters, Lectures and Notes, 1928–1936,* from the Collected Works. Edited and translated by Edwin H. Robertson and John Bowden. Vol. 1. New York: Harper and Row, 1965.

———. *Predigten Auslegungen Meditationen, 1935–1945.* Munich: Christian Kaiser Verlag, 1985.

———. *Sanctorum Communio.* Translated by Ronald Gregor Smith et al. London: Collins, 1963. (*Sanctorum Communio.* Munich: Christian Kaiser Verlag, 1986.)

———. *Spiritual Care.* Translated by Jay C. Rochelle. Philadelphia: Fortress Press, 1985.

———. *A Testament to Freedom: The Essential Writings of Dietrich Bonhoeffer.* Edited by Geffrey B. Kelly and F. Burton Nelson. San Francisco: Harper, 1990.

———. *True Patriotism: Letters, Lectures and Notes, 1930–1945, from the Collected Works.* Edited and translated by Edwin H. Robertson. Vol. 3. New York: Harper and Row, 1973.

———. *The Way to Freedom: Letters, Lectures, and Notes, 1935–1939.* Edited and translated by Edwin H. Robertson. New York: Harper and Row, 1966.

Bonsanquet, Mary. *The Life and Death of Dietrich Bonhoeffer.* New York: Harper and Row, 1968.

Brunner, Emil. *The Divine Imperative.* London: Lutterworth, 1937.

Bubner, Rudiger. *Modern German Philosophy.* Translated by Eric Matthews. Cambridge: Cambridge University Press, 1981.

Buck-Morss, Susan. *The Origin of Negative Dialectics.* New York: Free Press, 1977.

Burtness, James H. *Shaping the Future: The Ethics of Dietrich Bonhoeffer.* Philadelphia: Fortress Press, 1965.

Cajetan de Vio, Thomas. *De L'Analogie et du Concept d'Etre.* Translated by H. Robillard. Montreal: Presses L'Universitee de Montreal, 1963.

Carter, Guy, et al., eds. *Bonhoeffer's Ethics. Old Europe and New Frontiers.* Kampen: Kok Pharos, 1991.

Chavanne, Henri. *L'Analogie entre Dieu et le Monde selon Saint Thomas D'Aquin et selon Karl Barth.* Paris: Editions du Cerf, 1969.

Clements, Keith W. *What Freedom? The Persistent Challenge of Dietrich Bonhoeffer.* Birmingham: Church Enterprise Print, 1990.

Cochrane, J. R., and G. O. West, eds. *The Three-fold Cord: Theology, Work, and Labour.* Pietermaritzburg: Cluster Publications, 1991.

Cone, James H. *Black Theology and Black Power.* New York: Seabury Press, 1969.

Dallmeyr, Fred. *Twilight of Subjectivity: Contributions to a Post-Individualist Theory of Politics.* Amherst: University of Massachusetts Press, 1981.

Day, Thomas I. *A Bonhoeffer Legacy: Essays in Understanding.* Grand Rapids, Mich.: Eerdmans, 1981.

Derrida, Jacques. *Dissemination.* Chicago: University of Chicago Press, 1981.
———. *Of Grammatology.* Baltimore: Johns Hopkins University Press, 1974.
———. *Margins of Philosophy.* Chicago: University of Chicago Press, 1982.
———. *Positions.* Chicago: University of Chicago Press, 1981.

Dilthey, Wilhelm. *Weltanschuung und Analyse des Menschen seit Renaissance und Reformation.* Gesammelte Schriften, 2. Stuttgart and Göttingen: Teubner and Vandenhoeck and Ruprecht, 1960.

Dreyfus, Hubert, Paul Rabinow, and Michel Foucault. *Beyond Structuralism and Hermeneutics.* Chicago: University of Chicago Press, 1983.

Dulles, Avery. *Models of the Church.* Garden City, N.J.: Image Books, 1974.

Dumas, Alexandre. *Dietrich Bonhoeffer: Theologian of Reality.* London: SCM, 1971.

Ebach, Jürgen. *Theologische Reden, mit denen man keinen Staat machen kann.* Bochum: Selbstverlag des Sozialwissenschaftlichen Instituts der EKD, 1989.

Erdozain, Placido. *Archbishop Romero: Martyr of Salvador.* Translated by J. McFadden and R. Warner. Maryknoll, N.Y.: Orbis, 1981.

Fackenheim, Emil. *Wie eine Flachenpost. Okumenische Briefe und Beiträge für Eberhard Bethge.* Edited by H. H. Todt. Munich: Christian Kaiser Verlag, 1979.

Feil, Ernst. *The Theology of Dietrich Bonhoeffer.* Translated by M. Rumscheidt. Philadelphia: Fortress Press, 1985.

Floyd, Wayne Whitson. *Theology and the Dialectics of Otherness: On Reading Bonhoeffer and Adorno.* Lanham, N.Y.: University Press of America, 1988.

Forster, E. M. *A Passage to India.* Middlesex: Penguin, 1978.

Foucault, Michel. *Discipline and Punishment: The Birth of the Prison.* Translated by Alan Sheridan. New York: Random House, 1979.

Fukuyama, Francis. *The End of History.* New York: Free Press, 1992.

Gadamer, Hans-Georg. *Truth and Method.* Translated by G. Barden and J. Cumming. New York: Seabury Press, 1975.

Giordano, Ralph. *Die zweite Schuld oder Von der Last Deutscher zu sein.* Hamburg: Rash und Rohring Verlag, 1987.

Green, Clifford. *The Sociality of Christ and Humanity.* Missoula, Mont.: Scholars Press, 1975.

Greenberg, Irving. "Cloud of Smoke, Pillar of Fire: Judaism, Christianity and Modernity after the Holocaust." In *Auschwitz: Beginning of a New Era?* ed. Eva Fleishner. New York: KTAV, 1974.

Gremmels, Christian. *Die Prasenz des verdrangten Gottes. Glaube, Religionslosigkeit und Weltverantwortung nach Dietrich Bonhoeffer.* Munich: Internationales Bonhoeffer Forum, 1987.

———. *Wur Sozialgestalt des Luthertums in der Moderne.* Munich: Christian Kaiser Verlag, 1983.

Gruchy, John W. de. *Bonhoeffer and South Africa. Theology in Dialogue.* Grand Rapids, Mich.: Eerdmans, 1984.

———. *Dietrich Bonhoeffer: Witness to Jesus Christ.* London: Collins, 1987.

———. *Liberating Reformed Theology.* Grand Rapids, Mich.: Eerdmans, 1991.

Gutierrez, Gustavo. *The God of Life.* Maryknoll, N.Y.: Orbis, 1991.

———. *The Power of the Poor in History.* Maryknoll, N.Y.: Orbis, 1988.

———. *A Theology of Liberation.* Translated by Sister Caridad Inda and John Eagleson. Maryknoll, N.Y.: Orbis, 1973.

———. *The Truth Shall Make You Free: Confrontations.* Maryknoll, N.Y.: rbis, 1990.

Habermas, Jurgen. *Die Moderne—in unvollendetes Projekt. Philosophisch-politische Aufsatze, 1977–1990.* Leipzig: Reclam-Verlag, 1990.

Hall, Douglas John. *The Reality of the Gospel and the Unreality of the hurches.* Philadelphia: Westminster Press, 1984.

———. *Reinhold Niebuhr and the Issues of Our Time.* London: Mowbray, 1986.

Stanley. *After Christiandom?* Nashville: Abingdon Press, 1991.

Haval, Vaclav, "The Power of the Powerless." In *Living in Truth*, ed. Jan Vladislav. Boston: Faber and Faber, 1987.

Huber, Wolfgang. *Konflikt und Konsens, Studien zur Ethik der Verantwortung.* Munich: Christian Kaiser Verlag, 1990.

———. "Der Protestantismus und die Ambivalenz der moderne." In *Religion der Freiheit. Protestantismus in der Moderne,* ed. Jürgen Moltmann. Munich: Christian Kaiser Verlag, 1990.

Jaspers, Karl. *Die geistige Situation der Zeit.* Berlin: Goschen, 1932.

Jay, Martin. *Adorno.* Cambridge: Harvard University Press, 1984.

———. *Marxism and Totality: The Adventures of a Concept from Lukacs to Habermas.* Boston, Little: Brown, 1973; Berkeley: University of California Press, 1984.

Johnson, Roger A. *Psychohistory and Religion: The Case of Young Man Luther.* Philadelphia: Fortress Press, 1977.

Jones, L. Gregory, and Stephen Fowl. *Reading in Communion.* Grand Rapids, Mich.: Eerdmans, 1991.

Kelly, Geffrey B., ed. *Ethical Responsibility: Bonhoeffer's Legacy to the Churches.* New York: Edwin Mellen, 1981.

———. *Liberating Faith: Bonhoeffer's Message for Today.* Minneapolis: Augsburg, 1984.

Kelly, Geffrey B., and Burton Nelson. *A Testament to Freedom: The Essential Writings of Dietrich Bonhoeffer.* San Francisco: Harper, 1990.

Klassen, A. J., ed. *A Bonhoeffer Legacy.* Grand Rapids, Mich.: Eerdmans, 1981.

Kodalle, Klaus-Michael. *Dietrich Bonhoeffer, Zur Kritik seiner Theologie.* Gutersloh: Guterloher Verlagshaus Gerd Mohn, 1991.

Lash, Nicholas. *Easter in Ordinary: Reflections on Human Experience and the Knowledge of God.* Charlottesville: University of Virginia Press, 1988.

———. *Theology on the Way to Emmaus.* London: SCM Press, 1986.

Lehmann, Paul L. *Ethics in a Christian Context.* New York: Harper and Row, 1963.

Leibholz, Gerhard. *Das Wesen der Repräsentation unter besonderer Berücksichtigung des Repräsentativsystems.* Berlin: W. de Gruyter, 1929.

Lentricchia, Frank. *Criticism and Social Change.* Chicago Press: University of Chicago, 1983.

Levinas, Emmanuel. "Ethics as First Philosophy." In *The Levinas Reader,* ed. Sean Hand. Oxford: Basil Blackwell, 1987.

Lindbeck, George A. *The Nature of Doctrine.* Philadelphia: Westminster Press, 1984.

Lovin, Robin W. *Christian Faith and Public Choices: The Social Ethics of Barth, Brunner, and Bonhoeffer.* Philadelphia: Fortress Press, 1984.

Lowe, Walter. *Theology and Difference: The Wound of Reason.* Bloomington: Indiana University Press, 1993.

Lyotard, Jean-François. *Le Different.* Paris: Edition Minuit, 1983.

———. *L'inhumain: Causerie sur le temps.* Paris, 1980.

MacIntyre, Alasdair. *After Virtue: A Study in Moral Theology.* London: Duckworth, 1985.

Marlé, René. *Bonhoeffer: The Man and His Work.* Translated by R. Sheed. London: Geoffrey Chapman, 1968.

Marsh, Charles. "Bonhoeffer on Heidegger and Togetherness." *Modern Theology* 8 (July 1992).

Marx, Karl. "Contribution to the Critique of Hegel's *Philosophy of Right.*" In *The Marx-Engels Reader,* ed. Robert C. Tucker. New York: Norton, 1978.

Meeks, Wayne A. *The First Urban Christians: The Social World of the Apostle Paul.* New Haven: Yale University Press, 1983.

Meerson-Aksenov, Michael. *The Political, Social, and Religious Thought of Russian "Samizdat"—An Anthology.* Belmont, Mass.: Nordland, 1977.

Metz, Johann Baptist. *Faith in History and Society: Toward a Practical Fundamental Theology.* Translated by David Smith. New York: Seabury Press, 1980.

Meyendorf, John. *The Byzantine Legacy in the Orthodox Church.* Crestwood, N.Y.: St. Vladimir's Seminary Press, 1982.

Milbank, John, "The Second Difference: For a Trinitarianism without Reserve." *Modern Theology* 2 (1986).

———. *Theology and Social Theory.* Cambridge: Basil Blackwell, 1990.

Moltmann, Jürgen. *Herrschaft Christi und soziale Wirklichkeit nach Dietrich Bonhoeffer.* Munich: Christian Kaiser Verlag, 1959.

———. *The Way of Jesus Christ.* San Francisco: Harper, 1990.

Müller, Hanfried. *World Come of Age.* Philadelphia: Fortress Press, 1967.

Nalbandian, Louise. *The Armenian Revolutionary Movement.* Berkeley: University of California Press, 1963.

Nancy, Jean-Luc. *L'imperatif categorique.* Paris: Flammarion, 1983.

Niemoller, Wilhelm. *Die Bekennende Kirche sagt Hitler die Wahrheit. Die Geschichte der Denkschrift der vorlaufigen Leitung vom Mai 1936.* Bielefeld: Ludwig Bechauf Verlag, 1954.

Nietzsche, Friedrich. *The Portable Nietzsche.* Edited and translated by W. Kaufman. New York: Viking Press, 1968.

Ott, Heinrich. *Reality and Faith: The Theological Legacy of Dietrich Bonhoeffer.* Translated by A. A. Morrison. Philadelphia: Fortress Press, 1972.

Peck, William J. *New Studies on Bonhoeffer's Ethics.* Toronto Studies in Theology. Lewiston: Edwin Mellen, 1987.

Polanyi, Michael. *Personal Knowledge: Toward a Post-Critical Philosophy.* Chicago: University of Chicago Press, 1962.

Poteat, William. *Polanyian Meditations: In Search of a Post-Critical Logic.* Durham, N.C.: Duke University Press, 1985.

Rades, Jörg. "Bonhoeffer and Hegel: From *Sanctorum Communio* to the Hegel Seminar, with Some Perspectives for the Later Works." Unpublished ms., University of St. Andrews.

Rasmussen, Larry L. *Dietrich Bonhoeffer—His Significance for North Americans.* Minneapolis: Fortress Press, 1990.

———. *Dietrich Bonhoffer: Reality and Resistance.* Nashville: Abingdon Press, 1972.

Ratschow, Carl Heinz. *Von den Weindlungen Gottes. Beitraege wur systematische Theologie zum Geburtstag Carl Heinz Ratschow.* Berlin: W. de Gruyter, 1986.

Ringer, Fritz K. *The Decline of the German Mandarins: The German Academic Community.* Cambridge: Harvard University Press, 1969.

Romero, Oscar. *The Church's Mission amid the National Crisis.* Maryknoll, N.Y.: Orbis, 1985.

Rorty, Richard, *Essays on Heidegger and others.* Cambridge: Cambridge University Press, 1991.

———. *Objectivity, Relativism, and Truth.* Cambridge: Cambridge University Press, 1991.

Rose, Gillian. *The Melancholy Science: An Introduction to the Thought of Theodor W. Adorno.* New York: Columbia University Press, 1978.

Rosen Stanley. *Hermeneutics as Politics.* New York: Oxford University Press, 1987.

Rouse, Joseph. *Knowledge and Power: Toward a Political Philosophy of Science.* Ithaca, N.Y.: Cornell University Press, 1989.

Rubenstein, Richard. *The Cunning of History: The Holocaust and the American Future.* New York: Harper and Row, 1975.

Schmitt, Carl. *Political Theology: Four Chapters on the Concept of Sovereignty.* Translated by George Schwab. Cambridge: MIT Press, 1985.

Smith, Adam. *The Theory of Moral Sentiments.* Edited by D. D. Raphael and A. L. Macfie. Oxford: Clarendon Press, 1979.

Staten, Harry. *Wittgenstein and Derrida.* Lincoln: University of Nebraska Press, 1984.

Surin, Kenneth. *The Turning of Light and Dark: Essays in Philosophical and Systematic Theology.* New York: Cambridge University Press, 1989.

Taylor, Charles. *Sources of the Self. The Making of the Modern Identity.* Cambridge: Harvard University Press, 1989.

Taylor, Mark C. *Alterity.* Chicago: University of Chicago Press, 1987.

——. *Deconstructing Theology.* New York: Crossroads, 1982.

——. *Erring.* Chicago: University of Chicago Press, 1984.

Todorov, Tzvetan. *The Conquest of America: The Question of the Other.* New York: HarperPerennial, 1992.

Torres, Sergio, and Virginia Fabella. *The Emergent Gospel.* Maryknoll, N.Y.: Orbis, 1978.

Van Leeuwen, Arend T. *De nacht van het kapitaal.* Nijmegen: SUN, 1984.

Vattimo, Gianni. *The End of Modernity.* Baltimore: Johns Hopkins University Press, 1988.

West, Charles. *The Power to Be Human: Toward a Secular Theology.* New York: Macmillan, 1971.

Williams, Rowan. "Postmodern Judgement and the Judgement of the World." In *Postmodern Theology,* ed. Fredric B. Burnham. San Francisco: Harper and Row, 1989.

——. *Resurrection: Interpreting the Easter Gospel.* New York: Pilgrim Press, 1984.

Wolterstorff, Nicholas. *Until Justice and Peace Embrace.* Grand Rapids, Mich.: Eerdmans, 1983.

Yoder, John H. "Sacrament as Social Process: Christ the Transformer of Culture." *Theology Today* 48 (April 1991).

INDEX

German Christians (*Deutsche Christen*), 112, 178

Germany, 16, 27, 28, 33, 60, 87, 92, 94, 181, 192, 270, 276, 277, 284, 285, 297, 300

"Die Geschichte und das Gute" (Bonhoeffer), 148 n. 43

Gestalt Christi, 52–55

Gift. See *Donum*

Giordano, Ralph, 302

Gland, Switzerland, 94

Gland, World League Meeting, 144

God, 11, 12, 22, 28, 36, 39, 45, 47, 52, 80, 91, 103, 128, 152, 203, 211, 220 n. 15, 225, 226, 230, 231, 233, 234; being of, 137, 143; doctrine of, 138; hiddenness in world, 135, 136, 139, 140, 146, 148 n. 34; idea of, 255; image of, 25, 95; kingdom of, 49, 51, 145, 157, 162, 200; messianic rule of, 48; of metaphysics, 208; mysteries of, 51, 120; powerless, 99, 273; presence of (*see* Presence of God); as *Primum agens*, 138; self-revelation of, 140; as subject of history, 25; suffering, 53, 99; who suffers in Jesus Christ, 119; word of (*see* Word of God); as working hypothesis, 13, 14, 23, 29, 122, 130 n. 34, 277; and world, 136, 138, 145, 146

Godlessness, 180

Golgotha, 67

Good, the, 11, 49, 113, 138, 152, 219, 229, 271

Gospel, the, 114, 155, 172, 189, 219; proclamation of, 141, 162, 262, 263

Gospel, social, 199

"The Gospel and the New Order" (Bonhoeffer), 105 n. 16

Gottwald, Norman, 108

Government: human 30; as mandate, 111

Gräbe, Herrmann, 302

Grace, 12, 41, 50, 65, 91, 99, 152, 160, 164, 166 n. 11, 167 n. 16, 197, 265 n. 7; cheap, 83, 101, 149, 151, 153, 155, 160, 165, 271; costly, 15, 101, 151, 153, 157, 163

Grande, Rutilio, 89

Great Britain, 126

Greco-Roman antiquity, 26

Greece, 183

Green, Clifford, 19 n. 15, 169 n. 67

Greenberg, Rabbi Irving, 83–84, 303

Gregory, St., the Illuminator, 177

Gremmels, Christian, 122, 125, 130 n. 31

Grotius, Hugo, 44, 122, 135

Guilt, 12, 49, 83, 87, 88, 91, 149, 158–60, 277, 278

Gutierrez, Gustavo, 57 n. 28, 84, 102, 105 n. 47, 114, 115 n. 25, 117, 119, 121, 124–26, 128, 129 *passim*, 130 n. 30, 131 *passim*, 168 n. 43

Habermas, Jürgen, 305 n. 21

Habitus, 197

Haig, Alexander, 81

Harlem, 86

Harnack, Adolf von, 47, 117, 241

Hate, 12, 94; of Jews, 88

Hauerwas, Stanley, 52, 57 n. 42, 63

Havel, Václav, 7, 18 n. 4, 57 n. 16

Hebrew prophets, 27

Hebrew scripture, 24, 26, 37 n. 18, 201

Hegel, G.W.F., 17, 21, 23–25, 29–34, 164, 221 n. 22, 230, 231, 244, 245, 274

Heidegger, Martin, 203, 224, 232, 233, 253–56, 257, 264 n. 1, 265 n. 8

Heideggerian ontology, 199

Heideggerian project, 261

Henkys, J., 304 n. 3

Herbert, Lord, of Cherbury, 130 n. 33

Heresy, 77, 243

Hermeneutics, 107, 146, 198, 256; biblical, 111; black, 109; of community, 136, 144; liberation, 109; materialist, 108, 112; of suspicion, 208, 216; theological, 135; turn (*kehre*), 200

Jones, L. Gregory, 280 n. 5
Judaism, 26
Judeo-Christianity, 47
Judgment, 15, 41, 51, 149, 151, 152, 153, 164, 166; moral, 228
Jugend und Studium, 1918–1927 (Bonhoeffer), 249 n. 5
Jüngel, Eberhard, 148 n. 42
Justice, 52, 85, 101, 103, 141, 158, 159, 228, 234, 287
Justification, 130 n. 39; by grace through faith, 64

Kairos, 200
Kant, Immanuel, 12, 117, 121, 202, 218, 219, 230, 231, 236 n. 20, 244, 255, 272
Karekin II, Catholicos of Cilicia, 182
Kelley, James P., 110
Kelly, Geffrey B., 104 n. 1, 105 n. 41, 148 n. 34, 168 n. 60, 280 n. 13, 292 n. 4
Kelsen, Hans, 198
Kerygma, 141, 200, 256, 263
Khachadrian, Ludwig, 175
Kierkegaard Renaissance, German, 197
Kierkegaard, Soren, 16, 25, 34, 216, 219, 245, 256
Kirchenkampf (Church Struggle), 24, 283
Knowledge, 44, 45, 123, 125, 233, 255
Koch, Werner, 301
Kodalle, Klaus-Michael, 16
Koinonia, 54
Kojève, Alexandre, 21, 30, 33, 35
K'tutyune, 193
Kuske, Martin, 37 n. 18

Land acts, South African, 289
Language, 144, 217, 257, 263; spoken, 211; theological, 160–61, 163
Lash, Nicholas, 42, 56 nn. 10, 12, 58 n. 54
Latin America, 77, 81, 84, 93, 102; liberation theologies of, 168 n. 43
Law, 15, 16, 114

Leeuwen, Arend Th. van, 237 n. 37
Legislation, anti-Jewish, 88
Lehmann, Paul L., 50
Leibholz, Gerhard, 110, 197, 198, 204 n. 3
Lentricchia, Frank, 57 n. 24
Lessing, G. E., 121
Letters and Papers from Prison (Bonhoeffer), 5, 11, 13, 20, 21, 29, 47, 107, 117, 126–28, 136, 140, 149, 155, 160–63, 165, 179, 180, 201, 224, 240–41, 246–47, 295, 298
Levinas, Emmanuel, 156
Liberalism, 32, 117, 127, 209
Liberation, 10, 33, 36, 98, 102, 107, 108, 154, 287; from below, 111; movements, 285
Liberation theologies, 11, 77, 80, 82, 84, 93, 101, 102, 104, 113, 117, 118, 120; of Latin America, 168 n. 43
Life, 49, 272, 274, 275; polyphony of, 50, 51, 141, 240, 247, 275
Life Together (Bonhoeffer), 149, 155, 157, 163–65, 241
Lindbeck, George A., 59, 62
Linguistics, structuralist, 210
Littel, Franklin, 191
Locke, John, 227
Logocentrism, 244
Logology, 217, 220
Logos, 219, 245, 248; Christ, the Word, 215; crucified, 207, 220; human, 215, 216
Love, 12, 98, 99, 119, 152, 156; of enemies, 49, 157, 161; God's, for the world, 141
Lovin, Robin W., 281 n. 24
Luther, Martin, 21, 24, 25, 27, 28, 29, 64, 67, 83, 70, 139, 140, 141, 143, 198, 262, 277. *See also* Reformation; Two kingdoms
Lutheran Orthodoxy, 291
Lutherans, 28, 178, 271
Lyotard, Jean-François, 18 n. 13, 232

National Party, South African, 285, 290

National security, 93; idolatry of, 90, 94, 95

National Socialism, 25, 34, 121, 126, 244, 288

Nation state, 179

Native Americans, 78, 82

Natural, the, 28, 12, 197

Natural knowledge of God's essence, 137

Natural science, 127

Nature, 15, 21, 40, 44, 126, 136, 141, 143, 144, 227, 276

"The Nature of the Church" (Bonhoeffer), 200

Navarro, Father Alfonso, 89

Nazi Germany, 93, 98, 112, 158, 159, 160, 244

Nazis, Nazism, 29, 85, 107, 108, 110, 171, 178, 179, 181, 239, 249, 270, 284

Nehemiah, 112

Nersissian, Karekin, Bishop of Yerevan, 193

Nersoyan, Archbishop Tiran (Primate of the Diocese of the Armenian Church in America), 185–90

New Age, 230

New Creation, 55

New Testament, 52, 123, 179, 298

New World, 21

New world order, 21, 173, 284

Nicholas of Cusa, 130 n. 33

Niebuhr, Reinhold, 59, 67, 73, 304 n. 5

Niemöller, Wilhelm, 304 n. 15

Nietzsche, Friedrich, 27, 113, 166 n. 10, 208, 218, 224, 230, 232–34, 243, 245, 250 n. 17, 274

Nihilism, 29, 41, 121, 214, 230, 233

North America, 30, 59, 60, 61, 63, 66, 81, 126, 187, 275; churches in, 62

North German Patriarchalism, 111

Noumenon, 203

Object, 36, 43

Obligation, 275, 276

Old Testament, 52, 67, 68, 112, 123, 130 n. 39, 297

"On Forgiveness" (Bonhoeffer), 167 n. 16

"On Repentance" (Bonhoeffer), 167 n. 15

Ontological, the, 254

Ontology: existential, 256; genuine, 264; Heidegger's, 199; theological, 253

Onto-theology, 145, 208

Order, 21, 158, 159, 230; ecclesial, 98; moral, 228; secular, 173

Orders, 110, 144, 145, 201; of Preservation, 141

Organization, 44, 124, 127, 227, 228; technical, 40

Other, the, 17, 51, 79, 145, 190, 199, 220 n. 9, 243, 244, 246, 272

Otherworldliness, 66, 67, 69

Ott, Heinrich, 239, 249 n. 1

Ottoman Empire, 173, 182, 184, 185, 187

"Outline for a Book" (Bonhoeffer), 71, 226, 227, 248, 298, 300

Papacy, 27

Parable, 101, 114, 153, 212

Partiality, 209, 213, 215

Passio Christi, 67

Past, the, 40, 247, 258, 259, 263

Pathos, divine, 67

Paul, Saint, 54, 64, 67, 92, 260

Peace, 10, 12, 96, 156, 159, 284, 286

Penultimate, 21, 24, 113, 158, 159, 160, 162, 163, 165, 166, 181, 278

Phenomenology, 233

Philosophy: existentialist, 42, 46, 227; Greek, 27; idealistic, 230; political, 274; postmodern, 235; transcendental, 199, 200, 245; Western, 240, 242

Pietism, 28, 45, 46, 60, 64, 189, 278, 291

Pinochet, Augusto, 81